Principles
of
LOGIC

Principles

of

LOGIC

Alex C. Michalos

Associate Professor of Philosophy
University of Guelph, Ontario

Prentice-Hall, Inc.
Englewood Cliffs, New Jersey

13-709402-7

Library of Congress Catalog
Card Number 70–77905

Printed in the United States of America

Current Printing (last digit):
10 9 8 7 6 5 4 3 2 1

Prentice-Hall International, Inc., *London*
Prentice-Hall of Australia, Pty. Ltd., *Sydney*
Prentice-Hall of Canada, Ltd., *Toronto*
Prentice-Hall of India Private Ltd., *New Delhi*
Prentice-Hall of Japan, Inc., *Tokyo*

To the memory of my Father
who wanted his sons to be gentlemen

and to my Mother
who wanted them to be happy

Preface

I have written this introductory logic text because no other text has been satisfactory for my interests and purposes. Other texts have been inadequate because they have not had enough to say about nondemonstrative problems; i.e., about the problems involved in the appraisal of arguments that are not supposed to *establish* their conclusions but merely to make them more or less *acceptable*. There is, in fact, much more to be said at an elementary level than I have been able to say here. Nevertheless, there is more in this text than there is in any other. If the quality is up to par (and every reader must judge that for himself), nothing further *needs* to be said to justify its publication. And if the quality is not up to par, nothing further *could* be said to justify its publication.

The book is divided into three parts. Roughly speaking, they are ordered from the logically "neat and mechanical" to the logically "messy and artistic"; i.e., from discussions of demonstrative to nondemonstrative to informal principles. In the following paragraphs I shall briefly summarize the parts.

Part One (Chapters 1–4) introduces the fundamental principles of demonstrative logic. Chapter 1 deals with truth-functional logic and validity. The only decision procedures presented are the truth-table and *reductio ad absurdum* tests. While a number of people prefer to begin with syllogistic theory and while the present text would permit such an approach, it should be emphasized that an attempt has been made to make the introduction of most of the ideas in Chapters 2–4 seem to be natural developments or extensions of the ideas presented in Chapter 1.

Chapter 2 introduces the elements of the calculus of terms in a somewhat novel fashion. Translation rules for "disguised" categorical sentences are presented before any decision procedure. This has the advantage of allowing the student to acquire some idea of the *variety* of arguments that may be appraised by the techniques to be considered. Without introducing immediate inferences, we move directly to the Venn diagram test, inconsistent triad, and syllogistic rules. (The weak square of opposition is presented in the discussion of the inconsistent triad.) The full battery of immediate inferences is introduced in the last section of the chapter. Although there are a couple of thousand years of precedent against this small change, it seems less confusing from the students' point of view. The *idea* of inferring a particular from a universal is not presented at all *before* we have finished discussing decision procedures that do *not* allow such inferences. Finally, it should be noted that those who prefer to consider only those parts of the calculus of terms that are useful for the monadic predicate calculus may do so by covering only Secs. 2.1 and 2.2.

Chapters 3 and 4 are devoted to the method of natural deduction, including the rules for conditional and indirect proofs. Chapter 3 is quite standard, although it contains more than the usual number of examples and exercises. Chapter 4 differs from most introductions to a restricted monadic predicate calculus because it considers the *reductio ad absurdum* test *before* natural deduction. This has the advantage of giving the student some idea of the complications of quantificational validity before mastering the additional rules of natural deduction.

The terminology and symbols used in this part are borrowed from Willard van Orman Quine. Hence, the transition from the present text to, say, Quine's *Methods of Logic* for a second course is greatly facilitated.

Part Two (Chapters 5–9) introduces the fundamental principles of non-demonstrative logic. Section 5.1 sets the stage by separating the four problems of the *meaning* of 'probability' and the *measure, calculation,* and *application* of probability-values. This is followed by discussions of three interpretations of probability sentences including seven methods of obtaining initial probability-values.

Chapter 6 presents the basic theorems of the calculus of probability in a fairly general fashion. The variables are introduced as place holders for *elements* which may be thought of as sentences or propositions or terms or classes or events, etc., and appropriate interpretations of the operator signs are suggested. Bayes's theorem and the so-called 'method of Bayesian inference' are considered in detail. The chapter ends with a discussion and comparison of Laplace's rule of succession (and an important corollary), Reichenbach's straight rule, and Carnap's singular predictive inference rule.

Chapter 7 introduces some basic notions of descriptive and inferential statistics. After outlining procedures for measuring central tendencies and variety, Chebyshev's theorem is presented to give the student some idea of *how* distribution summaries may be used to make probabilistic inferences. The rules for combinations and permutations are considered as useful techniques for constructing distributions. Then they are employed in the exposition of the formula for the binomial distribution. Finally, it is shown how the formula and some knowledge of the properties of the normal distribution curve may be used to make probabilistic inferences.

Chapter 8 contains discussions of fourteen more or less plausible rules for the determination of acceptable hypotheses (where 'hypothesis' is used in a very broad sense to cover ordinary sentences as well as scientific laws and theories) *and* courses of action, *relative to* certain premises or circumstances. Such rules are referred to as 'acceptance rules' and the inferences justified by them are called 'nondemonstratively valid' ('*n*-valid', for short). Acceptance rules are used to *n*-validate or justify nondemonstrative inferences much the same as (deductive) inference rules are used to validate or justify demonstrative inferences. Whatever the merits of this attempt to highlight the similarities between acceptance rules and (deductive) inference rules (without losing sight of their differences), most of the acceptance rules themselves seem to be interesting to most people. They include ideas drawn from philosophy (e.g., Reichenbach's weight of hypotheses), game and statistical decision theory (e.g., Wald's minimax and Savage's minimax regret principles), and mathematics (e.g., least squares and expected utility).

The discussion of Mill's canons in Chapter 9 includes only the three canons of agreement, difference, and concomitant variations. The section on analogy is devoted entirely to analogical arguments. The notion of relative plausibility introduced in the final section is borrowed from G. Polya.

Part Three (Chapters 10 and 11) is concerned with some fairly informal issues in logic. In Chapter 10, twenty fallacies are distinguished. The discussion of definitions in Chapter 11 is heavily dependent upon Richard Robinson's classic *Definition* (though Professor Robinson would not agree with everything here).

The usual conventions are followed of *mentioning* a word (except in definitions) by putting it between single quotation marks (e.g., 'boy' has three letters), *using* a word with special emphasis by italicizing it (e.g., *everyone* dies), and using a word in an extraordinary fashion (or using a borrowed sentence or phrase) by putting it between double quotation marks (e.g., Arnold is "impossible"). Words or phrases that are being defined appear in boldface type (e.g., **bachelor** means an unmarried male).

The review problems (exercises) are designed to help the reader master the material by bringing it to his attention in different contexts. There are well over 1800 review questions and since they are primarily intended as reviewing aids, it is unlikely that anyone will want to cover all of them. The solutions of about half of the problems are given in the back of the book. (A *Solutions Manual* for the remaining problems may be obtained from the publisher.)

Suggestions for further reading appear at the end of every chapter and serve a twofold purpose: namely, to supply the student with a list of alternative presentations of the material and to indicate original sources and/or recognized classics. I owe a special debt to the authors whose works are cited.

Since, for many reasons, some classes move more rapidly than others, each instructor has to decide for himself which of the topics introduced here have a place in any given course. However, the following outlines may be useful.

1. *Freshman course for semester or quarter:* Ch. 1, 2, 5.1, some of 8, 9.1 and 9.2, 10, 11.

2. *Sophomore or junior course for semester or quarter:*
   a) Well-balanced: Ch. 1, some of 2, 3, 4, 5.1, some of 8, 9.1 and 9.2, some of 10, 11.
   b) Largely demonstrative and formal: Ch. 1, 2.1–2.3, 3, 4, 5.1, 5.2 a–b(i), 6.1–6.3, some of 8, 9.
   c) Largely nondemonstrative: Ch. 1, 2.1–2.3, 3, 5.1, 5.2 a–b(i), 6.1–6.3, 8, 9.

    d)   Wholly nondemonstrative: Part Two, perhaps adding and/or eliminating certain topics.

3. *Sophomore or junior year-long course:* The whole book, adding or deleting to suit one's needs.

Part Two should provide a worthwhile supplement for courses in the methodology or philosophy of science, probability and induction, decision theory, and hypothesis appraisal. Social scientists who have no particular interest in mathematically sophisticated discussions of hypothesis appraisal but who would like (or feel obliged) to become familiar with some of the essentials of, say, probability or decision theory should also find this part useful. Aside from the few theorems of the calculus of probability which are thoroughly explained and illustrated, the only mathematics required is arithmetic. Physical scientists engaged in designing "general education" courses for "nonscience majors" may also find this part useful.

Acknowledgments

A number of people have contributed to this enterprise in one way or another, and I am happy to take this opportunity to express my sincere gratitude to all of them.

My friends George Yoos, Ted Newton, Scott A. Kleiner, Tom W. Settle, and Jim van Evra read various parts of the manuscript, and freely offered their advice and encouragement.

Stan Evans, Jim Clark, Alan Lesure, and John White of Prentice-Hall, Inc. were constant sources of information, support, and good counsel. The dozen or so anonymous reviewers and critics provided by these men must be credited for helping me to eliminate many more errors than I imagined I could make.

Mrs. Kristina Casalini typed the final draft of the entire manuscript. It was hardly a picnic, and I am grateful for the care, patience, and skill she displayed throughout the ordeal. Mrs. Barbara Rumsey, Miss Stella Tchorzewski, and Mrs. Mabel Skeates conscientiously typed various parts of the manuscript at various stages.

My children, Cindy, Ted, and Stephanie, reluctantly but persistently denied their natural tendencies to make noise. I have appreciated both their silent service and their companionship.

Finally, I must say that my wife Bobbie typed, read, commented on, and criticized quite a bit of the manuscript at various stages. On the side she has been employed full time by our mathematics department; she has kept her family fed, clothed, cleaned, and comforted; and she has usually remained sane and pleasant from sunup till sundown. I am grateful to her for everything.

Alex C. Michalos

Guelph, Ontario

Contents

part TWO   Nondemonstrative Principles

part THREE   *Informal Principles*

The only complete safeguard against reasoning
ill, is the habit of reasoning well; familiarity
with the principles of correct reasoning,
and practice in applying those principles.

John Stuart Mill

Part

ONE

Demonstrative

Principles

Chapter

1

The Calculus of Sentences

1.1 Truth-functions and sentence schemata

The sentence

(1)   Jimmy Brown plays football.

is true if, and only if, Jimmy Brown plays football. One might say that sentence (1) has a **truth-value** of truth or falsity which is immediately dependent upon or a of function of some particular state of affairs. Similarly, to determine the truth-value of

(2)   Venus is larger than Mars.

one must examine some particular part of the universe, namely, the planets Venus and Mars. Hence the truth-value of (2) is immediately dependent upon or a function of the size of the planets.

If (1) and (2) are true then 'Jimmy Brown does not play football' or

(3)   It is not the case that Jimmy Brown plays football.

and 'Venus is not larger than Mars' or

(4)   It is not the case that Venus is larger than Mars.

must be false. However, the sentences

(5)   Amos believes that Jimmy Brown plays football.

and

(6)   Andy said that Venus is larger than Mars.

may be true or false.

There is a crucial logical distinction between (3) and (4) on the one hand and (5) and (6) on the other. The distinction is this: If 'it is not the case that' is prefixed to a sentence whose truth-value is determined, then the truth-value of the new sentence is also determined. If 'Amos believes that' or 'Andy said that' is prefixed to a sentence whose truth-value is determined, then the truth-value of the new sentence is still *not* determined. If we know that Jimmy Brown plays football and that Venus is larger than Mars, we still do not know the truth-value of (5) and (6) because we do not know what Amos believes or Andy said. While the truth-value of

(3)   It is not the case that Jimmy Brown plays football.

is *a function of the truth-value of*

(1)   Jimmy Brown plays football.

the truth-value of

(5)   Amos believes that Jimmy Brown plays football.

is *not* a function of the truth-value of (1). The truth-value of (5) is determined by examining another particular part of the world, namely Amos, to find out whether or not he believes that Jimmy Brown plays football.

Similarly, while the truth-value of

(2)   Venus is larger than Mars.

is *a function of some state of affairs* and the truth-value of

(6)   Andy said that Venus is larger than Mars.

is a function of *another* state of affairs, the truth-value of

(4)   It is not the case that Venus is larger than Mars.

is a function of the truth-value of (2).

The sentences (3)–(6) are formed by prefixing phrases to the simple sentences (1) and (2). The addition of these phrases creates slightly more complicated sentences whose meanings and truth-values are affected in different ways. We shall call such phrases **sentential operators.** So far, the only sentential operators we have considered are prefixes, but in the sections that follow we shall introduce operators which do not precede but *connect* sentences.

A **truth-operator** (or 'truth-functor') is a sentential operator which is such that when it is applied to sentences whose truth-values are determined, new sentences are created whose truth-values are also determined. The sentence or sentences to which truth-operators are applied will be called **component sentences.** (They are frequently called 'arguments', but we are reserving this name for something else.) Component sentences may be as simple as (1) or more complicated than even (10) below. We may say, then, that the operator 'it is not the case that' is a truth-operator that yields (3) when it is applied to the component sentence (1). When the same truth-operator is applied to the component sentence (2), the result is (4).

As we noted above, the truth-value of (3) is a function of the truth-value of (1), and the truth-value of (4) is a function of the truth-value of (2). Any sentence whose truth-value is a function of the values of its component sentences is called a **truth-functional sentence,** or simply a **truth-function;** i.e., its truth-value is a truth-function of its component sentences. Thus sentences (3) and (4) are, but (5) and (6) are *not*, truth-functional sentences. The operators 'Amos believes that' and 'Andy said that' are not truth-operators. When they are applied to sentences whose truth-values are determined [e.g., (1) and (2)], new sentences [(5) and (6)] are created whose truth-values are *not* also determined.

The sentence

(2)   Venus is larger than Mars.

is different from the sentence

(7)   Mars is smaller than Venus.

although both sentences have the same *meaning*. The meanings of declarative sentences are often referred to as **propositions** or **statements.** We might say, then, that a person who *uttered* either sentence (2) or (7) would be *asserting* one and the same proposition or statement. There are certain advantages and disadvantages involved in talking about sentences on the one hand and propositions or statements on the other; however, these will not be introduced here. Instead we shall simply note that in this text we are going to talk about sentences rather than propositions or statements. If two sentences have the same meaning, we shall treat them as the same sentence; e.g., we shall say that (2) and (7) are the same (because they have the same meaning), although the *words* and the *order* of the words in both sentences are different.

If we *abbreviate* sentence (1) by the capital letter '*J*' and the truth-operator 'it is not the case that' by the bar '$-$', then sentence (3) may be abbreviated thus:

(3′) $-J$.

Similarly, if we abbreviate sentence (2) by the capital letter '*V*', then sentence (4) may be abbreviated

(4′) $-V$.

In view of our agreement to treat sentences (2) and (7) the same, '*V*' is also an abbreviation of (7).

Any capital letter may be used as an abbreviation, but we usually select the first letter of some key word in the sentence for ease of reference. Letters used to *abbreviate specific sentences* will be called **sentence letters.** In the sections that follow we shall frequently find it convenient to abbreviate sentences and operators. It not only saves time and space, but it often increases the lucidity of very complicated sentences.

Letters used as *place holders* for *unspecified sentences* will be called **sentence variables.** Usually lowercase letters '*p*', '*q*', '*r*', and '*s*' are used for this purpose. A sentence variable is *not* an abbreviation of any specific sentence. It is a letter which *represents any unspecified sentence.* For example, the letter '*p*' may be thought of as ambiguously representing

Jimmy Brown plays football.

and

(8)   Either Henry is bald or not.

and

(9)   When I was seventeen, it was a very good year.

and

(10)   You can fool all of the people some of the time and some of the people all of the time, but you cannot fool all of the people all of the time.

etc. The function of sentence *variables* such as '*p*' then is quite different from the function of sentence *letters* such as '*V*'. While it makes sense to say that a specific *sentence,* say (2), or an abbreviation of that sentence (i.e., a sentence *letter*) '*V*' is true or false, a sentence *variable* such as '*p*' cannot be true or false. At best '*p*' may *represent* or be regarded as a *place holder* for sentences we may suppose or assume or imagine are true or false. But '*p*' cannot *be* true or false. Only sentences (or abbreviations of sentences) may be true or false.

An expression which becomes a *sentence* when its variables are appropriately replaced is called a **sentence schema** (plural, **schemata**). Sentence schemata constitute the *forms* of sentences; they reveal nothing about the *content* of sentences.

Examples of sentence schemata are '*p*', 'it is not the case that *p*', 'if *p* then *q*', '*p* and *q*', etc. The sentence schema '*p*' (which also happens to be merely a sentence variable) becomes a sentence when some sentence such as (1)–(10) replaces '*p*'. Similarly, the sentence schema 'if *p* then *q*' becomes a sentence when some sentence such as (1)–(10) replaces '*p*' and '*q*'. It does not matter whether we replace '*p*' and '*q*' with the same sentence, say (1), or with different sentences. In the first case we would obtain the trivial sentence

(11)   If Jimmy Brown plays football then Jimmy Brown plays football.

In the second case we might have

(12)   If Jimmy Brown plays football then Venus is larger than Mars.

In both cases a sentence is obtained from the sentence schema 'if *p* then *q*' by appropriately replacing the place holders '*p*' and '*q*'. Notice that although sentences (11) and (12) are obtained from the same schema and, therefore, may be said to have the same *form*, (11) and (12) have different *contents*. They do not mean the same thing. For the most part we shall be primarily concerned with the *forms* of sentences (i.e., sentence *schemata*) and only secondarily concerned with their *contents* (i.e., what particular sentences mean).

The relation between sentence variables and sentence schemata is perfectly straightforward. All sentence variables may be regarded as sentence schemata; e.g., '*p*' may be regarded as both. Many sentence schemata cannot be regarded as sentence variables; e.g., 'if *p* then *q*' cannot be regarded as a variable. *Both* sentence variables and sentence schemata represent or are place holders for sentences.

Sentences and *truth-values* of sentences obtained from a sentence schema by replacing sentence variables with sentences or truth-values of sentences will be called **interpretations** of that schema. An interpretation is **uniform** when each distinct variable is replaced by the same sentence or truth-value throughout the schema. For example, a uniform interpretation of the schema

If *p* and *q*, then *p*.

would be such that each occurrence of '*p*' is replaced with the same sentence or truth-value. Moreover, if each occurrence of '*p* *and* *q*' in the schema above is replaced by the *very* same sentence or truth-value, the interpretation is still regarded as uniform. If, say, the first occurrence of '*p*' is interpreted as a true sentence and the second is interpreted as a false one, the interpretation is *not* uniform.

As we noted in other words above, *uniform interpretations* of the *same schema* may be said to have the *same form*, though this tells us nothing about their *content* or what the interpretations mean. Each of the sentences (1)–(12) may be regarded as an interpretation of the sentence schema '*p*'. Each of those sentences may be obtained from the schema '*p*' by replacing the sole sentence variable '*p*' in that schema with each of the sentences (1)–(12). Of course, calling these sentences 'interpretations' of the schema '*p*' and, therefore, regarding them as having the same form is not particularly informative or interesting. But some of these sentences may also be regarded as interpretations of other schemata, and this is where things begin to become interesting. Consider

(3)   It is not the case that Jimmy Brown plays football.

Sentence (3) may be obtained from the sentence schema '−*p*' by replacing the sole sentence variable '*p*' in that schema by sentence (1) (and again letting the bar abbreviate 'it is not the case that'). Hence (3) may be regarded as an interpretation of the schema '−*p*' as well as of the schema '*p*' depending on what we choose to regard as a replacement for the sentence variable '*p*'.

Again, while sentences (11) and (12) may be regarded as interpretations of the schema '*p*', we have just seen that they may also be regarded as interpretations of the more complicated schema 'if *p* then *q*'. When (12), say, is regarded as an interpretation of the sentence schema '*p*', we are regarding the sentence variable '*p*' as a place holder for (12). When (12) is regarded as an interpretation of the sentence schema 'if *p* then *q*', we are regarding the sentence variable '*p*' as a place holder for (1) and the variable '*q*' as a place holder for (2).

The points we have been making in the last few paragraphs may be summarized thus: A given sentence may be regarded as an intrepretation of more than one sentence schema *and* a given sentence schema may have more than one interpretation. As our work progresses and we consider more complicated schemata and sentences, we shall have more to say about both of these points.

The **calculus of sentences** may now be defined as the class consisting of all schemata which contain only sentence variables and truth-operators, and their rules of use. If we were going to talk about propositions or statements, we would have entitled the chapter 'the calculus of propositions' or 'the calculus of statements'.

Review problems for Sec. 1.1.

1. Define the following.

   a) truth-operator   d) sentence schema
   b) truth-function   e) uniform interpretation
   c) sentence variable

2. What are the main differences between sentence variables and sentence letters?

3. State which of the following are sentence schemata and which are sentences.

   a) North Carolina is south of Washington, D. C.

    b)   If *p* and *q*, then *r*.

    c)   It is not the case that 'U.N.C.L.E.' is the name of a real organization.

    d)   It is not the case that *p*, and John belongs to the Y.M.C.A.

    e)   Edgar believes that *p*, although he doubts that *q* and *r*.

4.   What is the difference between sentences and propositions (or statements)?

5.   Which of the following are truth-functions?

    a)   Jerry knows that Beatrice is sick.

    b)   It is not the case that Little Jack Horner sat in the corner.

    c)   It is not the case that Carl is convinced that Judy is dead.

    d)   It is not the case that Frank believes that Carl thinks that John knows that Tom is dead.

6.   Give two interpretations with different *contents* for each of the following *schemata*.

    a)   *p* or *q*.   c)   If *r*, then *p* and *q*.

    b)   *p*, or *q* and *r*.   d)   *p* and *q*, if *r*.

7.   What is the calculus of sentences?

1.2   Negation, conjunction, and disjunction

In this section we are going to introduce three of a total of five truth-operators to be considered in this chapter.

If

(1)   Peter Rabbit eats cabbage.

is false then

(2)   It is not the case that Peter Rabbit eats cabbage.

must be true. If sentence (1) is true, then (2) must be false. Sentence (2) is used to deny or *negate* exactly what is affirmed or asserted by (1). Or, what amounts to the same thing, (2) is the negation of (1). The negation of a sentence is a truth-functional sentence; it is a truth-function of the sentence negated. The negation of a true sentence is false, and the negation of a false sentence is true.

We may generalize our discussion in the last paragraph thus: If '*p*' represents a true sentence then the schema '−*p*' represents a false one, and vice versa. The content of the last sentence is graphically illustrated by the diagram in Figure 1.21 which is called a **truth-table definition** of a negation schema. The truth-table definition of a negation schema tells us the conditions under which any sentence patterned after that schema is true or false. Let us review the parts of Figure 1.21 and examine this claim more carefully.

$$\begin{array}{c|c} p & -p \\ \hline \text{1.} \quad t & f \\ \text{2.} \quad f & t \end{array}$$

Figure 1.21

In the upper left-hand corner of the table we put the variable 'p'. In the upper right-hand corner we put the schema '$-p$'. Hereafter the bar '$-$' which we have been using to abbreviate the truth-operator 'it is not the case that' will be called a **negation sign**. Any sentence schema having the form '$-p$' will be called a **negation schema** and any appropriate interpretation of a negation schema will be called a **negation**. The lowercase 't's' and 'f's' in the table are short for 'true' and 'false', respectively. Since 'p' may represent a true or a false sentence, we put a lowercase 't' below it and a lowercase 'f' below the 't'. Line 1 of the table tells us that when the interpretation of 'p' is true, the interpretation of '$-p$' is false. Line 2 tells us that when the interpretation of 'p' is false, the interpretation of '$-p$' is true.

The sentence

(3)   Sid and Jill went up the hill.

means

(4)   *Both* Sid *and* Jill went up the hill.

which is to say

(5)   *Both* Sid went up the hill *and* Jill went up the hill.

If (5) [or its equivalents (3) and (4)] is a truth-functional sentence, then its truth-value must be completely determined by the truth-values of its component sentences 'Sid went up the hill' and 'Jill went up the hill'. Now, when there are N elements that may have one of two attributes, there are 2^N possible combinations (of elements and attributes). Hence, since we have two sentences which may be true or false, only $2^N = 4$ possible combinations of truth-values may result. The four combinations are

> 'Sid went up the hill' is true *and* 'Jill went up the hill' is true.
>
> 'Sid went up the hill' is true *and* 'Jill went up the hill' is false.
>
> 'Sid went up the hill' is false *and* 'Jill went up the hill' is true.
>
> 'Sid went up the hill' is false *and* 'Jill went up the hill' is false.

If (5) asserts that both Sid and Jill went up the hill and it is true that they both went up the hill, then (5) must be true. In other words, if both of the component sentences of (5) are true, then (5) is true. Again, if, according to (5), *both*

Sid and Jill went up the hill, but, in fact, not both but only one went up the hill, then (5) must be false. That is, if either one of the component sentences of (5) is false then (5) must be false. Finally, from what has just been said, it follows that if *both* of the component sentences of (5) are false then (5) must be false. This particular kind of truth-functional sentence is called a **conjunction.** The sentences conjoined by the truth-operator 'and' are called **conjuncts.** A conjunction is true only when *all* its conjuncts are true; a conjunction is false when at least one of its conjuncts is false.

We may generalize our discussion in the last two paragraphs thus: A sentence schema of the form '*p and q*' represents a true sentence only when the sentences represented by '*p*' and by '*q*' are true; if either of the sentences represented by '*p*' and '*q*' is false then '*p and q*' represents a false sentence. We shall use the dot '·' to abbreviate the truth-operator 'and' (as well as its grammatical equivalents 'but', 'still', 'although', 'besides', 'also', etc.). The technical term for the dot is a **conjunction sign.** Any sentence schema having the form '*p·q*' will be called a **conjunction schema.** Figure 1.22 is a truth-table definition of a conjunction schema. It tells us the conditions under which any sentence patterned after that schema is true or false.

$$p \quad \cdot \quad q$$

	p	$\cdot$	q
1.	t	t	t
2.	t	f	f
3.	f	f	t
4.	f	f	f

Figure 1.22

Since we have two variables '*p*' and '*q*' (and two possible truth-values), we have $2^2 = 4$ combinations. Each combination is represented by one of the four rows in the table. The column of 't's' and 'f's' under the conjunction sign indicates the truth-value of any interpretation of a conjunction schema for each of the four combinations. Line 1 tells us that when the interpretations of both '*p*' and '*q*' are true, the interpretation of '*p·q*' is true. Line 2 tells us that when the interpretation of '*p*' is true and the interpretation of '*q*' is false, the interpretation of '*p·q*' is false. Line 3 tells us that when the interpretation of '*p*' is false and the interpretation of '*q*' is true, the interpretation of '*p·q*' is false. Line 4 tells us that when the interpretations of both '*p*' and '*q*' are false, the interpretation of '*p·q*' is false.

In the sentences

(6)   Either there is something rotten in Denmark or not.

and

(7)   Either there is something rotten in Denmark or there is something rotten in the refrigerator.

the sentential operator 'either–or' is used in two different ways. In (6) the operator evidently has the sense of "either one or the other *but not both*", since nothing in Denmark could be both rotten and not rotten. On the other hand, there is no reason why something could not be rotten in both Denmark and the refrigerator. The refrigerator, after all, might be in Denmark. Thus in (7) the operator has the sense of "either one or the other *or both*." The sense of 'either–or' in (6) is called exclusive; i.e., the third possibility, the possibility that both alternatives are true is excluded. The 'either–or' in (7) is *inclusive;* i.e., the possibility that both alternatives are true is included. We shall ignore the exclusive sense of 'either–or' for now and concentrate on the inclusive sense.

Consider (7). If, according to (7), it is true that *either* there is something rotten in Denmark *or* there is something rotten in the refrigerator *or* there is something rotten in *both* Denmark and the refrigerator, then (7) might be true for any of three different reasons. That is, if at least one (or possibly both) of the component sentences of (7) is true then (7) must be true. Sentence (7) is false only when both of its component sentences are false. This particular kind of truth-functional sentence is called a **disjunction** (or 'alternation'). The sentences disjoined by the truth-operator 'either–or' are called **disjuncts** (or 'alternates'). A disjunction is true when *at least one* of its disjuncts is true; a disjunction is false when all its disjuncts are false.

We may generalize our discussion in the last two paragraphs thus: A sentence schema of the form '*p or q*' represents a true sentence only when *at least one* of the sentences represented by '*p*' and by '*q*' is true; if both of the sentences represented by '*p*' and '*q*' are false then '*p or q*' represents a false sentence. We shall use the wedge '∨' to abbreviate the truth-operator 'either–or'. The technical term for the wedge is a **disjunction sign.** Any sentence schema having the form '$p \lor q$' will be called a **disjunction schema.** Figure 1.23 is a truth-table definition of a disjunction schema. It tells us the conditions under which any sentence patterned after that schema is true or false.

p	$\lor$	q
t	t	t
t	t	f
f	t	t
f	f	f

Figure 1.23

The construction of this truth-table is exactly the same as the construction of that in Figure 1.22 with the exception of the middle column. The middle column here indicates the truth-value of any interpretation of a disjunction schema for each of the four combinations of truth-values. The first line tells us that when the interpretations of both '*p*' and '*q*' are true, the interpretation of '$p \lor q$' is true. The second line tells us that when the interpretation of '*p*' is true and the interpretation of '*q*' is false, the interpretation of '$p \lor q$' is true, etc.

Review problems for Sec. 1.2.

1. Define the following.

   a) negation schema
   b) negation sign
   c) negation

2. Complete the following truth-table definition of a negation schema.

$$\begin{array}{c|c} p & -p \\ \hline t & \\ f & \end{array}$$

3. Define the following.

   a) conjunction schema   c) conjunction
   b) conjunction sign   d) conjunct

4. Complete the following truth-table definition of a conjunction schema.

$$\begin{array}{cc} p & \cdot & q \\ \hline t & \\ t & \\ f & \\ f & \end{array}$$

5. If we are given N variables each with one of two values (i.e., true or false), how many combinations of truth-values may be formed?

6. What is the difference between the exclusive and the inclusive 'or'?

7. Define the following.

   a) disjunction schema   c) disjunction
   b) disjunction sign   d) disjunct

8. Complete the following truth-table definition of a disjunction schema.

$$\begin{array}{cc} p & \vee & q \\ \hline & t \\ & f \\ & t \\ & f \end{array}$$

9. Which of the following are not well-formed (i.e., do not make sense), and why?

   a) $\cdot p$ d) $p \cdot -q$
   b) $p - q$ e) $p \vee$
   c) $- \cdot -$ f) $p -$

1.3 Truth-value analysis of complex sentences

Before considering more truth-operators, let us briefly appraise our progress so far. With the help of our truth-operators we may determine the truth-value of extremely complex sentences in a fairly mechanical fashion. Consider the following examples.

EXAMPLE 1

What is the truth-value of the following sentence?

> Either Chicago is a city or Mary Poppins is not a paratrooper, and the Nile River is shorter than the Allegheny.

Solution. In the given sentence, the comma is used to emphasize the break between the disjunction 'Either Chicago is a city or Mary Poppins is not a paratrooper' and the sentence 'the Nile River is shorter than the Allegheny'. That is, the comma tells us that the sentence is a *conjunction* with a disjunctive component. If the comma followed 'city' then we would have a *disjunction* with a conjunctive component; i.e., 'Either Chicago is a city, or Mary Poppins is not a paratrooper and the Nile River is shorter than the Allegheny'.

If we use 'C' as an abbreviation for 'Chicago is a city', 'M' for 'Mary Poppins is a paratrooper', and 'N' for 'the Nile River is shorter than the Allegheny', our example may be abbreviated to

$$(1) \qquad (C \vee -M) \cdot N.$$

If the comma in our example followed 'city', we would slide the parentheses to the right,

$$(2) \qquad C \vee (-M \cdot N).$$

The parentheses in (1) and (2) serve roughly the same purpose that the commas serve in ordinary English sentences; i.e., they set off various components from others. In (1) and (2) the compound components '$C \vee -M$' and '$-M \cdot N$' are set off from the simple components 'N' and 'C', respectively. In the schema

$$(3) \qquad -p \cdot \{r \vee [p \cdot (q \vee s)]\},$$

the braces set off the complex schema

$$(4) \qquad r \vee [p \cdot (q \vee s)]$$

from '$-p$'. They tell us that (3) is a conjunction schema with the disjunctive component (4). The brackets set off

(5) $p \cdot (q \lor s)$

from 'r'. They tell us that (4) is a disjunction schema with a conjunctive component (5), etc.

    The **scope of application** of a negation sign is the sentence or sentence schema it negates. This scope is always the shortest complete sentence or sentence schema to its right. For example, in sentence (2) the scope of the negation sign is 'M', *not* '$M \cdot N$'. To negate the latter, we would write '$-(M \cdot N)$'. In the schema

(6) $-\{-[-(-p \lor q)]\}$

the scope of the first negation sign on the left is the whole schema within the braces

(7) $-[-(-p \lor q)]$.

The scope of the second negation sign is the whole schema within the brackets

(8) $-(-p \lor q)$.

The scope of the third negation sign in (6) is '$-p \lor q$' and the scope of the fourth is just 'p', *not* '$p \lor q$'.

    In order to determine the truth-value of a complex truth-functional sentence such as (1), we begin by finding the values of its *shortest components first;* i.e., we find the values of its simple sentences, then its compound sentences, then its complex sentences, and so on until the value of the whole sentence is found. Hence, given

(1) $(C \lor -M) \cdot N,$

we begin by finding the values of 'C', 'M', and 'N', then the negation '$-M$', then the disjunction '$C \lor -M$', and finally the whole conjunction (1).

    We begin by replacing the sentences with their truth-values. Since 'C' is true, 'M' is false, and 'N' is false, we have

(9) $(t \lor -(f)) \cdot f.$

The lowercase 't's' and 'f's' in (9) again are abbreviations of 'true' and 'false', respectively. In accordance with our definition of 'interpretation' in Sec. 1.1., expressions like (9), which merely record the truth-values of some sentences, are regarded as *interpretations* of sentence schemata. It will be proper, then, to refer to (9) as a conjunction (instead of a conjunction schema) and to say that it is true or false.

Now, '— (f)' may be replaced by 't'; so we have

(10) $(t \lor t) \cdot f$.

The disjunction 't ∨ t' may be replaced by 't'. So (10) may be shortened to

(11) $(t) \cdot f$.

Sentence (11) is a conjunction with a false conjunct. So (11) may be reduced to

(12)   f.

Sentence (12) tells us the truth-value of our original sentence (1). Sentence (1) is false.

Just to emphasize the importance of proper grouping and parentheses, let us determine the truth-value of

(2) $C \lor (-M \cdot N)$.

To begin with, we have

(13) $t \lor (-(f) \cdot f)$.

Replacing '— (f)' with 't', we have

(14) $t \lor (t \cdot f)$.

A conjunction with a false conjunct is false. So (14) may be shortened to

(15) $t \lor (f)$.

But a disjunction with a true disjunct is true. Hence (15) is true, and that means that (2) is true. Clearly, then, commas and parentheses are not only important aids for the elimination of ambiguity, but they may play a crucial role in the determination of a sentence's truth-value.

EXAMPLE 2

Find the truth-value of the following sentence.

> Either it is not the case that (both) the
> Nile River is not shorter than the Allegheny
> and Chicago is not a city, or (both) Mary
> Poppins is not a paratrooper and the Nile
> River is shorter than the Allegheny.

Solution. Let '*C*', '*M*', and '*N*' be as in Example 1. Then the given sentence may be abbreviated by the following *disjunction* of conjunctions.

$$-(-N\cdot-C) \vee (-M\cdot N).$$

We replace the sentences with their values as given in Example 1.

$$-(-(f)\cdot-(t)) \vee (-(f)\cdot f).$$

Replace negated 't's' with 'f's' and vice versa.

$$-(t\cdot f) \vee (t\cdot f).$$

Since a conjunction with a false conjunct is false, we have

$$-(f) \vee (f).$$

Replacing the negated 'f', we obtain

$$t \vee f$$

which is true. Hence our original sentence is true.

EXAMPLE 3

Suppose the variables '*p*' and '*r*' are interpreted as true sentences and '*q*' is interpreted as a false one. What will be the truth-value of the sentence obtained from the following schema.

$$-\{-[-q \vee (p\cdot-r)]\cdot(-p \vee q)\}.$$

Solution. Begin by replacing variables with 't's' and 'f's'.

$$-\{-[-(f) \vee (t\cdot-(t))]\cdot(-(t) \vee f)\}.$$

Replace negated 't's' with 'f's' and vice versa.

$$-\{-[t \vee (t\cdot f)]\cdot(f \vee f)\}.$$

A conjunction with a false conjunct is false: so

$$-\{-[t \vee (f)]\cdot(f \vee f)\}.$$

Since a disjunction with only false disjuncts is false, we have

$$-\{-[t \vee (f)]\cdot f\}.$$

And since a disjunction with a true disjunct is true,

$$-\{-[t]\cdot f\}.$$

A negated 't' may be replaced by an 'f', so

$$-\{f\cdot f\}$$

which is, finally, the negation of a false conjunction. Thus, the truth-value of the sentence obtained from the given schema with the given interpretations of its variables is true.

Review problems for Sec. 1.3.

1. Express the following in symbolic notation using the suggested abbreviations. *Note:* Be sure parentheses clearly indicate main connectives.

    > '*M*' for 'Mary has been making mud pies'.
    > '*J*' for 'Junior has been playing with his chemistry set'.
    > '*B*' for 'Barry has been making mud pies'.

    a) Either Mary has been making mud pies or Junior has been playing with his chemistry set.
    b) Junior has not been playing with his chemistry set, but both Mary and Barry have been making mud pies.
    c) Either both Mary and Barry have been making mud pies, or Mary has but Barry has not been making mud pies.
    d) It is not the case that both Junior has been playing with his chemistry set and Barry has not been making mud pies.

2. Express the following in symbolic notation. Again, be careful with your parentheses, brackets, and braces.

    a) the negation of Prob. 1(a)
    b) the disjunction of Prob. 1(a) and 1(b)
    c) the conjunction of Prob. 1(b) and 1(c)
    d) the conjunction of Prob. 1(c) and the negation of Prob. 1(a)
    e) the disjunction of Prob. 1(b) and 1(c), with Prob. 1(d)
    f) the negation of the disjunction of Prob. 1(c) and 1(d)
    g) the negation of the conjunction of the negation of Prob. 1(d) and 1(b)
    h) the conjunction of the negations of Prob. 1(b) and 1(d)
    i) the conjunction of the negation of Prob. 1(a) with the disjunction of Prob. 1(b) and 1(c)
    j) the disjunction of the conjunction of the negation of Prob. 1(a) and 1(b), with Prob. 1(c)

3. Make up ordinary English sentences that could be regarded as interpretations of the following schemata. Be sure your commas and semicolons clearly indicate proper grouping.

    a) $p \cdot (q \vee r)$
    b) $(p \cdot q) \vee r$
    c) $-p \cdot (q \vee -r)$
    d) $-(p \cdot q) \vee r$

    e) $-[-(p \cdot q)]$
    f) $(p \cdot -q) \vee -r$
    g) $(p \cdot q) \vee -(p \cdot -r)$
    h) $(r \vee p) \cdot -q$

4. Suppose '*p*' and '*q*' are interpreted as true and '*r*' is interpreted as false, and find the truth-values of the sentences represented by Prob. 3(a)–3(h).

5. Suppose

    a) 'Mary has been making mud pies' is true;
    b) 'Barry has been making mud pies' is false;
    c) 'Junior has been playing with his chemistry set' is true;

    and determine the truth-value of Prob. 2(a)–2(j).

6. If '*p*' is interpreted as true and '*p·q*' as false, what, if anything, do we know about the interpretation of '*q*'?

7. If '*p*' and '*p* ∨ *q*' are interpreted as true, what, if anything, do we know about the interpretation of '*q*'?

8. If '*p*' and '−(*p·q*)' are interpreted as true, what, if anything, do we know about the interpretation of '*q*'?

9. If '*p*' and '*p* ∨ (*q·* −*p*)' are interpreted as true, what, if anything, do we know about the interpretation of '*q*'?

10. If '−*p*', '*q*', and '(*p·* −*q*) ∨ (*r·* −*p*)' are interpreted as true, what, if anything, do we know about the interpretation of '*r*'?

11. If '−*p*' and '*q*' are interpreted as true and '−(*p* ∨ −*q*)· −(−*r* ∨ −*p*)' is interpreted as false, what, if anything, do we know about the interpretation of '*r*'?

1.4 Material conditional and biconditional

We have reached the most important truth-operator we have to consider, namely, 'if–then'. Consider the sentence

(1)   If Mrs. Wolf serves duck for dinner then there is a party at Charlie's house.

Sentence (1) may be regarded as an interpretation of the schema

(2)   If *p* then *q*.

when

       Mrs. Wolf serves duck for dinner.

is regarded as an interpretation of '*p*' and

       There is a party at Charlie's house.

is regarded as an interpretation of '*q*'.

The schema (2) will be called a **conditional schema.** Any sentence that may be regarded as an interpretation of (2) will be called a **conditional sentence** or, for short, a **conditional.** (Some authors prefer the terms 'implication' or 'hypothetical sentence'.) The sentence following 'if' (or its grammatical equivalents) is called the **antecedent** and the sentence following 'then' (or its grammatical equivalents) is called the **consequent** of the conditional. We shall consider some of the grammatical equivalents of 'if' and 'then' below.

There are many kinds of conditional sentences, not all of which are truth-functional. It may be said quite generally, however, that one uses a conditional to assert that its consequent is (or was, will be, would be, etc.) true *on the condition that* or *given the hypothesis that* its antecedent is (or was, will be, were, etc.) true. For example, (1) would generally be considered true if when Mrs. Wolf serves duck for dinner, there *is* a party at Charlie's house. Furthermore, if it is true that Mrs. Wolf serves duck for dinner but false that there is a party at Charlie's house, then (1) would generally be considered false. In other words, given any kind of conditional sentence, if the antecedent and the consequent both do happen, the sentence is considered true; if the antecedent happens but the consequent does not, the sentence is considered false.

All the last paragraph is fairly straightforward, but consider four more conditional sentences:

(3)   If wishes were horses then beggers would ride.

(4)   If you were a madman then I would be at your side.

(5)   If there is a third world war then there will be no survivors.

(6)   If there is a third world war then only the people living in New York will survive.

The antecedents of these four conditional sentences are false, but what are the truth-values of the conditional sentences themselves? We *suppose* (3) and (5) are true, while (4) and (6) are false. But why? Since each sentence has a false antecedent, we cannot say that (3) and (5) are true *because* their antecedents and consequents are true, and we cannot say that (4) and (6) are false *because* their antecedents are true while their consequents are false. But if we cannot determine the truth-values of (3)–(6) by considering the values of their component sentences, then (3)–(6) are not truth-functional conditional sentences. It happens that many ordinary English conditional sentences (including all contrary to fact or subjunctive conditionals, i.e., conditionals with the form, 'if ... were thus ... would be so') are simply not truth-functional sentences. These nontruth-functional sentences have exactly the same status as sentences beginning 'Amos believes that ... '. They *seem* to be more problematic because the English words 'if' and 'then' occur in both the truth-functional and the nontruth-functional conditionals. But as long as we are aware that the operator 'if–then' may be used in a nontruth-functional fashion, there need be no confusion.

The question remains: Granted that there are different kinds of conditional sentences, under what conditions is a truth-functional conditional sentence true or false? The answer is this: A truth-functional conditional is true when it has either a false antecedent or a true consequent. For example,

(7)   If rice is grown in China then two plus two equals four.

and

(8)   If two plus two equals five then rice is grown in Greenland.

are *both true* truth-functional conditionals. Sentence (7) is true because it has a true consequent and (8) is true because it has a false antecedent. Notice that it is not and *need not be* claimed that there is any relation between rice growing and arithmetical truths. Like all truth-functional sentences, the truth-value of a truth-functional conditional is a function of the *truth-values* of its component sentences. The *contents* or *meanings* of its components are irrelevant. Only their truth-values are important. Thus, unlike many other types of conditionals, the contents, senses, or meanings of the antecedents and consequents of truth-functional conditionals are frequently unrelated in any obvious fashion.

We may generalize our discussion of truth-functional conditionals thus: A sentence schema of the form 'if p then q' represents a true sentence when either the sentence represented by 'p' is false or the sentence represented by 'q' is true; if the sentence represented by 'p' is true and the sentence represented by 'q' is false then 'if p then q' represents a false sentence. Truth-functional conditional sentences will be called **material conditionals.** We shall use the horseshoe '$\supset$' to abbreviate the truth-operator 'if–then'. The technical name for the horseshoe is a **material conditional sign.** Any (truth-functional) sentence schema having the form '$p \supset q$' will be called a **material conditional schema.** Figure 1.41 is a truth-table definition of a material conditional schema. It tells us the conditions under which any sentence patterned after that schema is true or false.

$$p \quad \supset \quad q$$

t	t	t
t	f	f
f	t	t
f	t	f

Figure 1.41

The first line tells us that when the interpretations of both 'p' and 'q' are true, the interpretation of '$p \supset q$' is true. The second line tells us that when the interpretation of 'p' is true and the interpretation of 'q' is false, the interpretation of '$p \supset q$' is false, etc.

Before closing our discussion of material conditionals, we should consider a few other English locutions that may be used to express it. The following may be abbreviated by '$p \supset q$'.

If *p* then *q*.

q if *p*.

q provided that *p*.

q in case *p*.

p only if *q*.

Only if *q*, *p*.

In general, the sentence immediately following 'if' or some equivalent locution such as 'provided that' is the antecedent of a conditional. A sentence following 'only if' is a consequent.

The sentence

(9)   The Soviet Union wants peace if and only if the United States gets a smaller piece.

contains two conditional sentences, namely,

(10)   The Soviet Union wants peace *if* the United States gets a smaller piece.

and

(11)   The Soviet Union wants peace *only if* the United States gets a smaller piece.

This particular kind of truth-functional sentence will be called a **biconditional sentence** or, for short, a **biconditional.** (Some authors prefer to call it an 'equivalence sentence'.) Truth-functional biconditionals will be called **material biconditionals.** That is the only kind we shall discuss. As its name suggests and we have just shown, a biconditional is made up of two conditionals. Hence the name '*bi*conditional'. The claim behind a biconditional is that the sentences on either side of the truth-operator 'if and only if' have the same truth-value. That is, a biconditional is true when its component sentences are either both true or both false.

We may generalize our remarks in the last paragraph thus: A sentence schema of the form '*p* if and only if *q*' represents a true sentence when either both of the sentences represented by '*p*' and '*q*' are true or both of them are false. We shall use the three bars '$\equiv$' to abbreviate the truth-operator 'if and only if'. The technical name for the operator is **material biconditional sign.** Any sentence schema having the form '*p* $\equiv$ *q*' will be called a **material biconditional schema.** Figure 1.42 is a truth-table definition of a material biconditional schema. It tells us the conditions under which any sentence patterned after that schema is true or false.

$$
\begin{array}{ccc}
p & \equiv & q \\
\hline
t & t & t \\
t & f & f \\
f & f & t \\
f & t & f \\
\end{array}
$$

Figure 1.42

The first line tells us that when the interpretations of both 'p' and 'q' are true, the interpretation of '$p \equiv q$' is true. The second line tells us that when the interpretation of 'p' is true and the interpretation of 'q' is false, the interpretation of '$p \equiv q$' is false, etc.

Review problems for Sec. 1.4.

1. Define the following.

   a) material conditional schema   d) antecedent
   b) material conditional sign   e) consequent
   c) material conditional

2. Complete the following truth-table definition of a material conditional schema.

$$
\begin{array}{ccc}
p & \supset & q \\
\hline
 & t & \\
 & f & \\
 & t & \\
 & t & \\
\end{array}
$$

3. Give an example that proves that contrary to fact conditionals are not truth-functional.

4. Express the following in symbolic notation using the suggested abbreviations.

'L'	for	'Larry will marry Jerry'.
'M'	for	'Mary marries Harry'.
'T'	for	'Tommy will run home to his mommy'.
'C'	for	'Clyde turns from Jeckle to Hyde'.
'J'	for	'The jelly is smelly'.
'S'	for	'Shelly will have a sore belly'.

   a) Larry will marry Jerry only if Mary marries Harry.
   b) If Mary marries Harry then Tommy will run home to his mommy.
   c) Tommy will run home to his mommy provided that Clyde turns from Jeckle to Hyde.
   d) Only if Clyde turns from Jeckle to Hyde, Larry will marry Jerry.
   e) In case the jelly is smelly, Shelly will have a sore belly.
   f) Shelly will have a sore belly if Clyde turns from Jeckle to Hyde.

5. Define the following.

   a)   material biconditional schema
   b)   material biconditional sign
   c)   material biconditional

6. Complete the following truth-table definition of a material biconditional schema.

$$p \equiv q$$

p	$\equiv$	q
t		
	f	
f		
	f	

7. Suppose

   a)   'Larry will marry Jerry' is true.
   b)   'Mary marries Harry' is false.
   c)   'Tommy will run home to his mommy' is true.
   d)   'Clyde turns from Jeckle to Hyde' is false.
   e)   'The jelly is smelly' is true.
   f)   'Shelly will have a sore belly' is false.

   and determine the truth-value of Probs. 4(a)–4(f).

8. Make up English sentences that could be expressed by the following. Be sure commas and semicolons clearly indicate proper grouping.

   a) $p \supset (q \equiv r)$ 　　　　　　　f) $-(p \equiv q) \supset r$
   b) $(-r \vee p) \cdot q$ 　　　　　　　　g) $(p \vee q) \cdot (r \supset -p)$
   c) $(r \equiv p) \vee -q$ 　　　　　　　h) $(-p \supset -p)$
   d) $(q \supset p) \supset r$ 　　　　　　i) $p \vee (q \supset -r)$
   e) $-(q \supset -r)$ 　　　　　　　　j) $(-q \cdot -r) \equiv p$

9. If 'p' is interpreted as true and 'q' and 'r' are interpreted as false, find the values of Probs. 8(a)–8(j).

10. Express the following in symbolic notation using 'C' as an abbreviation of 'Clay will beat Patterson' and 'P' for 'Patterson uses a gun'.

   Clay will beat Patterson unless Patterson uses a gun.

11. If 'p' and '$p \supset q$' are interpreted as true, what, if anything, do we know about the interpretation of 'q'?

12. If 'p' and '$p \equiv q$' are interpreted as false, what, if anything, do we know about the interpretation of 'q'?

13. If 'p' and '$(p \supset q) \supset p$' are interpreted as false, what, if anything, do we know about the interpretation of 'q'?

14. If 'p' and '$(q \equiv p) \vee q$' are interpreted as true, what, if anything, do we know about the interpretation of 'q'?

15. If 'p' is given a false interpretation and '$(-p \lor q) \supset -q$' is given a true one, what, if anything, do we know about the interpretation of 'q'?

16. If 'p', 'q', and '$(p \lor -r) \equiv (-q \supset r)$' are given false interpretations, what, if anything, do we know about the interpretation of 'r'?

17. If 'p', 'q', and '$p \supset (r \supset -q)$' are given true interpretations, what, if anything, do we know about the interpretation of 'r'?

1.5 Tautologies and the truth-table test

A sentence schema from which only true uniform interpretations may be obtained is called a **tautologous schema.** Interpretations of tautologous schemata are called **tautologous sentences** or, for short, **tautologies.** Examples of tautologous schemata are '$p \lor -p$', '$p \supset (p \lor q)$', and '$(p \cdot q) \supset p$'.

A sentence schema from which only false uniform interpretations may be obtained is called a **contradictory schema.** Interpretations of contradictory schemata are called **contradictory sentences** or, for short, **contradictions.** Examples of contradictory schemata are '$p \cdot -p$', '$-(p \supset p)$', and '$-[p \supset (p \lor q)]$'.

A sentence schema from which at least one true and at least one false uniform interpretation may be obtained is called a **contingent schema.** Interpretations of contingent schemata are called **contingent sentences.** Examples of contingent schemata are 'p', '$p \lor q$', and '$p \supset -q$'.

In the remaining paragraphs of this section we shall introduce a method of testing sentence schemata to find out whether they are tautologous, contradictory, or contingent. Since it is merely an extension of what we already know about truth-tables, it may conveniently be referred to as the **truth-table test.**

The truth-table test is one of many methods or procedures designed to test schemata to see if they have a certain property, e.g., to see if they are tautologous or contradictory or contingent, etc. Logicians call such tests **decision procedures.** The logician's idea of a decision procedure is *narrower* than that employed by the man on the street. Ordinarily any procedure one might use to reach a decision could be correctly referred to as a decision procedure, e.g., flipping a coin, asking mother, appealing to a judge and jury, voting, etc. Different procedures may have different degrees of precision, reliability, lucidity, costs, etc. A decision procedure which is completely reliable, precise, and completable in a finite length of time is called **effective.** Frequently such procedures are described as *mechanical* to suggest the fact that they might be performed by some appropriately constructed machine. These are the procedures with which logicians *as* logicians (i.e., not as public citizens, board members, gamblers, etc.) are primarily concerned.

The so-called (effective) **decision problem** for a given class of schemata is the problem of *finding a decision procedure* for determining whether or not a certain property (e.g., that of being tautologous) belongs to each of the members of that class. If such a procedure can be found, the problem is said to be **solvable.** If it can be shown that it is impossible to construct such a procedure, the problem is said to be **unsolvable.** For example, we may say that the decision problem for the calculus of sentences is the problem of inventing an effective decision procedure for determining which of its schemata are tautologous and which are not. The truth-table test is just such a procedure. Therefore, for the calculus of sentences the decision problem is solvable.

Consider the following examples of the truth-table test.

EXAMPLE 1

Is the following schema tautologous?

$$p \vee -p$$

Solution. This particular schema was used as an example of a tautologous schema in the first paragraph. It is called the **law of excluded middle;** i.e., any sentence is either true or false. We may prove that '$p \vee -p$' is tautologous by listing *every* possible combination of truth-values for any uniform interpretation of this schema and showing that the truth-value of any such interpretation is always true. We learned in Sec. 1.2 that N variables which may have one of two attributes admit of 2^N combinations. So in order to list every possible combination of truth-values for any uniform interpretation of '$p \vee -p$', we need $2^N = 2^1 = 2$ rows. That is, our truth-table begins

$$
\begin{array}{ccc}
p & \vee & -p \\
\hline
t & & \\
f & &
\end{array}
$$

When the interpretation of 'p' is true, the interpretation of '$-p$' is false, and vice versa. So the letters under '$-p$' must be

$$
\begin{array}{ccc}
p & \vee & -p \\
\hline
t & & f \\
f & & t
\end{array}
$$

Finally, we may fill in the column under the disjunction sign according to the interpretations given and the truth-table definition of a disjunction schema. That is, when at least one disjunct is given a true interpretation, the interpretation of the whole schema is true. So the complete truth-table looks like this.

$$
\begin{array}{ccc}
p & \vee & -p \\
\hline
t \quad t & & f \\
f \quad t & & t
\end{array}
$$

The column below the disjunction sign has only 't's' in it. That means that only true uniform interpretations may be obtained from the schema '$p \lor -p$'; i.e., it means that '$p \lor -p$' is tautologous. Hence, any sentence having the form of this schema is a tautology, e.g.,

> Either Ralfe is a robot or Ralfe is not a robot.
>
> Sidney is going to college or not.
>
> Either John loves Mary and Sally is lonely, or it is not the case that (both) John loves Mary and Sally is lonely.

EXAMPLE 2

Is the following schema tautologous?

$$(p \lor q) \equiv -(-p \cdot -q)$$

Solution. Since we have two variables 'p' and 'q', we must have $2^N = 2^2 = 4$ rows. To determine the distribution of 't's' and 'f's' in each column, we employ the following rule: The xth column $(x = 1, 2, \ldots, N)$ of a sentence with N distinct variables begins with 2^{N-x} 't's' which are followed by as many 'f's'. The 2^{N-x} 't's' and 'f's' are alternated throughout each column. Thus, for example, under our first variable 'p' we have $2^{N-x} = 2^{2-1} = 2$ 't's' which are followed by 2 'f's'. Under our second variable 'q' we have $2^{N-2} = 2^{2-2} = 2^0 = 1$ 't' which is followed by as many 'f's', which is followed by a 't', which is followed by an 'f'. This brings us to the fourth and last row. We have then

(p	$\lor$	q)	$\equiv$	$-(-p$	$\cdot$	$-q)$
t		t				
t		f				
f		t				
f		f				

From here on everything is quite mechanical. The letters under the disjunction sign must be exactly the same as those in the truth-table definition of a disjunction schema. Thus

(p	$\lor$	q)	$\equiv$	$-(-p$	$\cdot$	$-q)$
t	t	t				
t	t	f				
f	t	t				
f	f	f				

We know that whenever 'p' is given a true interpretation, the interpretation of '$-p$' is false. Thus we may fill in the letters under '$-p$' on the right side of the biconditional sign in accordance with those under 'p' on the left side. That is,

$$(p \quad \lor \quad q) \quad \equiv \quad -(-p \quad \cdot \quad -q)$$

t	t	t		f
t	t	f		f
f	t	t		t
f	f	f		t

Similarly, we may fill in the letters under '$-q$' on the right in accordance with those under 'q' on the left; thus

$$(p \quad \lor \quad q) \quad \equiv \quad -(-p \quad \cdot \quad -q)$$

t	t	t		f		f
t	t	f		f		t
f	t	t		t		f
f	f	f		t		t

The letters under the conjunction sign may be filled in by recalling the truth-table definition of a conjunction schema; i.e., the interpretation of the whole schema is true only when the interpretations of both conjuncts are true. So only the last line has a 't' in the column under the conjunction sign.

$$(p \quad \lor \quad q) \quad \equiv \quad -(-p \quad \cdot \quad -q)$$

t	t	t		f	f	f
t	t	f		f	f	t
f	t	t		t	f	f
f	f	f		t	t	t

If '$-p \cdot -q$' is given a true interpretation then the interpretation of '$-(-p \cdot -q)$' is false, and vice versa. Hence below the negation sign in front of '$(-p \cdot -q)$' we have the new column of 't's' and 'f's' indicating the values of the negated conjunction for the four combinations.

$$(p \quad \lor \quad q) \quad \equiv \quad -(-p \quad \cdot \quad -q)$$

t	t	t		t	f	f	f
t	t	f		t	f	f	t
f	t	t		t	t	f	f
f	f	f		f	t	t	t
	*			*			

Finally, to find out whether or not the given schema is tautologous, we fill in the letters below the biconditional sign in accordance with the truth-table definition of a biconditional schema and the letters above the asterisks. That is, we imagine we have the following truth-table

?	≡	?
t		t
t		t
t		t
f		f
*		*

which must contain only 't's' in its center column.

?		≡		?
t	t	t	
t	t	t	
t	t	t	
f	t	f	
*		*	

That means that only true uniform interpretations may be obtained from the schema '$(p \lor q) \equiv -(-p \cdot -q)$'; i.e., it means that this schema is tautologous. Hence, any sentence having the form of this schema is a tautology, e.g.,

> Either Merl or Pearl is a lumberjack,
> if and only if, it is not the case that
> both Merl is not a lumberjack and Pearl
> is not a lumberjack.

> Lora will take the train or the bus, if
> and only if, Lora will not both fail to
> take the train and fail to take the bus.

> Maryland is near New York or Delaware,
> if and only if, Maryland is not both
> far from New York and far from Delaware.

EXAMPLE 3

Is the following schema tautologous, contradictory, or contingent?

$$[(p \supset q) \cdot (q \supset r)] \supset r$$

Solution. Since we have three distinct variables 'p', 'q', and 'r', we shall need a truth-table with $2^N = 2^3 = 8$ rows. The column under the first variable 'p' begins with $2^{N-1} = 2^{3-1} = 2^2 = 4$ 't's' which are followed by four 'f's'. The column under the second variable 'q' begins with $2^{N-2} = 2^{3-2} = 2^1 = 2$ 't's' which are followed by two 'f's'. The pairs of 't's' and 'f's' are alternated until the eighth and last row is reached. The column under the third variable 'r' begins with $2^{N-3} = 2^{3-3} = 2^0 = 1$ 't' which is followed by an 'f'. The 't's' and 'f's' are alternated until the eighth and final row is reached. We have, then,

$$[(p \supset q) \cdot (q \supset r)] \supset r$$

t	t	t	t	t
t	t	t	f	f
t	f	f	t	t
t	f	f	f	f
f	t	t	t	t
f	t	t	f	f
f	f	f	t	t
f	f	f	f	f

The second occurrence of '*q*' has a column of '*t*'s' and '*f*'s' under it that exactly matches the column under the first occurrence of '*q*'. Similarly, the column under the second occurrence of '*r*' matches the column under the first occurrence of '*r*'. The columns under the horseshoes in '*p* ⊃ *q*' and '*q* ⊃ *r*' can now be completed. There will be '*t*'s' to the right of all '*f*'s' in the antecedent columns and to the left of all '*t*'s' in the consequent columns, and '*f*'s' in the remaining places.

$$[(p \supset q) \cdot (q \supset r)] \supset r$$

t	t	t		t	t	t		t
t	t	t		t	f	f		f
t	f	f		f	t	t		t
t	f	f		f	t	f		f
f	t	t		t	t	t		t
f	t	t		t	f	f		f
f	t	f		f	t	t		t
f	t	f		f	t	f		f

The column under the conjunction sign may be completed by putting a '*t*' between every occurrence of '*t*'s' in the same row of *both* of the columns above the asterisks and '*f*'s' in the remaining places. Thus

$$[(p \supset q) \cdot (q \supset r)] \supset r$$

t	t	t	t	t	t	t		t
t	t	t	f	t	f	f		f
t	f	f	f	f	t	t		t
t	f	f	f	f	t	f		f
f	t	t	t	t	t	t		t
f	t	t	f	t	f	f		f
f	t	f	t	f	t	t		t
f	t	f	t	f	t	f		f
		*				*		

Finally, to find whether the given schema is tautologous, contradictory, or contingent, we fill in the letters below the conditional sign outside the brackets.

There will be 't's' to the left of every 't' in the column under '*r*' and to the right of all 'f's' in the column under the conjunction sign. The remaining places will contain 'f's'. As it turns out, there is only one 'f' in the column under this conditional sign, in the very last row.

[(*p*	⊃	*q*)	·	(*q*	⊃	*r*)]	⊃	*r*
t	t	t	t	t	t	t	t	t
t	t	t	f	t	f	f	t	f
t	f	f	f	f	t	t	t	t
t	f	f	f	f	t	f	t	f
f	t	t	t	t	t	t	t	t
f	t	t	f	t	f	f	t	f
f	t	f	t	f	t	t	t	t
f	t	f	t	f	t	f	f	f

That means that at least one false and at least one true uniform interpretation may be obtained from the schema '$[(p \supset q) \cdot (q \supset r)] \supset r$'; i.e., it means that this schema is contingent. Hence, any sentence having the form of this schema is contingent, e.g.

> If Liz is here then Dick is here, and if Dick is here then Eddie is gone; only if Eddie is gone.

> Charles will be King provided that Phillip dies, and if Charles will be King then Alexander must be assassinated; only if Alexander must be assassinated.

> If we shall need our coats in case Chicago is windy, and we shall need our gloves if Chicago is windy; then we shall need our gloves.

    Two schemata are truth-functionally equivalent if and only if the biconditional formed with one of them on either side is *tautologous*.

EXAMPLE 4

(1)   '$p \lor q$' is truth-functionally equivalent to '$-(-p \cdot -q)$'

if and only if

(2) $(p \lor q) \equiv -(-p \cdot -q)$

is *tautologous*. In Example 2 above we proved that (2) *is tautologous*. Hence (1) is true.

Notice that (1) and (2) are quite different. Sentence (1) is a *sentence* about two schemata and the relation of equivalence that obtains between them, but (2) is a sentence *schema*. Sentence (1) is true, but (2) cannot be true or false. Schema (2) can only have true or false interpretations.

EXAMPLE 5

(3)   '$p \supset q$' is truth-functionally equivalent to '$-(p \cdot -q)$'

if and only if

(4) $(p \supset q) \equiv -(p \cdot -q)$

is *tautologous*. As you will prove shortly (in the review problems), (4) *is* tautologous. Hence (3) is true. Again, (3) and (4) are quite different, because (3) is a *sentence* about two schemata and (4) is a sentence *schema*.

Sentences (1) and (3) suggest that we might eliminate the operators 'either–or' and 'if–then' in favor of two others, 'and' and 'it is not the case that'. Or, briefly, (1) and (3) suggest we might eliminate '$\vee$' and '$\supset$' in favor of '$\cdot$' and '$-$'. This is indeed the case. Moreover, we may also eliminate '$\equiv$' in favor of '$\cdot$' and '$-$'. That is,

(5) $(p \equiv q) \equiv [-(p \cdot -q) \cdot -(q \cdot -p)]$

is tautologous.

We may also eliminate '$\cdot$', '$\supset$', and '$\equiv$' in favor of '$\vee$' and '$-$' in view of the following tautologous schemata.

(6) $(p \cdot q) \equiv -(-p \vee -q)$.

(7) $(p \supset q) \equiv (-p \vee q)$.

(8) $(p \equiv q) \equiv -[-(-p \vee q) \vee -(-q \vee p)]$.

We may eliminate '$\vee$', '$\cdot$', and '$\equiv$' in favor of '$\supset$' and '$-$' in view of the following.

(9) $(p \vee q) \equiv (-p \supset q)$.

(10) $(p \cdot q) \equiv -(p \supset -q)$.

(11) $(p \equiv q) \equiv -[(p \supset q) \supset -(q \supset p)]$.

Finally, using only '$\supset$', we may express '$\vee$'.

(12) $(p \vee q) \equiv [(p \supset q) \supset q]$.

Review problems for Sec. 1.5.

1. Define the following.

   a) tautologous schema   d) contingent schema
   b) tautology   e) effective decision procedure
   c) contradictory schema   f) decision problem

2. To find out whether or not '$p \supset (r \vee q)$' is tautologous using the truth-table test, how many rows of 't's' and 'f's' are required? With how many 't's' does the *column* of 't's' and 'f's' under the first variable begin? The second? The third?

3. Complete the following truth-table.

$$p \quad \supset \quad (r \quad \vee \quad q)$$

t	t
t	t
t	t
t	f
f	t
f	t
f	t
f	f

   Is '$p \supset (r \vee q)$' tautologous, contradictory, or contingent?

4. Determine which of the following are tautologous, which are contradictory, and which are contingent.

   a) $p \equiv (p \cdot q)$ g) $-(p \vee -q) \supset (q \cdot -p)$
   b) $(q \vee p) \equiv (-q \supset p)$ h) $q \supset [(-p \supset q) \supset p]$
   c) $p \supset (-p \vee q)$ i) $(p \vee -q) \equiv (p \equiv -q)$
   d) $-q \cdot -(-p \vee -q)$ j) $-[-(-p \cdot q) \vee -p]$
   e) $(p \vee -q) \vee q$ k) $-(-p \supset q) \supset -p$
   f) $(p \vee -q) \cdot (-q \supset p)$ l) $(p \vee -q) \cdot (-p \supset -q)$

5. Explain or account for the following.

   a) The conjunction of a false sentence with any other sentence must be false.
   b) The conjunction of a true sentence with any other sentence must have the truth-value of the other sentence.
   c) The disjunction of a true sentence with any other sentence must be true.
   d) The disjunction of a false sentence with any other sentence must have the truth-value of the other sentence.
   e) The conditional sentence with a false antecedent and any consequent must be true.
   f) The conditional sentence with a true consequent and any antecedent must be true.

g)   The conditional sentence with a true antecedent must have the truth-value of its
consequent.

6. Using the suggested abbreviations and the truth-table test, decide which of the following are tautologies, which are contradictions, and which are contingent sentences.
(*Note:* To save time, instead of replacing sentence *letters* with *variables* to obtain the
proper *schema* to test, you may pretend that the letters are variables and apply the test
immediately.)

a)   If you drop your cup, then it will break only if you drop your cup. *D, B.*
b)   If you drop your cup then it will break, and you will cry. *C.*
c)   Either you do not drop your cup and it does not break, or it breaks.
d)   You drop your cup and it breaks, if and only if, you drop your cup only if it does
not break.
e)   If you do not drop your cup and it breaks, then you do not drop your cup.
f)   You drop your cup and it does not break, if and only if, either you do not drop
your cup or it breaks.
g)   Either you drop your cup, or it is not the case that both you drop your cup and
it does not break.
h)   You drop your cup only if it breaks, only if it breaks; only if you drop your cup.

7. Prove that (4)–(12) (in Sec. 1.5) are tautologous schemata.

8. Use the truth-table test to prove that the following biconditional schemata are
tautologous; i.e., prove that the schemata on either side of each biconditional sign are
truth-functionally equivalent.

a) $p \equiv -(-p)$

b) $[p \lor (q \lor r)] \equiv [(p \lor q) \lor r]$

c) $[p \cdot (q \cdot r)] \equiv [(p \cdot q) \cdot r]$

d) $(p \lor q) \equiv (q \lor p)$

e) $(p \cdot q) \equiv (q \cdot p)$

f) $-(p \lor q) \equiv (-p \cdot -q)$

g) $-(p \cdot q) \equiv (-p \lor -q)$

h) $[p \cdot (q \lor r)] \equiv [(p \cdot q) \lor (p \cdot r)]$

i) $[p \lor (q \cdot r)] \equiv [(p \lor q) \cdot (p \lor r)]$

j) $(p \supset q) \equiv (-q \supset -p)$

k) $p \equiv (p \cdot p)$

l) $p \equiv (p \lor p)$

m) $[(p \cdot q) \supset r] \equiv [p \supset (q \supset r)]$

9. Make up an ordinary English interpretation for each of the schemata in the last
question.

1.6   Arguments and validity

So far we have been primarily concerned with sentences and sentence schemata.
We have said nothing about arguments or inferences. But if we look up the word
'logic' in, say, *The American College Dictionary*, we find that logic is supposed to be
"the science which investigates the principles governing correct or reliable inference; reasoning or argumentation, or an instance of it". Some people would be
willing to defend the claim that the primary, if not the only, reason for studying

logic is to learn to distinguish correct from incorrect arguments or inferences. Whatever the status of such a claim, in this section we are going to begin our investigation of arguments and argument schemata.

An **argument** may be defined as a sequence of sentences divided in such a way that part of the sequence is supposed to be the warrant, reason, or guarantee for the rest of it. The *guaranteeing* or *warranting* part of an argument is called the **premiss(es)**. There may, of course, be more than one premiss. The *guaranteed* or warranted part is called the **conclusion.** Examples of arguments are

(premisses)	If Richard brought flowers then Jane is happy.
	Richard brought flowers.
(conclusion)	Therefore Jane is happy.
(premisses)	A horse is an animal.
(conclusion)	So the head of a horse is the head of an animal.
(premisses)	Most old men have grey hair.
	Aristotle is an old man.
(conclusion)	Hence it is probable that Aristotle has grey hair.

The word 'inference' is often used interchangeably with 'argument'. In this text we shall use **inference** to refer to the act or process of drawing a conclusion from some premiss(es). Since acts or processes are not sequences of sentences ordered in a certain fashion, inferences are not arguments.

An expression which becomes an *argument* when its variables are appropriately replaced is called an **argument schema.** Argument schemata constitute the *forms* of arguments; they reveal nothing about the *content* of arguments. Examples of argument schemata are

$$\begin{array}{cc} \text{(a)} & \text{(b)} \\[4pt] \dfrac{p}{p \text{ or } q} & \text{if } p \text{ then } q \\ & \dfrac{p}{q} \end{array}$$

In these schemata (a) and (b), the straight line is an abbreviation of 'therefore' (and its grammatical equivalents 'hence', 'so', 'thus', etc.). Schema (a), then, is short for

$$p. \text{ Therefore } p \text{ or } q.$$

By writing 'p' on the line below 'if p then q' in (b), we eliminate the need to write the word 'and'; i.e., (b) is short for

$$\text{If } p \text{ then } q, \text{ and } p. \text{ Therefore } q.$$

We frequently have arguments and argument schemata with more than two premisses in a column.

A **valid argument schema** is one for which *every* uniform interpretation that may be assigned to its variables is such that if its premisses are all true, then its conclusion *must* be true. An **invalid argument schema** is one for which there is *at least one* uniform interpretation such that the premisses are all true and the conclusion is false. The key word in our definition of 'valid argument schema' is '*must*'. The definition does *not* assert that any argument schema which happens to have a uniform interpretation with all true premisses and a true conclusion is valid. That is *false*. As we shall see shortly, an *invalid* argument schema *might* have many uniform interpretations with all true premisses and true conclusions. A valid argument schema is such that the *conjunction* of a true uniform interpretation of its premisses *and* the *negation* of the appropriate interpretation of its conclusion is a *contradiction*. If the interpretation of the premisses of a valid argument schema is true, then no one can assert those premisses *and* deny the conclusion without uttering a contradiction. Let us elucidate these points with three examples.

EXAMPLE 1

The argument schema

$$\frac{p \text{ and } q}{p}$$

is valid. Hence, *every* uniform interpretation which may be assigned to its variables is such that if its premiss is true, its conclusion *must* be true. For instance, if

(1)   Tom and Dick are singers.

is true, then according to the given schema and our definition of 'validity'

(2)   Tom is a singer.

must be true. The conjunction of (1) and the *negation* of (2) is a contradiction; i.e.,

Tom and Dick are singers, and Tom is not a singer.

is a contradiction.

EXAMPLE 2

The argument schema

$$\frac{p}{p \text{ or } q}$$

is valid. Hence, if

(3)   Tex is a dog.

is true, then

(4)   Tex or Rex are dogs.

must be true. The *conjunction* of (3) and the negation of (4), namely,

(5)   Tex is a dog, and it is not the case that either Tex or Rex are dogs.

is a contradiction.

EXAMPLE 3

The argument schema

$$\frac{p}{p \text{ and } q}$$

is invalid. Hence there is *at least one* uniform interpretation of this schema such that its premiss is true and its conclusion is false. For instance,

Chicago is in Illinois.

is true, but

Chicago and Tokyo are in Illinois.

is false.

As we mentioned above, an invalid argument schema *might* have many uniform interpretations with all true premisses and true conclusions; e.g., the given schema may be given the following interpretations.

Chicago is in Illinois.
Chicago and Urbana are in Illinois.

Mars is a planet.
Mars and Earth are planets.

What must be remembered about *invalid* argument schemata is that they *always* admit of *at least one* interpretation with all true premisses and a false conclusion. What must be remembered about valid argument schemata is that they never admit *even one* interpretation with all true premisses and a false conclusion.

Only uniform interpretations of valid argument schemata will be called **valid arguments.** Only uniform interpretations of invalid argument schemata will be called **invalid arguments.** For examples, the interpretations of the valid argument schemata in Examples 1 and 2 are valid arguments; the interpretations of the invalid argument schema in Example 3 are invalid arguments.

If an argument is valid *and* has only true premisses it is called **sound.** (Some authors prefer to call such arguments 'proofs'.) An **unsound** argument is either invalid or else valid with at least one false premiss. (In Part Three we shall consider a third type of unsound argument, one which might be *neither* invalid *nor* valid with at least one false premiss.) The interpretations of the argument schemata in Examples 1 and 2 are sound arguments. The interpretations of the schema in Example 3 are unsound *because* they are *invalid*. The following two arguments are unsound *because* they each have a false premiss. They *are*, however, valid; they may be regarded as interpretations of valid argument schemata.

> Detroit is in Japan.
> Detroit is in Japan or New York.

> If apples grow on vines then Canada is a small country.
> Apples grow on vines.
> Canada is a small country.

An argument whose premisses include a sentence and its negation is said to have **inconsistent premisses.** Such arguments must contain a *false* premiss since either the sentence or its negation must be false. Hence, such arguments are *unsound*. Because they are patterned after schemata that can *never* yield interpretations with all true premisses and false conclusions, however, they cannot be invalid. They must be valid. But they are nevertheless unsound, because they must contain a false premiss.

If the *content* of the premisses *and* conclusion of an argument is such that the conclusion *must* be true if the premisses are all true, *but* the argument cannot be regarded as an interpretation of a valid argument schema, then it is *invalid*. For examples, consider the following arguments.

> This object is a pear.
> This object is a fruit.

> John drew two squares.
> John drew two polygons.

The *content* of these arguments is such that their conclusions *must* be true if their premisses are true. Anyone who knows that all pears are fruits and that all squares are polygons would "see" that the truth of the premisses of these arguments guarantees the truth of their conclusions. If we had defined a 'valid argument' merely as one whose conclusion *must* be true when its premisses are true, we would have to regard the given arguments as valid. We would have to say, however, that they are *valid in virtue of their content*, *not* in virtue of their *form*. Because our definition of a 'valid argument' is *based on* our definition of a 'valid argument schema', we are able to say that the given arguments and all others like them are *invalid;* i.e., they may *not* be regarded as interpretations of valid argument schemata.

The premisses of a valid *argument schema* will be said to **imply** its conclusion. The conclusion of a valid argument schema will be said to **follow from** its premisses (with complete certainty). Hence, in Example 1, we say '*p* and *q*' implies '*p*'; in Example 2 we say '*p*' implies '*p* or *q*'; etc. Similarly, the premisses of a valid *argument* may be said to *imply* its conclusion, and the conclusion may be said to *follow from* its premisses. For examples, the premisses of the arguments in

Examples 1 and 2 imply their conclusions; the conclusions follow from their premisses.

If the conclusion of an argument schema is supposed (claimed, or alleged) to *follow from* its premisses (with complete certainty), then the schema will be called **demonstrative** (or 'deductive'). If the conclusion of an argument schema is supposed (claimed, or alleged) to be *more or less acceptable* relative to its premisses, then the schema will be called **nondemonstrative.** Interpretations of demonstrative and nondemonstrative argument schemata will be called **demonstrative** and **nondemonstrative arguments,** respectively. (We shall have nothing further to say about nondemonstrative argument schemata until Part Two.) The schemata and their interpretations in Examples 1–3 are all demonstrative. Because the schemata and their interpretations in Examples 1 and 2 are valid, they *do* exactly what they are supposed to do. Because the schema and its interpretations in Example 3 are invalid, they do *not* do what they are supposed to do. Nevertheless, all the schemata and interpretations in these examples are referred to as 'demonstrative' because their premisses are supposed to do the same thing, namely, *imply* their conclusions.

These definitions are *not* based on *formal* distinctions. They are based on distinctions of *supposition* or *allegation*. Using these definitions, we cannot always decide whether an argument is demonstrative or nondemonstrative by merely examining its *form*. For example, given the argument

> This apple is red.
> ――――――――――――――――――
> This apple and the one next to it are both red.

we could not decide whether it was supposed to be demonstrative or not. If we regard it as demonstrative, then, because it is invalid, we should reject it. If we regard it as nondemonstrative then it must be *appraised by some other principles*. It must be appraised by principles that are introduced in Part Two of this text. The principles introduced in Part One of this text are, as the title suggests, especially relevant to demonstrative arguments.

Review problems for Sec. 1.6.

1. Define the following.

   a) argument
   b) argument schema
   c) valid argument schema

2. What are the main differences between

   a) valid arguments and valid argument schemata
   b) valid and invalid argument schemata
   c) sound and unsound arguments

    d)   demonstrative and nondemonstrative arguments

    e)   arguments and inferences

    f)   validity in virtue of *content* and validity in virtue of *form*

3. Answer each of the following with 'true' or 'false'. Whenever your answer is 'false', prove it by constructing a counterexample (i.e., an example whose truth demonstrates the falsity of the given claim).

    a)   All the premisses of a valid argument must be true.

    b)   Some demonstrative arguments are sound.

    c)   An unsound argument may be invalid.

    d)   An argument with all true premisses and a true conclusion must be valid.

    e)   An argument with all true premisses and a false conclusion must be invalid.

    f)   Every interpretation of an invalid argument schema is invalid.

    g)   All sound arguments have true conclusions.

    h)   If the conclusion of any argument is false then at least one of its premisses must be false.

    i)   Every true sentence is a valid argument.

    j)   The conclusion of a demonstrative argument *follows from* its premisses.

    k)   At least one premiss of an invalid argument must be false.

    l)   The premiss(es) of a nondemonstrative argument is supposed to make its conclusion more or less acceptable.

    m)   An argument cannot have three premisses.

    n)   At least one premiss of an unsound argument must be false.

1.7   The reductio ad absurdum test

    A **truth-functional argument schema** is an argument schema which contains only truth-functional sentence schemata; i.e., it contains sentence schemata made up entirely of sentence variables and truth-operators. Truth-functional argument schemata, then, fall within the calculus of sentences as the latter was defined in Sec. 1.1. The validity of such schemata may be determined by decision procedures designed to cope with truth-functional schemata; e.g., the truth-table test.

    An argument schema is **truth-functionally valid** if and only if its premiss(es) *truth-functionally implies* its conclusion. Its premiss(es) **truth-functionally implies** its conclusion if and only if the material conditional schema that is formed using its premiss(es) as antecedent and its conclusion as consequent is *tautologous*. If that conditional schema is either *contingent* or *contradictory*, then the argument schema is **truth-functionally invalid** and its premiss(es) does *not* truth-functionally imply its conclusion.

EXAMPLE 1

(1) $\dfrac{p}{p \text{ or } q}$

is a truth-functionally valid argument schema if and only if

(2)   'p' truth-functionally implies 'p or q'.

Sentence (2) is true if and only if

(3)   If p, then p or q

is *tautologous.* Schema (3) may be abbreviated in the usual way; i.e.,

(4) $p \supset (p \lor q)$.

Hence, (2) is true if and only if (4) is tautologous, and the truth-table test may be used to prove that (4) *is* tautologous. Thus (2) is true, and, what amounts to the same thing, (1) is a truth-functionally valid argument schema. Again, it should be noticed that (2) and (3) are not the same. Sentence (2) is a *sentence* about two schemata 'p' and 'p or q' and about the relation of implication that obtains between them; while (3), on the other hand, is *not* a sentence at all, but a sentence *schema.*

Example 2

(5) $\dfrac{p \text{ and } q}{\text{not } p}$

is truth-functionally valid if and only if

(6)   'p and q' truth-functionally implies 'not p'.

Sentence (6) is true if and only if

(7)   If p and q, then not p

or, for short,

(8) $(p \cdot q) \supset -p$

is *tautologous.* But the truth-table test may be used to prove (8) is *contingent.* So (5) is a truth-functionally *invalid* argument schema.

    Examples 1 and 2 illustrate the use of the truth-table test to establish the validity or invalidity of truth-functional argument schemata. The truth-table test provides a solution to the decision problem of finding an effective decision procedure for determining the validity or invalidity of every truth-functional argument schema. Given any truth-functional argument schema, we may test it for validity by applying the truth-table test to the conditional schema formed using the premiss(es) and conclusion of the given argument schema as antecedent and consequent, respectively. If the conditional schema is tautologous, the argument schema is truth-functionally valid. If the conditional schema is contingent or contradictory, the argument schema is truth-functionally invalid.

While the truth-table test has the advantage of familiarity, it becomes extremely cumbersome as the premisses become more numerous and complex. For instance, if an argument schema contained five variables we would need a truth-table with $2^5 = 32$ rows. So it would be helpful to have a shorter method of testing for validity. The method we are going to introduce will be called the **reductio ad absurdum test;** i.e., the reduction to absurdity test. The steps of this method are as follows.

a)   Assume the argument schema is *invalid;* i.e., assume that it may be given a uniform interpretation such that its premisses are all true and its conclusion is false.

b)   Try to *justify* this assumption by giving the premisses and conclusion just such an interpretation.

c)   If it is *impossible* to justify the assumption that the schema is invalid (i.e., if every attempt leads to a contradiction), then the schema is *valid.*

Consider the following examples.

EXAMPLE 3

Test the following schema for validity by the *reductio ad absurdum* test.

$$\frac{p}{p \vee q}$$

Solution. Begin by assuming that it may be given a uniform interpretation such that the premiss is true and the conclusion is false. Thus:

$$\frac{p \qquad\qquad \text{t}}{p \vee q \qquad\quad \text{f}}$$

The lowercase 't' and 'f' to the right of each line are shorthand reminders of our original assumptions. The next step is to try to justify these assumptions by interpreting each of the variables in a manner consistent with the assumptions. It is usually convenient to begin with the conclusion. Since we have assumed that '$p \vee q$' is given a false interpretation, we must suppose both 'p' and 'q' are given false interpretations. This is plainly consistent with our assumption. We record this move by putting lowercase 'f's' beside each variable that is given a false interpretation.

$$\frac{p \qquad\qquad \text{t}}{p^{\text{f}} \vee q^{\text{f}} \qquad\quad \text{f}}$$

To make our interpretation *uniform*, we must give every variable the same interpretation throughout the schema; e.g., if 'p' is given a false interpretation in the conclusion then it must be given a false interpretation everywhere else in the schema, etc. So the premiss 'p' must be given a false interpretation. But this immediately produces a contradiction.

We have, in effect, reduced our assumption to absurdity by showing that it leads us to a contradiction. The assumption that the given schema is invalid (i.e., the assumption that it might be given a uniform interpretation with all true premisses and a false conclusion) has been reduced to absurdity (i.e., it has been shown that the assumption leads to a contradiction). Thus, since it is *impossible* to justify the assumption that the schema is invalid, it must be valid.

Three points should be emphasized. *First*, we begin by *supposing* the variables in the conclusion are given false interpretations *because* we are trying to justify our original assumption. If we supposed they represented true sentences, we would be deliberately violating our assumption. We would not, that is, be *trying to justify our assumption*. For the same reason we always try to interpret each variable in a premiss so that the interpretation of the premiss as a whole is true. *Try* to make every premiss represent a true sentence. *Second*, the fact that it is possible to give some or every premiss a *false* interpretation proves nothing as long as it is *also* possible to provide a uniform interpretation with all true premisses and a false conclusion. If the latter is possible, then the schema is invalid, whether or not the former is possible. *Finally*, recall that a schema with N distinct variables admits of exactly 2^N different uniform truth-value interpretations. So, *at most* 2^N trials may be required. Hence, while we are trying to "guess" the interpretation that will prove a schema's invalidity, we should keep track (mentally or on paper) of each combination of truth-values examined. In this way we may be sure of a correct decision in the shortest possible time.

EXAMPLE 4

Test the following schema for validity.

$$\frac{p \cdot q}{p}$$

Solution. Begin by assuming the schema may be given a uniform interpretation with a true premiss and a false conclusion; i.e., assume

$$\frac{p \cdot q}{p} \quad \begin{array}{c} t \\ f \end{array}$$

Try to justify this assumption by interpreting each variable, beginning with the conclusion, in accordance with the assumption. It must be supposed, then, that '*p*' represents a false sentence.

$$\frac{p \cdot q}{p^f} \qquad \begin{array}{c} t \\ f \end{array}$$

To ensure uniformity, '*p*' is given the same interpretation throughout the schema.

$$\frac{p^f \cdot q}{p^f} \qquad \begin{array}{c} t \\ f \end{array}$$

We have just contradicted ourselves! We assumed that '*p·q*' represents a true sentence. But if '*p*' represents a false sentence then '*p·q*' also represents a false sentence. So '*p·q*' represents a sentence that is *both* true *and* false, which is absurd. The contradiction may be illustrated thus.

(contradiction)

$$\frac{p^f \cdot q}{p^f} \qquad \begin{array}{c} t \\ f \end{array}$$

The assumption that this schema is invalid has led us to a contradiction. It is impossible to provide a uniform interpretation for this schema that has a false conclusion and a true premiss because the very fact that the interpretation of the conclusion is false *guarantees* that the interpretation of the premiss is false. In short, the argument is valid.

EXAMPLE 5

Test the following schema for validity.

$$\begin{array}{c} p \supset q \\ q \cdot r \\ \hline p \cdot r \end{array}$$

Solution. Begin by assuming the schema is invalid.

$$\begin{array}{cc} p \supset q & t \\ q \cdot r & t \\ \hline p \cdot r & f \end{array}$$

Try to justify these assumptions. We may justify the assumption that the conclusion may be given a false interpretation in *three* different ways. We might give only '*p*', only '*q*', or both '*p*' and '*q*' false interpretations. There is no need to interpret both '*p*' and '*q*', and, as a general rule of strategy, we should *make as few interpretations as possible to justify an assumption.* For the case at hand the rule of strategy would prescribe interpreting only '*p*' or only '*q*' as false. If '*r*' is given a false interpretation then the conclusion *and* the second premiss '*q·r*' must be interpreted as false. Thus

$$
\begin{array}{ll}
p \supset q & \text{t} \\
q \cdot r^{\text{f}} \longleftrightarrow & \text{t} \qquad \text{(contradiction)} \\
\hline
p \cdot r^{\text{f}} & \text{f}
\end{array}
$$

This would give us a contradiction, *but* this contradiction is *avoidable.* Now, we are supposed to try to justify our assumptions. Hence we should try to avoid this contradiction; i.e., we should consider alternative interpretations which might justify our assumptions *and* avoid contradictions. An obvious alternative in this case is to interpret '*p*' as false. This is sufficient to give the conclusion '*p·r*' a false interpretation.

$$
\begin{array}{ll}
p^{\text{f}} \supset q & \text{t} \\
q \cdot r & \text{t} \\
\hline
p^{\text{f}} \cdot r & \text{f}
\end{array}
$$

This move "killed two birds with one stone" because not only did it justify our assumption about the conclusion, it also justified our assumption about the first premiss. That is, because '*p* $\supset$ *q*' represents a true sentence when '*p*' is given a false interpretation, the first premiss has been given a *true* interpretation. This has been done without even interpreting '*q*' and it is in complete accord with our rule of strategy.

If both '*q*' and '*r*' are interpreted as true sentences then the second premiss '*q·r*' represents a true sentence.

$$
\begin{array}{ll}
p^{\text{f}} \supset q & \text{t} \\
q^{\text{t}} \cdot r^{\text{t}} & \text{t} \\
\hline
p^{\text{f}} \cdot r & \text{f}
\end{array}
$$

Thus, we have successfully justified our assumption that the given schema is invalid; i.e., we have shown that it is *possible* to interpret the variables in such a way that all the premisses are true and the conclusion is false.

The following are examples of English interpretations of the given schema whose truth-values match those required to show the schema's invalidity.

> If California is an ocean then Cleveland is in Ohio.
> Cleveland and Oberlin are in Ohio.
> California is an ocean and Oberlin is in Ohio.

> If two plus two equals five then two plus one equals three.
> Two plus one equals three and two plus two equals four.
> Two plus two equals both five and four.

Instead of using lowercase 't's' and 'f's' to test a schema, we might use ordinary English sentences. As the examples above suggest, the latter technique would be very cumbersome in most cases.

EXAMPLE 6

Test the following argument for validity.

> If Robinson Crusoe meets Friday on Thursday then Thursday is Friday.
> But Thursday is not Friday.
> Hence Robinson Crusoe is not meeting Friday on Thursday.

Solution. The given argument is valid if and only if it may be regarded as an interpretation of a valid argument schema. To find out whether or not it may be regarded as such an interpretation, we begin by abbreviating its sentences. Let '*R*' be short for 'Robinson Crusoe meets Friday on Thursday' and '*T*' for 'Thursday is Friday'. Then the argument may be abbreviated

$$R \supset T$$
$$\frac{-T}{-R}$$

This argument may be regarded as an interpretation of the following schema.

$$p \supset q$$
$$\frac{-q}{-p}$$

Hence we must test this schema for validity in order to determine the validity of the given argument. Begin by assuming the schema is invalid.

$$
\begin{array}{ll}
p \supset q & \text{t} \\
\underline{-q} & \text{t} \\
-p & \text{f}
\end{array}
$$

Try to justify these assumptions. First, suppose '*p*' represents a true sentence; so '−*p*' represents a false one.

$$
\begin{array}{ll}
p^{t} \supset q & \text{t} \\
\underline{-q} & \text{t} \\
[-p^{t}]^{f} & \text{f}
\end{array}
$$

'*q*' must be interpreted as false in order to give the second premiss '−*q*' a true interpretation.

$$p^t \supset q^f \longleftrightarrow t \qquad \text{(contradiction)}$$
$$[-q^f]^t \qquad\qquad t$$
$$\overline{[-p^t]^f} \qquad\qquad f$$

Then a contradiction results between our assumption that the first premiss represents a true sentence and the fact that it has been given a false interpretation. The only other alternative is to interpret 'q' as a true sentence in the first premiss. That would give '$p \supset q$' a true interpretation, but then the interpretation of the second premiss '$-q$' would be false. This would produce another contradiction.

$$p^t \supset q^t \qquad\qquad t$$
$$[-q^t]^f \longleftrightarrow t \qquad \text{(contradiction)}$$
$$\overline{[-p^t]^f} \qquad\qquad f$$

In short, *every* attempt to provide a uniform interpretation for the given schema that has all true premisses and a false conclusion leads directly to a contradiction. Hence, the schema and, therefore, the given argument must be pronounced '*valid*'.

Review problems for Sec. 1.7.

1. Define the following.

   a)   truth-functional argument schema
   b)   truth-functionally valid argument
   c)   truth-functional implication

2. Test the following schemata for validity by the *reductio ad absurdum* test.

   a) $p \lor q$
        $\overline{p}$

   b) $p \supset q$
        $\overline{-q}$

   c) $-p \supset q$
        $\overline{p}$

   d) $-p \supset (q \lor r)$
        $\overline{-q \lor p}$

   e) $p \equiv r$
        q
        $\overline{-r}$

   f) $r \equiv -q$
        p
        $\overline{-p \supset r}$

   g) $q \equiv -p$
        $-r \supset -q$
        $\overline{p \lor r}$

   h) $q \supset -p$
        $-r \lor -p$
        $\overline{p \supset -q}$

   i) $r \lor (q \cdot p)$
        $p \supset -r$
        $\overline{-q \lor -p}$

   j) $p \equiv (q \lor r)$
        $-q \supset -r$
        $\overline{q \lor -p}$

3. Using the suggested abbreviations, test the following arguments for validity by the *reductio ad absurdum* test. (*Note:* To save time, instead of replacing sentence *letters* with *variables* to obtain the proper schema to test, you may pretend that the letters are variables and apply the test immediately.)

a) If Rocky is kind and rich, then there is no problem. There is a problem. So, either Rocky is not kind or Rocky is not rich. *K, R, P.*

b) Big Shorty recovered the jewels if and only if Short Biggie escaped from prison. It is not the case that (both) Short Biggie escaped from prison and Howard the Coward confessed. Hence, if Howard the Coward confessed then Short Biggie did not escape from prison. *B, S, H.*

c) If Agent 006 finds the spy from B.O.T.C.H. (Big Organization to Control Humanity), then either the spy will destroy Agent 006 or 006 will destroy the spy. The spy from B.O.T.C.H. will not destroy Agent 006. Therefore, Agent 006 will not find the spy. *A, S, D.*

d) The lights in the gym were growing dim and Jim decided to go for a swim. In case Jim did not decide to go for a swim, Tim satisfied his whim by crawling out on a slim limb. Either Tim satisfied his whim by crawling out on a slim limb or the lights in the gym were not growing dim. So, Tim did not satisfy his whim by crawling out on a slim limb. *G, J, T.*

e) If it is not the case that Jethro let the cows wander through Granny's kitchen then a stranger must have done it. If a stranger did it, then he was either foolish or trying to prove something to Granny. A stranger would have nothing to prove to Granny. Hence, either a stranger did not do it or he was foolish. *J, S, F, T.*

f) If Anthony loved Cleopatra then he was not happy. If he was happy, then Brutus sold the tobacco shop and burned the wooden Indian. Anthony was happy but the wooden Indian was not burned. Hence, Brutus neither sold the tobacco shop nor did Anthony love Cleopatra. *A, H, B, I.*

g) The rain in Spain slows down the train as it crosses the plain. The main train in Spain never crosses the plain if the engineer develops a pain from the falling rain. If the engineer does not develop a pain from the falling rain, then either he gets a pain from Lady Jane or the rain in Spain does not slow down the train as it crosses the plain. It follows that the main train in Spain crosses the plain if and only if the engineer does not get a pain from Lady Jane. *R, E, M, J.*

h) Either a ghost knocked Marty down the stairs, or Marty was drunk and fell down. If Marty was drunk, then there is no need to believe that ghosts exist unless Casper appears. Thus, if Marty fell down then there is no need to believe that ghosts exist. *G, D, F, B, C.*

i) Sayers runs, passes, blocks, and even blows up the football. He runs if and only if, he is neither blocking nor passing. He blocks provided that he does not blow up the football. Therefore, if Sayers blows up the football, then he passes but does not run. *R, P, B, O.*

j) It is not the case that a man succeeds if and only if he has ability. A man has ability provided that he displays it once in awhile. If a man displays his ability once in awhile but does not succeed, then either he is unlucky or someone is against him. In case a man is unlucky, he can not display his ability. Thus, if someone is not against him, a man will be successful. *S, A, D, U, G.*

4. Test the following schemata for validity by the *reductio ad absurdum* test.

a) $p \supset (r \lor -s)$
   $-r \lor q$
   $-q$
   _____
   $-p$

b) $-r \equiv p$
   $r \lor -s$
   s
   _____
   $-p$

c) $-p \lor -q$
   $(-q \equiv r) \cdot -p$
   _____
   $r \supset -p$

d) $p \equiv (q \cdot -r)$
   $-r \equiv -p$
   $q \supset r$
   _____
   $p \supset -r$

e) $(q \lor r) \supset -p$
   $(p \cdot q) \lor (r \cdot -p)$
   $-p \supset q$
   _____
   $p \lor -r$

f) $(q \cdot -r) \equiv -p$
   $p \equiv (r \lor s)$
   $-s \lor (-r \supset p)$
   $-q$
   _____
   s

g) $(r \supset -p) \lor (q \cdot -s)$
   $-q \equiv (p \supset s)$
   $p \cdot -r$
   _____
   $p \supset (s \lor -q)$

h) $-q \supset -r$
   $(s \equiv p) \lor -q$
   $-(p \supset r)$
   _____
   $-s \lor p$

5. A number of truth-functionally valid argument schemata play such important roles in our subject that they have been given names. Many of these are listed below. (The names are explained in Chapter 3.) Using the *reductio ad absurdum* test, prove that the schemata *are* truth-functionally valid.

a) Modus ponens

   $p \supset q$
   p
   _____
   q

b) Modus tollens

   $p \supset q$
   $-q$
   _____
   $-p$

c) Conjunction

   p
   q
   _____
   $p \cdot q$

d) Addition

   p
   _____
   $p \lor q$

e) Simplification

   $p \cdot q$
   p

f) Elimination

   $p \lor q$
   $-p$
   _____
   q

g) Transitivity

   $p \supset q$
   $q \supset r$
   _____
   $p \supset r$

h) Constructive Dilemma

   $p \supset q$
   $r \supset s$
   $p \lor r$
   _____
   $q \lor s$

i) Destructive Dilemma

   $p \supset q$
   $r \supset s$
   $-q \lor -s$
   _____
   $-p \lor -r$

Suggestions for further reading related to Chapter 1.

Barker, Stephen F., *The Elements of Logic*. New York: McGraw-Hill Book Company, 1965, Chapters 1 and 3.

Carnap, Rudolph, *Introduction to Semantics*. Cambridge, Mass.: Harvard University Press, 1961, Appendix No. 37.

Copi, Irving M., *Introduction to Logic*. New York: The Macmillan Co., 1961, Chapters 1 and 8.

Quine, Willard van Orman, *Methods of Logic*. New York: Holt, Rinehart and Winston, Inc., 1950, Part I.

Rescher, Nicholas, *Introduction to Logic*. New York: St. Martin's Press, Inc., 1964, Chapters 1, 4, and 12.

Suppes, Patrick, *Introduction to Logic*. Princeton, N.J.: D. Van Nostrand Co., Inc., 1957, Chapter 1.

> The business of Logic is with the relations of classes, and with the modes in which the mind contemplates those relations.
>
> *George Boole*

The Calculus of Terms

2.1 Categorical sentences and schemata

An argument schema containing only sentential variables and truth-operators is called 'truth-functional'. A truth-functionally *valid* argument *schema* is a truth-functional argument schema such that given any uniform interpretation of its variables, its conclusion *must* be true if its premisses are all true. Any *argument* which may be regarded as an interpretation of a truth-functionally valid argument schema is called a 'truth-functionally valid argument'. The following argument is *not* truth-functionally valid, but it *is* valid.

(1)   All ruminants are animals.
        All camels are ruminants.
        All camels are animals.

If we let '*R*' be short for 'all ruminants are animals, '*C*' for 'all camels are ruminants' and '*A*' for 'all camels are animals', then (1) may be abbreviated thus:

(2) R
        $\dfrac{C}{A}$

Argument (2) may be regarded as an interpretation of the following *truth-func-tionally invalid* argument schema.

(3)   *p*

             q
             ———
             r

Hence (2) is clearly *truth-functionally* invalid.

Nevertheless, (2) *is valid*. It may be regarded as an interpretation of the following valid argument schema.

(4)   All *M* are *P*.
             All *S* are *M*.
             —————————
             All *S* are *P*.

In (4), '*M*', '*S*', and '*P*' are place holders for unspecified *terms*. **Terms** are nothing more than *nouns*. Proper nouns are called **singular terms;** e.g., 'Socrates', 'Sidney', 'San Diego', 'Sahara', etc. Common nouns are called **general terms;** e.g., 'man', 'men', 'mother', 'milk shake', 'moth', etc. The terms in (1) are all general; i.e., 'ruminants', 'animals', and 'camels'.

When we say that '*M*', '*S*', and '*P*' represent or are place holders for unspecified terms, we mean to say that they are *variables*. Since we call the lowercase letters '*p*', '*q*', '*r*', and '*s*' sentence variables because they are place holders for *sentences*, we should call the capital letters '*M*', '*S*', and '*P*' **term variables** because they are place holders for *terms*. We interpret *sentence variables* by specifying either *sentences or truth-values* that they may be regarded as representing. We interpret *term variables* by specifying either *terms* that they may be regarded as *representing* or *things denoted* by such terms. (A word **denotes** each and every *thing* to which it applies; e.g., the word 'horse' denotes each and every horse.) For example, we may interpret the term variable '*S*' in 'All *S* is *P*' by specifying *terms* such as 'men', 'moths', 'mothers', etc., *or* by specifying the *things* these terms denote, namely, men, moths, mothers, etc.

Some authors prefer to say that terms denote *classes* of things instead of just *things*. They would say, for example, that 'man' denotes the class consisting of all men, 'moth' denotes the class of all moths, etc. Occasionally these locutions are used in this text too. It should not be presumed, however, that, say, the *class* of all men is anything besides *each and every man*.

In this chapter all capital letters with the exception of '*M*', '*S*', and '*P*' may be used as abbreviations of specified terms. For examples, in (2) the letters '*R*', '*C*', and '*A*' are abbreviations for the terms 'ruminants', 'camels', and 'animals', respectively. Capital letters used to abbreviate terms may be called **term letters.** Unlike sentence letters, term letters cannot be regarded as true or false; e.g., '*C*' cannot be true or false any more than 'camels' can be true or false.

Using the term letters as suggested in the last paragraph, (1) may be abbreviated

(5)   All R are A.
           All C are R.
           _____
           All C are A.

Here (5), like (1), is an argument. It may be regarded as a uniform interpretation
of the schema (4); (5) has the same form as schema (4). In the sections that
follow we shall frequently abbreviate arguments to reveal their forms more
lucidly.

In order to test schemata such as (4) or their interpretations such as (1) or
(5) for validity, we must go beyond the calculus of sentences. In the remaining
paragraphs of this section we shall lay the foundation for our passage beyond
truth-functional sentences and truth-functional validity. (We shall have more
to say about validity in Sec. 2.7.)

To begin with, we must become familiar with four nontruth-functional
sentence schemata which we shall call **categorical sentence schemata.** They
are

    A All S are P.
    E No S are P.
    I Some S are P.
    O Some S are not P.

The expressions above are clearly sentence schemata, because they *become* sentences when their variables are appropriately replaced. For example,

    Some S are not P.

becomes a sentence when 'S' is replaced by 'clowns' and 'P' is replaced by 'Greeks';
i.e., it becomes the true sentence

    Some clowns are Greeks.

Interpretations of categorical sentence schemata are called **categorical sentences;**
e.g., all the sentences in (1) are categorical.

The expressions above are *not* truth-functional schemata because the truth-
values of their interpretations cannot be functions of the truth-values of their
component *sentences.* Their interpretations *have no* component *sentences;* they only
have component *terms* and terms cannot be true or false.

The boldface capital letters **'A', 'E', 'I',** and **'O'** before the categorical schemata
are their traditional *names;* e.g., any sentence having the form of the **A** schema

    All S are P.

is called an '**A** sentence'; any sentence having the form of the **E** schema

    No S are P.

is called an '**E** sentence'; etc.

Sentences having any of these four basic forms are *categorical* in the ordinary sense of this word; i.e., in each case the predicate is definitely affirmed or denied by the subject, without qualifications or conditions. They may be distinguished **quantitatively** by indicating whether they are about *everything or else* at least *one* thing denoted by their subjects and **qualitatively** by indicating whether they *affirm or deny* something of the things denoted by their subjects. The quantity of **A** and **E** schemata (and sentences) is said to be **universal** because sentences having either of these forms are used to make assertions about *everything* denoted by '*S*', whatever '*S*' happens to represent. For example, if '*S*' is replaced by 'frogs' and '*P*' is replaced by 'green' then the **A** and **E** sentences

> All frogs are green.

and

> No frogs are green.

are about each and every frog. The quantity of **I** and **O** schemata (and sentences) is said to be **particular** because sentences having either of these forms are used to make assertions about *at least one thing* denoted by '*S*'; e.g.,

> Some frogs are green.

and

> Some frogs are not green.

are about at least one frog.

The quantifying words 'all', 'no', and 'some' (and their grammatical equivalents; e.g., 'every', 'at least one', etc.) are called **quantifiers.** 'Some' (and its grammatical equivalents) is called an **existential quantifier.** 'All' (and its grammatical equivalents) is called a **universal quantifier.**

The quality of **A** and **I** schemata (and sentences) is said to be **affirmative** because sentences having these forms are used to affirm something of the things denoted by their subjects; e.g.,

> All frogs are green.

and

> Some frogs are green.

affirm the property of being green of every and at least one frog, respectively. The quality of **E** and **O** schemata (and sentences) is said to be **negative** because sentences having these forms are used to deny something of the things denoted by their subjects; e.g.,

> No frogs are green.

and

> Some frogs are not green.

deny the property of being green to every and at least one frog, respectively.

The last few paragraphs are conveniently summarized in Figure 2.11.

Quality

Quantity	Affirmative	Negative
Universal	Universal affirmative All *S* are *P*. **A**	Universal negative No *S* are *P*. **E**
Particular	Particular affirmative Some *S* are *P*. **I**	Particular negative Some *S* are not *P*. **O**

Figure 2.11

We shall assume, following what seems to be ordinary usage, that **I** and **O** sentences are used to assert the *existence* of the things denoted by their terms. Hence, for example, the **I** sentence

Some frogs are green.

means

There *exists* at least one green frog.

and the **O** sentence

Some frogs are not green.

means

There *exists* at least one frog that is not green.

I and **O** sentences, then, may be described as sentences with **existential import;** i.e., sentences that are used to assert existence.

On the other hand, we shall assume that **A** and **E** sentences are *not* used to assert the existence of the things denoted by their terms; i.e., they do not have existential import. For example, the **A** sentence

All chickens are birds.

means

If anything is a chicken then it is a bird.

and the **E** sentence

No chickens are birds.

means

If anything is a chicken then it is not a bird.

There are certainly chickens and birds, but these **A** and **E** sentences, unlike their **I** and **O** counterparts, are not used to *assert* that there are either.

A term that does not apply to anything that exists is called an **empty term;** e.g., 'mermaid', 'man over 9 feet tall', 'inhabitant of Mercury', etc. Some of the terms used in this chapter *may* be empty. In Sec. 2.7 we shall consider sentences and arguments with *only* *non*empty terms. There we shall presuppose or assume that *every* term used is such that there is at least one thing to which it applies. However, no such presupposition will be made for the rest of the chapter. If we are given an **I** or an **O** sentence then the existence of at least one thing denoted by their terms is, as we have just seen, *asserted*. It does not have to be presupposed or assumed. If we are given an **A** or an **E** sentence then nothing is asserted about existence. But nothing *has* to be presupposed either; so nothing will be. The terms used in **A** and **E** sentences *may* be empty.

By the term **calculus of terms,** which is the title of this chapter, we mean the class consisting of the four categorical sentence schemata with only term variables and their rules of use. In particular, sentence variables, truth-operators, and truth-functional schemata are excluded from the calculus of terms. We shall still use the operators 'and', 'if–then', etc. to *talk about* expressions in the calculus of terms, but these are not *included in* that calculus. The situation here is similar to that in the first chapter. There we used the quantifiers 'all' and 'some' to *talk about* expressions in the calculus of sentences, but these were not *included in* that calculus.

The technical name of a *language* that is used to *talk about* a language is a **metalanguage.** In this text we use a single metalanguage, English, to talk about various calculi which we may regard as simple artificial languages. A language which is an *object* of discussion is called an **object language.** So far, then, we have introduced two object languages, namely, the calculus of sentences and the calculus of terms. The former contains truth-functional schemata and sentence variables but no categorical schemata and term variables; the latter contains categorical schemata and term variables but no truth-functional schemata and sentence variables. The former is more *fundamental* than the latter in the sense that its *smallest* components are *sentence variables* or the outermost forms of sentences; the smallest components of the latter are *term variables* or mere *parts* of sentence schemata. In the former our analysis never becomes *fine* enough to consider the subjects and predicates of sentence schemata; in the latter the subjects and predicates of sentence schemata are practically our starting point. What we are here calling the 'calculus of terms' may be regarded as an elementary fragment of the mathematical theory of sets (classes, or groups) and of what we shall later come to know as the 'monadic predicate calculus'.

Review problems for Sec. 2.1.

1. Define the following.

    a) term
    b) term variable
    c) quantifier
    d) denote

    e) categorical sentence schema
    f) existential import
    g) empty term
    h) calculus of terms

2. *If it is possible*, give examples of the following kinds of categorical sentences.

   a) two affirmatives of the same quantity
   b) a negative whose quantity is universal
   c) a particular whose quality is negative
   d) two particulars with different qualities
   e) a universal whose quality is affirmative
   f) a universal and a particular whose qualities are negative

3. What is the difference between particular and universal categorical sentences with respect to the assertion of the existence of objects?

4. Name the following categorical sentences.

   a) No Americans are Koreans.   e) No professors are fascists.
   b) Some butchers are neurotics.   f) Some fascists are not Americans.
   c) Some clowns are not neurotics.   g) Some Americans are butchers.
   d) All chess players are neurotics.   h) All butchers are chess players.

5. What is the difference between an object language and a metalanguage?

6. Identify the quantity and quality of the sentences in Prob. 4.

7. Which of the following are schemata and which are sentences?

   a) All members of the Y.M.B.A. are Buddhists.
   b) Some *A* are *B*.
   c) No *S* are *M*.
   d) Some girl from the U. S. S. R. is neat.
   e) Some *P* are not *S*.
   f) No *A* are *S*.

2.2 Disguised categorical sentences

In Chapter 1 we saw that there were a number of English words that might be abbreviated by the conjunction sign and that there were quite a few ways to express conditional sentences. Similarly (and fortunately) a number of sentences that *prima facie* are not categorical may be easily translated into categorical sentences. We shall call these **disguised categorical sentences,** and in this section some useful translating principles will be introduced.

To begin with, let us agree that a categorical sentence will be said to be in **standard form** if and only if it is an interpretation of one of the four categorical schemata such that a) it begins with 'all', 'no', or 'some'; b) it has the copula 'are' or 'are not'; c) the terms of both its subject and predicate are noun substantives; i.e., *words* or *phrases* denoting persons, places, and things, but not properties.

Requirements a) and b) are straightforward; e.g.,

> *Every* boy *is* a ballplayer.
> Some vampire *is not* flying.

are *not*, while

> *All* boys *are* ballplayers.
> Some vampires *are not* flyers.

are in standard form. According to requirement c),

> No alligators are *ferocious*.
> Some roses are *secondhand*.

are *not*, while

> No alligators are *ferocious animals*.
> Some roses are *secondhand flowers*.

are in standard form.

The translating principles to be introduced should be treated as *suggestions* and not as hard and fast rules. In a given case there may be a number of correct ways to turn a disguised categorical sentence into standard form.

a)   *Change Predicates to Nouns*.   This suggestion applies to two types of cases. The *first* type was considered under requirement b) above. That is, if the copula 'are' is present but the predicate is an adjective, change the adjectival predicate to a noun; e.g.,

> All crows are *black*.
> Some lovers are *cowardly*.

are *not*, while

> All crows are *black birds*.

or

> All crows are *black things*.

or

> All crows are *black flyers*.

etc.

> Some lovers are *cowards*.

are in standard form. In the *second* type, the copula 'are' is not present. The copula must be added and the whole predicate must be changed into a noun; e.g.,

> No prisoners *escape*.
> Some fighters *take dives*.

are *not*, while

No prisoners are *escapers.*

or

No prisoners are *people who escape.*

or

No prisoners are *inmates who leave illegally.*

etc.

Some fighters are *dive-takers.*

or

Some fighters are *men who purposely lose fights.*

etc. are in standard form. Notice that we are not bound to use exactly the same phrase or words in our translation, and this, in fact, is our second suggestion.

b) *Introduce or Eliminate Synonyms.* As long as it is not misleading, in any given context synonyms or synonymous phrases may be eliminated or introduced. For example, we introduced 'inmates who leave illegally' in place of 'escapers' above. Very often it is necessary to eliminate *synonyms* of the quantifiers 'all', 'no', and 'some' in favor of the quantifier. For example,

Whoever spies, dies.
Whatever Lola wants, Lola gets.
Whenever we kiss, I worry and wonder.
He who sits in jelly, gets into jam.

are *not*, while

All people who spy are people who die.
All things that Lola wants are things that Lola gets.
All times when we kiss are times when I worry and wonder.
All men who sit in jelly are men who get into jam.

are in standard form. Again,

Nobody loves swindlers.
Nothing Charlie Brown could do could please Lucy.

are *not*, while

No people who are loved are swindlers.
No acts Charlie Brown could perform are acts that could please Lucy.

are in standard form. And finally,

Many men mash meatballs.
A few arthropods are cute.
At least one fox is not an artist.

are *not*, while

> *Some men* are meatball mashers.
> *Some arthropods* are cute insects.
> *Some foxes* are not artists.

are in standard form.

Some words function as universal quantifiers in some contexts but as particular quantifiers in others. Consider

> *A bear* is an animal.
> *A bear* went over the mountain.

The former means

> *All bears* are animals.

The latter means

Some bears (i.e., there is at least one) are animals that went over the mountain.

Again,

> *An early bird* catches the worm.
> *An early bird* caught the worm.

should be translated

> *All early birds* are birds that catch the worms.
> *Some early birds* are birds that caught the worm.

respectively.

c) *Rearrange or Add Quantifiers.* Strictly speaking, we have already suggested the addition of quantifiers for sentences beginning with the articles 'a' and 'an'. There are two other kinds of cases in which a quantifier may properly be introduced. First, singular sentences such as

> *Richard* is a bachelor.
> *This woman* is married.

are treated as universal affirmative or **A** sentences. Hence, these become,

> *All persons identical with Richard* are bachelors.
> *All persons identical with this woman* are married persons.

respectively.

The second kind in which a quantifier must be introduced requires a bit more thought.

> *College men* are suave.
> *College men* are human.

have the same grammatical form, but the former is probably intended as a particular sentence

> *Some college men* are suave men.

while the latter is a universal

> *All college men* are humans.

We suggest that the former should be treated as an **I** sentence because that seems
to make it true or, at least, more plausible. Again,

> *Lizards* are not rodents.
> *Lizards* are not wet.

are translated

> *No lizards* are rodents.
> *Some lizards* are not wet reptiles.

respectively.
   In the move from

> *Lizards* are not rodents.

to

> *No lizards* are rodents.

we have illustrated the fact that in some sentences the quantifier needs to be
rearranged to obtain a standard form categorical. Similarly,

> *Motorcycles are all* very dangerous.
> *Newspapers are some* kinds of mass media.

become

> *All motorcycles are* very dangerous vehicles.
> *Some kinds of mass media are* newspapers.

respectively.
   d) *Interchange Subject and Predicate of Exclusive Sentences.* An **exclusive** sentence is one in which the predicate applies *exclusively* or *only* to the subject. When
we considered alternative ways of expressing a conditional sentence (see Sec. 1.4),
it was pointed out that a *sentence* following 'only' is generally a consequent. Similarly, a *term* following 'only' (or its grammatical equivalents 'none but', 'alone',
'solely', etc.) is generally a predicate. Thus the exclusive sentences

> *Only Adam* dated Eve.
> *Nobody but the President* can make that decision.

are translated

All persons who dated Eve are *persons identical with Adam.*

All persons who can make that decision are *persons identical with the President.*

respectively.

Review problems for Sec. 2.2.

1. What are the three requirements of a standard form categorical sentence?

2. Change the following sentences into standard form categoricals.

   a) Only icemen carry ice.
   b) A little loving goes a long way.
   c) Nobody likes a poor loser.
   d) At least one government official is not corrupt.
   e) When in doubt, punt.
   f) An apple a day is a starvation diet.
   g) There is a slippery mermaid.
   h) Quitters are never winners.
   i) Owls are wise.
   j) Nothing but a Greek dog could be named Pluto.
   k) He who makes a mistake and fails to correct it makes a second mistake.
   l) Squirrels are friendly.
   m) You can't cheat a cheater.
   n) There is no substitute for trickery.
   o) Few frogs are intelligent.
   p) A little mouse ate the cheese.
   q) Mancini studies.
   r) Whatever Moose does, stinks.
   s) Somebody stole my gal.
   t) Sprinters are all nervous.

2.3   Venn diagram test of validity

A **syllogistic argument schema** is an argument schema consisting of exactly three categorical sentence schemata (two of which are premises and the third of which is a conclusion) and three term variables, each of which appears in two of the categoricals. For example,

(1)   All M are P.
         All S are M.
         ————————
         All S are P.

Any argument that may be regarded as an interpretation of a syllogistic argument schema is called a **syllogistic argument** or, briefly, a **syllogism;** e.g.,

(2)   All rodents are animals.
           All rats are rodents.
           All rats are animals.

    Traditionally, the subject of the conclusion of a syllogism is called its **minor term** and the predicate is called its **major term;** e.g., in (2) the minor term is 'rats' and the major term is 'animals'. The term that appears in both premisses but not in the conclusion is called the **middle term** of the syllogism; e.g., in (2) the middle term is 'rodents'. Extending this usage, we may say that a syllogistic argument *schema* has minor, major, and middle *term variables;* e.g., in (1) the minor term variable is 'S' (the *subject* of the conclusion), the major term variable is 'P' (the *predicate* of the conclusion), and the middle term variable is 'M'. The premiss containing the minor term (or term variable) is called the **minor premiss.** The premiss containing the major term (or term variable) is called the **major premiss.** For examples, the minor premisses of (1) and (2) are 'All S are M' and 'All rats are rodents', respectively. The other premisses are major.
    The middle term variable of a syllogistic schema may be situated in the schema in four different ways. Each of these ways is called a **figure.** Figure 2.31 illustrates the four possible figures.

Figure I	Figure II	Figure III	Figure IV
MP	*PM*	*MP*	*PM*
SM	*SM*	*MS*	*MS*
SP	*SP*	*SP*	*SP*

Figure 2.31

For example, when a given syllogistic schema is described as *in the first figure* (Figure I), it is understood that the middle term variable 'M' is the subject of the major premiss (abbreviated 'MP' under Figure I) and the predicate of the minor premiss (abbreviated 'SM' under Figure I). The schema (1) is in the first figure. The schema

(3)   No M are P.
           Some M are S.
           Some S are not P.

is in the third figure (Figure III), and

(4)   All P are M.
           No S are M.
           Some S are P.

is in the second figure, etc. Any *syllogism* is said to be in the same *figure* as the schema of which it may be regarded as an interpretation; e.g., (2) is in the first figure because it may be regarded as an interpretation of the first figure schema (1).

The **mood** of a syllogistic schema is specified by listing the names of its component sentence schemata. Schemata (1), (3), and (4) all have different moods. The mood of (1) is **A A A,** the mood of (3) is **E I O,** the mood of (4) is **A E I.** Any syllogism is said to have the same mood as the schema of which it may be regarded as an interpretation; e.g., (2) has the mood **A A A** because it may be regarded as an interpretation of schema (1) which has that mood.

Nearly all the technical terms we have introduced in the last few paragraphs have a rather remarkable relation to the validity of syllogistic argument schemata and syllogisms. Because every syllogistic schema consists of *three sentence schemata* which may have any of *four* different *forms*, there are $4 \times 4 \times 4 = 64$ possible syllogistic moods. Because there are *four figures*, there are four different ways for a middle term to be situated in each of the 64 moods. Hence, there are exactly $4 \times 64 = 256$ possible different syllogistic schemata. *Therefore*, the *decision problem* for syllogistic schemata is simply that of devising a mechanical method for determining which of these 256 schemata are valid and which are not. The problem has been solved in a number of ways. Given our assumption that some of the terms replacing term variables *may be empty*, there are 15 *valid* schemata. These are recorded in Figure 2.32.

Figure I	Figure II	Figure III	Figure IV
A A A	**E A E**	**I A I**	**A E E**
E A E	**A E E**	**A I I**	**I A I**
A I I	**E I O**	**O A O**	**E I O**
E I O	**A O O**	**E I O**	

Figure 2.32

With Figure 2.32 before us we have a very simple *decision procedure* for syllogistic schemata and syllogisms. All we have to do is match any given schemata or syllogism against the schemata summarized in Figure 2.32. If it has one of those forms, it is valid; otherwise it is invalid. Alternatively, we would learn a decision procedure that would relieve us of the burden of carrying Figure 2.32 around either on paper or in our heads. We are going to consider three such procedures: the Venn diagram test, the inconsistent triad, and syllogistic rules. Each of these constitutes a *solution* to the decision problem for syllogistic schemata. In the remaining paragraphs of this section we shall introduce the test that was invented by the nineteenth-century philosopher John Venn.

To begin with, we shall need a method of diagraming categorical schemata and sentences. We shall use the following.

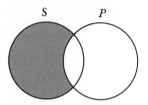

All S are *P*.

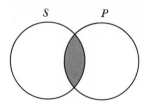

No S are *P*.

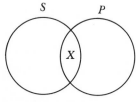

Some S are *P*.

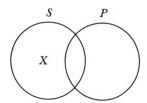

Some S are not *P*.

In these diagrams *shading represents emptiness* and the 'X' *represents the existence of at least one thing*. The *lune* is shaded in the diagram for

All *S* are *P*.

to indicate that there are *no S* that are *not P*; i.e., if anything is *S* then it is *P*. The diagram, like the **A** schema it represents, does not tell us that there are *S* or *P*. It merely tells us that if there are *S* they *must* be *P*. Similarly, the *lens* is shaded in the diagram for

No *S* are *P*.

to indicate that there are *no S* that *are P*; i.e., if anything is *S* then it is *not P*. The diagram, like the **E** schema it represents, does not tell us that there are *S* or *P*. It merely tells us that *if* there are *S* they must *not* be *P*.

The 'X' is put in the *lens* of the diagram above

Some *S* are *P*.

to indicate that there *exists* at least one *S* that is *P*; i.e., something is *both S* and *P*. Similarly, the 'X' is put in the lune of the diagram above

Some *S* are not *P*.

to indicate that there *exists* at least one *S* that is not *P*; i.e., something is *S* but *not P*.

Using these diagrams then, we would represent

All men are clowns.

by

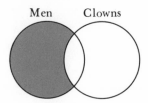

We would represent

Some men are not clowns.

by

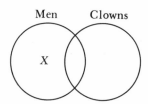

And so on. Let us apply these techniques to determine validity.

EXAMPLE 1

Test the following schema for validity by the Venn diagram method.

$$\text{All } M \text{ are } P.$$
$$\underline{\text{All } S \text{ are } M.}$$
$$\text{All } S \text{ are } P.$$

Solution. We begin with three interlocking circles.

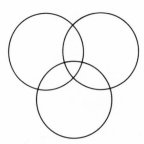

Let the upper left circle represent any S, the upper right circle any P, and the lower middle circle any M.

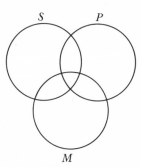

We do not know if there *are* any *S*, *P*, or *M*, but we have a place for each in our diagram.

Concentrating on only *two circles at a time*, diagram the *premisses* of the given schema. *First*, concentrate on the *M* and *P* circles. These must be shaded to represent the first premiss

All M are P.

Thus:

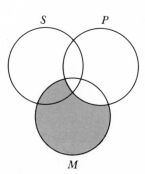

Some of the *S* circle was shaded but that was necessary in order to properly represent the first premiss. *Second*, concentrate on the *S* and *M* circles. These must be shaded to represent the second premiss

Thus:

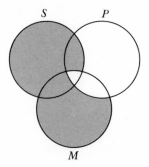

Some of the *P* circle was shaded but that was necessary in order to properly represent the second premiss. *Nothing* else has to be done to the diagram.

The schema is *valid* if and only if the conclusion

All *S* are *P*.

has been diagramed. Does the final diagram show that if anything is *S*, then it is *P*? To answer this question, concentrate on the *S* and *P* circles. The only part of the *S* circle that is *not* shaded is a part that overlaps the *P* circle. If there are any *S*, they *must* be *P*; i.e., the conclusion *has* been diagramed. Therefore the schema is *valid*.

Interpretations of this schema include the following.

All ruminants are animals.
All camels are ruminants.
All camels are animals.

All men are mortal.
Socrates is a man.
Socrates is mortal.

A gentleman is a man who washes.
He who can afford it is a gentleman.
Whoever can afford it, washes.

The first of these syllogisms is our argument (1) from Sec. 2.1. It contains *only* standard form categorical sentences, so we may call it a **syllogism in standard form.** The other two are not in standard form. Frequently we may avoid confusion by putting an argument into standard form before testing it for validity. In all our examples we shall follow this policy.

EXAMPLE 2

Use the Venn diagram test to determine the validity of the following argument.

No amoebas are television stars.
Some one-celled animals are amoebas.
Some one-celled animals are not television stars.

Solution. We shall begin by abbreviating its terms. Let '*A*' be short for 'amoebas', '*T*' for 'television stars', and '*O*' for 'one-celled animals'. The abbreviated argument looks like this.

No *A* are *T*.
Some *O* are *A*.
Some *O* are not *T*.

This syllogism is valid if and only if it may be regarded as an interpretation of a valid syllogistic schema. Instead of replacing the term letters in the syllogism with variables to obtain a *schema*, we may pretend the letters are variables and apply the test immediately. We label three interlocking circles so that the upper left circle represents the subject of the conclusion, the upper right circle represents the predicate of the conclusion, and the lower middle circle represents the middle term.

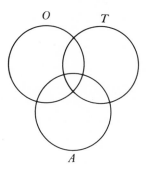

Concentrating on only *two* circles at a time, diagram the premisses. This time we have a universal and a particular premiss. In such cases we *always diagram the universal* (**A** or **E**) *premiss before the particular* (**I** or **O**). *First*, concentrate on the *A* and *T* circles. These must be shaded to represent the first premiss

No A are T.

Thus:

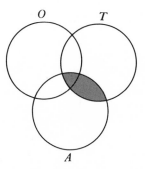

Some of the *O* circle was shaded but that was necessary in order to properly represent the first premiss. *Second*, concentrate on the *O* and *A* circles. These must be *crossed* to represent the second premiss

Some O are A.

That is,

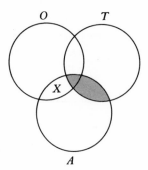

None of the *T* circle was crossed and this was necessary in order to properly represent the second premiss. If we had crossed any other lens or lune we could *not* have properly represented the second premiss. The other (erroneous) possibilities are as follows.

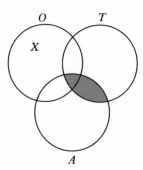

Some *O* are *not A.*
Some *O* are not *T.*

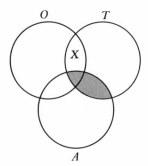

Some *O* are *T.*
Some *O* are *not A.*

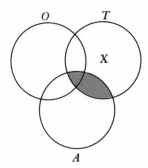

Some *T* are not *A.*
Some *T* are not *O.*

Clearly the other possibilities do *not* properly represent the second premiss.

The given argument is *valid* if and only if the conclusion

Some O are not T.

has been diagramed. Does the final diagram show that there exists at least one O that is not T? To answer this question, concentrate on the O and T circles. There is an 'X' in the O circle that is *outside* the T circle; i.e., at least one O is *not* T. So the conclusion has been diagramed, and the given argument is valid.

EXAMPLE 3

Test the following argument for validity.

> Batman apprehends criminals.
> Some policemen apprehend criminals.
> _____
> Some policeman is Batman.

Solution. The sentences of this argument are not in standard form. Hence our first step will be to translate the sentences into standard form.

> All persons identical with Batman are persons who apprehend criminals.
> Some policemen are persons who apprehend criminals.
> _____
> Some policemen are persons identical with Batman.

Substitute letters for the terms; e.g., 'B' for 'persons identical with Batman', 'A' for 'persons who apprehend criminals', and 'O' for 'policemen'. The syllogism, then, may be abbreviated,

> All B are A.
> Some O are A.
> _____
> Some O are B.

Again, by pretending the letters are variables, we may treat the argument above as a *schema* and apply the test immediately. We lable three interlocking circles and diagram the first premiss

All B are A.

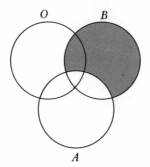

The second premiss presents an inescapable ambiguity. The universal (affirmative) premiss is properly diagramed first, but there is still a difficulty inserting the 'X'. Instead of making a choice between putting the 'X' in the overlapping part of *all three* circles, thus,

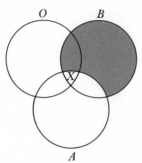

and putting the 'X' in the overlapping part of *only two* circles, so,

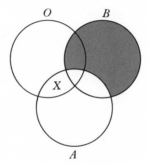

we put the 'X' on the line separating these alternatives.

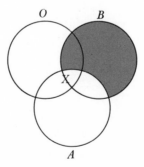

The given argument is valid if and only if the conclusion

Some *O* are *B*.

has been diagramed. Does the diagram show that there exists at least one *O* that is *B*? *No.* The diagram *does* show that there exists at least one *O* that *might* be

B and *might not* be *B*. But the mere *possibility* of an *O* being a *B* is not good enough. The given argument must be pronounced '*invalid*'.

EXAMPLE 4

Is the following argument valid?

> Only brain surgeons mumble.
> Ben Casey doesn't mumble.
> ---
> Ben Casey is not a brain surgeon.

Solution. We begin by rewriting the argument in standard syllogistic form.

> All persons who mumble are brain surgeons.
> No persons identical with Ben Casey are persons who mumble.
> ---
> No persons identical with Ben Casey are brain surgeons.

Letting '*R*' be short for 'persons who mumble', '*B*' for 'brain surgeons', and '*C*' for 'persons identical with Ben Casey', we have

> All *R* are *B*.
> No *C* are *R*.
> ---
> No *C* are *B*.

Labeling three circles and diagraming the first premiss,

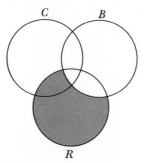

and then the second, we have

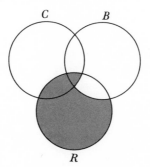

Has the conclusion

No *C* are *B*.

been diagramed? No. In order to diagram that conclusion, we must have the lens between the *C* and *B* circles *completely* shaded. But it is not completely shaded. So the given argument is *invalid*.

We may summarize the Venn diagram method of testing syllogistic schemata and syllogisms for validity in three basic steps.

a)   Draw and label three overlapping circles.

b)   Diagram each premiss (taking universals before particulars).

c)   The schema or syllogism is valid if and only if the conclusion is shown on the diagram.

For illustrative purposes we have always begun by putting the sentences of a syllogism into standard form and replacing terms with letters. These steps are pedagogically useful, but unnecessary.

Review problems for Sec. 2.3.

1.   Define the following.

   a)   syllogistic argument schema   d)   figure

   b)   major term   e)   mood

   c)   minor premiss

2.   How is it proved that there are 256 possible different syllogistic schemata?

3.   Make up syllogisms that have the following moods.

   a)   **A A A**   d)   **O A I**

   b)   **O E I**   e)   **E I E**

   c)   **E A O**   f)   **I A A**

4.   State the figure (i.e., I, II, III, or IV) of the following syllogisms.

   a)   Some generals are warmongers.   d)   All polecats are fighters.
        All warmongers are frightening people.   No Siamese cats are polecats.
        Some frightening people are generals.   No Siamese cats are fighters.

   b)   No bipeds are octopi.   e)   All philosophers are quiet.
        All bipeds are light-footed animals.   All powder puffs are quiet.
        No light-footed animals are octopi.   All powder puffs are philosophers.

   c)   No dogfish are swans.   f)   Some round things are bubbles.
        Some birds are swans.   Some heads are round things.
        Some birds are not dogfish.   Some heads are bubbles.

5. Make up syllogisms having the following figures and moods.

a) II **E I O**

b) III **A I I**

c) I **E A E**

d) IV **I A I**

e) II **A O O**

f) IV **A E E**

6. Test the syllogisms in Prob. 5 for validity by the Venn diagram method.

7. Test the following syllogisms for validity by the Venn diagram technique.

a) No children are apple blossoms.
   Some children are angels.
   Some angels are not apple blossoms.

b) All werewolves need haircuts.
   Some cucumbers do not need haircuts.
   Some cucumbers are not werewolves.

c) No airplanes are dirigibles.
   No dirigibles are snowmen.
   Some snowmen are not airplanes.

d) All hats are feathered.
   Whatever is feathered is a bird.
   All hats are birds.

e) No man is an island.
   All oases are islands.
   No oases are men.

f) Good coffee is reheatable.
   Good coffee is unbeatable.
   Reheatable coffee is unbeatable.

g) A centipede has a hundred legs.
   Any bug with a hundred legs never dances.
   Some centipedes never dance.

h) Some medicine tastes terrible.
   No ham sandwiches taste terrible.
   No medicine is a ham sandwich.

i) Old women tire easily.
   Aunt Bee is an old woman.
   Aunt Bee tires easily.

j) There is no business like show business.
   A few businesses are illegal.
   Some illegal business is not like show business.

8. Usually one does not find syllogisms in nice neat packages. A conclusion may be written first or between premises or after both premises. There are some fairly reliable signs of an intended conclusion. The words 'thus', 'therefore', 'hence', 'so', and 'it follows that' are generally signs of an intended conclusion. On the other hand, words like 'because', 'for', and 'since' are generally signs of intended premises. By keeping these guides in mind and attending to the sense of the sentences, one can

usually separate the warrant offered for a claim from the claim itself. Sometimes, of course, no clear distinction between warrant and claim has been made. In these cases there simply is no argument. Such cases may be spotted immediately by the *absence* of premiss or conclusion signs and by the abundance of conjunctions such as 'and', 'while', and 'however'. Decide which of the following are arguments and test them for validity. Where there is no argument, answer NA.

a) All crazy people bark at the moon; hence all coyotes are crazy people, since all coyotes bark at the moon.

b) Some grapefruits are not balloons, because balloons are not grown in Florida and some things that are grown in Florida are grapefruits.

c) While no football players are pansies and every pansy is a flower, some flowers are not football players.

d) Most corn is yellow, so, since whatever is yellow is sweet, it follows that some corn is sweet.

e) Chocolate sundaes are always cold and things that are always cold are frozen. Therefore some chocolate sundaes are frozen.

f) Whoever enjoys algebra is sweet; so no paperhangers enjoy algebra, for paperhangers are never sweet.

g) Circus performers do not hold seminars. But some doctors hold seminars and a few doctors are circus performers.

h) Many soldiers do not mind saluting, because many infantry men do not mind saluting and every infantry man is a soldier.

i) He who is passionate is pleasant and some passionate people are gentlemen. So a few gentlemen must be pleasant.

j) Some cars are not planets, although no one's hot rod is a planet and everyone's hot rod is a car.

2.4   Inconsistent triad test

In this section we shall introduce an alternative decision procedure for determining the validity of syllogistic schemata and syllogisms. It was discovered and called the **antilogism** by Mrs. C. Ladd Franklin, and here it is (following C. I. Lewis and C. H. Langford) called the **inconsistent triad test.**

To begin with, we must introduce a new word. The **complement** of a term denotes *everything* that is not denoted by that term. The complement of 'man' denotes *everything* that is not a man (e.g., wood, horses, mud, electrons, etc.); the complement of 'horse' denotes *everything* that is not a horse; etc. We form the complement of a term by prefixing the term with 'non'; e.g., the complement of 'man' is 'nonman'; the complement of 'horse' is 'nonhorse'; etc. If we begin with a term that is already prefixed by 'non', we form its complement by *dropping* the prefix; e.g., the complement of 'noncow' is 'cow'; the complement of 'nonboy' is 'boy'; etc. In general, then, if '*P*' represents any term, 'non-*P*' represents its complement, and vice versa. We shall use the bar above a capital letter

$$\overline{P}$$

to abbreviate the phrase

The complement of *P*.

The technical name for this bar is **complement sign.** It is a *term* operator, *not a* sentential operator.

We shall represent categorical schemata (and sentences) according to the equalities and *in*equalities in Figure 2.41.

Weak Square of Opposition

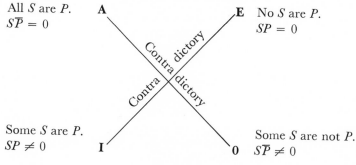

All *S* are *P*.   **A**   **E**   No *S* are *P*.
$S\overline{P} = 0$ $SP = 0$

Some *S* are *P*.   Some *S* are not *P*.
$SP \neq 0$ **I**   **0** $S\overline{P} \neq 0$

Figure 2.41

The equality

$$SP = 0$$

tells us that *nothing* is both *S* and *P*. The *in*equality

$$SP \neq 0$$

tells us that *something* is both *S* and *P*. The equality

$$S\overline{P} = 0$$

tells us that *nothing* is both *S* and non-*P*. The *in*equality

$$S\overline{P} \neq 0$$

tells us that *something* is both *S* and non-*P*.

Figure 2.41 is called a **Weak Square of Opposition** because it summarizes a minimum number of ways categorical sentences may be *opposed* to one another. (In Sec. 2.7 we shall consider a *Strong Square*.) The only opposition recorded in

Figure 2.41 is that of contradictories. Two sentences are said to be **contradictories** if whenever one is true (false), the other must be false (true). **A** and **O** are contradictories. If, for example,

All ships are at sea.

is true (false) then

Some ships are not at sea.

must be false (true). Similarly, **E** and **I** are contradictories. If, for example,

No ships are at sea.

is true (false) then

Some ships are at sea.

must be false (true).

Now, with the help of some examples we shall introduce the inconsistent triad test of validity.

EXAMPLE 1

Determine the validity or invalidity of the following syllogistic schema by the inconsistent triad test.

No M are P.

Some M are S.

Some S are not P.

Solution. We begin by expressing each categorical schema as an equality or inequality in accordance with Figure 2.41.

$MP = 0$ (No M are P.)

$MS \neq 0$ (Some M are S.)

$S\overline{P} \neq 0$ (Some S are not P.)

The concluding *in*equality must be replaced by an equality. This is accomplished by erasing the line through the equality sign. (This step always involves drawing or erasing a single line.)

$MP = 0$ (No M are P.)

$MS \neq 0$ (Some M are S.)

$S\overline{P} = 0$ (All S are P.)

The schema is valid if and only if *each* of the following conditions is met:

a)   The triad consists of exactly two equalities and one inequality.

b)   Each variable in the inequality appears in one or the other of the equalities.

c)   One of the variables appears in one equality with an overbar and in the other equality without the bar.

In the given schema we have a) two equalities, '$MP = 0$' and '$S\overline{P} = 0$', and one inequality, '$MS \neq 0$'; b) 'M' appearing in '$MP = 0$' and 'S' appearing in '$S\overline{P} = 0$'; and c) 'P' in one equality '$MP = 0$' but '$\overline{P}$' in the other '$S\overline{P} = 0$'. Hence the three conditions are met. So the schema is valid.

EXAMPLE 2

Is the following argument valid?

> Some dancers are not hairy.
> All dancers love music.
> Some music lovers are not hairy.

Solution. We begin by translating the sentences into standard form.

> Some dancers are not hairy people.
> All dancers are music lovers.
> Some music lovers are not hairy people.

Then we replace terms with letters,

> Some D are not H.
> All D are L.
> Some L are not H.

and sentences with equalities or inequalities.

$$\begin{array}{ll} D\overline{H} \neq 0 & \text{(Some } D \text{ are not } H.) \\ \underline{D\overline{L} = 0} & \text{(All } D \text{ are } L.) \\ L\overline{H} \neq 0 & \text{(Some } L \text{ are not } H.) \end{array}$$

The inequality representing the conclusion is replaced by that representing the contradictory of the conclusion.

$$\begin{array}{ll} D\overline{H} \neq 0 & \text{(Some } D \text{ are not } H.) \\ \underline{D\overline{L} = 0} & \text{(All } D \text{ are } L.) \\ L\overline{H} = 0 & \text{(All } L \text{ are } H.) \end{array}$$

This triad contains a) two equalities, '$D\overline{L} = 0$' and '$L\overline{H} = 0$', and one inequality '$D\overline{H} \neq 0$'; b) 'D' in the inequality and in '$D\overline{L} = 0$' and '$\overline{H}$' in the inequality and in '$L\overline{H} = 0$'; c) 'L' in one equality and '$\overline{L}$' in the other. If we think of the letters as *variables*, we may say that we have established the validity of the *schema* of which the given syllogism may be regarded as an interpretation. Hence the given syllogism is also valid.

EXAMPLE 3

Is the following argument valid?

> Some scarecrows are brainless.
> An orange is brainless.
> Some orange is a scarecrow.

Solution. Translate the sentences into standard form.

> Some scarecrows are brainless objects.
> All oranges are brainless objects.
> Some oranges are scarecrows.

Replace terms with letters. Let 'C' be short for 'scarecrows', 'B' for 'brainless objects', and 'O' for 'oranges'.

> Some C are B.
> All O are B.
> Some O are C.

Express these sentences as equalities and inequalities.

$$CB \neq 0 \qquad \text{(Some } C \text{ are } B.\text{)}$$
$$O\bar{B} = 0 \qquad \text{(All } O \text{ are } B.\text{)}$$
$$OC \neq 0 \qquad \text{(Some } O \text{ are } C.\text{)}$$

Replace the conclusion.

$$CB \neq 0$$
$$O\bar{B} = 0$$
$$OC = 0 \qquad \text{(No } O \text{ are } C.\text{)}$$

This triad contains a) two equalities and one inequality. But it lacks b) because 'B' appears in the inequality but *not* in either equality; and it lacks c) because 'O' is common to both equalities but does not have an overbar in one of them. If we think of the letters as variables, we may say that we have established the *invalidity* of the *schema* of which the given syllogism may be regarded as an interpretation. Hence the given syllogism is invalid.

EXAMPLE 4

Test the following argument for validity.

> All rabbits are nearsighted.
> Nearsighted animals are fearless.
> Some rabbits are fearless.

Solution. Translate each sentence into a categorical.

> All rabbits are nearsighted animals.
> All nearsighted animals are fearless animals.
> _____
> Some rabbits are fearless animals.

Replace terms with letters. Let '*R*' be short for 'rabbits', '*N*' for 'nearsighted animals', and '*F*' for 'fearless animals'. That gives us

> All *R* are *N*.
> All *N* are *F*.
> _____
> Some *R* are *F*.

Express each sentence as an equality or inequality.

$$R\bar{N} = 0 \qquad \text{(All } R \text{ are } N.)$$
$$N\bar{F} = 0 \qquad \text{(All } N \text{ are } F.)$$
$$\overline{RF \neq 0} \qquad \text{(Some } R \text{ are } F.)$$

Replace the conclusion.

$$R\bar{N} = 0$$
$$N\bar{F} = 0$$
$$\overline{RF = 0} \qquad \text{(No } R \text{ are } F.)$$

This triad fails the first test, because it lacks an inequality. Therefore the syllogism is invalid.

We may summarize the inconsistent triad test in three steps.

a) Express each sentence as an equality or inequality.
b) Replace concluding equalities with inequalities and vice versa.
c) The schema or syllogism is valid if and only if the triad is such that

  i)   It has two equalities and one inequality.
  ii) Each letter in the inequality appears in one or the other equality.
  iii) One letter is common to both equalities and has an overbar in one of them.

Review problems for Sec. 2.4.

1. Express the following as equalities or inequalities.

  a) Euripides took his pants to Herzig the tailor.
  b) Nobody knows the trouble I've seen.
  c) Many are the times I have dreamed of your kiss.
  d) Some people never smile.

e) Anytime you're thinking of me is a time when I shall not be thinking of you.

f) Only by trying can one succeed.

g) Some people have a lot of success without trying.

h) When the moon hits your eye like a big pizza pie, it's time for a cold shower.

i) There is at least one man named 'Vecchio' who would like to be named 'Jonathon Taylor.'

j) All boys are clowns.

2. Test the following syllogisms for validity by the inconsistent triad method.

a) Metaphysicians are always poets.
Many Spaniards are metaphysicians.
Some Spaniards are poets.

b) Angels never have horns.
Some winged creatures are angels.
There is at least one winged creature without horns.

c) At least one horseman is headless.
Headless people are truncated.
Some truncated object is a horseman.

d) No jack-o'-lanterns are talkative.
Whoever is talkative is dangerous.
A few dangerous things are not jack-o'-lanterns.

e) Sandy pitches.
Whoever pitches perspires.
Sandy perspires.

f) Gingerbread men are fictitious.
Fictitious people are not real.
No gingerbread men are real.

g) Every examination is designed by an authority figure.
Most examinations are a waste of time.
Some time-wasters are designed by authority figures.

h) No slum lords are nice guys.
A slum lord sucks blood from unsuspecting victims.
Some bloodsuckers are not nice guys.

i) Fireplugs are not bathrooms.
Some bathrooms are in beautiful homes.
There is at least one thing in a beautiful home that is not a fireplug.

j) No bathing suits are submarines.
All bikinis are bathing suits.
No bikinis are submarines.

3. Decide which of the following are arguments, and test them by the inconsistent triad method. If there is no argument, answer NA.

a) All Russians drink vodka, so, since all Russians are happy people, a few happy people drink vodka.

b) Some warriors are Frenchmen, but every warrior is a geologist and one or two geologists are Frenchmen.

c) Governors are never segregationists; so some salesmen are not governors because at least one salesman is a segregationist.

d) All heavy eaters have indigestion and many neurotics have indigestion. Hence, some neurotics are not heavy eaters.

e) No Communist is a Republican. Furthermore, most Communists are mad and Republicans are not mad.

f) A person born in August cannot fall in love with a person born in January, because everyone who can fall in love with a person born in January is bound to be unhappy and no one who is born in August is bound to be unhappy.

g) Marinelli fouled out, because Sarbiewski fouled out and Marinelli is not Sarbiewski.

h) Snails love to play in cool water. However, snakes are not snails and no snake will play in cool water.

i) Pirates are not poets and some pilots are pirates. Therefore, some pilots are not poets.

j) No atomic particles smell like fish eggs. So neutrons do not smell like fish eggs, for all neutrons are atomic particles.

4. Construct syllogisms which meet the following specifications and test them for validity by the inconsistent triad technique.

	Figure	Mood	Major term	Minor term	Middle term
a)	I	A A A	cows	ruminants	animals
b)	II	A A A	teddy bears	stuffed animals	toys
c)	III	I A I	states	cities	countries
d)	IV	A E E	lakes	oceans	rivers
e)	I	E I O	paintings	poems	statues
f)	II	E I O	flowers	lilies	roses
g)	III	A I I	novels	magazines	books
h)	IV	A E I	microscopes	stethoscopes	telescopes
i)	I	O A I	midgets	dwarfs	giants
j)	II	E E O	chickens	eggs	hens

2.5 Syllogistic rules

With the help of another technical term we may introduce another decision procedure for syllogistic schemata and syllogisms. In order to keep our explanations and rules fairly uncomplicated, in the next two sections we shall only talk about syllogisms. It is understood, of course, that a syllogism is valid or not depending on whether or not it may be regarded as an interpretation of a valid syllogistic schema. While the procedure we are going to introduce has the slight disadvantage of requiring a new word to denote a somewhat problematic notion, it also has the advantage of not requiring any paperwork. It is presented here because of its historical importance and because it is particularly useful in dealing with the syllogistic chains of the next section.

A term is said to be **distributed** in a categorical sentence if and only if the sentence makes an assertion about every object denoted by the term. For example, when we assert

All roses are flowers.

we mean that every object denoted by the term 'rose' is a flower. Thus, the subject of this **A** sentence is distributed. On the other hand, since we are not making a claim about *every* flower, the predicate is not distributed. Both the subject and predicate of

No roses are flowers.

are distributed; i.e., *nothing* denoted by the subject of an **E** sentence may be identical to *anything* denoted by its predicate. When we assert

Some roses are flowers.

our claim is merely about *some* roses and *some* flowers. Hence, neither term of an **I** sentence is distributed. Finally, only the predicate of the **O** sentence

Some roses are not flowers.

is distributed; i.e., given *any* flower at all, only *some* are roses. The following table summarizes our discussion of the distribution of terms.

	Subject	Predicate
A	distributed	undistributed
E	distributed	distributed
I	undistributed	undistributed
O	undistributed	distributed

The six syllogistic rules for *invalidity* are as follows.

   I. A syllogism with only universal premisses and a particular conclusion is invalid.

  II. A syllogism with only affirmative premisses and a negative conclusion is invalid.

 III. A syllogism with only negative premisses is invalid.

 IV. A syllogism with one negative premiss and an affirmative conclusion is invalid.

V. A syllogism with its middle term undistributed in both premisses is invalid.

VI. A syllogism with a term distributed in its conclusion but not in some premiss is invalid.

All other syllogisms are *valid*. Let us consider some examples.

EXAMPLE 1

Is the following syllogism valid?

> All hamburgers are sandwiches.
> No golf balls are hamburgers.
> _____
> No golf balls are sandwiches.

Solution. Substitute letters for terms. Let '*H*' be short for 'hamburgers', '*W*' for 'sandwiches', and '*G*' for 'golf balls'. Then the argument may be abbreviated:

> All *H* are *W*.
> No *G* are *H*.
> _____
> No *G* are *W*.

Inspecting the conclusion, we find that both '*G*' and '*W*' are distributed. However, '*W*' is not distributed in either premiss. Thus, according to Rule **VI,** this syllogism is invalid. Since, as we noted in Sec. 2.3, the predicate of the conclusion is traditionally called the '*major* term' of the syllogism, the erroneous inference illustrated above is called the **Fallacy of Illicit Process of the Major Term.**

EXAMPLE 2

Prove that the following syllogism is *invalid.*

> All sprinters are athletes.
> All sprinters are lovers.
> _____
> All lovers are athletes.

Solution. Let '*B*' be short for 'sprinters', '*A*' for 'athletes', and '*L*' for 'lovers'. That gives us

> All *B* are *A*.
> All *B* are *L*.
> _____
> All *L* are *A*.

Because '*L*' is distributed in the conclusion but not in either premiss, according to Rule **VI,** this argument is invalid. Since, as we noted earlier, the subject of the conclusion is traditionally called the '*minor* term' of the syllogism, the erroneous inference illustrated here is called the **Fallacy of Illicit Process of the Minor Term.**

EXAMPLE 3

Is the following syllogism valid?

>All plumbers are strong men.
>Some strong men are Eskimos.
>Some Eskimos are plumbers.

Solution. Let '*B*' be short for 'plumbers', '*R*' for 'strong men', and '*E*' for 'Eskimos'. Then the syllogism may be abbreviated as follows.

>All *B* are *R*.
>Some *R* are *E*.
>Some *E* are *B*.

Because '*R*' is not distributed in either premiss, according to Rule **V**, this argument is *invalid*. Traditionally, the erroneous inference illustrated here is called the **Fallacy of the Undistributed Middle Term.**

Review problems for Sec. 2.5.

1. Which terms are distributed in the following sentences?
   a) Kangaroos are never used-car salesmen.
   b) There is at least one thermometer which does not measure temperatures above 200°F.
   c) All umbrellas are ugly.
   d) Many gunslingers are buried on Boot Hill.
   e) Some mice do not run up clocks.
   f) Only hygrometers measure rainfall.
   g) No one proselytizes like a convert.
   h) Some Sunday morning you'll be carried down the aisle.

2. Test the following arguments for validity by the syllogistic rules. If the argument is invalid according to more than one rule, name each one.
   a) Days are not weeks.
      Tuesdays are days.
      Tuesdays are not weeks.
   b) He who is born with a silver spoon in his mouth is uncomfortable.
      He who is born on a mountain top is uncomfortable.
      Anyone born on a mountain top is born with a silver spoon in his mouth.
   c) There are many green giants.
      Some giants own geese that lay golden eggs.
      No people who own geese that lay golden eggs are green.

d)   A toad is not a squirrel.
     A few toads belch.
     Some belchers are not squirrels.

e)   There is at least one bald buffalo.
     No buffaloes are loyal.
     Some loyal animals are bald.

f)   Buddhists are not Presbyterians.
     Many Buddhists are contemplative.
     Some contemplative people are not Presbyterians.

g)   There are no rectangular triangles.
     Every square is rectangular.
     There are square triangles.

h)   No gumdrops are secret weapons.
     Some secret weapons explode.
     Some explosive objects are not gumdrops.

i)   Spaceships are not made for tourists.
     Spaceships fly at speeds faster than sound.
     At least one ship that flies at speeds faster than sound is not made for tourists.

j)   Benny built a better baby bottle.
     Whoever built a better baby bottle burped.
     Benny burped.

3. Decide which of the following are arguments, and test them for validity by the syllogistic rules. If the argument is invalid according to more than one rule, name each one. Write 'NA' for 'no argument'.

a)   Most psychologists are not psychiatrists, because psychiatrists are not Hindus and some psychologists are Hindus.

b)   As long as all flags are highly symbolic and few handkerchiefs are highly symbolic, it must follow that few handkerchiefs are not flags.

c)   There is at least one blue whale that sings and every blue whale has a calf. Therefore some calves are not singers.

d)   Since Christmas trees are always pretty and every Christmas tree is expensive, many expensive trees are pretty.

e)   While candles give enough light for some purposes and whatever gives enough light for some purposes is surely useful, a lot of useful things are candles.

f)   Whoever makes his living by farming is ambitious and he who is ambitious is rich. So all rich people make their living by farming.

g)   No fair maidens are in distress and whoever is in distress is not a karate expert. Hence, karate experts are not fair maidens.

h)   Some sailors swim. Hence some sailors do not dive, for some swimmers are divers.

i)   If it is granted that anyone who builds railroads is industrious and anyone who polishes glass is industrious, then it must be granted that whoever polishes glass builds railroads.

j)   Slaveholders are never very sensitive. Moreover, sensitive people are foolish and slaveholders are foolish too.

4. Construct syllogisms which meet the following specifications, and test them for validity by the Syllogistic Rules.

	Figure	Mood	Major term	Minor term	Middle term
a)	I	E A E	squares	triangles	polygons
b)	II	A E E	Athenians	barbarians	Romans
c)	III	O A O	dogfish	starfish	goldfish
d)	IV	E A O	high schools	universities	colleges
e)	I	E I I	bakers	electricians	blacksmiths
f)	II	A O O	doctors	lawyers	judges
g)	III	I O E	preachers	mathematicians	logicians
h)	IV	I A I	raspberries	blueberries	cranberries

2.6   Syllogistic chains

By suggesting various ways of turning disguised categoricals into standard form, we significantly increased our stock of syllogistic arguments. Syllogisms occur more frequently than one would expect. Similarly, by linking syllogisms together to form **syllogistic chains** (or, traditionally, **sorites**), we can increase the applicability of syllogistic arguments even further. Consider the following examples.

EXAMPLE 1

Show that the following argument is valid.

> All merchants are paupers.
> All fishermen are merchants.
> Some fishermen are women.
> ——————————————
> Some women are paupers.

Solution. Replace all terms with letters. Let 'W' be short for 'women', 'A' for 'paupers', 'C' for 'merchants', and 'F' for 'fishermen'. Then the argument may be abbreviated.

> 1.   All C are A.
> 2.   All F are C.
> 3.   Some F are W.
> ——————————————
> c.   Some W are A.

This argument is *not* a syllogism. We may construct two valid syllogisms out of it, however, which lead to the conclusion (c). We have, in fact, at least two possibilities. We could *argue* first from

> 1.   All C are A.
> 2.   All F are C.
> ——————————————

to

       c1.   All *F* are *A*.

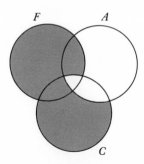

and then, using c1. as the first premiss of a second argument, from

       c1.   All *F* are *A*.
        3.   Some *F* are *W*.
                          ‾‾‾‾‾‾‾‾‾‾‾‾‾‾‾‾

to

        c.   Some *W* are *A*.

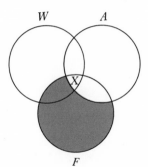

    An *alternative* reconstruction or *chain* of syllogisms for this argument would run from

        2.   All *F* are *C*.
        3.   Some *F* are *W*.
                          ‾‾‾‾‾‾‾‾‾‾‾‾‾‾‾‾

to

       c1.   Some *W* are *C*.

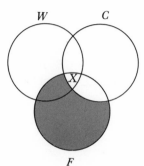

to

    c1. Some *W* are *C*.

      1. <u>All *C* are *A*.</u>

to

    c. Some *W* are *A*.

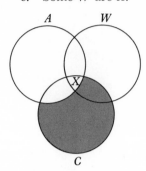

The validity of each of these arguments is demonstrated by the Venn diagram beside it. We could, of course, use the inconsistent triad or the syllogistic rules for the demonstration. The important point is that the validity of an argument which is *not* a syllogism has been demonstrated by reconstructing it into a *chain* of syllogisms.

The procedure involves some trial and error, but it is not entirely that. We know, for instance, that a syllogism must have a middle term. So we *begin by adjoining sentences with common terms.* Our *rules* tell us that certain combinations of sentences cannot be premises of valid arguments; e.g., **E E, O O, I O,** etc. These possibilities, then, are immediately eliminated. Thus, keeping one eye on what we know about valid syllogisms and one eye on the given possible combinations, we construct syllogistic chains.

Example 2

Show that the following argument is valid.

> No mothers are thieves.
> Some mothers are weight lifters.
> All weight lifters are barrel-chested people.
> <u>All barrel-chested people are scholars.</u>
> Some scholars are not thieves.

Solution. Begin by substituting letters for terms. Let '*O*' be short for 'mother', '*T*' for 'thieves', '*W*' for weightlifters, '*B*' for 'barrel-chested people', and '*C*' for 'scholars'. The argument, then, may be abbreviated.

    1. No *O* are *T*.

    2. Some *O* are *W*.

    3. All *W* are *B*.

    4. <u>All *B* are *C*.</u>

    c. Some *C* are not *T*.

One way (not the only way) to proceed is as follows. We might argue from

1. No *O* are *T*.
2. Some *O* are *W*.
c1. Some *W* are not *T*.

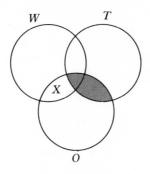

to

c1. Some *W* are not *T*.
3. All *W* are *B*.
c2. Some *B* are not *T*.

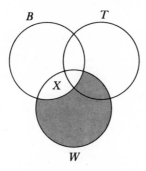

to

c2. Some *B* are not *T*.
4. All *B* are *C*.
c. Some *C* are not *T*.

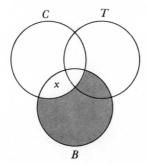

Thus, using three syllogistic arguments, we may show that a nonsyllogistic argument is valid.

While the construction of a chain of valid syllogisms leading to the desired conclusion proves that the argument is valid, the failure to construct such a chain *might not* prove that the argument is invalid. Perhaps we have not been *clever* enough to find a combination of valid syllogisms leading to the desired conclusion, although such a combination in fact exists. If it is shown, however, that *no* combination of given premisses can lead to the required conclusion, that *does* prove that the argument is invalid. Thus by a process of elimination, we may show that some nonsyllogistic arguments are invalid. Consider the following cases.

Example 3

Prove that the following argument is *invalid*.

> All ducks are amphibians.
> Some trucks are amphibians.
> Some swans are amphibians.
> ─────────────────────────
> No ducks are swans.

Solution. Replace terms with letters. Let '*D*' be short for 'ducks', '*T*' for 'trucks', '*W*' for 'swans', and '*A*' for 'amphibians'.

> 1.   All D are A.
> 2.   Some T are A.
> 3.   Some W are A.
> ──────────────────
> c.   No D are W.

Here the syllogistic rules are extremely helpful. This argument has a *negative* conclusion but only *affirmative* premisses. According to Rule **II**, then, no valid syllogism, and hence no *chain* of them, can be constructed which leads from these premisses to the desired conclusion. So the argument is invalid.

Example 4

Test the following argument for validity.

> No students are critical.
> Administrators are never wise.
> Some good students are not persecuted.
> A wise man never criticizes.
> ─────────────────────────────────
> Administrators are persecuted.

Solution. Translate the sentences into standard form.

> 1.   No students are critical people.
> 2.   No administrators are wise men.

3. Some students are not persecuted people.
4. No wise men are critical people.

   c. No administrators are persecuted people.

There is no need to go any further. Because all the premises are negative, according to Rule **II,** *no* valid syllogism could be constructed. The argument is invalid.

Review problems for Sec. 2.6.

1. Construct syllogistic chains to prove that the following arguments are valid.

   a) Hotheads are never patient.
       A few doctors are patient.
       All paranoids are hotheads.

       Some doctors are not paranoids.

   b) To be a fireman one must be courageous.
       Every citizen is a fireman.
       Many citizens are well-educated.

       Many well-educated people are courageous.

   c) All nuclear physicists play golf.
       Everyone who loses in a toothpaste test becomes introverted.
       Whoever becomes introverted enjoys music.
       There is at least one nuclear physicist who lost in a toothpaste test.

       There is at least one person who enjoys music and plays golf.

   d) When you wish upon a star, your dreams come true.
       Dreamers are time-wasters.
       Many dreamers wish upon stars.
       Whenever your dreams came true, you need a vacation.

       Some time-wasters need a vacation.

   e) Some man-eating savages are sophisticated.
       He who is sophisticated enjoys good cooking.
       Every man-eating savage is a cannibal.
       Whoever enjoys good cooking uses mustard.

       There is at least one cannibal who uses mustard.

   f) Nothing but eggs are gifts of Easter Bunnies.
       Whoever is a fanatical patriot is an assassin.
       Some gifts of Easter Bunnies are fanatical patriots.
       All eggs are hidden in cakes.

       Some assassins are hidden in cakes.

   g) No spectators are competitors.
       Winners are always hardworking people.

He who is lonely is a competitor.

Some winner is a spectator.

Some hardworking people are not lonely.

h) Goober goes for girls.

Only Goober is loved by Gwendolyn.

Every giraffe is loved by Gwendolyn.

Some grown-up animals are giraffes.

Some grown-up animals go for girls.

i) No exotic dancers study symbolic logic.

There is at least one sorority girl who reads Pali.

Anyone who reads Pali has a high IQ.

Whoever has a high IQ studies symbolic logic.

All well-paid dancers are exotic dancers.

Some sorority girl is not a well-paid dancer.

2. Test the following arguments for validity.

a) Anyone who enjoys playing chess is shrewd.

He who is shrewd plays poker on Saturday night.

There is at least one person who enjoys playing chess and is late for church.

Everyone who plays poker on Saturday night comes home late Sunday morning.

Someone who comes home late Sunday morning is late for church.

b) No British diplomats are called 'Tarzan'.

Princeton men are not wild men.

All Princeton men are physical education majors.

Anyone who majors in physical education is called 'Tarzan'.

There is at least one wild man called 'Tarzan'.

c) He who has smelly feet sits near open windows.

No one who sits near open windows can avoid catching a cold.

Some famous scullery maid is called 'Cinderella'.

Someone who can avoid catching a cold is not a famous scullery maid.

At least one famous scullery maid sits near open windows.

Anyone called 'Cinderella' has smelly feet.

d) Any object that falls from outer space is a meteorite.

All good fairies fall from outer space.

Carrots are vegetables.

Meteorites always contain nickel.

Vegetables never contain nickel.

No carrots are good fairies.

e) Only people who survive death have pure souls.

Every administrator is an executive.

Important people do not survive death.

All executives are important people.

No administrators have pure souls.

f) James Bond is a secret agent.

Only James Bond can apprehend Goldfinger.

Some schoolteachers stand for honesty, truth, and beauty.

Every schoolteacher is a lovable creature.

No molly-milktoast type of person is a secret agent.

Anyone who stands for honesty, truth, and beauty can apprehend Goldfinger.

There is at least one lovable creature who is not a molly-milktoast type of person.

g) All cowboys ride horses.

Broncobusters are cowboys.

Some outlaw is a broncobuster.

All Northwest Mounted Policemen ride horses.

Some broncobusters do not ride horses.

h) No electricians are liars.

There is at least one liar who sold the Brooklyn Bridge.

Some cocker spaniels have warm noses.

All angels have wings.

All electricians have wings.

i) Healthy-minded people never complain.

Only termites eat wood.

Anyone who eats bananas has indigestion.

Some wood-eaters are healthy-minded people.

Whoever has indigestion, complains.

Some termites do not eat bananas.

2.7 Immediate inferences

Throughout this chapter we have assumed that the term variables '*S*', '*P*', and '*M*' may represent terms that do not apply to anything that exists; e.g., 'mermaids', 'centaurs', etc. Such terms are said to be *empty*. Given this assumption, we have had to regard argument schemata such as

(1)   All *S* are *P*.

Some *S* are *P*.

as *invalid*. Schema (1) *may* be given a uniform interpretation such that its premiss is true and its conclusion is false; e.g.,

(2)   All mermaids have fins.

Some mermaids have fins.

The premiss of (2) asserts that if anything is a mermaid, it has a fin. That is true, *although* there are no mermaids. The conclusion of (2) asserts that there *exists* at least one mermaid with a fin. That is false, *because* there are no mermaids.

If we presuppose or assume that term variables *cannot* represent *empty* terms, then (1) will become valid. Schema (1) will become valid because every *permitted* interpretation of its variables will be such that if its premiss is true, its conclusion *must* be true. Of course, this sort of validity is "narrower" than the sort we considered in the other sections of this chapter. In the other sections *no* restrictions were put on the terms represented by our term variables. They may or may not have been standing in place of empty terms. The schemata pronounced 'valid' in those sections are valid even if *some* or *all* of their interpretations involve empty terms. Schema (1), however, is *not* valid unless it is presupposed that none of its interpretations may involve empty terms. Or, to put this important point in a slightly different way, if it is presupposed that the term variables in (1) must be interpreted by *nonempty* terms then (1) may be regarded as *valid*. Given this presupposition, (1) may be regarded as valid because all interpretations like (2) are excluded.

Similarly, consider

(3)   No *S* are *P*.
        ―――――――――
        Some *S* are not *P*.

In previous sections we would have pronounced it '*invalid*' and that would have been the end of it. We might have established its invalidity with the following interpretation.

(4)   No centaurs have wings.
        ―――――――――――――――
        Some centaur does not have wings.

The premiss of (4) is true. If anything is a centaur it does not have wings. (A centaur is a mythological creature with the trunk, head, and arms of a man, and the body and legs of a horse.) But the conclusion is false. It is false that there *exists* at least one centaur without wings.

Suppose, however, that we *prohibit* interpretations of (3) that involve empty terms. That is, we shall assume that the term variables of (3) must be interpreted by *nonempty* terms. Then (4) and every similar interpretation is excluded. In that case, (3) will always yield valid inferences.

When it is presupposed that the term variables of categorical schemata must be interpreted by *nonempty* terms, we say that the schemata are given an **existential interpretation.** The name 'existential interpretation' is fairly descriptive, since it denotes an assumption to the effect that *every term* used to interpret the variables of categorical schemata applies to at least one *existing* thing. Given a **hypothetical interpretation,** the variables may be interpreted by empty *or* nonempty terms; i.e., no assumption is made about the existence or nonexistence of anything.

The upshot of this discussion so far is this: The class of valid argument schemata contains at least three subclasses, namely, the familiar class of truth-functionally valid schemata, the class of schemata that are valid given an existential interpretation, and the class of schemata that are valid given a hypothetical interpretation. We examined truth-functional validity in the first chapter and validity given a hypothetical interpretation in the preceding sections of this chapter. In this section we shall take a closer look at validity given an existential interpretation.

The inferences in (1)–(4) have traditionally been called **immediate inferences.** They are inferences from one sentence to another without the *mediation* of any other sentences or terms. These are contrasted with **mediate inferences** (mediated inferences) that require other sentences or terms, e.g., syllogistic inferences. In the remaining paragraphs of this section we are going to introduce a few useful immediate inferences. On the way we shall have to note whether they are valid given a hypothetical interpretation or merely valid given an existential interpretation.

Figure 2.71 is a summary of five types of immediate inferences that are valid given an existential interpretation. It is called a **Strong Square of Opposition** because three of those types are types of opposition.

Strong Square of Opposition

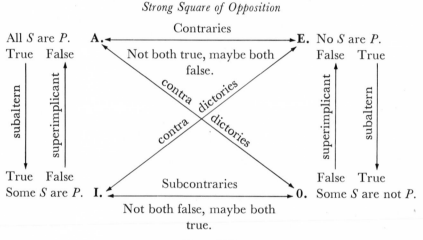

Figure 2.71

'Contradictories' are defined exactly as in Sec. 2.4. One must be true and the other false.

Two sentences are called **contraries** if both cannot be true, but both can be false. **A** and **E** sentences are contraries. If, for example,

All clocks are timepieces.

is true, then

No clocks are timepieces.

must be false. On the other hand, *both* contraries *might* be false; e.g.,

All men are doctors.

and

No men are doctors.

are both false.

Two sentences are called **subcontraries** if both cannot be false but both can be true. **I** and **O** sentences are subcontraries. If, for example,

Some lawyers are Indians.

is false, then

Some lawyers are not Indians.

must be true. On the other hand, *both* subcontraries *might* be true, as those just suggested.

I and **O** sentences are said to be the **subalterns** of **A** and **E** sentences, respectively. As we saw earlier, the subaltern of a true sentence is true; i.e., if **A** is true, then its corresponding **I** must be true; and if **E** is true, then its corresponding **O** must be true.

A and **E** sentences are said to be the **superimplicants** of **I** and **O** sentences, respectively. The superimplicant of a false sentence is false; e.g., if the **I** sentence

Some men are sad.

is false, then its superimplicant **A** sentence

All men are sad.

must be false, and if the **O** sentence

Some men are not sad.

is false, then its superimplicant **E** sentence

No men are sad.

must be false.

So far we have emphasized the fact that given the truth or falsity of certain sentences, the falsity or truth of certain others follows. But there are also some implicit limitations that should be mentioned. Given the truth or falsity of any sentence, the falsity or truth of its contradictory follows with certainty. Contradictories, then, present no immediate problem. But given the *falsity* of one of two contraries or the *truth* of one of two subcontraries, the truth-value of the other (contrary or subcontrary) is simply unknown. For example, if

All pencils are lions.

is false then

No pencils are lions.

may be true *or* false; and if

Some cows are herbivores.

is true then

Some cows are not herbivores.

may be true *or* false. Again, given the *falsity* of a universal sentence, the truth-value of its subaltern particular sentence is unknown; e.g., if

All Italians are singers.

is false then

Some Italians are singers.

may be true *or* false. Finally, given the *truth* of a particular sentence, the truth-value of its superimplicant universal sentence is unknown; e.g., if

Some leaders are tyrants.

is true then

All leaders are tyrants.

may be true *or* false.

The **converse** of an **E** or an **I** sentence is formed by interchanging the subjects and predicates. For example, the converse of

No men are owls.

is

No owls are men.

and the converse of

Some owls are men.

is

Some men are owls.

Since the converse of an **E** or **I** sentence is an *equivalent* **E** or **I** sentence, the inference from an **E** or **I** sentence to its converse is valid given a hypothetical interpretation.

The converse of an **A** sentence is formed by interchanging its subject and predicate, and substituting 'some' for 'all'. This is called **conversion by limitation;** e.g., the "limited" converse of

All boys are brutes.

is

Some brutes are boys.

Clearly, such an inference cannot be sanctioned given a hypothetical interpretation (because there may not be any brutes or boys). Hence, conversion by limitation is an inference that is merely valid given an existential interpretation.

An **O** sentence has *no* converse. The schema

$$\frac{\text{Some } S \text{ is not } P.}{\text{Some } P \text{ is not } S.}$$

admits of a uniform interpretation such that its premiss is true and its conclusion is false; e.g.,

$$\frac{\text{Some mammals are not whales.}}{\text{Some whales are not mammals.}}$$

Hence, **O** sentences cannot be converted.

To form the **obverse** of a categorical sentence, replace its predicate with its complement and change its quality (i.e., change affirmatives to negatives and vice versa). Thus to form the obverse of

> All mice are rodents.

replace the predicate 'rodents' with its complement 'nonrodents' to obtain

> All mice are nonrodents.

and change the quality, which is (universal) affirmative to (universal) negative,

> No mice are nonrodents.

To form the obverse of

> No mice are rodents.

we replace the predicate with its complement,

> No mice are nonrodents.

and change the quality from negative to affirmative:

> All mice are nonrodents.

The obverse of

> Some mice are rodents.

is

> Some mice are not nonrodents.

and the obverse of

> Some mice are not rodents.

is the obviously equivalent

Some mice are nonrodents.

Since the obverse of a sentence is an *equivalent* sentence, the inference from any sentence to its obverse is valid given a hypothetical interpretation.

To form the **contrapositive** of an **A** or an **O** sentence, we interchange its subject and predicate and replace each term with its complement. For example, to form the contrapositive of the **A** sentence

All moons are satellites.

we interchange the terms to obtain

All satellites are moons.

and replace each term with its complement,

All nonsatellites are nonmoons.

To form the contrapositive of

Some moons are not satellites.

we interchange the terms to obtain

Some satellites are not moons.

and replace each term with its complement,

Some nonsatellites are not nonmoons.

These two steps *do not* lead to true sentences from an **E** or an **I** sentence; e.g., applying the two steps to the **E** sentence

No eggs are bathtubs.

which is true, we find

No nonbathtubs are noneggs.

which is false (e.g., ice cubes are nonbathtubs *and* noneggs). If we obvert, convert, and then obvert this **E** sentence, however, we arrive at its contrapositive without any difficulty; e.g., if we obvert

No eggs are bathtubs.

we find

All eggs are nonbathtubs.

If we convert that, we find

> Some nonbathtubs are eggs.

which by obversion again gives

> Some nonbathtubs are not noneggs.

which is the contrapositive of the **E** sentence. This three-step procedure has the advantage of applying to all three sentences, **A, E,** and **O.** The **I** sentence has no contrapositive.

Since the contrapositive of an **A** or **O** sentence is an *equivalent* sentence, the inference from an **A** or an **O** sentence to its contrapositive is valid given a hypothetical interpretation. On the other hand, the inference from an **E** sentence to its contrapositive is merely valid given an existential interpretation.

The following table summarizes our discussion of conversion, obversion, and contraposition.

Immediate Inferences

Categorical schema	Converse	Obverse	Contrapositive
A All *S* are *P*.	Some *P* are *S*.	No *S* are non-*P*.	All non-*P* are non-*S*.
E No *S* are *P*.	No *P* are *S*.	All *S* are non-*P*.	Some non-*P* are not non-*S*.
I Some *S* are *P*.	Some *P* are *S*.	Some *S* are not non-*P*.	None
O Some *S* are not *P*.	None	Some *S* are non-*P*.	Some non-*P* are not non-*S*.

Before closing this discussion of immediate inferences and validity given an existential interpretation, it should be mentioned that there are nine syllogistic schemata that are valid given this sort of interpretation, but *invalid* given a hypothetical interpretation. These are indicated in Figure 2.72.

Figure I	Figure II	Figure III	Figure IV
A A I	A E O	A A I	A E O
E A O	E A O	E A O	E A O
			A A I

Figure 2.72

Notice that each of these schemata involves an inference from universals to particulars. Every conclusion is particular and every premiss is universal. If these schemata are added to the fifteen that are valid given a hypothetical interpretation, we have a total of twenty-four syllogistic schemata that are valid given an existential interpretation.

We already have all the tools required to test syllogistic schemata and syllogisms for validity given an existential interpretation. One way is to match them against the schemata summarized in Figures 2.32 and 2.72. Alternatively, we might apply the Venn diagram, inconsistent triad, or syllogistic rules tests *with* an appropriate immediate inference. Let us look at this possibility more carefully.

To prove that a schema in Figure I with a mood **A A I** (hereafter, I **A A I**) is valid given an existential interpretation, we may prove I **A A A** is valid given a hypothetical interpretation by, say, a Venn diagram and then note that **I** is the subaltern of **A**. Hence, if we may infer **A** from the premisses **A A** in Figure I, we may also infer **I** given an existential interpretation.

To prove II **A E O** is valid given an existential interpretation, we begin by proving II **A E E** is valid given a hypothetical interpretation. Then, since **O** is the subaltern of **E**, II **A E O** is valid given an existential interpretation.

This technique is applicable to the four schemata in Figures I and II that are valid given an existential interpretation and to IV **A E O.** Each of these schemata may be described as a **weakened mood** of a schemata that is valid given a hypothetical interpretation. The four remaining schemata recorded in Figure 2.72 may be described as **strengthened moods** of schemata that are valid given a hypothetical interpretation. In each of the latter cases a premiss of a schema that is valid given a hypothetical interpretation is replaced by its superimplicant. For example, III **A A I** is valid given an existential interpretation because III **I A I** is valid given a hypothetical interpretation and the **I** premiss in the latter is merely replaced by the stronger **A** premiss (its superimplicant) in the former. Hence, to prove III **A A I** is valid given an existential interpretation, we prove III **I A I** is valid given a hypothetical interpretation and note that the first premiss in the former implies the first premiss in the latter given an existential interpretation. Similar justifications may be constructed for III **E A O** (using III **O A O** or **E I O**), IV **E A O** (using IV **E I O**), and IV **A A I** (using IV **I A I**).

Review problems for Sec. 2.7.

1. What is the difference between

    a) validity given a hypothetical interpretation and validity given an existential interpretation

    b) mediate and immediate inferences

    c) contradictories and contraries

    d) the Weak and the Strong Squares of Opposition

    e) conversion and conversion by limitation

2. Using the Strong Square of Opposition, fill in the blanks below. (*Note:* The answers will be 'true', 'false', or 'undetermined'.)

Given: **A** is true.

a) **E** is _____.
b) **I** is _____.
c) **O** is _____.

Given: **E** is true.

d) **A** is _____.
e) **I** is _____.
f) **O** is _____.

Given: **I** is true.

g) **O** is _____.
h) **A** is _____.
i) **E** is _____.

Given: **O** is true.

j) **I** is _____.
k) **A** is _____.
l) **E** is _____.

Given: **A** is false.

m) **E** is _____.
n) **I** is _____.
o) **O** is _____.

Given: **E** is false.

p) **A** is _____.
q) **I** is _____.
r) **O** is _____.

Given: **I** is false.

s) **O** is _____.
t) **A** is _____.
u) **E** is _____.

Given: **O** is false.

v) **I** is _____.
w) **A** is _____.
x) **E** is _____.

3. Given an existential interpretation, translate the following into standard form and *convert* them.

a) A brave person only dies once.
b) There is at least one Swiss Family Clyde.
c) Thinking stinks.
d) A little bird told me that you love me.
e) No men are perfect.
f) Some things are not for sale.

4. Translate the following into standard form and *obvert* them.

a) Kilroy is dead.
b) Few people are saints.
c) No lovers are mad.
d) Some battles are not profitable.
e) Nothing transient is permanent.
f) Superman is a fink.

5. Translate the following into standard form and *contrapose* them.

a) Some sloths are not lazy.
b) Love is grand.
c) No fat rats are rotten rodents.
d) There is at least one purple pillow.
e) All tests are pests.
f) No pork chops are hills.

6. If 'All generals are clowns' is *true*, what is the truth-value of each of the following sentences?

a) Some generals are not clowns.
b) No nonclowns are generals.
c) Some nonclowns are not nongenerals.
d) No generals are clowns.
e) Some clowns are generals.
f) All clowns are nongenerals.
g) No clowns are nongenerals.
h) All nonclowns are nongenerals.

7. Explain why IV **A E O** is valid given an existential interpretation.

Suggestions for further reading related to Chapter 2.

Barker, Stephen F., *The Elements of Logic.* New York: McGraw-Hill Book Company, 1965, Chapter 2.

Bird, Otto, *Syllogistic and Its Extensions.* Englewood Cliffs, N. J.: Prentice-Hall, Inc., 1964.

Carroll, Lewis, *Symbolic Logic and the Game of Logic.* New York: Dover Publications, Inc., 1958.

Copi, Irving M., *Introduction to Logic.* New York: The Macmillan Co., 1961, Chapters 5, 6, and 7.

Hughes, G. E., and Londey, D. G., *The Elements of Formal Logic.* New York: Harper & Row, Inc., 1965, Part IV.

Rescher, Nicholas, *Introduction to Logic.* New York: St. Martin's Press, Inc., 1964, Chapters 2 and 7–11.

In so far as rigour is lacking in a proof, the proof is defective; it is no defence to urge that common sense shows the result to be correct, for if we were to rely upon that, it would be better to dispense with argument altogether, rather than bring fallacy to the rescue of common sense. No appeal to common sense, or "intuition", or anything else except strict deductive logic, ought to be needed after the premisses have been laid down.

Bertrand Russell

Chapter

3

Natural Deduction in the Calculus of Sentences

3.1 Inference rules

In the first chapter we used the truth-table and *reductio ad absurdum* tests to prove that certain argument schemata were truth-functionally valid. The premisses of truth-functionally valid argument schemata were said to *truth-functionally imply*

Modus ponens (mp): '$p \supset q$' and 'p' imply 'q'.
Modus tollens (mt): '$p \supset q$' and '$-q$' imply '$-p$'. √
Conjunction (conj): 'p' and 'q' imply '$p \cdot q$'.
Addition (add): 'p' implies '$p \vee q$'.
Simplification (simp): '$p \cdot q$' implies 'p'.
Elimination (elim): '$p \vee q$' and '$-p$' imply 'q'.
Transitivity (trans): '$p \supset q$' and '$q \supset r$' imply '$p \supset r$'. √
Constructive dilemma (cd): '$p \supset q$', '$r \supset s$', and '$p \vee r$' imply '$q \vee s$'.
Destructive dilemma (dd): '$p \supset q$', '$r \supset s$', and '$-q \vee -s$' imply '$-p \vee -r$'.

Rules of Inference

Figure 3.11

their conclusions. For Prob. 5 in Sec. 1.7, you demonstrated the validity of nine such schemata. Each of these was given a name. Figure 3.11 contains a summary of the results obtained from that exercise.

A **rule of inference** is a rule that is designed to justify or validate inferences from certain schemata or sentences to certain others. Each of the sentences in Figure 3.11 may be regarded as a rule of inference. The first rule, *Modus ponens* or, for short, mp, tells us that '$p \supset q$' and 'p' *together* (truth-functionally) imply 'q'. In other words, the inference *from* '$p \supset q$' and 'p' *to* 'q' is valid. Similarly, any appropriate uniform interpretation of the schemata '$p \supset q$' and 'p' implies the corresponding interpretation of 'q'. For examples, consider the following arguments.

$$
\begin{array}{lll}
F \supset H & L \supset (I \equiv O) & (M \supset U) \supset N \\
F & L & M \supset U \\
\hline
H & I \equiv O & N
\end{array}
$$

'*Modus ponens*' is an abbreviation of the Latin phrase '*modus ponendo ponens*' which means the mood which affirms by affirming. The name is quite appropriate. In each of the arguments above we begin with a material conditional; e.g., the first begins with '$F \supset H$'. The antecedents of those conditionals are affirmed as second premisses; e.g., the second premiss of the first argument is 'F'. Then the consequents of those conditionals are *detached* and *affirmed;* e.g., the consequent 'H' is detached from the first premiss and affirmed. Thus, using mp, we do affirm (consequents) *by* affirming (antecedents). Since the consequents are *detached* from conditionals, mp is often called the 'Law of Detachment'.

Notice that mp *does not* validate the inference of the antecedent 'p' from the conditional schema '$p \supset q$' and the affirmation of its *consequent* 'q'. The following *reductio ad absurdum* shows that such an inference would be *invalid*.

$$
\begin{array}{lll}
p \supset q^t & t & \\
q^t & t & \text{(invalid)} \\
\hline
p^f & f &
\end{array}
$$

That is, when 'p' is given a false interpretation and 'q' is given a true one, the interpretation of the schema above will have all true premisses and a false conclusion. Traditionally one who uses an argument patterned after this schema is said to commit the **fallacy of affirming the consequent.** This is an appropriate description since the mistake or fallacious move is the affirmation of the consequent instead of the antecedent in the second premiss.

When a sentence is inferred from some others in accordance with a rule of inference, we shall say it has been **derived** or **deduced** from the others. A sequence of sentences leading from *given* premisses to a *derived* conclusion will be called a **formal proof.** The procedure of constructing formal proofs from given premisses and validating (justifying) every derivation by the rules listed in Figure 3.11 and/or others to be introduced in this and the next chapter is known as the

method of natural deduction. It was first introduced by Gerhard Gentzen and Stanislaw Jaskowski in 1934. This method will be the focus of our attention for the remainder of Part One. Let us begin with some simple examples.

EXAMPLE 1

Derive '$I \equiv O$' from the following premisses.

$$1. \quad L \supset (I \equiv O)$$
$$2. \quad L$$

Solution. Each line of our deduction must be validated or *justified;* i.e., we must *give a reason* for writing every line. Premisses 1 and 2 are *given,* so *this* is their justification. Hence, to the right of each premiss we write 'Given'.

1.	$L \supset (I \equiv O)$	Given
2.	L	Given

Since the conclusion we wish to derive is the consequent of the first premiss and since the second premiss *matches* the antecedent of the first premiss, we may write the consequent '$I \equiv O$' as our third line.

1.	$L \supset (I \equiv O)$	Given
2.	L	Given
3.	$I \equiv O$	

The third line is justifiable because it *completes the pattern* of mp. In other words, given premisses 1 and 2, according to mp, line 3 may be written as a new line. To the right of '$I \equiv O$' on line 3 we write '1, 2, mp' which is short for 'from lines 1 and 2 according to (or following the pattern of) mp'. The complete formal proof, then, looks like this.

1.	$L \supset (I \equiv O)$	Given
2.	L	Given
3.	$I \equiv O$	1, 2, mp

Notice that in this proof we regarded

'L' as an interpretation of 'p'.
'$I \equiv O$' as an interpretation of 'q'.

Examples of arguments that might be abbreviated by the given letters are

If Louis took the bus, then Igor walked if and only if Otto walked.
Louis took the bus.
Igor walked if and only if Otto walked.

If Alice is alone, then she is insane if and only if she is out to get Charlie.
Alice is alone.

She is insane if and only if she is out to get Charlie.

Usually, as we shall see shortly, more than one rule (or pattern) must be employed to reach a desired conclusion. Hence, lines which are originally introduced as conclusions of given premises are frequently used as premises to derive other conclusions. In short, a *chain* of valid arguments is constructed leading from the given premises to the desired conclusion.

EXAMPLE 2

Derive '$(A \cdot B) \supset C$' from

$$
\begin{array}{ll}
1. & (A \cdot B) \supset (D \supset E) \\
2. & (D \supset E) \supset C.
\end{array}
$$

Solution. We begin by writing the justification for each premiss.

$$
\begin{array}{lll}
1. & (A \cdot B) \supset (D \supset E) & \text{Given} \\
2. & (D \supset E) \supset C & \text{Given}
\end{array}
$$

Next, examine the nine rules to find one that seems applicable to the given premises. More precisely, we are looking for a rule that will validate an inference from *two conditionals* to another conditional. Is there such a rule? Yes. According to the *transitivity* rule or, for short, trans, '$p \supset q$' and '$q \supset r$' *together* imply '$p \supset r$'. Hence any uniform interpretation of '$p \supset q$' and '$q \supset r$' implies the corresponding interpretation of '$p \supset r$'. That is, according to trans, we may write line 3 of our demonstration.

$$
\begin{array}{lll}
3. & (A \cdot B) \supset C & 1, 2, \text{trans}
\end{array}
$$

This completes the demonstration.

Notice that in this proof we regarded

'$A \cdot B$' as an interpretation of 'p'.
'$D \supset E$' as an interpretation of 'q'.
'C' as an interpretation of 'r'.

An example of an argument that might be abbreviated by the given letters is

If Al and Bob are dead, then if Don is dead then Ed is dead.
If Don is dead then Ed is dead, only if Carl is dead.

Al and Bob are dead, only if Carl is dead.

EXAMPLE 3

Derive the conclusion of this argument from its premises.

If Able loved his brother then Baker bought a banana.
Baker did not buy a banana and Charlie was glad.

Able did not love his brother.

Solution. Begin by abbreviating the argument. Let '*A*' be short for 'Able loved his brother', '*B*' for 'Baker bought a banana', and '*C*' for 'Charlie was glad'. Hence, we must derive '$-A$' from

1. $A \supset B$ Given
2. $-B \cdot C$ Given

Having justified each of the premisses, examine the nine rules to see which one (or *ones* if there are more than one) might be used to derive '$-A$'. None of the rules validates an inference from a conditional and a conjunction to a negation. So we shall not be able to derive the conclusion '$-A$' in *one* step.

The rule of *modus tollens*, or mt, may be used to validate an inference *from* a conditional and the negation of its consequent *to* the negation of its antecedent· '*Modus tollens*' is short for the Latin phrase *modus tollendo tollens* which means the mood which denies (the antecedent) by denying (the consequent). We have a conditional in our first premiss, '$A \supset B$'. '$-B$' in the second premiss is the negation of the consequent of that conditional. If we had '$-B$' on a line by itself, we could derive '$-A$' according to mt. The question is, How can we place '$-B$' on a line by itself?

Examining the rules again, we find that the rule of *simplification*, or simp, may be used to validate an inference from a conjunction to *any* of its conjuncts. '$-B$' is the left-hand conjunct of the second premiss '$-B \cdot C$'. Hence, according to simp, we may write '$-B$' as a new line.

3. $-B$ 2, simp

(*Note:* simp could also be used to validate the inference to '*C*', but we do not *need* '*C*' to derive our conclusion '$-A$'.)

Now, with '$-B$' and the first premiss '$A \supset B$' we may derive the desired conclusion according to mt.

4. $-A$ 1, 3, mt

This completes the demonstration.

Notice that mt *does not* validate the inference of the negated consequent '$-q$' from the conditional schema '$p \supset q$' and its negated antecedent '$-p$'. The following *reductio ad absurdum* shows that such an inference would be *invalid*.

$$
\begin{array}{ll}
p \supset q^{t} & t \\
-p^{t} & t \\
\hline
-q^{f} & f
\end{array}
$$

That is, when '*p*' is given a false interpretation and '*q*' is given a true one, the interpretation of the schema above will have all true premisses and a false conclusion. Traditionally one who uses an argument patterned after this schema is said to commit the **fallacy of denying the antecedent.** This is an appropriate description since the mistake or fallacious move is the denial of the antecedent instead of the consequent in the second premiss.

EXAMPLE 4

Demonstrate the validity of the following argument by natural deduction.

> Either Henry rides or Julie walks.
> Henry never rides.
> ———————————————
> Either Julie walks or Paul prays.

Solution. Put the argument into symbolic form. Let '*H*' be short for 'Henry rides', '*J*' for 'Julie walks', and '*P*' for 'Paul prays'. Thus, we must derive '$J \lor P$' from

$$1. \quad H \lor J \qquad \text{Given}$$
$$2. \quad -H \qquad \text{Given}$$

Begin by examining the rules to see if one of them may be used to validate an inference from a disjunction and the negation of one of its disjuncts to another disjunction. The rule of *elimination*, or elim, may be used to validate an inference from a disjunction and the negation of *either* of its disjuncts to the other disjunct. The application of elim will not be sufficient to obtain the desired conclusion '$J \lor P$', but it will help. Hence, we shall apply elim to obtain

$$3. \quad J \qquad 1, 2, \text{elim}$$

The question is, How can we obtain '$J \lor P$' from '*J*'? To answer this question, we *return to the rules of inference.* The rule of *addition*, or add, may be used to validate an inference from any sentence to the disjunction of that sentence with any other sentence. Thus, we may derive

$$4. \quad J \lor P \qquad 3, \text{add}$$

EXAMPLE 5

Demonstrate the validity of the following argument.

> Either the pie burns, or if the pan is heated to 200°F then the cake will burn.
> The pie does not burn, and if the pie burns then there will be no dessert.
> The pan is heated to 200°F.
> ———————————————
> Either the cake will burn or there will be no dessert.

Solution. Put the argument into symbolic form. Let '*P*' be short for 'the pie burns', 'H' for 'the pan is heated to 200°F', 'C' for 'the cake will burn', and 'D' for 'there will be no dessert'. The argument, then, looks like this.

$$
\begin{array}{lll}
1. & P \vee (H \supset C) & \text{Given} \\
2. & -P \cdot (P \supset D) & \text{Given} \\
3. & H & \text{Given} \\
\hline
& C \vee D &
\end{array}
$$

Since the conclusion is a disjunction, if we could derive either disjunct by itself, we could then introduce the other by add. So we shall try to derive 'C'. How can we do that? 'C' appears in the premisses as the consequent of '$H \supset C$', and the third premiss is 'H'. So if we could place '$H \supset C$' on a line by itself, then we could obtain 'C' by mp.

The question now is, How can we place '$H \supset C$' on a line by itself? '$H \supset C$' is a disjunct of the first premiss '$P \vee (H \supset C)$'. The other disjunct of the first premiss is 'P' and the negation of 'P' appears in the second premiss '$-P \cdot (P \supset D)$'. Now, the path is clear. If we drop '$-P$' from the second premiss by simp, then we may drop '$H \supset C$' from the first premiss by elim. Here, then, is how the complete demonstration looks.

$$
\begin{array}{lll}
1. & P \vee (H \supset C) & \text{Given} \\
2. & -P \cdot (P \supset D) & \text{Given} \\
3. & H & \text{Given} \\
4. & -P & \text{2, simp} \\
5. & H \supset C & \text{1, 4, elim} \\
6. & C & \text{5, 3, mp} \\
7. & C \vee D & \text{6, add}
\end{array}
$$

Notice that our strategy was to begin with the conclusion and repeatedly raise the question, How can we obtain *this* line? Step by step each answer yielded a line of the demonstration.

EXAMPLE 6

Derive '$(-E \cdot -B)$' from the following premisses.

$$
\begin{array}{ll}
1. & -B \\
2. & C \supset D \\
3. & E \supset -D \\
4. & A \vee C \\
5. & A \supset B
\end{array}
$$

Solution. Since the conclusion we wish to derive is a conjunction, we may derive *one conjunct at a time* and then conjoin them. We already have '$-B$' in premiss 1. So all we need is '$-E$'. We could obtain '$-E$' from premiss 3, '$E \supset -D$', by mt if we had 'D'. So how can we obtain *that?* We could obtain 'D' from premiss

2, '$C \supset D$', by mp if we had 'C'. 'C' could be eliminated from the fourth premiss, '$A \lor C$', if we had '$-A$'. And '$-A$', finally, could be detached from premiss 5, '$A \supset B$', if we had '$-B$'. And, fortunately, we have '$-B$'!

This, then, is the complete proof.

1.	$-B$	Given
2.	$C \supset D$	Given
3.	$E \supset -D$	Given
4.	$A \lor C$	Given
5.	$A \supset B$	Given
6.	$-A$	5, 1, mt
7.	C	4, 6, elim
8.	D	2, 7, mp
9.	$-E$	3, 8, mt
10.	$-E \cdot -B$	9, 1, conj

Again it should be noted that our strategy was to begin with the conclusion and ask repeatedly, How might *this* line be obtained? Step by step we worked our way back to the premisses.

In general, then, we have used two types of strategies based on two different questions. In the first place, we raised the question, Do any of our rules validate an inference from the given premisses to the given conclusion or to any part of that conclusion? Alternatively, we considered the conclusion and asked, How might *this* line be derived? There is no reason why *both* strategies might not be used on the same argument. Of course, until the rules become fairly familiar, your strategy will be *largely* a matter of *trial and error*. But it is hardly ever completely trial and error. Usually a cursory inspection of the given premisses immediately reveals the inapplicability of certain rules, and in a short time you will be able to make a number of moves "in your head". Hence, the trial and error technique is supplemented with some handy information practically from the beginning.

Review problems for Sec. 3.1.

1. Define the following.

   a) rule of inference   c) fallacy of affirming the consequent
   b) method of natural deduction   d) fallacy of denying the antecedent

2. The following exercise is designed to help you become familiar with the nine rules of inference. *Do not worry about the strategy yet.* Just *fill in the blanks* and then *reread each proof* to try to discover recurring patterns.

   a)   1. $C \supset (A \supset B)$ _____
           2. $C \cdot A$ Given

    3. C _____, simp

    4. _____ $\supset B$ 1, _____, mp

    5. A 2, simp

    6. _____   4, 5, mp

    7. $B \vee D$ 6, _____

b)   1. $A \supset -(C \vee B)$ Given

    2. $C \supset (D \cdot E)$ _____

    3. $A \cdot C$ Given

    4. A 3, _____

    5. $A \vee C$ _____, add

    6. $-(C \vee B) \vee$ _____   1, _____, 5, cd

    7. C _____, simp

    8. _____ $\vee B$ 7, add

    9. $D \cdot$ _____   6, _____, elim

c)   1. $(A \equiv B) \supset D$ _____

    2. $D \supset (A \supset C)$ Given

    3. $(A \equiv B) \cdot -C$ Given

    4. $(A \equiv B) \supset (A \supset C)$ _____, _____, trans

    5. _____ $\equiv B$ 3, _____

    6. $A \supset$ _____   4, _____, mp

    7. $-C$ _____, simp

    8. _____   6, 7, mt

d)   1. $A \supset -C$ Given

    2. $D \supset E$ _____

    3. $C \cdot A$ Given

    4. C _____, _____

    5. _____ $\vee -E$ 4, add

    6. _____ $\vee -D$ 1, 2, _____, dd

    7. A 3, _____

    8. $-D$ 6, _____, elim

e)   1. $A \supset -(C \equiv$ _____$)$ Given

    2. $(C \equiv D) \vee B$ Given

    3. $(B \supset E) \cdot -E$ Given

    4. $B \supset$ _____   _____, simp

    5. $-E$ 3, _____

    6. _____   4, 5, mt

    7. _____   2, _____, elim

    8. $-A$ 1, _____, _____

f)   1. $(-B \supset C) \cdot (C \supset E)$ Given

    2. $-E$ Given

    3. $-B \supset$ _____   1, _____

    4. _____ $\supset E$ _____, simp

    5. $-B \supset E$ 3, 4, _____

    6. _____   4, 2, mt

7. _____   5, 2, _____
8. $B \cdot -C$ 6, 7, _____

g) 1. $(F \supset -E) \cdot (B \supset -D)$ Given
    2. $D \cdot (B \vee E)$ Given
    3. $B \supset -D$ Given
    4. D _____, _____
    5. _____   3, 4, mt
    6. $B \vee E$ 2, _____
    7. _____   6, _____, elim
    8. $F \supset -E$ _____, simp
    9. _____   8, 7, _____

h) 1. $-(-C \vee -E) \vee (A \equiv B)$ _____
    2. $(C \supset -D) \cdot D$ _____
    3. $(E \supset F)$ Given
    4. D 2, _____
    5. _____ $\vee -F$ 4, add
    6. $C \supset -D$ _____, simp
    7. $-C \vee$ _____   _____, _____, _____, dd
    8. _____   1, 7, elim
    9. $(A \equiv B)$ _____ $(D \cdot E)$ _____, add

i) 1. $(A \equiv -B) \supset C$ Given
    2. $E \supset (D \vee -F)$ Given
    3. $(A \equiv -B) \cdot (-C \cdot -D)$ Given
    4. $(A \equiv -B)$ 3, _____
    5. _____ $\vee E$ 4, _____
    6. _____ $\vee ($ _____ $\vee -F)$ 1, 2, 5, _____
    7. $-C \cdot -D$ _____, simp
    8. $-C$ _____, _____
    9. _____   6, 8, elim
    10. $-D$ 7, _____
    11. $-F$ 9, _____, elim

j) 1. $(A \cdot B) \supset (B \supset D)$ Given
    2. $(-A \supset E) \cdot B$ _____
    3. $-E$ Given
    4. $-A \supset$ _____   _____, simp
    5. _____   4, _____, mt
    6. B 2, _____
    7. $A \cdot$ _____   _____, 6, conj
    8. $B \supset D$ _____, _____, mp
    9. _____   8, 6, _____
    10. $A \cdot D$ _____, _____, _____

k) 1. $-[-(E \supset D) \supset -C] \supset B$ _____
    2. $(-B \cdot C) \cdot (D \supset E)$ Given
    3. $-B \cdot$ _____   2, _____

4. $-B$ _____, _____

5. $-($ _____ $) \supset -C$ _____, _____, mt

6. C 3, simp

7. _____ 5, 6, mt

8. $D \supset E$ 2, simp

l) 1. $(A \equiv B) \supset (C \equiv D)$ _____

2. $(E \equiv F) \supset L$ _____

3. _____ $\cdot (A \equiv B)$ Given

4. $-L$ 3, simp

5. $-L \vee -(C \equiv D)$ _____, _____

6. _____ $\vee -(E \equiv F)$ 1, 2, _____, _____

7. $A \equiv B$ _____, simp

8. _____ 2, 4, mt

9. _____ 1, 7, mp

m) 1. _____ $\supset -C$ Given

2. $(-D \vee -E) \supset -F$ _____

3. _____ $\cdot C$ Given

4. $-A$ 3, simp

5. _____ $\vee -B$ 4, _____

6. $(-A \vee -B) \vee (-D \vee -E)$ _____, add

7. _____ 1, 2, 6, _____

8. C 3, simp

9. _____ 7, 8, elim

10. _____ 1, 8, mt

11. $-(-A \vee -B) \vee G$ 10, _____

12. G _____, _____, _____

n) 1. $A \supset [B \supset (C \supset D)]$ Given

2. $D \supset [B \supset (F \supset C)]$ Given

3. _____ $\cdot (B \cdot C)$ Given

4. A _____, _____

5. _____ 1, 4, _____

6. $B \cdot C$ _____, _____

7. B _____, _____

8. $C \supset D$ 7, _____, _____

9. $C \supset$ _____ 8, 2, _____

10. C _____, _____

11. $B \supset ($ _____ $\supset C)$ _____, _____, mp

12. _____ 7, 11, _____

13. $F \supset D$ _____, _____, trans

14. $F \supset$ _____ 13, 2, _____

o) 1. $(-A \cdot -B) \cdot -C$ Given

2. $(A \vee B) \vee C$ Given

3. $-C$ _____, _____

4. _____ $\vee B$ _____, _____, elim

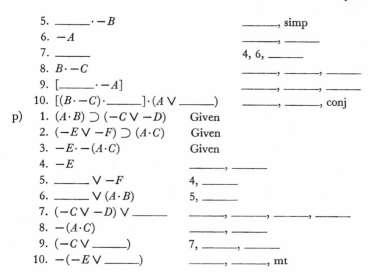

5. _____·−B   _____, simp
6. −A   _____, _____
7. _____   4, 6, _____
8. B·−C   _____, _____, _____
9. [_____·−A]   _____, _____, _____
10. [(B·−C)·_____]·(A ∨ _____)   _____, _____, conj

p)   1. (A·B) ⊃ (−C ∨ −D)   Given
     2. (−E ∨ −F) ⊃ (A·C)   Given
     3. −E·−(A·C)   Given
     4. −E   _____, _____
     5. _____ ∨ −F   4, _____
     6. _____ ∨ (A·B)   5, _____
     7. (−C ∨ −D) ∨ _____   _____, _____, _____, _____
     8. −(A·C)   _____, _____
     9. (−C ∨ _____)   7, _____, _____
    10. −(−E ∨ _____)   _____, _____, mt

3. Construct formal proofs for the following arguments.

a) $A ⊃ −(B ∨ C)$
     B
     $\overline{−A}$

b) $(A ≡ B) ∨ C$
     $\overline{B·−C}$
     $\overline{B·(A ≡ B)}$

c) $(A ∨ −B) ⊃ C$

     $C ⊃ −(D ≡ E)$

     A
     $\overline{−(D ≡ E)}$

d) $A ⊃ (B ⊃ C)$
     $−(B ⊃ C)$
     $\overline{−A ∨ −C}$

e) $B ⊃ (A ∨ D)$
     $D ⊃ −(C ⊃ F)$
     $B·−A$
     $\overline{−(C ⊃ F)}$

f) $(A ≡ C) ∨ D$
     $(A ≡ C) ⊃ B$
     $−B$
     $\overline{D·−B}$

g) $B ∨ D$
     $−(A ⊃ −B) ⊃ −C$
     $C·A$
     $\overline{D}$

h) $[(B ∨ C)·E] ⊃ F$
     $D ∨ (B ∨ C)$
     $E·−D$
     $\overline{(F·E)·−D}$

i) $(C ⊃ D) ⊃ [(D ⊃ E)·(B ⊃ A)]$
     $(D·B)·(C ⊃ D)$
     $\overline{E·A}$

j) $(F ⊃ C)·(C ⊃ D)$
     $(−B ∨ −D)·(F·A)$
     $\overline{D}$

4. Put the following arguments into symbolic form, and construct formal demonstrations of their validity.

a) Either Alfie is working or Cyril's horse did not come in first. If Bannister was the jockey then Cyril's horse came in first. Alfie is working only if Bannister was not the jockey. But Bannister was the jockey. Thus, Alfie is not working and Bannister was not the jockey. Use *A, C, B*.

b) If Arnold did not buy the pork chops then Berferd's charcoal burner is useless. Berferd's charcoal burner is not useless provided that Charlie shows up with the can opener. Arnold did not buy the pork chops. If either Elmer's beer tastes good or Doda's dancing entices us, then Charlie is bound to show up with the can opener. Hence, it is not the case that either Elmer's beer will taste good or Doda's dancing will entice us. *A, B, E, C, D.*

c) Freddy never freeloads and Eugene pays his bills. If Carl gets into trouble then Freddy will freeload. If Carl does not get into trouble and Eugene pays his bills, then Carl gets into trouble. Therefore, Freddy does freeload. *F, E, C.*

d) Angels live good lives and boy scouts do good deeds. If angels live good lives, then if boy scouts do good deeds then circus clowns are happy. Circus clowns are not happy if dogs are barking. Thus, dogs are not barking. *A, B, C, D.*

e) If aardvarks eat ants, then baboons laugh if and only if crocodiles cry. Baboons laugh only if crocodiles do not cry. Aardvarks eat ants and crocodiles cry. Hence, baboons laugh if and only if crocodiles cry, and baboons do not laugh. *A, B, C.*

f) If Billy the Kid and Dirty Dan are in the territory, then Eunice must close the saloon. If Klondike Sam is in town then Billy the Kid is in the territory. Dirty Dan is in the territory and Klondike Sam is in town. So, Eunice must close the saloon. *B, D, E, C.*

g) If the bride is late for her wedding, then if she is not a coward she is an alcoholic. She is not an alcoholic but the bride is late for her wedding. Either she just doesn't give a damn or she is an alcoholic, provided that she is a coward. Hence, she just doesn't give a damn. *B, C, A, D.*

h) Antisthenes was a good friend of Pericles, and Beepinese loved her Pekingese if Celeries picked a peck of peas. Celeries picked a peck of peas. If Dafidese bought a piece of cheese, then it is not the case that both Antisthenes was a good friend of Pericles and Beepinese loved her Pekingese. Thus, Dafidese did not buy a piece of cheese. *A, B, C, D.*

i) Beggers can be choosers if and only if choosers can be beggers, or dullards can be administrators. Dullards cannot be administrators and extroverts can be obnoxious. Beggers can be choosers if and only if choosers can be beggers, only if free men are in chains. If both free men are in chains and extroverts can be obnoxious, then beggers cannot be choosers. Therefore, beggers cannot be choosers. *B, C, D, E, F.*

3.2   Equivalent schemata

In the first chapter we used the truth-table test to prove that certain schemata were *truth-functionally equivalent*. For Prob. 8 in Sec. 1.5, you demonstrated the equivalence of a number of schemata. Figure 3.21 contains a summary of the results obtained from that exercise.

Double negation (dn):
'p' is equivalent to '$-(-p)$'.

Association (assn):
'$p \lor (q \lor r)$' is equivalent to '$(p \lor q) \lor r$'.
'$p \cdot (q \cdot r)$' is equivalent to '$(p \cdot q) \cdot r$'.

Commutation (comm):
'$p \lor q$' is equivalent to '$q \lor p$'.
'$p \cdot q$' is equivalent to '$q \cdot p$'.

De Morgan's laws (dem):
'$-(p \lor q)$' is equivalent to '$-p \cdot -q$'.
'$-(p \cdot q)$' is equivalent to '$-p \lor -q$'.

Distribution (dist):
'$p \cdot (q \lor r)$' is equivalent to '$(p \cdot q) \lor (p \cdot r)$'.
'$p \lor (q \cdot r)$' is equivalent to '$(p \lor q) \cdot (p \lor r)$'.

Transposition (transp):
'$p \supset q$' is equivalent to '$-q \supset -p$'.

Implication (imp):
'$p \supset q$' is equivalent to '$-p \lor q$'.
'$p \supset q$' is equivalent to '$-(p \cdot -q)$'.

Idempotence (idem):
'p' is equivalent to '$p \cdot p$'.
'p' is equivalent to '$p \lor p$'.

Exportation (exp):
'$(p \cdot q) \supset r$' is equivalent to '$p \supset (q \supset r)$'.

Biconditional (bic):
'$p \equiv q$' is equivalent to '$(p \supset q) \cdot (q \supset p)$'.
'$p \equiv q$' is equivalent to '$(p \cdot q) \lor (-p \cdot -q)$'.

Equivalent Schemata

Figure 3.21

Each of the sentences in Figure 3.21 may be *used* as a rule of inference. The first rule, *double negation*, or dn, tells us that 'p' implies '$-(-p)$' *and* that '$-(-p)$' implies 'p'. In other words, *both* the inferences from 'p' to '$-(-p)$' *and* from '$-(-p)$' to 'p' are valid. Similarly, any appropriate uniform interpretation of the schema 'p' implies the corresponding interpretation of '$-(-p)$', and vice versa.

Sometimes it is useful to replace *only part* of a complex sentence with an equivalent part. For examples, the inference from '$(A \lor B) \cdot C$' to '$(B \lor A) \cdot C$' may be validated by *commutation*, or comm; the move from '$A \supset (-B \lor C)$' to '$A \supset (B \supset C)$' may be justified by *implication*, or imp; '$(A \lor A) \lor B$' implies '$A \lor B$' according to *idempotence*, or idem; etc. *Note*, however, that the rules of inference summarized in Figure 3.11 *cannot* be applied to only parts of complex sentences. For examples, the inference from '$A \supset B$' to '$B \vee C$' cannot be validated by add; the move from '$(A \cdot B) \supset C$' and 'B' to 'C' cannot be justified by mp; etc. The application of the *reductio ad absurdum* test to the following reveals their invalidity.

$$\frac{A \supset B}{B \vee C} \qquad \frac{(A \cdot B) \supset C}{\quad B \quad} \\ \overline{\quad C \quad}$$

Quite generally, whenever there is any doubt about the validity of an inference from some line(s) to another line, apply the *reductio ad absurdum* test. It cannot provide any new rules, but it can swiftly eliminate errors.

Consider some derivations involving rules obtained from the equivalent schemata summarized in Figure 3.21.

EXAMPLE 1

Derive '$-A \vee -C$' from

$$\begin{array}{ll} 1. & -A \vee B \\ 2. & -(C \cdot -D) \\ 3. & -(B \cdot D) \end{array}$$

Solution. If imp is applied to the first two premisses '$-A \vee B$' and '$-(C \cdot -D)$', we obtain

$$\begin{array}{lll} 4. & A \supset B & \text{1, imp} \\ 5. & C \supset D & \text{2, imp} \end{array}$$

Applying one of *De Morgan's laws*, or dem, to the third premiss, '$-(B \cdot D)$,' we have

$$\begin{array}{lll} 6. & -B \vee -D & \text{3, dem} \end{array}$$

Using the rule of *destructive dilemma*, or dd, we may derive the conclusion from the last three lines.

$$\begin{array}{lll} 7. & -A \vee -C & \text{4, 5, 6, dd} \end{array}$$

This completes the demonstration.

An example of an argument that might be abbreviated by the given letters is

> Alvin is not rich or Bill is rich.
> It is not the case that both Carl is rich and Don is not rich.
> It is not the case that both Bill and Don are rich.
> Either Alvin is not rich or Carl is not rich.

EXAMPLE 2

Demonstrate the validity of the following argument.

> If Paul and George play guitar, then Ringo plays drums.
> Either Ringo does not play drums or John sings.
> _____
> If Paul plays guitar, then if George plays guitar then John sings.

Solution. Begin by abbreviating the argument. Let 'P' be short for 'Paul plays guitar', 'G' for 'George plays guitar', 'R' for 'Ringo plays drums', and 'J' for 'John sings'. The argument, then, has the following form.

$$(P \cdot G) \supset R$$
$$-R \lor J$$
$$\overline{P \supset (G \supset J)}$$

If imp is applied to the second premiss, '$-R \lor J$', we have

1.	$(P \cdot G) \supset R$	Given
2.	$-R \lor J$	Given
3.	$R \supset J$	2, imp

Applying trans to the first premiss, '$(P \cdot G) \supset R$', and the third line, '$R \supset J$', we find

4.	$(P \cdot G) \supset J$	1, 3, trans

Applying *exportation*, or exp, to line 4, we arrive at the desired conclusion.

5.	$P \supset (G \supset J)$	4, exp

EXAMPLE 3

Prove that the following argument is valid by natural deduction.

> Either Kitchen Sink will not win or Pleasant Moon will win, or Apple Blossom will win.
> Pleasant Moon will not win and Apple Blossom will not win.
> _____
> If Dixie Star wins then Kitchen Sink will not win.

Solution. Put the argument into symbolic form. Let 'K' be short for 'Kitchen Sink will *not* win', 'P' for 'Pleasant Moon will win', 'A' for 'Apple Blossom will win', and 'D' for 'Dixie Star wins'. Then the argument has the following form.

$$(K \lor P) \lor A$$
$$-P \cdot -A$$
$$\overline{D \supset K}$$

Let us employ the strategy of beginning from the conclusion and ask, How can we find '$D \supset K$'? Since, according to imp, '$D \supset K$' is equivalent to '$-D \vee K$', we may aim for the latter. We can find '$-D \vee K$' from either one of its disjuncts, and since '$-D$' does not appear in the premisses, we should aim for 'K'. 'K' appears in a disjunction with 'P' in the first premiss, '$(K \vee P) \vee A$', and the negation of 'P' appears in the second premiss, '$-P \cdot -A$'. Hence, if we could obtain '$K \vee P$' from the first premiss, that would complete the demonstration. On the other hand, if by *association*, or assn, we slid the parentheses in the first premiss to the right, 'K' would be disjoined to '$P \vee A$'. Since premiss 2, '$-P \cdot -A$', is equivalent to '$-(P \vee A)$', 'K' could be obtained by elim. We shall use this alternative course.

1.	$(K \vee P) \vee A$	Given
2.	$-P \cdot -A$	Given
3.	$K \vee (P \vee A)$	1, assn
4.	$-(P \vee A)$	2, dem
5.	K	3, 4, elim
6.	$K \vee -D$	5, add
7.	$-D \vee K$	6, comm
8.	$D \supset K$	7, imp

EXAMPLE 4

Demonstrate the validity of the following argument.

$$(E \cdot F) \cdot (B \equiv E)$$
$$-[A \cdot (B \vee C)]$$
$$\overline{-A}$$

Solution. There is only one occurrence of 'A' in the given premisses. If the 'A' could be negated and taken out of the second premiss '$-[A \cdot (B \vee C)]$', we would have the conclusion '$-A$' isolated. Let us begin by applying dem to the second premiss.

1.	$(E \cdot F) \cdot (B \equiv E)$	Given
2.	$-[A \cdot (B \vee C)]$	Given
3.	$-A \vee -(B \vee C)$	2, dem

From this point, a backward strategy looks fairly promising. If we had '$B \vee C$', we could find '$-A$' by elim. We can find '$B \vee C$' from either one of its disjuncts, and since 'B' appears in the first premiss, we shall aim for that. The question is, How can we take 'B' out of the first premiss, '$(E \cdot F) \cdot (B \equiv E)$'? There are a couple of possibilities. Let us begin by *simplifying* line 1.

4.	$B \equiv E$	1, simp

Applying the *biconditional* rule, or bic, we have

5.	$(B \supset E) \cdot (E \supset B)$	4, bic

This may be simplified to

6. $E \supset B$ 5, simp

We have an 'E' in the first premiss which may be obtained in two steps.

7. $E \cdot F$ 1, simp
8. E 7, simp

Applying mp to lines 6 and 8, we have

9. B 6, 8, mp

The conclusion follows as planned.

10. $B \lor C$ 9, add
11. $-A$ 3, 10, elim

Review problems for Sec. 3.2.

1. Fill in the blanks in the following demonstrations.

   a) 1. $-(B \cdot -C)$ Given
       2. $A \supset (B \cdot D)$ Given
       3. $-A \lor (B \cdot D)$ 2, _____
       4. $(-A \lor B) \cdot$_____   3, dist
       5. _____ $\lor B$ _____, simp
       6. $A \supset B$ _____, _____
       7. $B \supset C$ 1, _____
       8. $A \supset C$ _____, _____, _____

   b) 1. $-(A \lor C)$ Given
       2. $(A \lor -B) \lor C$ Given
       3. _____ $\lor (-B \lor C)$ _____, assn
       4. $(-B \lor C) \lor A$ _____, _____
       5. _____ $\lor A$ 4, imp
       6. $-A \cdot$_____   1, _____
       7. $-A$ _____, _____
       8. $B \supset C$ 5, _____, _____
       9. $-C$ _____, simp
       10. _____   8, _____, mt

   c) 1. $(-A \lor B) \supset C$ Given
       2. $-(-A \lor B) \lor C$ 1, _____
       3. $(A \cdot$_____$) \lor C$ 2, dem
       4. $C \lor (A \cdot -B)$ _____, _____

5. _____ $\cdot (C \vee -B)$ 4, _____
6. $C \vee -B$ _____ , _____
7. _____   6, comm
8. _____   7, imp

d)   1. $C \supset (E \supset F)$ Given
2. $A \equiv -C$ Given
3. $(A \supset -C) \cdot$ _____   _____ , bic
4. $-C \supset A$ _____ , _____
5. _____ $\supset C$ 4, _____
6. $-A \supset ($ _____ $\supset F)$ 5, _____ , _____
7. $(-A \cdot$ _____ $) \supset F$ 6, _____
8. $-($ _____ $\vee -E) \supset F$ _____ , _____
9. $-F \supset (A \vee -E)$ _____ , _____
10. $-F \supset$ _____   9, comm
11. $-F \supset (E \supset A)$ _____ , _____

e)   1. $(-(-A) \cdot B) \supset C$ Given
2. $($ _____ $\cdot B) \supset C$ 1, _____
3. $A \supset$ _____   _____ , _____
4. _____ $\vee (B \supset C)$ _____ , imp
5. $-A \vee (-B \vee$ _____ $)$ 4, _____
6. $(-B \vee C) \vee$ _____   _____ , _____
7. _____ $\vee (C \vee -A)$ _____ , _____
8. $-B \vee$ _____   _____ , comm
9. _____ $\supset (-A \vee C)$ _____ , _____
10. $B \supset$ _____   9, imp

f)   1. $(-E \equiv F) \cdot (D \supset E)$ _____
2. $-(E \cdot -F)$ Given
3. $-E \equiv F$ _____ , _____
4. _____ $\vee (-(-E) \cdot -F)$ _____ , _____
5. $(-E \cdot F) \vee ($ _____ $\cdot -F)$ _____ , _____
6. $-E \cdot F$ 5, 2, _____
7. $D \supset E$ 1, _____
8. $-E$ _____ , _____
9. _____   7, _____ , mt
10. F 6, _____
11. $-D \cdot F$ _____ , _____ , _____

g)   1. $(-A \vee B) \cdot (-A \vee C)$ _____
2. $(B \cdot C) \supset D$ Given
3. $-A \vee (B \cdot$ _____ $)$ _____ , _____
4. _____ $\supset (B \cdot C)$ 3, _____
5. $A \supset$ _____   _____ , _____ , trans
6. $-D \supset$ _____   5, _____
7. $D \vee -A$ 6, _____

h)   1. $A \supset (B \supset C)$ Given

2. $-(B \supset C) \supset$ _____   _____ , _____

3. $-[-(\underline{\quad} \cdot -C)] \supset -A$ 2, _____

4. $(B \cdot \underline{\quad}) \supset -A$ 3, _____

5. $-(B \cdot -C) \vee -A$ 4, _____

6. $(\underline{\quad} \vee C) \vee -A$ _____ , dem

7. $-B \vee \underline{\quad}$ 6, _____

8. $\underline{\quad} \supset (C \vee -A)$ _____ , _____

9. $B \supset \underline{\quad}$ _____ , comm

10. $B \supset (A \supset C)$ _____ , _____

i)   1. $-B \equiv (D \vee C)$ Given

2. $[-B \supset (D \vee C)] \cdot [(D \vee C) \supset -B]$ _____ , _____

3. $-B \supset (D \vee C)$ _____ , _____

4. $B \vee \underline{\quad}$ 3, _____

5. $\underline{\quad} \vee C$ 4, _____

6. $C \vee \underline{\quad}$ _____ , _____

7. $\underline{\quad} \supset (B \vee D)$ 6, _____

8. $(D \vee C) \supset \underline{\quad}$ 2, _____

9. $-(D \vee C) \vee -B$ 8, _____

10. $\underline{\quad} \vee -B$ _____ , dem

11. $-B \vee (\underline{\quad} \cdot -C)$ 10, _____

12. $(-B \vee \underline{\quad}) \cdot (\underline{\quad} \vee -C)$ _____ , _____

13. $-B \vee -C$ _____ , simp

14. $\underline{\quad} \supset -C$ _____ , _____

j)   1. $(-A \cdot -B) \cdot -C$ Given

2. $-A \cdot (-B \cdot -C)$ 1, _____

3. $-A \cdot \underline{\quad}$ 2, dem

4. $-(\underline{\quad} \vee C) \cdot -A$ 3, _____

5. $-[\underline{\quad} \vee A]$ 4, _____

6. $-[B \vee (\underline{\quad})]$ 5, _____

7. $-B \cdot \underline{\quad}$ _____ , _____

8. $-B \cdot (-C \cdot \underline{\quad})$ 7, _____

9. $(-B \cdot -C) \cdot \underline{\quad}$ _____ , _____

k)   1. $(C \vee -D) \cdot (C \vee -E)$ Given

2. $C \supset (F \cdot G)$ Given

3. $C \vee (\underline{\quad} \cdot -E)$ _____ , _____

4. $(-D \cdot \underline{\quad}) \vee C$ 3, _____

5. $-(\underline{\quad}) \vee C$ _____ , dem

6. $\underline{\quad} \supset C$ 5, _____

7. $(D \vee E) \supset \underline{\quad}$ _____ , _____ , trans

8. $-(D \vee E) \vee (F \cdot G)$ 7, _____

9. $[-(D \vee E) \vee F] \cdot \underline{\quad}$ 8, dist

10. $-(D \vee E) \vee F$ _____ , _____

11. $\underline{\quad} \supset F$ _____ , _____

12. $-F \supset -(D \vee E)$ 11, _____

l)
1. $-[A \cdot -(B \equiv -D)]$ Given
2. _____ $\vee (B \equiv -D)$ _____ , _____
3. $-A \vee [(B \supset -D) \cdot (-D \supset B)]$ 2, _____
4. $[-A \vee (B \supset -D)] \cdot [-A \vee (-D \supset B)]$ _____ , _____
5. _____ $\vee (B \supset$ _____ $)$ _____ , _____
6. $-A \vee ($ _____ $\vee -D)$ 5, _____
7. _____ $\vee -D$ 6, _____
8. $-(A \cdot B) \vee -D$ _____ , dem
9. $(A \cdot B) \supset -D$ _____ , _____

m)
1. $(A \vee B) \supset (C \supset D)$ _____
2. $-D \cdot A$ Given
3. $[(A \vee B) \cdot C] \supset D$ _____ , _____
4. $-D$ _____ , _____
5. $-[$ _____ $\cdot C]$ _____ , _____ , mt
6. $-(A \vee$ _____ $) \vee$ _____   5, _____
7. $-C \vee$ _____   6, _____
8. _____ $\supset -(A \vee B)$ 7, _____
9. A _____ , _____
10. $A \vee B$ _____ , _____
11. $-C$ _____ , _____ , _____

n)
1. $-A$ Given
2. $(A \equiv B) \equiv C$ Given
3. _____ $\cdot [C \supset (A \equiv B)]$ _____ , _____
4. $(A \equiv B) \supset C$ _____ , _____
5. $[(A \supset B) \cdot$ _____ $] \supset C$ 4, _____
6. _____ $\supset [(B \supset A) \supset$ _____ $]$ 5, _____
7. _____ $\vee B$ 1, _____
8. $A \supset B$ _____ , _____
9. $(B \supset$ _____ $) \supset C$ _____ , _____ , _____

o)
1. $[(A \supset C) \cdot A] \supset D$ _____
2. $(A \cdot -D) \cdot (E \supset C)$ Given
3. _____ $\supset (A \supset D)$ 1, _____
4. $A \cdot$ _____   _____ , simp
5. $-($ _____ $)$ 4, dem
6. $-(A \supset D)$ 5, _____
7. $-($ _____ $\supset C)$ _____ , _____ , _____
8. $-($ _____ $\vee C)$ 7, _____
9. _____ $\cdot -C$ 8, _____
10. $-C$ _____ , _____
11. $E \supset C$ _____ , _____
12. _____   11, _____ , mt
13. A _____ , _____
14. $A \cdot -E$ _____ , _____ , _____

2. Construct formal proofs for the following arguments.

a) $A \supset (B \supset D)$
$\overline{B \supset (A \supset D)}$

b) $-(A \cdot B) \vee D$
$D \supset (F \cdot C)$
$\overline{A \supset (B \supset F)}$

c) $A \cdot (B \cdot C)$
$\overline{B \cdot (A \cdot C)}$

d) $-A \supset (B \equiv C)$
$\overline{(-A \cdot B) \supset C}$

e) $-E \supset B$
$C \supset B$
$\overline{(-E \vee C) \supset B}$

f) $[(C \cdot -B) \cdot A]$
$\overline{-[(B \vee -A) \vee -C]}$

g) $-C \cdot -(A \cdot B)$
$(A \equiv B) \equiv (C \cdot D)$
$\overline{-[(A \supset B) \cdot (B \supset A)]}$

h) $-G \cdot [-F \supset (B \cdot E)]$
$(-F \vee G) \cdot (-F \vee C)$
$\overline{-(E \supset G)}$

i) $-A \supset (C \supset D)$
$-A \supset (E \equiv F)$
$\overline{-A \supset [(C \supset D) \cdot (E \supset F)]}$

j) $(-B \cdot -C) \vee D$
$-D \cdot (-B \supset A)$
$\overline{(-D \cdot A) \cdot -C}$

3. Put the following arguments into symbolic form, and construct formal proofs of their validity.

a) It is not the case that both Abraham loved Isaac and Benjamin did not love Lillie. Benjamin did not love Lillie. Hence, if Abraham loved Isaac then Clarence had no friends at all. *A, B, C.*

b) Florence is the most beautiful city in Italy if and only if Bologna is in Spain. It is not the case that either Florence is the most beautiful city in Italy or Rome is in Brooklyn. Thus, if Bologna is in Spain then Anthony visited Egypt. *F, B, R, A.*

c) If your friends forsake you then it is better to have enemies, only if your enemies are harmless. If your enemies are harmless, then Leibniz was right and this is the best of all possible worlds. So, either your friends forsake you or Leibniz was right. *F, B, H, L, W.*

d) Confucius never washed his own laundry if and only if Yoo Wan Won closed his shop. Hee Wan Won was not related to Yoo Wan Won. Day Wan Won was a cousin of Yoo Wan Won if and only if Hee Wan Won was related to Yoo Wan Won. Thus, if Day Wan Won was a cousin of Yoo Wan Won then Yoo Wan Won did not close his shop. *C, Y, H, D.*

e) If Claire went to the fair, then it is not the case that the mare was both there and bare. Hence, if Claire went to the fair and the mare was there, then the mare was not bare. *C, M, B.*

f) Jill is not ill and Bill is not ill, or Phil is not ill. It is not the case that both Jill and Phil are ill, only if Bill is ill. Therefore, Jill is ill provided that Phil is ill. *J, B, P.*

g) Either Fidel runs the country, or better relations with the United States are established and Cuba does not suffer economic ruin. If Fidel runs the country and better relations with the United States are established, then Communism is finished in the Western Hemisphere. Hence, if Cuba suffers economic ruin and better relations with the United States are established, then Communism is finished in the Western Hemisphere. *F, R, U, C.*

h)   The Buddha did not watch television and Danny Thomas does watch television, only if Anthony Perkins is playing a dramatic role. The Buddha did not watch television. If Anthony Perkins is playing a dramatic role then Mrs. Perkins is content. Thus, if Evelyn plays according to the rules and Danny Thomas watches television, then Mrs. Perkins is content. *B, D, A, C, E.*

i)   England swings if and only if pendulums do, or France swings. Pendulums do not swing. Hence, if England swings then France swings. *E, P, F.*

j)   It is not the case that ham tastes good if and only if it is served with spaghetti. Ham is not served with spaghetti. So, if ham does not taste good then a wise man eats hamburger. *H, S, W.*

3.3   Conditional proof

In 1929 Alfred Tarski demonstrated the validity of the now somewhat famous (among logicians) *deduction theorem*. The theorem will be introduced here as the rule of

Conditional proof (cp): If a set of premises '$p_1, p_2, \ldots, p_n$' and 'q' together imply 's' then '$p_1, p_2, \ldots, p_n$' implies '$q \supset s$'.

The rule may be used to simplify demonstrations which end in conditionals. Schematically, the prodedure runs as follows. Given an argument patterned after the schema

$$
\begin{array}{l}
p_1 \\
p_2 \\
\vdots \qquad\qquad \text{(given premisses)} \\
\underline{p_n} \\
q \supset s \qquad \text{(conclusion)}
\end{array}
$$

we may *assume* the antecedent 'q' of the conclusion as an additional premiss and derive 's' alone. That is, we construct a new argument patterned after the following schema.

$$
\begin{array}{l}
p_1 \\
p_2 \\
\vdots \qquad\qquad \text{(given premisses)} \\
p_n \\
\underline{q} \qquad\qquad \text{(assumed premiss)} \\
s \qquad\qquad\ \text{(new conclusion)}
\end{array}
$$

Having derived the conclusion 's' from 'q' and some set of premisses '$p_1, p_2, \ldots, p_n$', the rule of *conditional proof*, or cp, validates the inference to the desired conclusion '$q \supset s$' from the set of premisses alone.

Consider the following examples.

EXAMPLE 1

Use cp to derive '$C \supset (C \cdot E)$' from '$C \supset E$'.

Solution. Begin by assuming the antecedent of the conclusion as a new premiss.

$$
\begin{array}{lll}
1. & C \supset E & \text{Given} \\
2. & C/(C \cdot E) & \text{Assumed}
\end{array}
$$

Notice that to the right of the *slash* at the right of the assumed premiss (antecedent), we put the conclusion (consequent) which must be derived to *complete the conditional proof*. When cp is used more than once in a demonstration, it is very helpful to have a reminder of the consequents that must be derived for the various assumed premisses.

The conclusion (consequent) '$C \cdot E$' that must be derived to complete the cp of this argument follows from mp and conj in two steps.

$$
\begin{array}{lll}
3. & E & 1, 2, \text{mp} \\
4. & C \cdot E & 2, 3, \text{conj} \\
5. & C \supset (C \cdot E) & 2, 4, \text{cp}
\end{array}
$$

Notice that the *justification* for line 5 contains the line numbers of the *assumed* premiss (antecedent) and the *new* conclusion (consequent), followed by 'cp'.

EXAMPLE 2

Use cp to demonstrate the validity of the following argument.

> If money can't buy happiness then I'll settle for a new house.
> If money can't buy happiness and we both know it, then I'll settle for a new house and we both know it.

Solution. Put the argument into symbolic form. Let 'M' be short for 'money can't buy happiness', 'W' for 'we both know it', and 'S' for 'I'll settle for a new house'. Then the argument has this form.

$$
\frac{M \supset S}{(M \cdot W) \supset (S \cdot W)}
$$

Begin by assuming the antecedent of the conclusion as a new premiss.

$$
\begin{array}{lll}
1. & M \supset S & \text{Given} \\
2. & M \cdot W/(S \cdot W) & \text{Assumed}
\end{array}
$$

The first conclusion that must be derived is '$S \cdot W$'. 'W' follows immediately from the assumed premiss and 'S' may be obtained in two more steps.

$$
\begin{array}{lll}
3. & W & 2,\ \text{simp} \\
4. & M & 2,\ \text{simp} \\
5. & S & 1,\ 4,\ \text{mp}
\end{array}
$$

The demonstration is completed by conj and cp.

$$
\begin{array}{lll}
6. & S \cdot W & 5,\ 3,\ \text{conj} \\
7. & (M \cdot W) \supset (S \cdot W) & 2,\ 6,\ \text{cp}
\end{array}
$$

EXAMPLE 3

Prove the validity of the following argument by cp.

$$
\frac{\begin{array}{l}(A \cdot D) \supset C \\ E \supset D\end{array}}{A \supset (E \supset C)}
$$

Solution. Begin by assuming the antecedent of the conclusion as a new premiss.

$$
\begin{array}{lll}
1. & (A \cdot D) \supset C & \text{Given} \\
2. & E \supset D & \text{Given} \\
3. & A/(E \supset C) & \text{Assumed}
\end{array}
$$

Since the new conclusion '$E \supset C$' is a conditional, we may assume *its* antecedent as a new premiss.

$$
\begin{array}{lll}
4. & E/C & \text{Assumed}
\end{array}
$$

The first conclusion, then, is 'C'. How do we obtain that? 'C' is the consequent of the first premiss '$(A \cdot D) \supset C$'. So if we had the antecedent '$A \cdot D$', we could detach 'C' by mp. We already have 'A' in line 3, so all we need is 'D'. We may detach 'D' from the second premiss, '$E \supset D$', by mp; i.e.,

$$
\begin{array}{lll}
5. & D & 2,\ 4,\ \text{mp}
\end{array}
$$

The remaining lines of the derivation run as planned.

$$
\begin{array}{lll}
6. & A \cdot D & 3,\ 5,\ \text{conj} \\
7. & C & 1,\ 6,\ \text{mp} \\
8. & E \supset C & 4,\ 7,\ \text{cp} \\
9. & A \supset (E \supset C) & 3,\ 8,\ \text{cp}
\end{array}
$$

It should be emphasized that a) so far cp is the only inference rule which requires the *assumption* of a new line and b) the number of every assumed line (e.g., 3 and 4 above) appears finally in some justification with 'cp'. In the next section we shall consider a second inference rule which requires an assumed premiss and a modification of b). For the present, however, it is well to remember that there is *only one reason to introduce an assumption* and there is only *one way to correctly dispose of it*, namely, by completing a cp.

Review problems for Sec. 3.3.

1. Demonstrate the validity of the following arguments using cp.

a) $\dfrac{-A \lor B}{-B \supset -A}$

b) $\dfrac{A \supset B}{B \supset (A \lor B)}$

c) $\dfrac{A}{-(A \cdot B) \supset (A \cdot -B)}$

d) $\dfrac{A \supset B}{(A \cdot C) \supset B}$

e) $\dfrac{\begin{array}{l}B \supset C \\ B \supset D\end{array}}{B \supset (C \cdot D)}$

f) $\dfrac{A \cdot (B \lor C)}{-(A \cdot B) \supset (A \cdot C)}$

g) $\dfrac{A \lor (B \lor C)}{-(A \lor B) \supset (A \lor C)}$

h) $\dfrac{A \supset (B \lor C)}{-(A \supset B) \supset (A \supset C)}$

2. Put the following arguments into symbolic form, and demonstrate their validity using cp.

a) Humpty Dumpty sat on a wall, only if the King's men were asleep only if the Queen was having tea. Hence, if Humpty Dumpty sat on a wall then the King's men were asleep, only if the Queen was having tea provided that Humpty Dumpty sat on a wall. *H, K, Q.*

b) Moths fly and sparrows die, but the sun is in the sky. Thus, if moths fly then sparrows die, only if the sun is in the sky in case sparrows die. *M, S, U.*

c) If Floyd becomes a doctor then George will become a coach. Therefore, if Floyd and Sebransky become doctors, then either George will become a coach or Cramer will sell business machines. *F, G, S, C.*

d) If your sweetheart sends a letter of goodbye then it will bring a tear to your eye. Hence, if you do not expect it then your sweetheart sends a letter of goodbye, only if you do expect it provided that it will not bring a tear to your eye. *S, T, E.*

e) Edgar was mad, or both Edgar and Lear were mad. Thus, if Edgar was not mad then Lear was mad. *E, L.*

f) Sid sells shoes if and only if both Sid and Saul sell shoes. Hence, if Sid sells shoes then Saul sells shoes. *I, A.*

g) If Africa is larger than Ohio, then if Brazil is larger than Chile then Chile is larger than Massachusetts. Thus, if Brazil is larger than Chile, then Africa is larger than Ohio only if Chile is larger than Massachusetts. *A, B, C.*

3.4   Indirect proof

When the *reductio ad absurdum* test is applied to an argument schema, it is assumed, to begin with, that the schema is invalid. If this assumption leads to an unavoidable contradiction then the argument is pronounced 'valid'. The *indirect proof* which will be introduced in this section involves exactly the same strategy with a different context. The new inference rule is called

Indirect proof (ip): If a set of premises '$p_1, p_2, \ldots, p_n$' and '$-s$' together imply '$q \cdot -q$', then the set of premises alone imply 's'.

Schematically, the procedure runs as follows. Given an argument patterned after the schema

$$p_1$$
$$p_2$$
$$\vdots \qquad \text{(given premisses)}$$
$$\underline{p_n}$$
$$s \qquad \text{(conclusion)}$$

we may *assume* '$-s$' as an additional premiss and derive '$q \cdot -q$', i.e., derive *any* contradiction. Having derived a contradiction from some set of premisses and '$-s$', the rule of *indirect proof*, or ip, validates the inference to 's' from the set of premisses alone. That is, a new argument is constructed patterned after the schema

$$p_1$$
$$p_2$$
$$\vdots \qquad\qquad \text{(given premisses)}$$
$$p_n$$
$$\underline{-s} \qquad\quad \text{(assumed negated conclusion)}$$
$$\underline{q \cdot -q} \qquad \text{(contradiction)}$$
$$s \qquad\qquad \text{(conclusion)}$$

Consider the following examples.

EXAMPLE 1

Demonstrate the validity of the following argument by ip.

$$A \supset B$$
$$C \supset B$$
$$\underline{A \vee C}$$
$$B$$

Solution. Begin by assuming the negation of the conclusion as a new premiss.

$$
\begin{array}{lll}
1. & A \supset B & \text{Given} \\
2. & C \supset B & \text{Given} \\
3. & A \lor C & \text{Given} \\
4. & -B & \text{Assumed}
\end{array}
$$

Since we have '$-B$' and two conditionals '$A \supset B$' and '$C \supset B$' with 'B's' as their consequents, we may apply mt to derive

$$
\begin{array}{lll}
5. & -A & 1, 4, \text{mt} \\
6. & -C & 2, 4, \text{mt}
\end{array}
$$

If 'C' is eliminated from the third premiss, '$A \lor C$', we have a contradiction.

$$
\begin{array}{lll}
7. & C & 3, 5, \text{elim} \\
8. & C \cdot -C & 7, 6, \text{conj}
\end{array}
$$

The desired conclusion follows immediately.

$$
\begin{array}{lll}
9. & B & 4, 8, \text{ip}
\end{array}
$$

Notice that with 'ip' we write the number of the *assumed* line and the number of the *contradictory* line. Furthermore, notice that we now have a *second* way to correctly dispose of an assumption, namely, by completing an ip. If the denial of a conclusion is assumed as an additional premiss, the number of the assumed line must finally appear as the first item in the justification with 'ip'.

EXAMPLE 2

Demonstrate the validity of the following argument by ip.

> If the ice melted then the ship could return home safely.
> The ice melted but the captain dropped dead.
> Though the captain dropped dead, the ship could return home safely.

Solution. Begin by putting the argument into symbolic form. Let 'M' be short for 'the ice melted', 'S' for 'the ship could return home safely', and 'C' for 'the captain dropped dead'. Then the argument has the following form.

$$
\begin{array}{l}
M \supset S \\
\underline{M \cdot C} \\
C \cdot S
\end{array}
$$

Assume the negation of the conclusion as a new premiss.

$$
\begin{array}{lll}
1. & M \supset S & \text{Given} \\
2. & M \cdot C & \text{Given} \\
3. & -(C \cdot S) & \text{Assumed}
\end{array}
$$

Applying dem to the assumed premiss, we find

$$
\begin{array}{lll}
4. & -C \lor -S & \text{3, dem}
\end{array}
$$

Now, we could aim for '$M \cdot -M$', '$S \cdot -S$' or '$C \cdot -C$', since each of these may be derived in roughly the same number of steps. Take '$S \cdot -S$'.

$$
\begin{array}{lll}
5. & C & \text{2, simp} \\
6. & -S & \text{4, 5, elim} \\
7. & M & \text{2, simp} \\
8. & S & \text{1, 7, mp} \\
9. & S \cdot -S & \text{8, 6, conj}
\end{array}
$$

Hence,

$$
\begin{array}{lll}
10. & C \cdot S & \text{3, 9, ip}
\end{array}
$$

EXAMPLE 3

Derive 'B' from the following premisses by ip.

$$
\begin{array}{lll}
1. & A \supset (B \lor C) & \text{Given} \\
2. & A \cdot -C & \text{Given}
\end{array}
$$

Solution. Begin by assuming the negation of the conclusion as a new premiss.

$$
\begin{array}{lll}
3. & -B & \text{Assumed}
\end{array}
$$

As in Example 2, we have three possible contradictions, namely, '$A \cdot -A$', '$B \cdot -B$' and '$C \cdot -C$'. Take '$A \cdot -A$'. 'A' may be obtained easily from line 2.

$$
\begin{array}{lll}
4. & A & \text{2, simp}
\end{array}
$$

So all we need is '$-A$'. If we had the negation of '$B \lor C$', we could obtain '$-A$' from the first premiss by mt. The former is obtained from

$$
\begin{array}{lll}
5. & -C & \text{2, simp} \\
6. & -B \cdot -C & \text{3, 5, conj}
\end{array}
$$

by dem.

$$
\begin{array}{lll}
7. & -(B \lor C) & \text{6, dem}
\end{array}
$$

Hence,

$$
\begin{array}{lll}
8. & -A & 1, 7, \text{mt} \\
9. & A \cdot -A & 4, 8, \text{conj} \\
10. & B & 3, 9, \text{ip}
\end{array}
$$

Review problems for Sec. 3.4.

1. Use the *reductio ad absurdum* test to show that the following schema is valid.

$$
\frac{(p \cdot -s) \supset (q \cdot -q)}{p \supset s}
$$

Compare this schema with ip.

2. Derive the conclusions of these arguments from their premisses using ip.

a) $E \supset (C \cdot -D)$
    $(A \cdot D) \cdot E$
    $\overline{C}$

d) $(-A \equiv B) \vee -C$
    $C \cdot -B$
    $\overline{A}$

b) $-E \vee (B \equiv C)$
    $E \cdot (F \supset D)$
    $-C$
    $\overline{C \supset -F}$

e) $-(C \supset A) \cdot (B \cdot -G)$
    $(A \vee -C) \vee [(B \cdot E) \supset G]$
    $\overline{-E}$

c) $(A \vee -C) \supset (D \cdot F)$
    $(-A \supset E) \cdot -F$
    $\overline{E}$

f) $D \supset (-E \cdot F)$
    $(B \vee E) \supset D$
    $\overline{B \supset F}$

3. Put the following arguments into symbolic form, and prove their validity by ip.

a) Either Mildred is a hypochondriac or Harland has not poisoned her tea. If Harland has not poisoned her tea then Mildred is a hypochondriac. Thus, Mildred is a hypochondriac. *M, H.*

b) If Columbus was afraid then his men were afraid. If his men were afraid then control of the ship was lost, only if Columbus was afraid. Hence, his men were afraid. *C, M, O.*

c) Either Mario stabbed Julio or Rosario lied about Rocco, only if both Antonio and Frederico joined the rodeo. Antonio did not join the rodeo. Therefore, Mario did not stab Julio. *M, R, A, F.*

d) California is a nice place to live provided that you can escape the smog. Denver is not a nice place to live if California is a nice place to live. Denver is a nice place to live or Oregon is a nice place to live. Oregon is not a nice place to live. Thus, you can not escape the smog. *C, E, D, O.*

e) If Shaw was clever then Milton was brilliant, only if Chaucer was spectacular. Therefore, either Milton was not brilliant or Chaucer was spectacular. *S, M, C.*

4. Some of the following arguments are valid and some are not. Determine which ones are valid by the *reductio ad absurdum* test, and construct formal proofs for them. Use *any* of the rules introduced so far.

a) $(-A \cdot B) \lor (-A \cdot C)$
$C \supset (-E \supset -D)$
$\overline{D \supset (B \lor E)}$

b)   If Joshua becomes a minstrel, then he will sell his house and horse. If Joshua either sells his horse or travels by camel, then Elijah will return to his parents. Hence, either Joshua will not become a minstrel or Elijah will return to his parents. *J, O, R, T, E.*

c)   Either a miracle did not occur or Oliver did not report the facts correctly. If Henry saw the fish, then Oliver reported the facts correctly if and only if Norman's story is false. Either Norman's story is false or a miracle did not occur. Hence, Oliver reported the facts correctly provided that Norman's story is not false. *M, O, H, N.*

d)   Nanking contains several universities only if there are universities in China, or the historians are fooling us. If the historians are not fooling us then Nanking contains several universities. Therefore, if the historians are not fooling us then there are universities in China. *N, U, H.*

e)   The shirt of Nessus killed Hercules if the Greek legend is accurate. Either Hercules shot Nessus with a poisoned arrow, or the Greek legend is not accurate and mothers must stop telling it to their children. If the shirt of Nessus killed Hercules then Hercules shot Nessus with a poisoned arrow. Thus, Hercules shot Nessus with a poisoned arrow. *S, G, H, M.*

f) $(C \equiv D) \lor -B$
$-C \cdot E$
$\underline{E \supset (D \supset C)}$
$B \cdot -D$

g)   Skip tripped and cut his lip, or Skip tripped and ripped his hip. If Skip cut his lip then Skip did not trip. Thus, Skip ripped his hip. *T, C, H.*

h)   If Rosie is cozy, then Harry is merry only if Bill is still. Either Rosie is cozy, or if Harry is merry then Bill is still. Harry is merry. Therefore, Bill is still. *R, H, B.*

i)   Symbolic logic is interesting but it is no substitute for sex, only if you are terribly introverted. If you are terribly introverted, you need help. Symbolic logic is no substitute for sex and you do not need help. Hence, symbolic logic is not interesting. *L, S, T, H.*

j) $A \supset E$
$\underline{(B \cdot E) \supset F}$
$A \supset \{B \supset [C \supset (F \lor D)]\}$

k) $N \supset -B$
$-C \lor -D$
$C \supset -N$
$\underline{B}$
D

l) There is a little good in the worst of us and a little evil in the best of us, or life is like a grapefruit. If there is not a little evil in the best of us, then there is a little good in the worst of us and life is not like a grapefruit. Hence, there is a little evil in the best of us. *G, E, L.*

m) If the first opera was not written in Italy, then it was written in Greece only if the lyric theater is a kind of opera. It is not the case that either the lyric theater is a kind of opera or the first opera was written in Italy. Thus, the first opera was not written in Greece. *I, G, L.*

n) If Henry I was the king of Germany in 936 A.D. then Otto the Great succeeded him. Otto became king of the Lombards provided that he married Adelaide. Hence, if Henry I was the king of Germany in 936 A.D. and Otto married Adelaide, then Otto the Great succeeded Henry I and became king of the Lombards. *H, O, L, M.*

o) Either the animal we saw was a panda, or it was a raccoon and raccoons resemble pandas. If the animal we saw was a panda then pandas live outside Burma. Raccoons resemble pandas provided that pandas live outside Burma. Therefore, raccoons resemble pandas. *A, R, E, L.*

p) If Robin Hood lived in Sherwood Forest then he must have been dirty most of the time. If Robin Hood did not live in Sherwood Forest then he lived in Shaker Heights. If he lived in Shaker Heights then he did not know Maid Marion. If he knew Friar Tuck then he was not dirty most of the time. Therefore, either he did not know Friar Tuck or he did not know Maid Marion. *R, D, S, A, T.*

q) If it was the night before Christmas, then not a creature was stirring and daddy was stoned. Daddy was not stoned or Santa Claus did not land on the roof, but mommy was stoned. Junior was stoned and mommy was stoned, or Santa Claus did not land on the roof. Thus, if Santa Claus did not land on the roof then it was not the night before Christmas. *N, C, D, S, M, J.*

r) The Sac and Fox Indians moved to Illinois if and only if they defeated the Illinois Indians. If the Sac and Fox Indians moved to Illinois and they defeated the Illinois Indians, then the Fox Indians enjoyed peace only if the Sac Indians enjoyed peace. Either the Fox Indians did not enjoy peace or the Sac Indians did not enjoy peace. The Sac and Fox Indians did not defeat the Illinois Indians. Hence, if the Fox Indians enjoyed peace then the Sac and Fox Indians moved to Illinois. *M, D, F, S.*

s) If there is a difference between your ideas and your brain then mental phenomena are not reducible to material phenomena. Hence, if there is a difference between your ideas and your brain and you agree with Descartes, then either mental phenomena are not reducible to material phenomena or you agree with Berkeley. *D, R, E, B.*

t) The volcano of Popocatepetl is in the area or the climate is mild, only if you are near Mexico City or the volcano of Ixtacihuatl. If you are near the volcano of Ixtacihuatl or the National Palace, then you are in Mexico City. Therefore, if the volcano of Popocatepetl is in the area then you are in Mexico City. *P, C, N, I, A, M.*

u)   Bees sneeze if and only if flees sneeze. If trees wheeze in the breeze then bees sneeze. Either bees do not sneeze or the cheese will freeze, and flees do not sneeze. Hence, trees wheeze in the breeze. B, F, T, C.

v) $A \vee -(D \supset C)$
$-D \cdot C$
$\dfrac{E \supset (C \supset -A)}{-E}$

w)   Herman is strange if and only if Lilly is strange. If Eddie is strange then Grandad is strange. Dorothy is not strange. Either Eddie is not strange or Lilly is not strange. Hence, Grandad is strange. H, L, E, G, D.

x)   If the masses are content then the government is secure. The President has it pretty soft. Either the government is secure or we need a new constitution. The President does not have it pretty soft if and only if the masses are not content. Therefore, we do not need a new constitution. M, G, P, C.

y) $(B \supset -E) \vee -F$
$(A \equiv B) \supset C$
$E \cdot (A \equiv B)$
$\dfrac{B \vee -C}{B}$

Suggestions for further reading related to Chapter 3.

Anderson, John M., and Johnstone, Henry W., *Natural Deduction*. Belmont, Calif.: Wadsworth Publications Co., Inc., 1963, Chapters 1 and 2.

Barker, Stephen F., *The Elements of Logic*. New York: McGraw-Hill Book Company, 1965, Chapter 3.

Copi, Irving M., *Introduction to Logic*. New York: The Macmillan Company, 1961, Chapter 9.

Neidorf, Robert, *Deductive Forms*. New York: Harper & Row, Publishers, 1967, Chapter 3.

Rescher, Nicholas, *Introduction to Logic*. New York: St Martin's Press, Inc., 1964, Chapter 13.

Suppes, Patrick, *Introduction to Logic*. Princeton, N.J.: D. Van Nostrand Co., Inc., 1957, Chapter 2.

Chapter

4

Natural Deduction
in the
Monadic Predicate Calculus

4.1 Quantifiers and sentential functions

In the second chapter, singular sentences such as

(1)   Kildare is in the hospital.

were translated into **A** sentences, e.g.,

All persons identical with Kildare are persons who are in the hospital.

While the translation was grotesque, it made it possible to demonstrate the validity of certain arguments which, given the available techniques, would have been otherwise impossible. In this section we shall introduce a way of abbreviating singular sentences which is not grotesque but is every bit as fruitful.

To begin with, let us use 'H' as an abbreviation for the *predicate* of (1), 'is in the hospital'. Letters used to *abbreviate specific predicates* will be called **predicate letters.** These may be contrasted with **predicate variables** which are letters used as *place holders* for *unspecified* predicates. We shall use the letters 'S', 'P', and 'M' as

139

predicate *variables*. Any other capital letter may be used as a predicate *letter*, but we usually select the first letter of some key word in the predicate for ease of reference.

The lowercase '*k*' will be used to abbreviate the subject of (1), 'Kildare'. Letters used to *abbreviate specific names* of individuals (persons, places, or things) will be called **individual constants**. These may be contrasted with **individual variables** which are letters used as *place holders* for *unspecified* individual names. We shall use the letters '*x*', '*y*', and '*z*' as individual *variables*. With the exception of '*a*', '*b*', and '*c*', which will have special assignments later, any other lowercase letter may be used as an individual *constant*.

Using these conventions, then, (1) may be abbreviated

(2)   *Hk.*

Similarly, if '*g*' is short for 'Gillespie' and '*o*' for 'Zoe', then

(3)   *Hg*

(4)   *Ho*

are abbreviations of

(5)   Gillespie is in the hospital.

(6)   Zoe is in the hospital.

respectively. If '*F*' is short for the predicate 'is on the third floor' then

(7)   *Fg*

is an abbreviation of

(8)   Gillespie is on the third floor.

The predicates 'is in the hospital' and 'is on the third floor' are called **one-place** or **monadic predicates** because only *one* name must be added to each to form a sentence. Schematically, the point may be illustrated as follows. The schemata

_____ is in the hospital.
_____ is on the third floor.

become sentences when the blanks are filled by the name of some individual, say 'Kildare'; e.g.,

Kildare is in the hospital.
Kildare is on the third floor.

The predicates

              _____ is the mother of _____.

              _____ is taller than _____.

are called **two-place** or **dyadic predicates** because *two* names must be added to each to form a sentence; e.g.,

              Harriet is the mother of Ricky.

              Mutt is taller than Jeff.

The predicate

              _____ is between _____ and _____.

is a **triadic** or **three-place predicate,** since *three* names must be added to it to form a sentence; e.g.,

              Cleveland is between New York and Chicago.

As the title of this chapter suggests, we are going to apply the method of natural deduction to arguments involving only monadic or one-place predicates.

Now, suppose we wanted to abbreviate

(9)   Everything is in the hospital.

Unlike 'Kildare', the quantifier 'everything' is not the name of some individual. So it would be extremely misleading to write a small '*e*' beside '*H*' to express (9). '*He*' would mean that there is some individual in the hospital named 'Everything', but that is not the meaning of (9). Sentence (9) may be precisely abbreviated in the following fashion.

First, we form an expression out of the predicate letter '*H*' and an individual variable, say '*x*'; i.e., we form

(10)   *Hx*.

This expression may be regarded as an abbreviation of

(11)   It is in the hospital.

Next, let '(x)' be short for the *universal quantifier* 'every x is such that' or, simply, 'everything is such that'. Then

(12) $(x)Hx$

is short for

(13)   Everything is such that it is in the hospital.

or (9).

(14) $(x)Fx$

abbreviates

(15)   Everything is such that it is on the third floor.

or, briefly,

(16)   Everything is on the third floor.

Suppose, now, that we wanted to abbreviate

(17)   Something is in the hospital.

'Something', like 'everything', is not the name of some individual. There is no individual in the hospital or anywhere else named 'Something'. Thus, to express (17) properly, we must first introduce some means of abbreviating 'Something'. Let '(Ex)' be short for the *existential quantifier* 'there is at least one x such that' or, briefly, 'something is such that'. Then

(18) $(Ex)Hx$

is short for

(19)   Something is such that it is in the hospital.

or, briefly, (17). Similarly,

(20) $(Ex)Fx$

may be regarded as an abbreviation of

(21)   Something is such that it is on the third floor.

or, briefly,

(22)   Something is on the third floor.

There is an important difference between 'Hk', '$(x)Hx$', and '$(Ex)Hx$' on the one hand and 'Hx' on the other. The first three expressions are (abbreviations of) *sentences* that must be true or false. 'Hk' is a sentence about *one specific* individual named 'Kildare'; '$(x)Hx$' is a sentence about *every* individual, and '$(Ex)Hx$' is a sentence about *at least one* individual. In each of these cases we know what it would take to show the truth or falsity of the sentence. 'Hk' is true if and only if a man named 'Kildare' is in the hospital. '$(x)Hx$' is true if and only if *every individual* is in the hospital, and '$(Ex)Hx$' is true if and only if *at least one* individual is in the hospital. But nothing comparable may be said for 'Hx'. Because the 'x' in 'Hx' is merely a place holder for unspecified names of individuals, 'Hx' has *no* truth-value.

An expression that becomes a sentence when a) its variables are replaced by constants, b) a universal quantifier is prefixed to it, or c) an existential quanti-fier is prefixed to it is called a **sentential function.** For example, 'Hx' is a sentential function because it becomes a sentence by replacing 'x' with 'k' to obtain (2), by prefixing '(x)' to it to obtain (12), and by prefixing '(Ex)' to it to obtain (18). Similarly, 'Fx' becomes a sentence by replacing 'x' with, say, 'g' to obtain (7), by prefixing '(x)' to it to obtain (14), and by prefixing '(Ex)' to it to obtain (20). Hence, 'Fx' is a sentential function. Since sentential functions are not sentences, they cannot be true or false.

The scope of application of a quantifier is similar to that of the negation sign; e.g., the scope of the quantifiers in (12) and (18) is 'Hx'; the scope of the quantifier in '$(x)Hx \cdot Fx$' is also 'Hx'; the scope of the quantifier in '$(x)(Hx \cdot Fx)$' is '$Hx \cdot Fx$'. (We shall have more to say about compound expressions like '$Hx \cdot Fx$' in the next section.) In the sections that follow, the scope of *every* quantifier will be the *whole expression* following it.

When a variable is within the scope of a quantifier which contains a matching variable, it is called **bound;** e.g., the 'x' beside 'F' in '$(x)Fx \cdot Hx$' and the 'y' beside 'H' in '$Fx \cdot (y)Hy$' are bound. Variables that are not bound are called **free;** e.g., the 'x' beside 'H' in '$(x)Fx \cdot Hx$' and the 'x' beside 'F' in '$Fx \cdot (y)Hy$' are free. It is possible, then, for a variable to be bound at one place in an expression and free at another; e.g., in '$(x)Fx \cdot Hx$' the 'x' beside 'F' is bound, but the 'x' beside 'H' is free. It cannot, of course, be both bound and free at the *same* place.

Review problems for Sec. 4.1.

1. Define the following.

   a) predicate letter   c) individual constant

   b) predicate variable   d) individual variable

2. How are the following phrases abbreviated symbolically?

   a) everything is such that   b) something is such that

3. Which of the following predicates are monadic?

   a) is the friend of   e) drinks

   b) is below   f) loves

   c) is honest   g) came earlier than

   d) equals   h) is a bird

4. Make up two examples of each of the following.

   a) sentential function
   b) free variable
   c) bound variable

5. Which of the following are schemata and which are sentences?

   a) *Fg*   d) That shoe belongs to *m*.
   b) *(x)(Sx ⊃ Px)*   e) *Md*
   c) *(Ex)Bx*   f) *(Ex)Hx·Ge*

4.2 Symbolizing English sentences

In this section we are going to introduce some suggestions and conventions that will be useful in translating ordinary English sentences into logical notation.
   If

(1)   Everything grows.

is true, then

(2)   It is not the case that something is such that it does not grow.

must be true, and vice versa. Sentence (2) is merely a long way of writing (1). If we use '*G*' to abbreviate the predicate 'grows', then (1) and (2) may be abbreviated

(3)   *(x)Gx*

(4)   *−(Ex) −Gx*

respectively. Here (3) is equivalent to (4), i.e.,

(5)   '*(x)Gx*' is equivalent to '*−(Ex) −Gx*'.

   Note that since the existential quantifier is an *operator* and not a sentence, the scope of the first negation sign in (4) is the whole expression following it. While (4) could be properly punctuated with brackets '*−[(Ex) −Gx]*', the brackets are omitted here to simplify the notation.
   If

(6)   Something grows.

is true, then

(7)   It is not the case that everything is such that it does not grow.

must be true, and vice versa. Sentences (6) and (7) may be abbreviated '$(Ex)Gx$' and '$-(x) -Gx$', respectively, and

(8)   '$(Ex)Gx$' is equivalent to '$-(x) -Gx$'.

The sentence

> It is not the case that something grows.

is equivalent to

> Everything is such that it does not grow.

Or, briefly,

(9)   '$-(Ex)Gx$' is equivalent to '$(x) -Gx$'.

And finally,

> It is not the case that everything grows.

is equivalent to

> Something does not grow.

Or,

(10)   '$-(x)Gx$' is equivalent to '$(Ex) -Gx$'.

Letting 'H', 'F', and 'k' abbreviate 'is in the hospital', 'is on the third floor', and 'Kildare', respectively,

> Kildare is in the hospital on the third floor.

or

> Kildare is in the hospital and Kildare is on the third floor.

may be expressed symbolically by the conjunction

$$Hk \cdot Fk.$$

Hence,

(11) $(Ex)(Hx \cdot Fx)$

is short for

(12)   Something is such that it is both in the hospital and on the third floor.

Sentence (12) is equivalent to the **I** sentence

> Some things in the hospital are things on the third floor.

or, simply,

> Something in the hospital is on the third floor.

The negation or contradictory of (11) is

(13) $-(Ex)(Hx \cdot Fx)$.

If we replace '$-(Ex)$' with a universal quantifier and negation sign as suggested by (9), then (13) becomes

(14) $(x) - (Hx \cdot Fx)$.

Sentence (14), in turn, is equivalent to

(15) $(x)(Hx \supset -Fx)$

because the sentential function '$-(Hx \cdot Fx)$' which follows the universal quantifier in (14) is equivalent to '$(Hx \supset -Fx)$'. Although (13), (14), and (15) are equivalent, (15) would generally be used to abbreviate the **E** sentence

> If anything is in the hospital then it is not on the third floor.

or, simply,

> Nothing in the hospital is on the third floor.

The **O** sentence

> Some things in the hospital are not things on the third floor.

or, more naturally,

> Something in the hospital is not on the third floor.

would be abbreviated

(16) $(Ex)(Hx \cdot -Fx)$.

The negation or contradictory of (16) is

(17) $-(Ex)(Hx \cdot -Fx)$.

If we replace '$-(Ex)$' with a universal quantifier and negation sign as suggested by (9), then (17) becomes

(18) $(x) - (Hx \cdot -Fx)$.

Because the sentential function '$-(Hx \cdot -Fx)$' following the quantifier in (18) is equivalent to '$(Hx \supset Fx)$', (18) is equivalent to

(19) $(x)(Hx \supset Fx)$.

While (17), (18), and (19) are equivalent, (19) would generally be used to abbreviate the **A** sentence

> If anything is in the hospital then it is on the third floor.

or, simply,

> Everything in the hospital is on the third floor.

Following our usage in the calculus of sentences, we shall call sentential functions involving a single predicate **simple sentential functions**; e.g., 'Hx', 'Fx', 'Gx'. Sentential functions involving two predicates (or two occurrences of the same predicate) will be called **compound sentential functions**; e.g., '$Hx \cdot Fx$', '$Fx \supset Hx$', etc. Those involving more than two predicates (or more than two occurrences of some predicate) will be called **complex sentential functions**; e.g., '$(Hx \cdot Fx) \supset Gx$', '$Hx \cdot (Fx \cdot Gx)$', etc.

Expressions that become sentential functions when their *predicate* variables are appropriately replaced will be called **sentential function schemata**; e.g., 'Sx', '$Sx \supset Px$', '$Mx \cdot Px$', etc. The sentential functions obtained from such schemata will be called their 'interpretations'. Just as we may regard simple, compound, and complex sentences as interpretations of the schema 'p', we may regard simple, compound, and complex sentential functions as interpretations of the schema 'Sx'. For examples, 'Fx', '$Fx \supset Hx$', '$(Fx \cdot Hx) \supset Gx$', etc., may all be regarded as interpretations of the schema 'Sx'. Again, '$Fx \supset Hx$' may also be regarded as an interpretation of '$Sx \supset Px$' if we think of 'Sx' as a place holder for 'Fx' and 'Px' as a place holder for 'Hx'.

Figure 4.21 contains the four categorical schemata and their symbolic abbreviations.

A	All S are P.	$(x)(Sx \supset Px)$
E	No S are P.	$(x)(Sx \supset -Px)$
I	Some S are P.	$(Ex)(Sx \cdot Px)$
O	Some S are not P.	$(Ex)(Sx \cdot -Px)$

Figure 4.21

In this Figure, the 'S's' and 'P's' in the left-hand column are *term* variables, while the 'S's' and 'P's' in the right-hand column are predicate variables. The difference is that a term variable, say 'S', is a place holder for terms such as 'man', 'mortal', and 'cat'; while the predicate variable 'S' is a place holder for predicates such as 'is a man', 'is mortal', and 'is a cat'.

If 'g' is short for 'Gillespie' then

(20) $Hg \equiv Fg$

is an abbreviation of

>   Gillespie is in the hospital if and only if Gillespie is on the third floor.

(21) $Hg \lor Fg$

is short for

>   Either Gillespie is in the hospital or Gillespie is on the third floor.

Sentence (20) results from replacing the variables in the sentential function

$$Hx \equiv Fx.$$

If we prefix a universal quantifier to that function, we obtain

$$(x)(Hx \equiv Fx),$$

i.e.,

>   Everything is such that it is in the hospital if and only if it is on the third floor.

To symbolize

>   Everything in the hospital is either on the third floor or not on the third floor.

we might first consider it as a universal affirmative sentence; i.e.,

>   Everything is such that if it is in the hospital, then either it is on the third floor or it is not on the third floor.

Then the universal quantifier and the operators may be abbreviated as usual.

(x) [it is in the hospital $\supset$ (it is on the third floor $\lor$ $-$(it is on the third floor))].

Finally, we abbreviate the sentential functions.

$$(x)[Hx \supset (Fx \lor -Fx)].$$

To abbreviate

>   Something is such that it is in the hospital and on the third floor, if and only if it grows.

we would begin by symbolizing the quantifier and operators; i.e.,

(Ex)(it is in the hospital $\cdot$ it is on the third floor) $\equiv$ it grows.

Then the functions are shortened to obtain

$$(Ex)[(Hx \cdot Fx) \equiv Gx].$$

When it is clear from the context that only a certain type of individual is being considered, the quantifiers and variables may be interpreted accordingly. For example, we might abbreviate

(22)   Everyone is laughing.

by

(23) $(x)Lx$.

In (23) '(x)' is short for 'every*one* is such that' instead of 'every*thing* is such that', and 'Lx' is short for '*he* (or *she*) is laughing' instead of 'it is laughing'. By permitting such interpretations, we may shorten our symbolic abbreviations considerably. In the present case, for instance, our alternative would have been to treat (22) as the **A** sentence

All persons are laughing.

and abbreviate it

$$(x)(Rx \supset Lx),$$

where 'Rx' is short for 'x is a person' and 'Lx' is short for 'x is laughing'.

Similarly, when the context makes it clear that we are only talking about, say, *numbers*, '(Ex)' may be used to abbreviate 'some *number* x is such that' instead of 'some x is such that', etc.

Review problems for Sec. 4.2.

1. Define 'sentential function schema', and give two examples.

2. Put the following sentences into symbolic notation.

    a) Everything is purple. (Use 'Qx'.)
    b) Nothing is purple.
    c) Something is either purple or red. Rx
    d) If anything is red then it is not purple.
    e) Most red things are not purple.
    f) Anyone who rides a horse needs a saddle. Hx, Nx
    g) Gillespie rides a horse. g
    h) Someone rides a horse.
    i) Everyone either rides a horse or flies an airplane. Fx
    j) Something is square if and only if it is not round. Ax, Ox
    k) No red squares are round.

l) Every square is red if and only if it is not round.

m) Most men sleep. Cx, Lx

n) Gillespie sleeps if and only if Gillespie either rides a horse or flies an airplane.

o) Only gentlemen prefer blonds. Gx, Bx

p) Something is not red.

q) Either Kildare prefers blonds or he is not a gentleman. k

r) Some gentleman either rides a horse or sleeps.

s) A blond gentleman is a blond gentleman. Dx

t) All gentlemen prefer blonds if and only if they (gentlemen) are not sleeping.

u) If Gillespie is a gentleman who rides a horse, then he prefers blonds and does not fly airplanes.

v) Anything purple is not both red and square.

w) Some men are squares.

x) It is not the case that both Kildare and Gillespie fly airplanes.

y) A few men are not sleeping.

z) Kildare sleeps if and only if Gillespie prefers blonds.

a$'$) Everyone prefers blonds.

b$'$) Blonds prefer blonds.

c$'$) Enough is enough. Ux

4.3   Reductio ad absurdum extended

By the term **monadic predicate calculus** in the title of this chapter, we mean the class consisting of all schemata containing only individual and monadic predicate variables with quantifiers for the former but *not* the latter, truth-operators, and their rules of usage. (Some authors might prefer the term 'lower functional calculus' and contrast this with 'higher functional calculi' in which predicate variables are also quantified.) Argument schemata in the monadic predicate calculus will be called **quantificational argument schemata,** and their interpretations will be called **quantificational arguments.**

The problem immediately before us is that of finding a decision procedure for the monadic predicate calculus to determine which quantificational argument schemata are valid and which are not. We shall use a variation of the *reductio ad absurdum* test for this purpose. As we shall see shortly, the test does not provide a *general* solution to the decision problem for the monadic predicate calculus; however, it is sufficient for the limited purposes at hand. In the following sections, we shall apply the method of natural deduction to arguments pronounced 'valid' (in a certain sense) by the *reductio ad absurdum* test.

Suppose the sequence of individual constants '$o_1, o_2, \ldots, o_n$' contains the names of every individual in some universe. (n may be any finite number greater than 0.) For *that* universe, the sentence

(1)   Everything freezes.

is equivalent to

(2) o_1 freezes *and* o_2 freezes *and* . . . *and* o_n freezes.

In symbols,

(3) $(x)Fx$

is equivalent to

(4) $Fo_1 \cdot Fo_2 \cdot \ \cdots \ \cdot Fo_n$

for the universe with n individuals.

Sentences (2) and (4) illustrate the fact that *universally* quantified sentences may be expressed as conjunctions provided, of course, that our universe contains only a *finite* number of individuals. If our universe contained only two individuals named 'm' and 'n', then (3) would be equivalent to the conjunction

$$Fm \cdot Fn.$$

In the universe containing only the individuals named by '$o_1, o_2, \ldots, o_n$'

(5)   Something freezes.

is equivalent to

(6)   Either o_1 freezes *or* o_2 freezes *or* . . . *or* o_n freezes.

In symbols,

(7) $(Ex)Fx$

is equivalent to

(8) $Fo_1 \lor Fo_2 \lor \cdots \lor Fo_n$

for the universe with n individuals.

Sentences (6) and (8) illustrate the fact that *existentially* quantified sentences may be expressed as *disjunctions*. If our universe contained only two individuals named 'm' and 'n', then (7) would be equivalent to the disjunction

$$Fm \lor Fn.$$

We may generalize these remarks in the following fashion. Given a universe containing only the individuals named by '$o_1, o_2, \ldots, o_n$', if 'Sx' represents any sentential function, then

(9)   '$(x)Sx$' is equivalent to '$So_1 \cdot So_2 \cdot \ \cdots \ \cdot So_n$'

and

(10)   '$(Ex)Sx$' is equivalent to '$So_1 \lor So_2 \lor \cdots \lor So_n$'.

According to (9), then, in a universe with only two individuals named 'm' and 'n',

(11) $(x)(Hx \supset Fx)$

is equivalent to

$$(Hm \supset Fm) \cdot (Hn \supset Fn).$$

According to (10), in such a universe

(12) $(Ex)(Hx \cdot -Fx)$

is equivalent to

$$(Hm \cdot -Fm) \lor (Hn \cdot -Fn).$$

In an n-membered universe, (11) is equivalent to

$$(Ho_1 \supset Fo_1) \cdot (Ho_2 \supset Fo_2) \cdot \cdots \cdot (Ho_n \supset Fo_n).$$

and (12) is equivalent to

$$(Ho_1 \cdot -Fo_1) \lor (Ho_2 \cdot -Fo_2) \lor \cdots \lor (Ho_n \cdot -Fo_n).$$

With the help of (9) and (10) we may apply the *reductio ad absurdum* test to argument schemata involving quantifiers. Let us begin with some examples.

EXAMPLE 1

Test the following schema for validity by the *reductio ad absurdum* method.

$$\frac{\begin{array}{c}(x)(Mx \supset -Px) \\ (x)(Sx \supset Mx)\end{array}}{(x)(Sx \supset Px)}$$

Solution. We begin by dropping the quantifiers in accordance with (9) *and* the assumption that our universe contains a single individual named, say, 'm'. In a one-membered universe, the given schema is equivalent to

$$\frac{\begin{array}{c}Mm \supset -Pm \\ Sm \supset Mm\end{array}}{Sm \supset Pm}$$

The *reductio ad absurdum* test may now be applied.

$$Mm \supset -Pm^t \qquad t$$
$$\frac{Sm \supset Mm^t}{Sm^t \supset Pm^f} \qquad \begin{array}{c} t \\ \hline f \end{array}$$

This schema is invalid. Hence, the *given* schema is *invalid in every one-membered* universe. But, as a general rule, if a schema is invalid in every *n*-membered universe then it is invalid in *every larger universe*. Hence, the given schema is invalid in *every nonempty* universe.

How does the given schema fare in an *empty* universe? The answer to this question is short and sweet. In an empty universe, every schema beginning with an *existential* quantifier 'there *exists* at least one individual such that' must be *false* (because there are *no* individuals in an empty universe). Every schema beginning with a *universal* quantifier may be regarded as the *negation* of an existentially quantified schema; i.e.

Everything is *S*.

is equivalent to the negation

It is not the case that there exists at least one individual such that it is not *S*.

or, briefly,

'$(x)Sx$' is equivalent to '$-[(Ex) -Sx]$'.

Hence, every universally quantified schema is *true* in an empty universe.

In an empty universe the given schema cannot be given an interpretation such that its premises are all true *and* its conclusion is false, because it contains only universally quantified sentence schemata. Hence, the given schema is *valid in an empty universe*.

The determination of validity in an empty universe is clearly a trivial problem. We interpret universally quantified schemata as true and existentially quantified schemata as false. Then, if the argument schema does not admit of an interpretation with all true premises and a false conclusion, it is valid; otherwise it is invalid. Hereafter we shall have nothing to say about validity in empty universes.

Interpretations of the schema in Example 1 include the following.

No men are poor.
All Greeks are men.
All Greeks are poor.

Geniuses are never happy.
Every great poet is a genius.
All great poets are happy.

No scientists are slow-thinking or cowardly.
Every biologist is a scientist.

Every biologist is slow-thinking or cowardly.

Having excluded empty universes from consideration, we may define validity for quantificational argument schemata as follows. A quantificational argument schema is valid if and only if, *every* uniform interpretation that may be assigned to its variables in *any nonempty* universe is such that if its premises are all true then its conclusion *must* be true. Such schemata and their interpretations will be called **quantificationally valid.** A **quantificationally invalid schema** is one for which there is *at least one* uniform interpretation in *some nonempty* universe such that the premises are all true and the conclusion is false. Armed with this new definition of validity, we may proceed to describe the application of the *reductio ad absurdum* test to quantificational argument schemata. Clearly, the schema presented in Example 1 is quantificationally invalid.

EXAMPLE 2

Test the following schema for validity.

$$(Ex)(Mx \cdot Px)$$
$$(Ex)(Mx \cdot Sx)$$
$$\overline{(Ex)(Sx \cdot Px)}$$

Solution. Begin by dropping the quantifiers in accordance with (10) *and* the assumption that our universe contains a single individual named '*m*'. The given schema is then equivalent to

$$Mm \cdot Pm$$
$$Mm \cdot Sm$$
$$\overline{Sm \cdot Pm}$$

Applying the *reductio ad absurdum* test to this schema, we find unavoidable contradictions; i.e., either

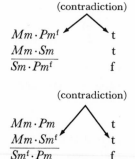

(contradiction)

$$Mm \cdot Pm^f \qquad t$$
$$Mm \cdot Sm \qquad t$$
$$\overline{Sm \cdot Pm^f} \qquad f$$

or

(contradiction)

$$Mm \cdot Pm \qquad t$$
$$Mm \cdot Sm^f \qquad t$$
$$\overline{Sm^f \cdot Pm} \qquad f$$

Therefore, we assume our universe contains *two* individuals named, say, '*m*' and '*n*' and expand the *given* schema according to (10); i.e., we *begin again* with

$$(Mm \cdot Pm) \lor (Mn \cdot Pn)$$
$$\underline{(Mm \cdot Sm) \lor (Mn \cdot Sn)}$$
$$(Sm \cdot Pm) \lor (Sn \cdot Pn)$$

This time it is possible to provide an interpretation such that its premises are all true and its conclusion is false.

$$\overset{\text{t}\quad\text{t}}{(Mm \cdot Pm)} \lor (Mn \cdot Pn) \qquad \text{t}$$
$$\underline{\overset{\quad\text{t}\quad\text{t}}{(Mm \cdot Sm)} \lor (Mn \cdot Sn)} \qquad \text{t}$$
$$\overset{\text{f}}{(Sm \cdot Pm)} \lor \overset{\text{f}}{(Sn \cdot Pn)} \qquad \text{f}$$

Hence, according to our definition above, the schema is *quantificationally invalid*. Interpretations of the given schema include the following.

> Some novels are exciting.
> Some novels are boring.
> ――――――――――――――――――
> Some boring things are exciting.

> There is at least one red herring.
> Some red things are noses.
> ――――――――――――――――――
> There is at least one nose that is also a red herring.

> Some rivers are long if and only if they are wide.
> There is at least one river such that it is good for fishing.
> ――――――――――――――――――
> Some river that is good for fishing is long if and only if it is wide.

EXAMPLE 3

Show that the following schema is quantificationally invalid.

$$(Ex)(Sx \cdot Px)$$
$$\underline{(Ex)(-Sx \cdot Px)}$$
$$(x)Px$$

Solution. First, we drop the quantifiers in accordance with (9) and (10) *and* the assumption that our universe contains only a single individual.

$$Sm \cdot Pm \qquad\qquad \text{t}$$
$$\underline{-Sm \cdot Pm^{\text{f}}} \qquad\qquad \text{t}$$
$$Pm^{\text{f}} \qquad\qquad\qquad \text{f}$$

(contradiction)

Having obtained a contradiction, we expand the given schema for a two-membered universe.

$$
\begin{array}{c}
\overset{f}{(Sm \cdot Pm)} \vee \overset{f}{(Sn \cdot Pn)} \\
\end{array}
$$

(contradiction)

$$
\begin{array}{c}
\overset{f}{(Sm \cdot Pm)} \vee \overset{f}{(Sn \cdot Pn)} \qquad\qquad\qquad t \\[4pt]
\underline{\overset{t}{(-Sm \cdot Pm)} \;\; \overset{t}{\vee} \;\; (-Sn \cdot Pn)} \qquad\qquad\qquad t \\
\overset{f}{} \\
Pm \cdot Pn \qquad\qquad\qquad f
\end{array}
$$

Again a contradiction! So we expand the given schema for a three-membered universe.

$$
\begin{array}{c}
\overset{t}{(Sm \cdot Pm)} \;\; \overset{t}{\vee} \;\; (Sn \cdot Pn) \vee (So \cdot Po) \qquad\qquad t \\[4pt]
\underline{\overset{t}{(-Sm \cdot Pm)} \vee \overset{t}{(-Sn \cdot Pn)} \vee (-So \cdot Po)} \qquad t \\
\overset{f}{} \\
Pm \cdot Pn \cdot Po \qquad\qquad\qquad f
\end{array}
$$

Given a three-membered universe, it is possible to provide an interpretation for the given schema such that its premisses are all true and its conclusion is false. Hence, the schema is quantificationally invalid.

It is apparent that the fact that an unavoidable contradiction is obtained from a schema in an *n*-membered universe ($n > 0$) by the *reductio ad absurdum* test is *no* guarantee that the schema is quantificationally valid. In this sense, then, the *reductio ad absurdum* test does not constitute a *general* solution to the decision problem for the monadic predicate calculus.

The decision problem for the monadic predicate calculus is solvable; i.e., there are general effective decision procedures for this calculus. But all of them require a few more technicalities than we have time to consider. It should be noted, however, that there is *no general* solution to the decision problem for the predicate calculus with *n*-placed predicates where $n > 1$. That is, if we admitted schemata containing dyadic, triadic, etc., predicate variables then it would be *impossible* to find a general effective decision procedure for determining validity. The *unsolvability* of the decision problem for such a calculus was demonstrated by the American logician Alonzo Church in 1936. According to **Church's theorem,** the decision problem for the *n*-adic ($n > 1$) predicate calculus is unsolvable.

Review problems for Sec. 4.3.

1. Define the following.

    a)   monadic predicate calculus

    b) quantificational argument schemata

    c) Church's theorem

2. Assuming a universe with exactly two members named '*m*' and '*n*', eliminate the quantifiers from the following sentences.

a) $(x)Rx$ e) $(x)[(Cx \cdot Dx) \lor Bx]$

b) $(Ex) - Cx$ f) $(Ex)(- Rx \supset - Bx)$

c) $(Ex)(Rx \equiv Bx)$ g) $(x)[(Ax \cdot Bx) \cdot Cx]$

d) $(x) - (Ax \lor Bx)$ h) $(Ex)[(Ax \cdot Cx) \lor - Dx]$

3. Test the following arguments for quantificational validity by the *reductio ad absurdum* method. If an argument yields a contradiction for a two-membered universe, regard it as "quantificationally valid".

a) $(x)Ax$ f) $(Ex) - Hx$
    $(x)(Bx \equiv Ax)$ $(Ex)(Cx \lor - Rx)$
    $(Ex)(Cx \lor - Bx)$ $(x)(Gx \equiv Hx)$
    $\overline{(Ex)(Ax \cdot Cx)}$ $\overline{(x) - Cx}$

b) $(Ex)(Bx \supset - Cx)$ g) $(x)[Gx \lor (Rx \cdot Bx)]$
    $(x)(- Dx \equiv - Bx)$ $(Ex)(- Rx \supset Bx)$
    $(x)Cx$ $\overline{(x)Bx}$
    $\overline{(Ex)(Bx \lor - Dx)}$

                                            h) $(Ex)(- Bx \equiv Cx)$

c) $(x)[Cx \supset (Bx \lor Ax)]$ $(Ex) - Dx$
    $(Ex) - Bx$ $(Ex)(- Ax \supset - Cx)$
    $\overline{(x)(Cx \cdot Bx)}$ $\overline{(Ex)(Bx \lor Ax)}$

d) $(Ex)(Dx \supset Rx)$ i) $(x)(Bx \lor - Cx)$
    $(x)(Ox \supset Rx)$ $(x)[Bx \supset (Gx \lor - Hx)]$
    $(Ex)(Ox \lor Dx)$ $(x)Gx$
    $\overline{(x)(Hx \lor Rx)}$ $\overline{(x)(- Cx \cdot Gx)}$

e) $(x)(Rx \supset - Gx)$ j) $(x)(- Cx \equiv Dx)$
    $(Ex)[Gx \equiv (Bx \lor Ax)]$ $(Ex)[Dx \supset (Bx \cdot Ax)]$
    $(x) - Ax$ $(Ex)(- Ax \cdot Dx)$
    $(x) - Rx$ $\overline{(x)(Bx \lor Cx)}$
    $\overline{(Ex)(- Gx \lor Bx)}$

4. Put the following arguments into symbolic form, and test them for validity as in Prob. 3.

    a) All heavy objects have mass. Everything either does not have mass or does not belong in this world. Everything belongs in this world. Therefore, nothing has mass. *Hx, Ax, Bx.*

    b) Everything is controlled by demons if and only if it is profitable. Something is not profitable or owned by a Hungarian Gypsy. Something is controlled by demons. Hence, something is both controlled by demons and owned by a Hungarian Gypsy. *Cx, Rx, Ox.*

    c) No Europeans are Australians. Everyone either is not Australian or is an existentialist. One is a European if and only if one is cosmopolitan. Hence, someone is an existentialist. *Ux, Ax, Xx, Cx.*

d)　Whoever flies cries if and only if he dies. Some birds die. Everything either does not die or does not fly. Something cries. Hence, either something does not fly or it is a bird. *Fx, Cx, Dx, Bx.*

e)　Whatever is fit for a king is expensive. Everything is suitable either for talented people or for rich people. Something is suitable for rich people only if it is suitable for talented people. Either something is suitable for rich people or it is expensive. Thus, something is not fit for a king only if it is suitable for talented people. *Fx, Xx, Tx, Rx.*

f)　Everything is blue. Something is thin. Something is square if and only if it is not circular. Everything is either square or not blue. Therefore, something is not circular provided that it is thin. *Bx, Tx, Ax, Cx.*

g)　What is unbearable is not terrible. Everything is intolerable if and only if it is unbearable. What is terrible is not intolerable. Everything is intolerable. Therefore, everything is either terrible or unbearable. *Ux, Tx, Ox.*

h)　Something is not beautiful provided that it is ugly. Something is either lovely or gorgeous, and inspiring. Something is inspiring only if it is not beautiful. Everything is lovely. Thus, something is either gorgeous or not beautiful. *Bx, Ux, Lx, Gx, Ix.*

i)　Laws are just if and only if they protect poor people. Something does not protect poor people and is not a law. Something is not a law only if it is not a just law. Therefore, something protects poor people. *Lx, Jx, Ox.*

j)　Something is either sweet smelling, or unpleasant and frightening. Something is either not frightening or not stimulating. Everything is either sweet smelling or unpleasant. Everything is stimulating. Hence, something is frightening only if it is not sweet smelling. *Wx, Ux, Fx, Tx.*

4.4　Universal specification and existential generalization

In the last section it was shown that, with one exception, the fact that a quantificational argument yields a contradiction when the *reductio ad absurdum* test is applied to it in some nonempty universe is *no* guarantee that the schema is quantificationally valid. However, every quantificational argument whose conclusion may be derived from its premises by the method of natural deduction is quantificationally valid in *every nonempty* universe. Hence, the latter method is a useful supplement to the former. More precisely, we shall unite the two methods as follows. First, every quantificational argument will be tested by the *reductio ad absurdum* method in a one-membered universe. If it shows up quantificationally invalid, that will be the end of it. If it yields a contradiction then it will be tested in a two-membered universe. Again, if it shows up invalid, there is nothing more to do. If it yields a contradiction however, then its conclusion will be derived from its premises by the method of natural deduction. (Ordinarily, aside from the exceptional case, the fact that an argument yields a contradiction by applying the *reductio ad absurdum* test would merely be considered as *some evidence* that it is quantificationally valid. The arguments in this and the following sections are *designed* such that their conclusions can be derived from their premises by natural deduction provided that they yield a contradiction when tested in a two-membered universe.)

In the remaining three sections of this chapter we are going to introduce five rules involving the elimination, addition, or exchange of quantifiers. We shall call them **quantification rules.** The quantification rules constitute the final addition to our rules of natural deduction.

In ordinary English, when we are unwilling or unable to refer to an individual by some particular class name or by his own proper name, we may refer to him (her, or it) by an *ambiguous name.* For example, suppose someone said

(1)   Napoleon is a dirty so-and-so.

Whoever used (1) evidently intended to call Napoleon something, but did not want to say *exactly what.* 'So-and-so' could denote anything or everything. Of course, the adjective 'dirty' informs us that the name which was replaced by 'so-and-so' was probably not complimentary. Perhaps 'so-and-so' was used instead of 'liar', 'louse', or some combination; e.g., 'lousy liar'. If Napoleon heard (1), he would know that he had been called something, perhaps even *everything,* but he would not know exactly what. In a few words, 'so-and-so' is just an *ambiguous* name.

Again, suppose someone said

(2)   So-and-so had a date with Rosie.

Whoever used (2) knew that Rosie had a date with someone but, perhaps, forgot the person's name. So he (or she) could not say *exactly who* had a date with Rosie. Alternatively, 'so-and-so' was used in place of the proper name of Rosie's date. Since 'so-and-so' could be the name of *anybody, everybody* is a possible candidate for Rosie's partner. That is, 'so-and-so' is merely an ambiguous name for any or every individual.

Similarly, in symbolic logic when we are unwilling or unable to assign a specific name to an individual, we may employ an ambiguous name. The first letter of the alphabet '*a*' will be used as an abbreviation for an ambiguous name; e.g., 'so-and-so', 'such-and-such', 'John Doe', etc. Thus, for example, if '*R*' is short for 'had a date with Rosie' then

(3)   *Ra*

is short for (2). When we want to introduce *distinct* ambiguous names, we shall use a prime '*a′*' or double prime '*a″*'. So

(4) Ra'

is short for (2) when it is understood that 'a' ' denotes a different so-and-so from 'a'.

Ambiguous names are unlike proper names because the latter denote specific individuals but the former denote *un*specified individuals. In this respect ambiguous names are like individual variables. But ambiguous names are unlike individual variables because the latter may be quantified, while the former cannot be quantified; i.e., we might say 'there is some x such that' or 'every x is such that', but *never* 'there is some a such that' or 'every a is such that'. (In this respect our ambiguous names differ from those in ordinary English.) Hence, we may define an **ambiguous name** as an unquantifiable name that denotes unspecified individuals.

To simplify our presentation of four of the quantification rules, we shall introduce three special signs. First, let us agree to use the small letter 'c' as an abbreviation for any *proper* name; e.g., 'c' will be short for 'Mickey', 'Kildare', 'Rosie', etc. Second, we shall use the small letter 'b' as an abbreviation of both 'a' and 'c', where 'c' is short for any proper name and 'a' is short for an ambiguous name. Both 'b' and 'c' will only be used to state the rules.

The first rule we have to consider is

Universal Specification (US):   '$(x)Sx$' implies 'Sb'. According to US, *both* of the following kinds of inferences are valid.

$$
\begin{array}{cc}
\text{a)} & \text{b)} \\[4pt]
(x)Sx & (x)Sx \\
\hline
Sa & Sc
\end{array}
$$

In both cases a) and b), we are given a universal schema to begin with; i.e., S is attributed to everything. Now, if

Everything is S.

represents a true sentence, then any or every individual we could *ambiguously name* is S. So

So-and-so is S.

must be interpreted as true, since 'so-and-so' is merely an ambiguous name for *any or every* individual. This is all that is asserted by a). Again, if

Everything is S.

is interpreted as true, then any or every individual we could *specify* is S. So

Mickey is S.

must be interpreted as true, since 'Mickey' is merely a proper name for *one* of the individuals we could specify. This is what is asserted by b).

Sometimes it is necessary to derive a sentence containing an ambiguous name and other times it is necessary to derive a sentence containing a proper name. Briefly, we may call these two types of sentences **ambiguous** and **proper sentences,** respectively. Hence, US may be roughly paraphrased for sentences as follows: Both ambiguous and proper sentences may be inferred from universally quantified sentences. Consider the following derivations requiring the use of US.

EXAMPLE 1

Demonstrate the validity of the following argument by natural deduction.

> Everything is hot and sticky.
> ─────────────────────
> Harvard is hot.

Solution. Begin by abbreviating the argument. Let '*Hx*' be short for '*x* is hot', '*Tx*' for '*x* is sticky' and '*h*' for 'Harvard'. Then the argument looks like this:

$$\frac{(x)(Hx \cdot Tx)}{Hh}$$

In order to apply simp to this argument, we must first eliminate the quantifier. Since we are trying to derive '*Hh*', we should use '*h*' in the application of US. That is, we begin with

$$
\begin{array}{lll}
1. & (x)(Hx \cdot Tx) & \text{Given} \\
2. & Hh \cdot Th & \text{1, US}
\end{array}
$$

The conclusion follows from line 2 immediately.

$$
\begin{array}{lll}
3. & Hh & \text{2, simp}
\end{array}
$$

EXAMPLE 2

By cp, derive '*Ho* ⊃ *Go*' from

$$(x)(Hx \supset Fx)$$
$$(x)(-Fx \lor Gx)$$

Solution. Begin by removing the quantifiers from the premisses. Since the individual constant '*o*' appears in the conclusion, we should use '*o*' in the application of US.

$$
\begin{array}{lll}
1. & (x)(Hx \supset Fx) & \text{Given} \\
2. & (x)(-Fx \lor Gx) & \text{Given} \\
3. & Ho \supset Fo & \text{1, US} \\
4. & -Fo \lor Go & \text{2, US}
\end{array}
$$

Now, assume the antecedent of the conclusion as a new premiss, derive '*Go*', and complete cp.

$$5. \quad Ho/Go \qquad \text{Assumed}$$
$$6. \quad Fo \qquad \text{3, 5, mp}$$
$$7. \quad Go \qquad \text{4, 6, elim}$$
$$8. \quad Ho \supset Go \qquad \text{5, 7, cp}$$

EXAMPLE 3

Prove that the following argument is valid by natural deduction.

$$(x)[-Fx \lor (Gx \cdot Hx)]$$
$$(x)[(Gx \cdot Hx) \supset Ix]$$
$$\frac{-Ia}{-Fa}$$

Solution. Since the ambiguous name '*a*' appears in the conclusion, we should use '*a*' in the application of US.

$$1. \quad (x)[-Fx \lor (Gx \cdot Hx)] \qquad \text{Given}$$
$$2. \quad (x)[(Gx \cdot Hx) \supset Ix] \qquad \text{Given}$$
$$3. \quad -Ia \qquad \text{Given}$$
$$4. \quad -Fa \lor (Ga \cdot Ha) \qquad \text{1, US}$$
$$5. \quad (Ga \cdot Ha) \supset Ia \qquad \text{2, US}$$

The conclusion follows in two steps.

$$6. \quad -(Ga \cdot Ha) \qquad \text{5, 3, mt}$$
$$7. \quad -Fa \qquad \text{4, 6, elim}$$

The second rule we have to consider is

Existential generalization (EG): '*Sb*' implies '*(Ex)Sx*'. According to EG, *both* of the following kinds of inferences are valid.

$$\begin{array}{cc} \text{a)} & \text{b)} \\ \dfrac{Sa}{(Ex)Sx} & \dfrac{Sc}{(Ex)Sx} \end{array}$$

In both cases a) and b) we derive an existentially quantified schema; i.e., *S* is attributed to at least one individual. Now, if

So-and-so is *S*.

represents a true sentence, then the (existentially) *generalized* schema

Something is *S*.

must be interpreted as true, since 'so-and-so' is merely an ambiguous name for *any or every* (some)thing. This is all that is asserted by a). Again, if

Jackie Gleason is *S*.

is interpreted as true, then the (existentially) *generalized* schema

Something is *S*.

must represent a true sentence, since 'Jackie Gleason' is merely the proper name of *some* individual. This is all that is asserted by b). Hence, EG might be roughly paraphrased for sentences as follows: Existentially quantified sentences may be inferred from both ambiguous and proper sentences. Consider the following examples requiring the use of EG and US.

EXAMPLE 4

Prove that the following argument is valid by natural deduction.

> Either Jersey Joe is not friendly or Arnold is gaining weight.
> Jersey Joe is friendly.
> ———————————————
> Someone is gaining weight.

Solution. Begin by putting the argument into symbolic form. Let '*j*' be short for 'Jersey Joe', '*Fx*' for '*x* is friendly', '*n*' for 'Arnold', and '*Gx*' for '*x* is gaining weight'. Then the argument has the following form.

$$-Fj \lor Gn$$
$$\underline{Fj}$$
$$(Ex)Gx$$

The derivation requires only two steps.

1.	$-Fj \lor Gn$	Given
2.	Fj	Given
3.	Gn	1, 2, elim
4.	$(Ex)Gx$	3, EG

EXAMPLE 5

Derive '$(Ex)(Hx \cdot Kx)$' from

$$Ha \cdot Fa$$
$$(x)[(Fx \lor Gx) \supset Kx].$$

Solution. Begin by eliminating the universal quantifier. Since '*a*' appears in the first premiss, we should use '*a*' in the application of US.

1.	$Ha \cdot Fa$	Given
2.	$(x)[(Fx \lor Gx) \supset Kx]$	Given
3.	$(Fa \lor Ga) \supset Ka$	2, US

Our strategy will be to derive 'Ka', add it to 'Ha', and apply EG. We find 'Ka' by mp once we have the antecedent of line 3. The latter is easily obtained.

4.	Fa	1, simp
5.	$Fa \lor Ga$	4, add

Then,

6.	Ka	3, 5, mp
7.	Ha	1, simp
8.	$Ha \cdot Ka$	7, 6, conj
9.	$(Ex)(Hx \cdot Kx)$	8, EG

EXAMPLE 6

By cp, derive '$(Ex)(Sx \supset Px)$' from

$$(x)(Mx \supset Px)$$
$$Sa \supset Ma.$$

Solution. Begin by eliminating the universal quantifier.

1.	$(x)(Mx \supset Px)$	Given
2.	$Sa \supset Ma$	Given
3.	$Ma \supset Pa$	1, US

Our strategy will be to derive '$Sa \supset Pa$' by cp and then apply EG.

4.	Sa/Pa	Assumed
5.	Ma	2, 4, mp
6.	Pa	3, 5, mp
7.	$Sa \supset Pa$	4, 6, cp
8.	$(Ex)(Sx \supset Px)$	7, EG

It may be noticed now that although we have confined our discussion of quantificational validity to nonempty universes and although we may obtain an existentially quantified sentence from a universally quantified one by US and EG, we cannot validate inferences from **A** to **I** or from **E** to **O** sentences. Given, say,

(5)   All mermaids have fins.

we may obtain

(6)   *If a is a mermaid then a* has a fin.

by US and

(7)   There exists at least one thing such that *if* it is a mermaid *then* it has a fin.

from that by EG, but we cannot obtain

(8)   There exists at least one thing such that it is a mermaid *and* it has a fin.

In order to obtain (8) from (5), we would have to assume that there are mermaids; i.e., we would have to give (5) an *existential interpretation*. Since there are no mermaids, however, such an interpretation is unwarranted. On the other hand, the derivation of (7) from (5) is both valid and plausible. According to (7), we are committed to the assertion that our universe contains at least one *thing*, but *not* necessarily one mermaid. Of course, *if* that thing *is* a mermaid then it must have a fin; i.e., it is either not a mermaid at all or it has a fin. But we simply cannot derive the existence of a mermaid or any other *specific thing* from an **A** or an **E** sentence. At best we are permitted to "derive" the existence of *something or other*.

Review problems for Sec. 4.4.

1.   Define the following.

     a)   ambiguous name

     b)   universal specification

     c)   existential generalization

2.   Derive the conclusions of the following arguments from the given premisses.

a) $(x)[(-Ax \equiv Cx) \cdot -Dx]$
$$-(De \cdot Ae)$$

b) $(-Af \lor Gf) \supset (Af \lor Df)$
$(x)(-Gx \supset Ax)$
$$\frac{(x) -Ax}{(Ex)Dx}$$

c) $Dh \cdot (-Fh \equiv Gh)$
$(x)(Cx \supset -Dx)$
$$\frac{(x) -Gx}{(Ex)(-Cx \lor -Fx)}$$

d) $(x)[(-Ax \cdot Fx) \cdot -Cx]$
$Gm \supset Cm$
$$\frac{-Hm \lor -Fm}{(Ex) -(Hx \lor Gx)}$$

e) $(x)[(Ax \supset Bx) \supset (Cx \supset Dx)]$
$-(Ae \cdot -Be) \cdot Ce$
$De \equiv He$
$$\frac{}{(Ex)Hx}$$

f) $(-Hg \equiv -Dg) \lor -Fg$
$Fg \cdot Dg$
$$\frac{-Hg \lor (Gg \supset -Fg)}{(Ex) -Gx}$$

g) $(x)\{Dx \supset [Hx \supset (Cx \supset Bx)]\}$
$(x)(Gx \supset Dx)$
$$\frac{(x)[(Gx \cdot Hx) \cdot -Bx]}{(Ex) -Cx}$$

h) $(x)[(Ax \cdot Dx) \cdot Gx]$
$(x)[Ax \supset (Dx \supset Hx)]$
$$\frac{-Hj \lor (Fj \equiv Dj)}{Fj \cdot Gj}$$

3. Put the following arguments into symbolic form, and construct formal proofs of their validity.

   a) Everything is not precious if and only if it is in demand. Whatever is precious is available in small quantities. Everything is not in demand. Hence, something is available in small quantities. *Rx, Dx, Ax.*

   b) Elmer is not painting and not eating, or he is listening to records. Everyone listens to records if and only if it is in style. Everything is not in style. Hence, Elmer is not painting. *e, Ax, Tx, Lx, Yx.*

   c) No hogs are dogs. Everything is either a hog and lost in the fog, or is a log. Pluto is not a log and is lost in the fog. Therefore, something is not a dog. *Hx, Dx, Lx, Ox, p.*

   d) All cads are sad. Whoever is sad is mad. If Lucius is not your dad, then Lucius is glad. Everyone is not mad and not glad. Hence, someone is your dad and not mad, and not a cad. *Cx, Ax, Dx, l, Fx, Gx.*

   e) Fred is dead if and only if he lost his head, if and only if he turned red. Everything turns red. Fred is dead and he did not lose his head. Thus, someone lost his head. *f, Dx, Lx, Tx.*

   f) Everyone either takes a bus, or does not walk but rides a bicycle. Whoever takes a bus, sleeps only if he takes a pill. Hoss does not take pills but he walks. Thus, someone does not sleep. *Bx, Wx, Rx, Lx, Ix, h.*

   g) All drones moan. Whoever moans is stoned. Whoever is stoned is alone. Everything known is shown. Jones is not stoned. Hence, someone is known only if he does not moan. *Dx, Ox, Tx, Ax, Kx, Hx, j.*

   h) No sportsmen are gunfighters if and only if they are not fishermen. He who hunts is a sportsman. If Jerome fishes then he is a fisherman. Jerome hunts and fishes. Thus, someone is a gunfighter. *Ox, Gx, Fx, Hx, Ix, j.*

   i) Everything falls if and only if it is not supported. Everything is supported but not taxed. Everything either falls, or is taxed or turns rotten. Hence, something turns rotten. *Fx, Ux, Tx, Rx.*

   j) Evelyn rose to power or gave up her children, and lost her fortune. If Evelyn lost her fortune, then she neither gave up her children nor inherited a bundle. Evelyn did not rise to power. So, someone inherited a bundle only if it was God's will. *e, Rx, Gx, Lx, Ix, Fx.*

4.5 Exchanging quantifying expressions

In Sec. 4.2 it was shown that a universal quantifier may always be eliminated in favor of an existential quantifier with a negation sign on both sides; a universal quantifier followed by a negation sign may be eliminated in favor of a negation sign followed by an existential quantifier; etc. It is frequently useful to exchange one quantifying expression for another. Hence, we introduce the following rule of

Exchanging Quantifying Expressions (EQ):

'$(x)Sx$'	is equivalent to	'$-(Ex)-Sx$'.
'$-(x)-Sx$'	is equivalent to	'$(Ex)Sx$'.
'$-(x)Sx$'	is equivalent to	'$(Ex)-Sx$'.
'$(x)-Sx$'	is equivalent to	'$-(Ex)Sx$'.

EQ is applied in the same way that the rules for truth-functionally equivalent schemata are applied. That is, the first sentence tells us that '$(x)Sx$' implies '$-(Ex)-Sx$', and vice versa; the second sentence tells us that '$-(x)-Sx$' implies '$(Ex)Sx$', and vice versa; etc. As the following examples show, EQ is especially useful when applying ip to an argument whose conclusion is a quantified sentence.

EXAMPLE 1

Demonstrate the validity of the following argument by ip.

$$(x)(Fx \supset -Gx)$$
$$(x)(Hx \cdot Gx)$$
$$\overline{(Ex)(Hx \cdot -Fx)}$$

Solution. We begin by assuming the negation of the conclusion as a new premiss.

1.	$(x)(Fx \supset -Gx)$	Given
2.	$(x)(Hx \cdot Gx)$	Given
3.	$-(Ex)(Hx \cdot -Fx)$	Assumed

Apply EQ to line 3.

4.	$(x)-(Hx \cdot -Fx)$	3, EQ

Now we may drop all quantifiers by US.

5.	$Fa \supset -Ga$	1, US
6.	$Ha \cdot Ga$	2, US
7.	$-(Ha \cdot -Fa)$	4, US

Applying dem to line 7,

8.	$-Ha \lor Fa$	7, dem

we find three possible contradictions, namely, '$Fa \cdot -Fa$', '$Ga \cdot -Ga$', and '$Ha \cdot -Ha$'. Take the middle one.

9.	Ga	6, simp
10.	Ha	6, simp
11.	Fa	8, 10, elim
12.	$-Ga$	5, 11, mp
13.	$Ga \cdot -Ga$	9, 12, conj
14.	$(Ex)(Hx \cdot -Fx)$	3, 13, ip

EXAMPLE 2

Prove the validity of the following argument by natural deduction.

$$-(Ex)(Fx \cdot -Gx)$$
$$\underline{-(Ex) -Fx}$$
$$Ga$$

Solution. We begin by replacing the negated quantified sentences by unnegated ones.

1.	$-(Ex)(Fx \cdot -Gx)$	Given
2.	$-(Ex) -Fx$	Given
3.	$(x) -(Fx \cdot -Gx)$	1, EQ
4.	$(x)Fx$	2, EQ

After the quantifiers are eliminated, the conclusion follows in two steps.

5.	$-(Fa \cdot -Ga)$	3, US
6.	Fa	4, US
7.	$Fa \supset Ga$	5, imp
8.	Ga	7, 6, mp

EXAMPLE 3

By ip, derive '$(Ex) -(Lx \cdot Fx)$' from

$$-(Ex) -(Fx \lor Gx)$$
$$-(Ex)Fx$$
$$(x)[Gx \supset (Hx \cdot Lx)].$$

Solution. We begin by replacing the negated quantified sentences by unnegated ones.

1.	$-(Ex) -(Fx \lor Gx)$	Given
2.	$-(Ex)Fx$	Given
3.	$(x)[Gx \supset (Hx \cdot Lx)]$	Given
4.	$(x)(Fx \lor Gx)$	1, EQ
5.	$(x) -Fx$	2, EQ

Then the negation of the conclusion is assumed as a new premiss.

6.	$-(Ex) -(Lx \cdot Fx)$	Assumed

Next, we exchange and then drop all quantifiers.

7.	$(x)(Lx \cdot Fx)$	6, EQ
8.	$La \cdot Fa$	7, US
9.	$Ga \supset (Ha \cdot La)$	3, US
10.	$Fa \lor Ga$	4, US
11.	$-Fa$	5, US

The conclusion follows in three steps.

12.	Fa	8, simp
13.	$Fa \cdot -Fa$	12, 11, conj
14.	$(Ex) - (Lx \cdot Fx)$	6, 13, ip

Review problems for Sec. 4.5.

1. Eliminate the negation sign before each of the following schemata according to EQ. Whenever possible, put the schema into one of the four categorical forms.

   a) $-(x)Sx$
   b) $-(Ex) -Sx$
   c) $-(Ex) -(Sx \lor -Px)$
   d) $-(Ex)(Sx \cdot -Px)$
   e) $-(x)(-Sx \cdot Px)$

   f) $-(x) -(Sx \lor Px)$
   g) $-(x) -(Sx \cdot -Px)$
   h) $-(Ex) -(Sx \supset -Px)$
   i) $-(x)(Sx \lor -Px)$
   j) $-(Ex) -[-(Sx \cdot -Px)]$

2. Derive the conclusions of the following arguments from the given premises.

   a) $-(Ex)[(Ax \lor Cx) \cdot -(Gx \cdot Hx)]$
       $(x)(-Hx \cdot Fx)$
       $(x)(Dx \supset Cx)$ _____
       $(Ex) -Dx$

   b) $(x)[-(Hx \supset Gx) \lor Dx]$
       $-Fe \lor (Ae \cdot Ce)$
       $-(Ex) -(-Cx)$
       $De \equiv Fe$ _____
       $-Ge$

   c) $(x)\{-[-(Ax \supset Ex) \supset (Cx \supset Dx)] \supset (Hx \supset Fx)\}$
       $-(Ex) -[(Hx \cdot -Fx) \cdot -Bx]$
       $Ce \cdot -De$ _____
       $Ae \supset Be$

   d) $-(Cg \equiv -Dg) \supset (Hg \cdot Fg)$
       $-(Ex) -(-Fx \cdot Dx)$
       $(x)[Cx \lor (Gx \cdot Fx)]$ _____
       $(Ex)Gx$

   e) $(x)[-Fx \supset (-Ax \cdot -Bx)]$
       $-(Ex) -[(Gx \cdot Fx) \supset Dx]$
       $(x)Ax$
       $(x)(Fx \equiv Gx)$ _____
       $(Ex)Dx$

   f) $-(Ex) -\{[(Fx \cdot Gx) \supset Hx] \supset Kx\}$
       $-(Ex) -[Hx \cdot (Bx \supset -Kx)]$ _____
       $(Ex) -Bx$

3. Put the following arguments into symbolic form, and construct formal proofs of their validity.

   a) Everything is expendable if and only if it is replaceable. Everything is marketable if and only if it is not expendable. Everything is changeable if and only if it is replaceable. It is false that something is not changeable. Hence, something is replaceable but not marketable. *Xx, Rx, Ax, Cx.*

   b) All policemen are useful public servants. Everyone either is not a detective or is a policeman. It is not the case that someone is either a useful public servant or a milkman. Therefore, it is not the case that Percy is either a detective or a milkman. *Ox, Ux, Dx, Ix, p.*

   c) No shipowner is a traveling salesman. All shipbuilders are honest men. Every honest man is a traveling salesman. It is not the case that there is not a ship-builder. Everyone is not a shipowner if and only if he is a pilot. Hence, there is at least one pilot. *Ix, Tx, Bx, Hx, Ox.*

   d) He who is punctual is responsible. Whoever is reliable deserves a raise. A person who uses an alarm clock is punctual. Everyone uses an alarm clock. It is false that someone is not reliable. Therefore, some responsible person deserves a raise. *Ux, Rx, Lx, Dx, Ax.*

   e) Honeymoons never last forever. No vacations are completely enjoyable. Everything is either a honeymoon or a vacation. It is not the case that something does not last forever. Thus, something is not completely enjoyable. *Hx, Lx, Vx, Cx.*

4.6 Existential specification and universal generalization

The fourth rule we have to consider is

Existential Specification (ES): '$(Ex)Sx$' implies 'Sa' provided that 'a' has no previous occurrence in the demonstration. According to ES, *only the first* of the following kinds of inferences is valid, and even that has an important restriction.

$$
\begin{array}{cc}
\text{a)} & \text{b)} \\
\dfrac{(Ex)Sx}{Sa \;\; \text{(restricted)}} & \dfrac{(Ex)Sx}{Sc \;\; \text{(invalid)}}
\end{array}
$$

In both cases a) and b), we are given an existentially quantified schema to begin with; i.e., S is attributed to at least one individual. Now, the following inter-pretation proves that b) is *invalid*. While

> Something is in Chicago.

is true,

> Hong Kong is in Chicago.

is false. Thus b) may be given an interpretation such that its premiss is true and its conclusion is false; i.e., b) is invalid. This might have been expected. It is one thing to know that *something* is in Chicago and quite another to know *exactly who or what* is in Chicago. Again, we would all be successful detectives if we could infer the *exact name* of a criminal from the mere statement that *someone* committed a crime.

On the other hand, a) is valid. If

Something is S.

represents a true sentence, then

So-and-so is S.

must also represent a true sentence, since 'so-and-so' is merely an ambiguous name for any or every (some) thing. Or, to put the point in a slightly different fashion,

So-and-so is S.

does not *go beyond* or *tell us more than*

Something is S.

This is *part* of what is asserted by a). But a) also carries an important restriction which may be elucidated with the help of the following *invalid* argument.

Something is square.
Something is not square.
<u>   </u>
Something is square and not square.

Clearly *both* of the premisses of this argument are true and its conclusion is false. But if we let 'Qx' stand for 'x is square' and *ignore the restriction* on ES, we may demonstrate the validity of this argument as follows.

1.	$(Ex)Qx$	Given
2.	$(Ex) -Qx$	Given
3.	Qa	1, ES
4.	$-Qa$ (erroneous)	2, ES
5.	$Qa \cdot -Qa$	3, 4, conj
6.	$(Ex)(Sx \cdot -Sx)$	5, EG

The restriction on ES prevents such moves as line 4. According to the restriction, line 4 is erroneous because the ambiguous name '*a*' may only be used in an application of ES *if it has not been used before* in the demonstration, and '*a*' *was used before* line 4, namely, in line 3. We might, then, roughly paraphrase ES for sentences as follows: An ambiguous sentence may be inferred from an existentially quantified sentence provided that the ambiguous name occurring in the former has not been used previously in the demonstration. Consider the following examples requiring the use of ES, EG, and/or US.

Example 1

Prove that the following argument is valid.

> Some horses are racehorses.
> Every horse loves its master.
> ————————————————
> Something loves its master.

Solution. Begin by putting the argument into symbolic form. Let '*Hx*' be short for '*x* is a horse', '*Rx*' for '*x* is a racehorse', and '*Lx*' for '*x* loves its master'. Then the argument has the following form.

$$(Ex)(Hx \cdot Rx)$$
$$(x)(Hx \supset Lx)$$
$$\overline{(Ex)Lx}$$

The next step is to eliminate the quantifiers from the premisses. Since both premisses will be needed to derive the conclusion, we must use the same name when ES and US are applied. Furthermore, since we may *only* use the ambiguous name '*a*' with ES and *that* only if '*a*' is not already used in the demonstration, we must apply ES *before* US. That is, we must begin the derivation as follows.

1.	$(Ex)(Hx \cdot Rx)$	Given
2.	$(x)(Hx \supset Lx)$	Given
3.	$Ha \cdot Ra$	1, ES
4.	$Ha \supset La$	2, US

Again, because an ambiguous sentence may be derived from an existentially quantified sentence *only if* the ambiguous name in the former has not appeared previously in the demonstration, it would have been impossible to apply US first and then ES, i.e.,

3.	$Ha \supset La$	2, US
4.	$Ha \cdot Ra$ (erroneous)	1, ES

would have been a violation of the restriction on ES.

There are only three more steps to our conclusion.

5.	Ha	3, simp
6.	La	4, 5, mp
7.	$(Ex)Lx$	6, EG

EXAMPLE 2

Derive '$(Ex)(-Fx \lor Lx)$' from

$$(x)[Hx \supset (Fx \equiv Gx)]$$
$$(Ex)(Hx \cdot -Gx).$$

Solution. Begin by dropping the quantifiers from the premisses.

1.	$(x)[Hx \supset (Fx \equiv Gx)]$	Given
2.	$(Ex)(Hx \cdot -Gx)$	Given
3.	$Ha \cdot -Ga$	2, ES
4.	$Ha \supset (Fa \equiv Ga)$	1, US

In order to arrive at the desired conclusion, we must first derive the disjunction '$-Fa \lor La$'. To begin with, either disjunct would do. Hence, our strategy will be to place the consequent of line 4 on a line by itself, change it into two conditionals, and detach '$-Fa$' from one of the latter. Thus,

5.	Ha	3, simp
6.	$Fa \equiv Ga$	4, 5, mp
7.	$(Fa \supset Ga) \cdot (Ga \supset Fa)$	6, bic
8.	$Fa \supset Ga$	7, simp
9.	$-Ga$	3, simp
10.	$-Fa$	8, 9, mt

The conclusion follows in two familiar steps.

11.	$-Fa \lor La$	10, add
12.	$(Ex)(-Fx \lor Lx)$	11, EG

The fifth and final rule we have to consider is

Universal Generalization (UG): 'Sa' implies '$(x)Sx$' provided that 'a' has not been introduced by ES. According to UG, *only the first* of the following kinds of inferences is valid, and even *that* has an important restriction.

a)   b)

$$\frac{Sa}{(x)Sx} \quad \text{(restricted)} \qquad \frac{Sc}{(x)Sx} \quad \text{(invalid)}$$

In both cases a) and b), we derive a universally quantified schema; i.e., S is attributed to everything. Now, the following interpretation proves that b) is *invalid*. Although

Los Angeles is in California.

is true,

Everything is in California.

is false. Thus b) may be given an interpretation with a true premiss and a false conclusion; i.e., b) is invalid. This might have been expected. We would all be millionaires if we could infer that *everyone* is a millionaire from the mere statement that *Rockefeller* is a millionaire.

On the other hand, a) is valid. If

So-and-so is in California.

is true, then

Everything is in California.

must be true, since 'so-and-so' is merely an ambiguous name for *any or every* thing. If *any* so-and-so we can name is in California, then *every* so-and-so we can name must be in California. This is *part* of what is asserted by a). But a) also carries an important restriction which may be elucidated with the help of the following *invalid* argument.

Something is square.
Everything is square.

Clearly the premiss of this argument is true, and the conclusion is false. But if we let 'Qx' be short for 'x is square' and *ignore the restriction* on UG, we may demonstrate the validity of this argument as follows.

1.	$(Ex)Qx$		Given
2.	Qa		1, ES
3.	$(x)Qx$	(erroneous)	2, UG

The restriction on UG prevents such moves as line 3. According to the restriction, line 3 is erroneous because the ambiguous name 'a' may only be used in an application of UG *if it has not been introduced by* ES, and 'a' *was introduced by* ES. We might, then, roughly paraphrase UG for sentences thus: A universally quantified sentence may be inferred from an ambiguous sentence provided that the ambiguous name in the latter has not been introduced by ES. Consider the following examples requiring the use of UG.

EXAMPLE 3

Demonstrate the validity of the following argument.

Impermanent things finally disappear.
Everything is impermanent.
Everything finally disappears.

Solution. Put the argument into symbolic form. Let 'Ix' be short for 'x is impermanent' and 'F*x*' for '*x* finally disappears'. Then the argument has the following form.

$$(x)(Ix \supset Fx)$$
$$(x)Ix$$
$$\overline{(x)Fx}$$

Once the quantifiers are removed, the conclusion follows in two steps. Since the conclusion is a universally quantified sentence and such a sentence may *only* be inferred from an ambiguous sentence, we must use the ambiguous name '*a*' in the application of US.

1.	$(x)(Ix \supset Fx)$	Given
2.	$(x)Ix$	Given
3.	$Ia \supset Fa$	1, US
4.	Ia	2, US
5.	Fa	3, 4, mp
6.	$(x)Fx$	5, UG

EXAMPLE 4

Derive '$(x)Gx$' from

$$(x)[(-Lx \cdot Hx) \supset Gx]$$
$$(x)(Lx \equiv Fx)$$
$$(x)(-Fx \cdot Hx).$$

Solution. Begin by eliminating quantifiers.

1.	$(x)[(-Lx \cdot Hx) \supset Gx]$	Given
2.	$(x)(Lx \equiv Fx)$	Given
3.	$(x)(-Fx \cdot Hx)$	Given
4.	$(-La \cdot Ha) \supset Ga$	1, US
5.	$La \equiv Fa$	2, US
6.	$-Fa \cdot Ha$	3, US

If 'Ga' could be detached from line 4, UG would yield the desired conclusion. To detach 'Ga', we must have '$-La \cdot Ha$'. 'Ha' follows immediately from line 6.

7.	Ha	6, simp

So all we need is '$-La$'. This is easily derived.

8.	$(La \supset Fa) \cdot (Fa \supset La)$	5, bic
9.	$La \supset Fa$	8, simp
10.	$-Fa$	6, simp
11.	$-La$	9, 10, mt

Then, according to our plan,

$$12. \quad -La \cdot Ha \qquad 11, 7, \text{conj}$$
$$13. \quad Ga \qquad\qquad 4, 12, \text{mp}$$
$$14. \quad (x)Gx \qquad\quad 13, \text{UG}$$

Review problems for Sec. 4.6.

1. Define the following.

   a) existential specification
   b) universal generalization

2. Why should ES be applied before UG?

3. Derive the conclusions of the following arguments from the given premises.

a) $(x)[(-Cx \lor -Dx) \lor -Hx]$
   $(x)(Hx \cdot -Gx)$
   $(x)[-Dx \supset (Fx \cdot Gx)]$
   —————————————
   $(x) -Cx$

b) $(Ex)[(Cx \supset -Bx) \supset Dx]$
   $(x) -(Ax \lor Dx)$
   $(x)(Bx \supset Hx)$
   —————————————
   $(Ex)(Hx \cdot Cx)$

c) $-(Ex) -[(Dx \cdot Cx) \cdot (Fx \cdot Gx)]$
   $(x)(-Bx \supset Cx)$
   $(x)(Hx \supset -Gx)$
   $(Ex)[(Bx \cdot -Hx) \supset Kx]$
   —————————————
   $(Ex)Kx$

d) $-(x) -[Ax \supset (Bx \supset Cx)]$
   $(x)[(Bx \supset Cx) \supset Dx]$
   $(x)[Dx \supset (Hx \supset Fx)]$
   $(x)(-Fx \cdot Hx)$
   —————————————
   $(Ex)(Ax \supset Gx)$

e) $(x)\{[Fx \supset (Hx \lor Kx)] \lor Bx\}$
   $(x)(Bx \equiv Gx)$
   $(x) -Gx$
   —————————————
   $(x)[-(Fx \supset Hx) \supset Kx]$

f) $(Ex)\{-Ax \supset [-Cx \supset (Dx \supset Hx)]\}$
   $-(Ex) -(Ax \supset Hx)$
   $-(Ex)(Bx \lor Hx)$
   $-(Ex)Cx$
   —————————————
   $(Ex)(-Hx \supset -Dx)$

g) $(x)[Hx \supset -(Fx \cdot -Cx)]$
   $-(x)(Hx \supset Tx)$
   $(x)[(Cx \supset Gx) \cdot Fx]$
   —————————————
   $(Ex)Gx$

h) $(x)[(Dx \lor Fx) \equiv (Gx \lor Hx)]$
   $-(Ex) -(Dx \cdot -Gx)$
   $(x)[Hx \supset (-Fx \equiv Bx)]$
   $-(Ex)Bx$
   —————————————
   $(x)Fx$

4. Some of the following arguments are valid in every nonempty universe and some are not. Determine which ones are valid in a two-membered universe by the *reductio ad absurdum* test, and derive their conclusions from their premises by natural deduction.

   a) All bees live in hives. Everyone is afraid of bees if and only if he does not understand them. Whoever lives in hives understands bees. Everyone is afraid of bees. Therefore, someone is afraid of bees, but is not a bee. *Bx, Lx, Ax, Ux.*

   b) No bees live in solitude. Something either lives in solitude, or it is a social insect if and only if it is not a prude. All bees are social insects. Hence, something is a prude only if it is lonely. *Bx, Lx, Ix, Ux, Ox.*

c) Whatever is a bee and is not in a hive is hunting for nectar. Benjamin is not in a hive, but is sitting on a flower. Whatever is sitting on a flower is a bee. Hence, something is hunting for nectar. *Bx, Ix, Hx, e, Tx.*

d) $-(Ex) - \{[Gx \supset (Bx \lor Cx)] \supset Dx\}$
    $-(Ex)(Ax \supset Dx)$
    _____
    $(x) - Bx$

e) $(Ex)\{[Bx \supset (Cx \supset Dx)] \supset Ax\}$
    $(x)(-Bx \lor Hx)$
    $(x)[(Hx \equiv -Ax) \cdot -Dx]$
    _____
    $(Ex)(-Ax \supset Cx)$

f) No queen is a small bee. Some workers are not builders. All foragers are more than 2 weeks old. No queens are workers. Nothing is more than 2 weeks old. Hence, something is not either a builder or a forager, and is not a queen. *Qx, Ax, Wx, Bx, Fx, Ox.*

g) Some bees are drones. No queens are workers. Something is not an ant if and only if it is a drone. All drones are queens. Therefore, something is a worker. *Bx, Dx, Qx, Wx, Ax.*

h) $(x)[-Ax \equiv (-Bx \supset Cx)]$
    $(x)[Ax \lor (Dx \cdot Gx)]$
    $(x)(Gx \supset Fx)$
    $(x)(-Fx \cdot -Cx)$
    _____
    $(x)Bx$

i) $(x)(Gx \lor Dx)$
    $(Ex)[(-Kx \lor Ax) \lor -Dx]$
    $(x)[-Gx \cdot (-Ax \lor Fx)]$
    _____
    $(Ex)[Hx \supset (Kx \supset Fx)]$

j) $(x)[Hx \lor -(Fx \supset Gx)]$
    $-(Ex)(Cx \supset Dx)$
    $(x)(Fx \supset Dx)$
    _____
    $(Ex)Hx$

k) All workers are either builders or hive cleaners. Every builder is more than 1 week old. Some workers are not more than 1 week old. Hence, some workers are hive cleaners. *Wx, Bx, Hx, Ox.*

l) All bees are either not queens or not workers. Everything is either a drone or not alone. All queens are alone. Everything is a bee if and only if it is industrious. Something is a worker. Hence, something is a queen. *Bx, Qx, Wx, Dx, Ax, Ix.*

m) $(x)[(-Dx \equiv Kx) \equiv Gx]$
    $(Ex)[Fx \supset (Ax \supset Bx)]$
    $(x)[-Kx \lor (Bx \cdot -Cx)]$
    $(x)(Cx \supset Fx)$
    _____
    $(Ex)(Gx \cdot Cx)$

n) Something is a bee, if and only if it is a worker only if it is more than 2 weeks old. Everything either is not an ant or is a bee. It is not the case that something is an ant only if it is strong. Everything is a worker. Hence, something is more than 2 weeks old. *Bx*, *Wx*, *Ox*, *Ax*, *Tx*.

o) No queens are workers. All builders are workers. Everything is a worker if and only if it is a female. Hence, everything is such that if it is a queen it is not a female, and if it is a builder then it is a female. *Qx*, *Wx*, *Bx*, *Fx*.

p) $-(Ex)(-Ax \lor -Bx)$
$(x)[(Cx \supset Dx) \supset Gx]$
$$\frac{(Ex)(-Gx \lor -Ax)}{(Ex) -(Bx \supset Dx)}$$

q) All bees are workers if and only if they are females. All drones are large. Something is a queen. All workers are large. Everything is either a female or not a bee. Hence, something is a queen only if it is not a bee. *Bx*, *Wx*, *Fx*, *Dx*, *Lx*, *Qx*.

r) All worker bees are not queens. Some worker bees are builders. Hence, something is a bee and a builder, but not a queen. *Wx*, *Bx*, *Qx*, *Ux*.

s) Whatever is either a worker or a queen is a female. Everything that is either a female or a builder is a bee. Hence, all workers are bees. *Wx*, *Qx*, *Fx*, *Ux*, *Bx*.

Suggestions for further reading related to Chapter 4.

Anderson, John M., and Johnstone, Henry W., Jr., *Natural Deduction*. Belmont, Calif.: Wadsworth Publishing Co., Inc., 1962, Chapter 5.

Barker, Stephen F., *The Elements of Logic*. New York: McGraw-Hill Book Company, 1965, Chapter 4.

Copi, Irving M., *Introduction to Logic*. New York: The Macmillan Company, 1961, Chapter 10.

Lemmon, E. J., *Beginning Logic*. London: Thomas Nelson & Sons Ltd., 1965, Chapter 3.

Neidorf, Robert, *Deductive Forms*. New York: Harper & Row, Publishers, 1967, Chapters 5 and 6.

Suppes, Patrick, *Introduction to Logic*. Princeton, N. J.: D. Van Nostrand Co., Inc., 1957, Chapters 3 and 4.

We may at once admit that any inductive inference
must be attended with some degree of uncertainty,
but this is not the same as to admit that such
inference cannot be absolutely rigorous, for the
nature and degree of the uncertainty may itself be
capable of rigorous expression.

Ronald A. Fisher

Part

TWO

Nondemonstrative

Principles

Chapter

5

Meaning and Measures of Probability

5.1 Nondemonstrative problems

An argument schema is called 'nondemonstrative' if its conclusion is *supposed* (or *claimed*, or *alleged*) to be more or less acceptable *relative to* its premises. Interpretations of nondemonstrative argument schemata are called 'nondemonstrative arguments'. An argument *schema* is **nondemonstratively valid (n-valid** for short) if and only if its conclusion *is* more or less acceptable *relative to* its premises. Interpretations of *n*-valid schemata are called **nondemonstratively valid (n-valid** for short) **arguments.** Nondemonstrative schemata whose conclusions are *not* more or less acceptable *relative to* their premises are **nondemonstratively invalid (n-invalid).** Interpretations of such schemata are **n-invalid arguments.**

As we shall see, every valid argument is *also* *n*-valid, but most *n*-valid arguments are not valid. In other words, every inference which we were able to validate by some demonstrative principle in Part One may also be *n*-validated by some nondemonstrative principle which will be introduced in this part; however, most of the inferences we shall be able to *n*-validate by some principle in this part cannot be validated by any demonstrative principle.

The situation here is analogous to that in Part One. *Given*, for example, the premisses of the *demonstrative* argument

All men are mortal.
Pericles is a man.

we say that the conclusion

Pericles is mortal.

is *supposed* to *follow* (with complete certainty). If the argument may be regarded as an interpretation of a *valid* schema then the conclusion *does* follow from the premisses, and the argument does what it is supposed to do. If the argument is patterned after an *invalid* schema then it does not do what it is supposed to do, but it is nonetheless demonstrative.

Similarly, *given* the premisses of the *nondemonstrative* argument

Most men are mortal.
Pericles is a man.

we say that the conclusion

Pericles is mortal.

is *supposed* to be *more or less acceptable*. If the argument may be regarded as an interpretation of an *n-valid* schema then the conclusion *is* more or less acceptable *relative to* the premisses, and the argument does what it is supposed to do. If the argument is patterned after an *n-invalid* schema then it does not do what it is supposed to do, but it is nonetheless nondemonstrative.

It must be emphasized that the demonstrative-nondemonstrative distinction we have drawn is *not* based on the *form* of arguments (or schemata). Rather, it is based on the *suppositions, allegations,* or *claims* made about arguments. A demonstrative argument must be appraised by demonstrative principles of the sort introduced in Part One. A nondemonstrative argument must be appraised by nondemonstrative principles of the sort to be introduced in (this) Part Two.

We have defined '*n*-validity' in terms of acceptability but we have not explained the latter. An adequate account of acceptability can only be given after a considerable amount of *necessary, important, and interesting* work has been done on the narrower topic of *probability*. (Some people seem to *identify* probability and acceptability, but there should be no doubt by the time we reach the end of Part Two that such an identification is at best a serious *oversimplification*.) The remaining sections of this chapter and the next two chapters are all about probability. In Chapter 8 we return to the problem of acceptability.

Our investigation will be organized about four problems. *First*, we shall consider the problem of the *meaning or interpretation of 'probability' and probability sentences*. Any sentence in which probability is ascribed to something will be called a **probability sentence.** Hence, for example, we shall want to know exactly what is asserted by the following probability sentences and, in particular, how the word 'probability' may be interpreted in each one.

There is a high probability that Fred is dead.
The probability of getting a head on a toss of this coin is 0.5.
The probability of getting a head on the very *next* toss of this coin is 0.5.

Solutions to this problem of meaning may be classified *genetically* into three types. That is, there are three *sources* or *origins* of probability sentences which yield three general interpretations of 'probability' and probability sentences. Here are the three interpretations.

a) 'Probability' may be interpreted as a *logical relation* between sentences (or propositions, or statements). Given this **logical interpretation** of 'probability', when we say that something is probable, we mean that relative to certain other sentences which we accept, the sentence describing some event has a certain number or range of logically possible ways of being true. This interpretation is explained in detail in Sec. 5.2.

b) 'Probability' may be interpreted as a *physical attribute* of certain sequences of events or of certain physical ranges. Given this **physical interpretation** of 'probability', when we say that something is probable, we mean that a particular event occurs with a certain frequency in some sequence of events of a certain kind or that a certain event has a certain number or range of physically possible ways of occurring. This interpretation is explained in detail in Sec. 5.3.

c) 'Probability' may be interpreted as a *psychological attitude* toward the occurrence of certain events. Given this **psychological interpretation** of 'probability', when we say that something is probable, we mean that we have a certain degree of belief in the occurrence of some event. This interpretation is explained in detail in Sec. 5.4.

Many writers prefer to talk about "objective" and "subjective" interpretations. The view we refer to as "psychological" would be classified as "subjective" and the view we refer to as "physical" would be classified as "objective". Usually the view we refer to as "logical" would be classified as "subjective", but it has also been classified as "objective".

The *second* problem we shall consider is that of *obtaining initial numerical values for probabilities.* Such values shall be called **probability values** or **probabilities,** and the methods used to obtain them shall be called **theories of measuring initial probability values,** or briefly, **theories of measuring probabilities.** There is general agreement that any such value should be a real number on the interval from 0 to 1, inclusive. When something is (logically or physically) necessary, it is assigned a probability of *one.* When something is (logically or physically) impossible, it is assigned a probability of *zero.* The probability of things that are neither necessary nor impossible is some *fraction* between 0 and 1.

We shall explain exactly how such values are obtained for the various interpretations in Secs. 5.2.–5.4.

Since we are investigating a concept of probability which is characterized by numerical values, we may say we are considering a **quantitative concept** of probability. As we shall see in the following chapter, the basic arithmetical operations of addition, subtraction, multiplication, and division are all applicable to these numerical values. Examples of other quantitative concepts to which these operations are applicable are length, density, temperature (Kelvin), volume, price, etc. Alternatively, we might investigate a concept of probability which is used merely to classify things into two kinds, namely, *probable or not probable;* i.e., we might consider a **qualitative concept** of probability. Examples of other qualitative concepts are hot or cold, large or small, male or female, rich or poor, etc. Finally, we might investigate a concept of probability which is used to compare things with respect to their being *more or less probable;* i.e., we might consider a **comparative concept** of probability. Examples of other comparative concepts are warmer, colder, larger, smaller, richer, poorer, etc. If we chose to investigate a *qualitative* concept of probability, then our second problem would be that of determining when something is probable and when it is not probable. If we chose to investigate a *comparative* concept of probability, then our second problem would be that of determining when something is more or less probable than something else. We are investigating a *quantitative* concept of probability, however, so we want to know how to obtain initial *numerical probability values given* either a logical, a physical, or a psychological interpretation of 'probability'.

The *third* problem we shall consider is that of *calculating with initially given probabilities to obtain others.* For example, having found the probability that Pericles is courageous and the probability that he is bald, we may wish to *use these* to calculate the probability that he is *both* bald and courageous. To solve this problem, we must become familiar with some of the fundamental principles of the *calculus of probability.* By the term **calculus of probability** we mean the class consisting of all probability sentence schemata that are regarded as *rules* for the calculation of probabilities from other probabilities. A **probability sentence schema** is an expression that becomes a probability sentence when its variables are appropriately replaced. We shall introduce such schemata in Chapter 6.

Since every schema contains *uninterpreted variables*, the calculus of probability may be called an **uninterpreted calculus.** Moreover, even *after* the variables in a probability sentence schema have been replaced, say, by terms or sentences, we have a sentence whose meaning is ambiguous because the word 'probability' is ambiguous. The ambiguity is eliminated by assigning 'probability' a single precise meaning or definition. By a fairly innocuous and useful extension of our definition of 'interpretation', we have referred to the latter process as "interpreting 'probability' and probability sentences".

The calculus of probability constitutes a set of *formal conditions* which any acceptable interpretation of 'probability' must satisfy; e.g., that probability values must be real numbers on the interval from 0 to 1, inclusive. An interpretation **satisfies** these conditions if the sentences expressing these conditions become *true* sentences *given* that interpretation. For example, suppose an interpretation was such that it produced probability values as high as 66. This would mean that the condition about values between 0 and 1 inclusive would be violated; i.e., *given* the interpretation in question, this condition would become a *false* sentence. Any interpretation which satisfies all those conditions is called **admissible.** Hence, the interpretation yielding values as high as 66 would *not* be admissible. The logical, physical, and psychological interpretations we shall consider are all *admissible.*

The fourth problem we shall consider is that of the *application of probabilities in the determination of the acceptability of hypotheses and courses of action.* Aside from a few passing references to hypotheses in discussions of *analogy* and *Mill's methods*, this problem has received very little attention in introductory logic texts. But from the "practical" point of view, it is the most exciting problem in the whole area of nondemonstrative inference.

Notice that we said "*hypotheses and courses of action*". There is an important distinction here. It is one thing to *believe* something and quite another to *do* something about what you believe. It is one thing to accept a *hypothesis* as an object of belief and another thing to accept a particular course of *action*. For example, there is a difference between believing that the state needs a new governor and taking some kind of action to obtain a new governor. The difference is that the action *must* have some consequences (though not necessarily the ones intended), but the belief *need not* (though beliefs frequently *do*) have consequences. Philosophers, poets, theologians, and other less respectable types of dreamers are frequently criticized for not *doing* anything. The criticism has some force, for ideas or beliefs are subject to a kind of sterility that people who are used to "getting things done" recognize immediately.

As you would expect, this difference between belief and action is reflected in the principles used to determine acceptability. In Chapter 8 we shall consider a number of such principles which we call 'acceptance rules'. Some of the rules are designed primarily to select acceptable hypotheses (objects of belief), while others (most of them) are intended to be used to select acceptable courses of action. In some of them, probabilities play a crucial role. In others, probabilities are *ex hypothesi* entirely irrelevant.

Review problems for Sec. 5.1.

1. How is the relation between the premisses and conclusion of a nondemonstrative argument different from the relation between the premisses and conclusion of a demonstrative argument?

2. Briefly define the following interpretations of 'probability' and probability sentences.

    a) logical   d) objective

    b) physical   e) subjective

    c) psychological

3. For each of the following, indicate whether it denotes a qualitative, comparative, or quantitative concept.

a)	mile	f)	cubit
b)	wiser	g)	sticky
c)	evergreen	h)	healthier
d)	more peaceful	i)	nondemonstrative
e)	teaspoonful	j)	fluid ounce

4. Define the following.

   a) calculus of probability
   b) probability sentence schema
   c) admissible interpretation

5. Why is the calculus of probability called an 'uninterpreted calculus'?

6. How does one decide whether or not an interpretation *satisfies* the formal conditions of the calculus of probability?

5.2   The logical interpretation

a)   THE PROBLEM OF MEANING

As we suggested earlier, according to the logical interpretation, 'probability' is interpreted as a *logical relation* between sentences (or propositions, or statements). For example, relative to the sentence

> Either a head or a tail will turn up.

the sentence

> A head will turn up.

may be assigned a probability of $\frac{1}{2}$. The relation between the given sentence(s) and the sentence whose probability is to be determined is considered *similar to* but *weaker than* the relation between the premises and conclusion of a valid demonstrative argument. In the latter case, we say the premises *imply* the conclusion. Here we say the premises *partially imply* the conclusion. The question of the existence, comparative strength, or degree of the relation of *partial implication* between two or more sentences is a purely logical one. That is, the answers to such questions must be determined by logical analysis, *not* by empirical investigation. Thus, probability sentences are *logically true* if they are true at all, and *logically false* (i.e., self-contradictory) if they are false at all. While certain experiences or empirical investigations may persuade us to abandon certain probability sentences which were determined *a priori*, such experience can not falsify these statements any more than they could verify them. Since the sentences are analytic or self-contradictory, strictly speaking, experience is irrelevant to them. (We shall consider this peculiarity in detail later.)

b) THE PROBLEM OF MEASUREMENT

Granting, then, that probabilities are to be determined by and based on logical considerations alone, the question is, *How do we obtain initial numerical probabilities?* A rough provisional answer to this question is this: *Count* logical possibilities and determine the ratios of certain numbers of these to certain numbers of others. We shall consider two theories of measuring probabilities within the logical interpretation which might be roughly characterized by this answer, namely, the *classical theory* and the *logical range theory*.

i) **The classical theory:** According to the **classical theory** *of measuring probabilities* which was created by Pierre Simon de Laplace in the latter half of the eighteenth century, we measure the probability of an event of a certain kind in three steps: 1. Count the total number of equally possible events of a certain kind. 2. Count the number of cases of these which are "favorable" to the event whose probability is to be measured. 3. The ratio of the number of "favorable" cases to the total number of equally possible events is the required numerical value; i.e.,

$$(A) \qquad \text{Measure of probability} = \frac{\text{number of favorable cases}}{\text{total number of equally possible events.}}$$

Since events may be described by *sentences*, we may rewrite (A) thus:

$$\text{Measure of probability} = \frac{\text{number of favorable sentences}}{\text{total number of equally possible sentences.}}$$

Consider some examples.

EXAMPLE 1

What is the probability of tossing a head with a fair coin? (A coin is **fair** if its design is such that its two faces have an equal chance of turning up on any toss.)

Solution. The sentence whose probability we wish to measure is

A head turns up.

There are two equally possible sentences (describing two equally possible events), namely,

A head turns up.
A tail turns up.

Hence, the denominator of our fraction is 2. There is one "favorable" sentence (describing one "favorable" event), namely,

A head turns up.

So the numerator of our fraction is 1. Hence, the probability of tossing a head with a fair coin is $\frac{1}{2}$, which is also the probability of the sentence describing that event. Dividing the numerator by the denominator, we may convert this ordinary fraction into a decimal fraction, namely, 0.5. Either expression '$\frac{1}{2}$' or '0.5' will do.

We have repeatedly emphasized the fact that probabilities are always *relative* to something. We shall call the set or collection of events (or sentences, or hypotheses), relative to which the probability of some event (or sentence, or hypothesis) is determined, a **sample space.** It is, after all, a "space" full of *samples* of a whole *population* (viz., the whole collection). Occasionally we shall speak of activities engaged in to obtain sample spaces as **experiments;** e.g., counting the total number of cards in a deck, tossing a coin, rolling a die, etc. Then the various events in such sample spaces will be called **outcomes** (e.g., a king, a queen, an ace, etc.; a head; a six; etc.) and the sample space itself will be called an **outcome space.** The sample or outcome space which happens to contain the *total number* of events under discussion, *whether or not* they are *equally possible,* will be called the **universe of discourse** or **universal set.** When the sample or outcome space contains *some* but not all of the events in the universal set, we sometimes refer to it as a **subset** of the universal set. *Every* probability value is relative to *some* or a *part* of some universe of discourse.

EXAMPLE 2

Suppose a fair *die* is tossed. What is the probability of the hypothesis that a face with six dots will turn up?

Solution. A die is a small cube with six different faces, namely,

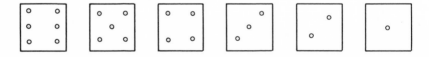

Our *sample space,* then, contains six events and is identical with our *universe of discourse.* The hypothesis whose probability we wish to measure is

A face with six dots will turn up.

There are six *equally possible* hypotheses, one for each face. Hence, the denominator of our fraction is 6. There is one "favorable" hypothesis. So the numerator of our fraction is 1. Hence, the probability of the hypothesis that a six will turn up is $\frac{1}{6}$.

This value $\frac{1}{6}$ is called the **initial** or **absolute** probability of the hypothesis that a six will turn up; it is the probability of the hypothesis relative to the *initially* *given universe of discourse or universal set.* It is contrasted with **conditional** or **relative** probability, which is the probability of a hypothesis relative to a *subset* of the universe of discourse. That is, although *all* probabilities are relative to some sample space, only those which are relative to a sample space which is a subset (part) of the (whole) universe of discourse are called 'relative' or 'conditional probabilities'. Consider the following example of relative or conditional probability.

EXAMPLE 3

Given the information that a die has been tossed and that a face with an *even* number of dots has turned up, what is the probability of the hypothesis that a six has turned up?

Solution. Because we know a face with an even number of dots has turned up, we can not use the universal set as our sample space. Instead, we must use only a subset of it, namely, the *three equally possible even-numbered* faces.

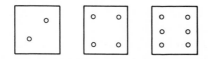

So the denominator of our fraction is 3. We still have only one "favorable" hypothesis; i.e., that a face with six dots has turned up. Hence, the numerator of our fraction is 1. Thus, the *relative* or *conditional* probability of the hypothesis that a six has turned up, *given* the information that a face with an even number of dots has turned up, is $\frac{1}{3}$.

The classical theory of measuring probabilities is useful *provided that* we have a set of *equally possible* events (or hypotheses, or sentences) to begin with. Therefore, it is imperative that we devise some criterion for determining exactly which events are equally possible and which are not. The criterion employed by Laplace was called **The Principle of Nonsufficient Reason;** i.e., in the absence of any reason for considering certain events to be *not* equally possible, they may be considered equally possible. John Maynard Keynes called this **The Principle of Indifference** and we shall use this term too, because it is shorter. Since "equally possible" events are events with equal initial probabilities, the principle prescribes the assignment of *equal numerical values* for all initial probabilities. This prescription, however, is *ambiguous* and leads directly to contradictions. For suppose we are interested in the probability of throwing a six with a fair die. Since the die is fair, we have *no reason* to believe that any of the six sides is more probable than any other. Hence, according to the principle, we must assign a probability of $\frac{1}{6}$ to the hypothesis that a face with six dots will turn up. But we also have *no reason* to expect a six rather than a nonsix. So, according to the principle, we must assign a probability of $\frac{1}{2}$ to the hypothesis that a face with six dots will turn up. But *this contradicts* our original assignment. Furthermore, we have no reason to expect a five rather than a nonfive. So the probability of the hypothesis that a face with five dots will turn up is ½. But applying the *Special Addition Principle* of the calculus of probability (which is explained in Sec. 6.2), we find that the probability of the hypothesis that *either* the face with five dots *or* the face with six dots will turn up is *one*. That is, it is *certain* that either a five or a six will turn up! Evidently the principle is taking too much for granted.

When contradictions and extravagant probabilities are obtained by applying the principle as we did in the last paragraph, most people suspect that it is *not* the principle which is at fault, but the application of that principle. Most people are unwilling to admit that we have no reason to expect a nonsix rather than a six. After all, they reason, nonsix *includes* or *is made up of* five other events, and what better reason could we want for *not* assigning six and nonsix equal initial probabilities? They suggest, then, that the principle might be modified somehow to block such misapplications or misunderstandings as we have just seen. Let us consider the possibility more carefully.

To begin with, we should distinguish divisible events from indivisible ones. **Indivisible events** are events which for *some* reason (e.g., logical, physical, technological, or practical) cannot be broken up into component events. They are *ultimate alternatives* or *simple* events in the sense that they are not composed (or compounded) of others, but all others are composed (or compounded) of them. For example, each of the faces of a die; the faces of a coin; births, deaths; (for some purposes) apples, men, automobiles; etc. Anything which for one reason or another we might wish to treat as an indivisible element or unit could serve as an example. Events which are *not* indivisible, then, are **divisible.** They are compound events, i.e., events which are composed of others; e.g., nonsix; even-numbered face; (for some purposes) bald men, bitter apples, blue automobiles; etc. Given this distinction between divisible and indivisible events, we may modify the Principle of Indifference thus: In the absence of any reason for considering certain *indivisible* events to be *not* equally possible, they may be considered equally possible. This modified principle is strong enough to withstand the *sort* of attacks we considered above (though *not all* attacks) *provided that* we can reach some agreement about which events are indivisible and which are not in any given experiment. Usually (and fortunately), as in the case of six and nonsix, nothing more than common sense or intuition is required for investigators to reach such an agreement. Hereafter when we refer to the Principle of Indifference, we shall always mean the modified version.

⬥

Review problems for Sec. 5.2 a–b: i)

1. What is the meaning of 'the logical interpretation of probability sentences'?

2. According to the classical theory of Laplace, how does one measure probabilities? Give an example.

Using the classical theory, answer the following.

3. One of John's four tires has a tack in it. What is the probability that the tack is in the left front tire?

4. Henry has one opportunity to try to guess a certain number between 1 and 10. What are his chances of guessing the right one?

5. Suppose a fair die is tossed. What is the probability that

   a) A face with two dots turns up?
   b) A face with more than two dots turns up? (*Note:* A face with three *or* four *or* five *or* six dots is a "favorable" case.)
   c) A face with less than two dots turns up?
   d) An even number turns up? (*Note:* A face with two *or* four *or* six dots is "favorable.")
   e) A number greater than two but less than five turns up?

6. There were 6 Fords and 10 Plymouths in Honest Ed's lot. Suppose he sold one car last week. What is the probability that it was a Ford? What is the probability that he sold a Plymouth?

7. A certain class has the following distribution of students.

	Freshmen	Sophomores	Juniors	Seniors	Total
Boys	12	8	6	4	30
Girls	18	12	4	16	50
Total	30	20	10	20	80

Suppose that you meet one of the students in this class in the cafeteria. What is the probability that the student is a

   a) sophomore
   b) freshman
   c) girl
   d) freshman boy
   e) junior boy

   f) sophomore girl
   g) boy or a girl
   h) junior or a senior
   i) freshman girl or a junior (boy or girl)
   j) senior boy or a sophomore (boy or girl)

8. Define the following.

   a) sample space
   b) experiment
   c) outcome

   d) universe of discourse
   e) initial (or absolute) probability
   f) conditional (or relative) probability

9. Make up examples of the following.

   a) a universe of discourse with exactly six members
   b) an experiment with exactly three possible outcomes

10. What is the Principle of Indifference?

11. How is the distinction between indivisible and divisible alternatives relevant to the Principle of Indifference?

ii) The logical range theory: The most thorough and systematic investigation of the theory of measuring probabilities by logical ranges has been given by the contemporary philosopher Rudolf Carnap. To begin with, we must imagine that we have some very simple world to describe. It is a world with only one primitive property, say the property of being red, and only two individuals, say Arf and Barf. The property is **primitive** in the sense that it is not to be defined in terms of any other properties in the little world, but another property (that of being nonred) is defined in terms of it. There are only four possible states of affairs in this world, namely,

S1   Arf is red and Barf is red.

S2   Arf is red and Barf is not red.

S3   Arf is not red and Barf is red.

S4   Arf is not red and Barf is not red.

(Notice the similarity between this table and ordinary truth-tables for two sentences with two possible truth-values.) Instead of talking about states of affairs, Carnap introduces the technical term 'state description'. A **state description** is a sentence which indicates, for *every* individual in the universe of discourse and for *every* primitive property, whether or not the individual has that property. Sometimes the term 'individual distribution' is used instead of 'state description'. The former is appropriate since the thing designated is a sentence describing the way in which *all* the properties in the universe of discourse are *distributed* among *all* the *individuals*. When there are n individuals in the universe and r primitive properties, there are 2^{nr} state descriptions. In the simple little world we are considering, we have $n = 2$ and $r = 1$; hence we have $2^{nr} = 2^{2 \times 1} = 2^2 = 4$ state descriptions S1, S2, S3, and S4.

The **logical range** of any *sentence* is the class consisting of all those state descriptions in which the sentence is true. Thus, for example, the *logical range* of the sentence

Arf is red.

is the class consisting of S1 and S2. These two state descriptions describe the only logically possible states of affairs in our little world in which the given sentence is true. That is, if the state of the world is such that either

S1   *Arf is red* and Barf is red.

or

S2   *Arf is red* and Barf is not red.

adequately describes it, then the given sentence is true. Again, the *logical range* of the sentence

Arf and Barf are red.

is the class consisting of the single state description

S1   *Arf is red* and *Barf is red.*

Here S1 describes the only logically possible state of affairs in our little world in which the given sentence is true. The *logical range* of the sentence

Either Arf is red or Barf is red.

is the class consisting of the three state descriptions

S1   *Arf is red* and *Barf is red.*

S2   *Arf is red* and Barf is not red.

S3   Arf is not red and *Barf is red.*

If any one of these state descriptions adequately describes the present state of our world, then the given sentence is true. Moreover, S1, S2, and S3 describe the only logically possible states of affairs in which the given sentence *may* be true in this world.

Notice, now, that the middle two state descriptions S2 and S3 are related to each other in a rather peculiar way, a way in which neither of them is related to either of the other state descriptions (S1 and S4) or in which neither of these (S1 and S4) are related to each other. If we substitute 'Barf' for 'Arf' and 'Arf' for 'Barf' in the middle two state descriptions, then S2 becomes S3 and S3 becomes S2. That is,

S2   Arf is red and Barf is not red.

becomes

S3   Barf is red and Arf is not red.

and

S3   Arf is not red and Barf is red.

becomes

S2   Barf is not red and Arf is red.

When state descriptions are related in such a way that one may be obtained from another by substituting the names of certain individuals for others (in the manner illustrated above), they are **isomorphic.** Thus, S2 and S3 are isomorphic state descriptions.

A **structure description** is a disjunction of all the state descriptions which are isomorphic to a given one. In the little world of our example there are three structure descriptions, namely,

St 1   Arf is red and Barf is red.

which is identical with S1;

St 2   Either Arf is red and Barf is not red, or Arf is not red and Barf is red.

which is the *disjunction* of S2 and S3; and

St 3   Arf is not red and Barf is not red.

which is identical with S4. While we happen to know *exactly which* individuals in our little world have which properties, all that is required for the complete characterization of a structure description is that we know *how many* individuals have which properties; e.g., we might characterize the second structure description St 2 by indicating that in it there is one red individual and one that is not red. It does not matter which individuals are or are not red. Sometimes the term 'statistical distribution' is used instead of 'structure description'. The former is appropriate since the thing designated is a sentence giving us a certain *statistic* about the *distribution* of properties in our world, namely, the number of individuals in this world which have *each* of the available properties. A census taker, for example, would only be interested in statistical distributions such as the number of men, women, boys, and girls living in a certain house; the number of automobiles purchased in a year; the number of deaths; etc.

According to the **logical range theory** *of measuring probabilities* as it was developed by Carnap, then, we measure the probability (Carnap would say the "degree of confirmation") of a hypothesis in three steps: a) Apply the Principle of Indifference to the structure descriptions of some universe of discourse. b) Apply the principle *again* to the isomorphic state descriptions which make up every structure description. The result of these two steps is that each *state description* has been assigned an *initial probability.* c) The measure of the initial probability of any hypothesis then is the *sum* of the initial probabilities of all the state descriptions in the *range* of that hypothesis. That is,

Measure of initial probability   _   sum of initial probabilities of state descriptions
of hypothesis   =   in range of that hypothesis.

Consider some examples.

EXAMPLE 4

Given the little world of Arf and Barf, what is the probability of the hypothesis that Barf is not red?

Solution. Let us begin by abbreviating our description of this world. Let '*a*' and '*b*' be short for the proper names 'Arf' and 'Barf', respectively; and let 'R' and '$\overline{R}$' be short for the predicates 'is red' and 'is not red', respectively. Using familiar logical notation, the abbreviated description of our world looks like this.

S1	$Ra \cdot Rb$
S2	$Ra \cdot \overline{R}b$
S3	$\overline{R}a \cdot Rb$
S4	$\overline{R}a \cdot \overline{R}b$

Following step a), we assign equal probabilities to the structure descriptions.

Structure Descriptions

St 1	$Ra \cdot Rb$	$\frac{1}{3}$
St 2	$\begin{cases} Ra \cdot \overline{R}b \\ \overline{R}a \cdot Rb \end{cases}$	$\frac{1}{3}$
St 3	$\overline{R}a \cdot \overline{R}b$	$\frac{1}{3}$

Next, according to step b), we assign equal probabilities to each of the state descriptions which make up every structure description.

		Structure Descriptions	*State Descriptions*
St 1	$Ra \cdot Rb$	$\frac{1}{3}$	$\frac{1}{3}$ (S1)
St 2	$\begin{cases} Ra \cdot \overline{R}b \\ \overline{R}a \cdot Rb \end{cases}$	$\frac{1}{3}$	$\begin{cases} \frac{1}{6} \ (S2) \\ \frac{1}{6} \ (S3) \end{cases}$
St 3	$\overline{R}a \cdot \overline{R}b$	$\frac{1}{3}$	$\frac{1}{3}$ (S4)

TABLE 5.21

The *range* of the hypothesis that Barf is not red, '$\overline{R}b$', is the class of those state descriptions in which it is true, namely, S2 and S4. The sum of the probabilities of these two state descriptions is $\frac{1}{6} + \frac{1}{3} = \frac{1}{2}$. Hence, the probability of the hypothesis that Barf is not red is $\frac{1}{2}$.

It should be emphasized that the *double application* of the Principle of Indifference is a somewhat problematic novelty of *Carnap's* logical range theory. Carnap's predecessors, Ludwig Wittgenstein and Johannes von Kries, and most people apply the principle directly to state descriptions. The result of such an application looks like this.

State Descriptions

S1	$Ra \cdot Rb$	$\frac{1}{4}$
S2	$Ra \cdot \bar{R}b$	$\frac{1}{4}$
S3	$\bar{R}a \cdot Rb$	$\frac{1}{4}$
S4	$\bar{R}a \cdot \bar{R}b$	$\frac{1}{4}$

In Sec. c) on page 200 we shall consider Carnap's argument in defense of the double application. We are presenting Carnap's position rather than that of, say, one of his predecessors because Carnap's position has been more thoroughly developed and discussed.

EXAMPLE 5

Suppose three fair coins are tossed. What is the probability of the hypothesis that *at least two* of them will turn up heads?

Solution. We have a little world with two properties, that of being a head and that of being a tail. There are three individuals, the three coins. If a coin turns up heads (tails) [i.e., has the property of being a head (tail)], then it is logically impossible for it to turn up tails (heads) at the same time. The two properties exclude one another and are, therefore, called 'mutually exclusive'. We might, then, consider the property of being a tail as simply the *lack* of the *primitive* property of being a head. Thus, when we determine the number of state descriptions in this world, we may assume we have $r = 1$ primitive property and $n = 3$ individuals. So we shall need $2^{nr} = 2^{3 \times 1} = 2^3 = 8$ state descriptions. Let us abbreviate 'is a head' by 'H', 'is a tail' by '$\bar{H}$', 'the first coin' by 'a', 'the second coin' by 'b', and 'the third coin' by 'c'. Then our abbreviated table of state and structure descriptions will look like this.

		Structure Descriptions	*State Descriptions*
St 1	$Ha \cdot Hb \cdot Hc$	$\frac{1}{4}$	$\frac{1}{4}$ (S1)
St 2	$\begin{bmatrix} Ha \cdot Hb \cdot \bar{H}c \\ Ha \cdot \bar{H}b \cdot Hc \\ \bar{H}a \cdot Hb \cdot Hc \end{bmatrix}$	$\frac{1}{4}$	$\begin{bmatrix} \frac{1}{12} & (S2) \\ \frac{1}{12} & (S3) \\ \frac{1}{12} & (S4) \end{bmatrix}$
St 3	$\begin{bmatrix} Ha \cdot \bar{H}b \cdot \bar{H}c \\ \bar{H}a \cdot Hb \cdot \bar{H}c \\ \bar{H}a \cdot \bar{H}b \cdot Hc \end{bmatrix}$	$\frac{1}{4}$	$\begin{bmatrix} \frac{1}{12} & (S5) \\ \frac{1}{12} & (S6) \\ \frac{1}{12} & (S7) \end{bmatrix}$
St 4	$\bar{H}a \cdot \bar{H}b \cdot \bar{H}c$	$\frac{1}{4}$	$\frac{1}{4}$ (S8)

TABLE 5.22

(Notice the similarity between this table and an ordinary truth-table for three sentences with two possible truth-values.) We have four structure descriptions since none, one, two, or all three coins might have the property of being a head.

Applying the Principle of Indifference to these structure descriptions [according to step a)], each one is assigned a probability of $\frac{1}{4}$. Applying the principle *next* to the state descriptions which make up these structure descriptions, we find the values listed under 'state descriptions' in Table 5.22. The *range* of the hypothesis that *at least two* coins will turn up heads is the class consisting of those state descriptions in which it is true, namely, S1–S4. The sum of the probabilities of these four state descriptions is $\frac{1}{4} + \frac{1}{12} + \frac{1}{12} + \frac{1}{12} = \frac{1}{2}$. Hence, the probability of the hypothesis that at least two coins will turn up heads is $\frac{1}{2}$.

Again, it should be noted that Carnap's predecessors and many other people would apply the Principle of Indifference directly to state descriptions. As a result, each state description in Table 5.22 would be assigned an initial probability of $\frac{1}{8}$.

So far we have seen how *initial* probability values are obtained with the logical range theory. Little more needs to be said to explain how *conditional* probabilities are obtained. We measure the (conditional) probability of a hypothesis represented by '*H*', *given* some evidence '*E*', by the fraction whose numerator is the sum of the initial probabilities for all the state descriptions in the range of '*H and E*' and whose denominator is the sum of the initial probabilities for all the state descriptions in the range of '*E*'; i.e.,

$$\frac{\text{Measure of probability}}{\text{of '}H\ given\ E\text{'}} = \frac{\begin{array}{l}\text{Sum of initial probabilities of state}\\ \text{descriptions in range of '}H\ and\ E\text{'}\end{array}}{\begin{array}{l}\text{sum of initial probabilities of state}\\ \text{descriptions in range of '}E\text{'.}\end{array}}$$

(We are using the capital letters '*H*' and '*E*' as sentential variables here because they seem to be more suggestive than, say, '*p*' and '*q*'.) Consider the following example.

EXAMPLE 6

Given the information that three coins have been tossed and that the first two have turned up heads, what is the probability that the third coin is a head?

Solution. We may use Table 5.22 as a description of our universe of discourse. The evidence '*E*' is interpreted as

(Coin) *a* is a head and *b* is a head.

That is,

$$Ha \cdot Hb.$$

The *range* of '*E*' is the class consisting of S1 and S2. The sum of the initial probabilities of S1 and S2 is $\frac{1}{4} + \frac{1}{12} = \frac{1}{3}$. So $\frac{1}{3}$ is the denominator of our fraction. The numerator is the sum of the initial probabilities in the range of '*H and E*'; i.e.,

(The third coin) *c* is a head *and* (coin) *a* is a head *and* *b* is a head.

This is just state description 1, which has an initial probability of $\frac{1}{4}$. Hence, the numerator of our fraction is $\frac{1}{4}$. Therefore, the (conditional) probability of the hypothesis that (the third coin) c is a head *given* the evidence that the first two are heads is $\left(\frac{1}{4}\right)/\left(\frac{1}{3}\right) = \frac{3}{4}$.

c)   Some Advantages and Disadvantages of the Logical Interpretation

There are at least five advantages to the logical interpretation of 'probability' and probability sentences when either the classical or the logical range theories (with a *single* rather than a *double* application of the Principle of Indifference) are used to obtain numerical values. In the *first* place, the interpretation usually allows us to obtain probabilities which agree with our *intuition*. Given, for example, a lottery ticket with 1 chance in 1000 of winning, most people do not *expect* to win. There are, after all, 999 "unfavorable" cases and only 1 "favorable." On the other hand, if someone had the 999 tickets, he would feel very confident about his chances of winning the lottery. Of course, given 1 ticket or 999, no one could be *certain* of the outcome. Nevertheless, in either case most people would have very little doubt about it. The logical interpretation is usually in complete agreement with such *intuitions*. In the *second* place, the interpretation frequently allows us to obtain probabilities which agree with our *observations*. Suppose, for example, that someone repeatedly played lotteries in either of the ways suggested above (i.e., always buying only 1 or else 999 of a total possible 1000), he would win with roughly the same frequency. That is, in the long run he would win just about *once* or else nearly 999 times in every 1000. We would observe, then, a *frequency* of wins which corresponds fairly closely to the probabilities obtained with the logical interpretation. Coins usually *do* turn up heads about half of the time in long-run experiments and each of the sides of a die *does* turn up roughly $\frac{1}{6}$ of the time. The logical interpretation agrees fairly well with such *observations*.

This second advantage leads directly to a *third*, namely, that we may use sentences about logical probability (or probabilities based only on logical considerations) to *appraise* predictions and actual frequencies *prior to observation*. To see how this is possible, we must be very clear about the meaning of probability sentences on the logical interpretation. We have said that sentences about logical probability are logically true (analytic) or logically false (self-contradictory); e.g.,

The probability of the hypothesis that a head will turn up is $\frac{1}{2}$.

is logically true if it is true at all or it is logically false. This is tantamount to saying that such probability sentences have no *predictive force*. They are not *about* what will or will not happen. Rather, as their name suggests, they are *about probability conceived as a logical relation;* e.g., the example above is an analytic sentence about the logical relation (probability) of a particular hypothesis, namely,

A head will turn up.

to some evidence (sentences) about the shape of a coin, etc. The latter hypothesis *has* predictive force; i.e., it is a prediction *about* what will or will not happen. It is an empirical sentence *about* the *appearance* of a particular face of a coin. Now, the fact that probability sentences (on the logical interpretation) are not predictions does *not* prevent us from using them to assess predictions *prior* to the observation of outcomes. If, for instance, Otto Optimist buys 1 of 1000 lottery tickets and *predicts* that he will win the lottery, we know just about what this prediction is worth. We know just about what it is worth *because* we have the (logical) probability sentence

> The probability of the hypothesis that a ticket numbered such and such will be drawn is $\frac{1}{1000}$.

The probability sentence has no predictive force, but it may be used to *assess* predictions.

Again, suppose Otto has always bought only 1 ticket for each lottery *and* that he has won roughly 50 percent of the time. Given our probability sentence, such success is incredible—unless, of course, the lotteries have been "fixed". Given Otto's purchases, his success, and our probability sentence, we *suspect* that there has been foul play. Nobody is *that* lucky. What we are doing, then, is using our probability sentence to appraise the actual frequency of success which Otto has been experiencing. *Before* we observe that frequency, we use the logical interpretation to *estimate* it. The more that frequency disagrees with our logical probability estimate, the more we suspect that chance alone is not responsible for Otto's success. Hence, while the probability sentence has no predictive force, it may be used to *assess actual frequencies.*

The *fourth* advantage of the logical interpretation is that it is always *applicable.* There is no particular problem applying the notion to such unique events as; e.g., the death of your Uncle Stanley on the last day of October 1980. Finally, we must list the comparatively *easy access* to probability values as the *fifth* advantage of this interpretation. We do not have to engage in any lengthy investigation of some part of the physical world or examine anyone's psychological characteristics; i.e., we do not have to consider the physical universe or anyone's psychology. We merely have to consider relevant logical possibilities and determine certain ratios among various numbers of them.

There are at least two *disadvantages* of the logical interpretation. In the *first* place, there is the problem of the *proper application* of the Principle of Indifference to obtain initial probabilities. According to Carnap's logical range theory, the principle should be applied first to *structure* descriptions and then to state descriptions. If it is applied this way, however, we may obtain very *inaccurate estimates* of actual frequencies. Suppose, for example, that we toss 10 fair coins all at once and ask for the probability of the hypothesis that all 10 will turn up heads. We have, then, a world with one primitive property (that of being a head) and 10 individuals. Hence, we have 11 possible structure descriptions, namely, all 10 individuals (coins) are heads, exactly 9 are heads, 8 are heads, . . . , none are heads. Hence, applying the principle to structure descriptions, the initial probability of the hypothesis that all 10 coins will turn up heads is $\frac{1}{11}$. But the actual frequency of the event described by this hypothesis is (or *would be* if we ran some experiments) *much closer* to $\frac{1}{1024}$. The application of the Principle of Indifference to structure descriptions, then, may yield very inaccurate estimates.

It *seems* that the way out of this problem is already before us, for if the principle is applied directly to *state* descriptions, as suggested by Wittgenstein and von Kries, we obtain an initial probability of $\frac{1}{1024}$ for the hypothesis in question. This is basically the approach taken by the classical theory of measuring probabilities. Carnap has insisted, however, that our problems cannot be eliminated in this fashion. His argument runs as follows. According to a generally accepted **Principle of Learning from Experience,** "other things being equal, a future event is to be regarded as the more probable, the greater the relative frequency of similar events observed so far under similar circumstances". But if the Principle of Indifference is applied directly to state descriptions, then we may be forced to violate the Principle of Learning from Experience. We may be forced to assign conditional probabilities to hypotheses which are *always identical* to their initial probabilities; i.e., we may be unable to alter probabilities by altering our evidence. Hence, we cannot apply the Principle of Indifference directly to state descriptions.

With the help of Example 5 in our discussion of the logical range theory, we may illustrate the problem Carnap has suggested. (Our illustration is the same in all important respects to one that Carnap constructed using black and white balls in an urn.) If the Principle of Indifference is applied directly to the state descriptions in Table 5.22, each state description will have an initial probability of $\frac{1}{8}$. If we know that three coins have been tossed and that the first two have turned up heads, then the probability of the hypothesis that the third coin is a head is *not* $\frac{3}{4}$ as before, but $\frac{1}{2}$. That is, now we have the probability of the evidence 'E'

$$Ha \cdot Hb$$

is $\frac{1}{4}$, the sum of the probabilities of S1 and S2 (i.e., the range of 'E'). The probability of 'H and E'

$$Ha \cdot Hb \cdot Hc$$

is now $\frac{1}{8}$, the probability of S1. Hence, the probability of 'H given E' is $(\frac{1}{8})/(\frac{1}{4}) = \frac{1}{2}$. Suppose, now, that *instead* of the evidence 'E', we are given 'E''

Coin a is not a head and b is a head.

That is, we know three coins have been tossed and

$$\overline{H}a \cdot Hb.$$

What is the probability of the hypothesis that c is a head? It is *still* $\frac{1}{2}$. The range of 'E' is S4 and S6. (See Table 5.22.) Hence, the probability of 'E' is $\frac{1}{8} + \frac{1}{8} = \frac{1}{4}$. '$H$ and E' is interpreted as

$$\overline{H}a \cdot Hb \cdot Hc$$

which is just S4. Hence, its probability is $\frac{1}{8}$. Dividing $\frac{1}{8}$ by $\frac{1}{4}$ we have $\frac{1}{2}$, the probability of the given hypothesis. Hence, given

$$Ha \cdot Hb$$

or

$$\overline{H}a \cdot Hb$$

the probability of 'Hc' is $\frac{1}{2}$. But the sum of the probabilities for the state descriptions in the range of 'Hc' *alone* is *also* $\frac{1}{2}$. Thus, the conditional probability of this hypothesis is *identical* to its initial probability; i.e., we are unable to alter the probability of the hypothesis by altering the evidence. Hence, the Principle of Learning from Experience is violated if the Principle of Indifference is applied directly to state descriptions. Therefore, according to Carnap, it would be a mistake to assume that the problem of the proper application of the Principle of Indifference is solved by applying the principle to state descriptions instead of structure descriptions.

The *second* disadvantage of the logical interpretation has been suggested by the philosopher Alfred Ayer. Ayer claims that regardless of the amount of evidence gathered, every correctly determined probability sentence is as good as every other. A probability sentence on this interpretation is *logically* true if it is true at all. Among equally analytically true sentences, we cannot select better or worse, more or less correct ones. They are all equally correct and, therefore, equally acceptable. It follows, then, that there is no reason for ever trying to *increase* the amount of *evidence* gathered for any hypothesis. Once we have any properly determined probability sentence, we should halt all investigation and the sooner the better. Consider the following example.

There is going to be a football game Saturday between the professional teams of Atlanta and Boston. We are interested in determining the probability of the hypothesis 'H' that Atlanta will win. If we assume that we know nothing about either team, we should say the probability of our hypothesis is $\frac{1}{2}$. *A priori* Atlanta's winning is as probable as not. Suppose, however, that we have three bits of information.

A: Six of Atlanta's better players are ill.
B: The game is going to be played in Boston's stadium.
C: Atlanta has lost seven games in a row.

Furthermore, suppose we know that the initial probability of 'H' is *higher* than the probability of 'H' relative to the initial evidence 'E and A'; that relative to 'E

and A and B', the probability of '*H*' is even *lower* than it is relative to '*E and A*';
and that relative to '*E and A and B and C*', the probability of '*H*' is *still lower*.
That is, as we increase our evidence, the probability of the hypothesis that Atlanta
will win is *decreased*. It is becoming less and less probable that Atlanta will win.
Now, most people would say that the probability of a hypothesis should be determined on *all* available relevant evidence. Carnap calls this the **Principle of
Total Evidence.** They would say that the most *accurate* probability sentence about
the outcome of the given game is that which is based on *all* our evidence '*E and
A and B and C*'. But there is *no warrant* at all for such claims on the logical interpretation. Each of the probability sentences suggested above would be as accurate as
every other, since each one is necessarily true. Thus, according to Ayer, there is
no reason to prefer the sentence involving *all* our evidence over that involving
only the *initially* given evidence. Any resources spent gathering evidence beyond
the initially given evidence are wasted.

Review problems for Sec. 5.2 b: ii)–c.

1. Define the following.

    a) state description
    b) logical range of a sentence
    c) isomorphic state descriptions

    d) structure description
    e) primitive property

2. Using Table 5.21 in Sec. b: ii) and the wedge '$\vee$' to abbreviate 'or', find the range of

    a) Rb
    b) $\bar{R}a$

    c) $Ra \cdot \bar{R}b$
    d) $Ra \vee Rb$

3. Using Table 5.22 in Sec. b ii), find the range of

    a) $\bar{H}c$
    b) $Ha \cdot Hb$
    c) $Ha \cdot \bar{H}c$
    d) $Ha \cdot \bar{H}b \cdot Hc$
    e) $\bar{H}b \cdot Hc$

    f) $Ha \vee Hc$
    g) $Hb \vee \bar{H}c$
    h) $\bar{H}a \vee Hb$
    i) $Ha \cdot Hb \cdot Hc$
    j) $Ha \vee \bar{H}b \vee Hc$

4. A world with *r* primitive properties and *n* individuals has 2^{nr} state descriptions. How
    many state descriptions do each of the following "little" worlds contain?

    a) $r = 2, n = 3$
    b) $r = 3, n = 4$

    c) $r = 2, n = 7$
    d) $r = 4, n = 4$

5. Which, if any, of the state descriptions in the following groups are isomorphic to
    others in the group? Explain.

    a) i) $Ba \cdot Bb \cdot Bc \cdot Bd$
        ii) $Ba \cdot \bar{B}b \cdot Bc \cdot Bd$
        iii) $Ba \cdot Bb \cdot Bc \cdot \bar{B}d$

  b)   i) $\bar{R}a \cdot Rb \cdot \bar{R}c \cdot Rd \cdot Re$
          ii) $Ra \cdot Rb \cdot Rc \cdot \bar{R}d \cdot \bar{R}e$
        iii) $\bar{R}a \cdot Rb \cdot \bar{R}c \cdot Rd \cdot Re$
  c)   i) $Ra \cdot \bar{R}b \cdot Sa \cdot \bar{S}b \cdot Ta \cdot Tb$
          ii) $\bar{R}a \cdot Rb \cdot \bar{S}a \cdot \bar{S}b \cdot Ta \cdot Tb$
        iii) $Ra \cdot Rb \cdot \bar{S}a \cdot Sb \cdot Ta \cdot Tb$

6. Using Table 5.21, find the probability of the following according to the logical range theory.

    a) $\bar{R}a$ e) $Ra \lor Rb$
    b) $\bar{R}a \cdot \bar{R}b$ f) Rb given Ra
    c) $\bar{R}a \lor Rb$ g) Rb given $\bar{R}a$
    d) $\bar{R}a \cdot Rb$

7. Using Table 5.22, find the probability of the following according to the logical range theory.

    a) Ha f) $Ha \lor Hb \lor Hc$
    b) $\bar{H}a \cdot Hb$ g) Hc, given $Ha \cdot Hb$
    c) $\bar{H}a \cdot \bar{H}b \cdot \bar{H}c$ h) $Hb \cdot Hc$, given Ha
    d) $Ha \cdot Hb \cdot \bar{H}c$ i) $\bar{H}b \cdot Hc$, given Ha
    e) $\bar{H}b \lor Hc$ j) $\bar{H}c$, given $Ha \cdot Hb$

8. What are three advantages of the logical interpretation?

9. What objection was raised against the application of the Principle of Indifference directly to state descriptions? What, if any, sort of a reply might be made to it?

10. What, if any, reply might be offered to the objection that one correctly determined logical probability sentence is as good as any other?

5.3   The physical interpretation

a)   The Problem of Meaning

As we suggested earlier, according to the physical interpretation, 'probability' is interpreted as a *physical attribute* of certain physical systems. The systems may be physical ranges, experimental arrangements, or sequences of events. Thus, for example, the probability sentence

         The probability of throwing a six with this fair die is $\frac{1}{6}$.

may be given any of the following (rough) physical interpretations.

The proportion of the *physical range* of the event of a six turning up to the *physical range* of the event of tossing a fair die is $\frac{1}{6}$.

The experimental arrangement of tossing a fair die has the *propensity* of turning up a six about $\frac{1}{6}$ of the time.

The *relative frequency* (in the long run) of tossing a six with a fair die is $\frac{1}{6}$.

The proportions of physical ranges, the propensities, and the relative frequencies are all physical attributes of certain physical systems. The question of the existence, comparative amount, or degree of the physical attributes possessed by any systems is an *empirical* or *factual* one. That is, the answers to such questions must be determined by empirical investigation, *not* by logical analysis. Thus, probability sentences are *empirically true* if they are true at all and *empirically false* if they are false at all. Their truth or falsity is determined *a posteriori* if it is determined at all. Hence, experience is highly relevant to these sentences.

b) THE PROBLEM OF MEASUREMENT

Granting, then, that probabilities are to be determined by and based on physical considerations alone, the question again arises, *How do we obtain initial numerical probabilities?* A rough provisional answer to this question is this: *Count* physical attributes and determine the ratios of certain numbers of these to certain numbers of others. We shall consider two theories of measuring probabilities within the physical interpretation which might be roughly characterized by this answer, namely, the *physical range theory* and *frequency theories*.

i) **The physical range theory.** The physical range theory of measuring probabilities, as it has been developed by the philosopher William Kneale, is similar to Carnap's logical range theory in two important respects. The notions of a *range* and a *Principle of Indifference* are fundamental for both theories. But it is precisely in these two fundamental ideas that the main *differences* between the two theories lie. In the next few paragraphs we shall explain these differences. We shall *not* present the physical range theory from the bottom up as it were. Rather we shall *assume* that the physical range theory is *exactly the same* as the logical range theory already discussed, and we shall merely make *two* changes in the latter.

To begin with, you recall that the *logical* range of a sentence is the class of those state descriptions in which the sentence is true and that we find out which state descriptions are in this class *a priori* by logical analysis. Now, we may say that the **physical range** of an *event* is the class of those states of affairs which contain that event and that we find out which states of affairs contain the event in question *a posteriori* by empirical investigation. Consider, for example, the little world described in Table 5.21. The *physically* possible states of affairs are described by the four state descriptions. To say that these states of affairs are **physically possible** is to say that given the existing laws of nature (e.g., the laws of physics, chemistry, biology, etc.), any of these states of affairs *may* occur. These are, to use Kneale's phrase, "real possibilities." The events *contained in* these states of affairs or the events which *constitute* these states of affairs *are* contained in or *do* constitute these states of affairs *as a matter of fact*, not as a matter of logic. The sentence

> The *physical range* of the event of Arf's being red is the class consisting of the states of affairs described by S1 and S2 (in Table 5.21).

is a factual (or empirical, or synthetic) one. We must examine the little world to find out whether or not the event in question is *physically* possible given those states of affairs. We know the event is *logically* possible because we know the sentence describing that event is not self-contradictory. But we must investigate the world to reach a decision about physical possibility. This, then, is the *first* fundamental difference between the physical and logical range theories: In the *physical* range theory, the range of an *event* is a *physical entity* (a physical possibility) which either exists as a matter of *fact* or does not. In the *logical* range theory, on the other hand, the range of a *sentence* is a *logical entity* (a logical possibility) which exists as a matter of *logic* or does not.

You recall that the Principle of Indifference is: In the *absence of any reason* for considering certain indivisible events (or sentences) to be *not* equally possible, they may be considered equally possible. The **Physical Principle of Indifference** suggested by Kneale is: In the *presence of a reason* for considering certain indivisible events to be equally possible, they must be considered equally possible. If we conduct a thorough investigation of certain events which, for one reason or another, we are treating as *indivisible* and find good reasons for considering them as equally possible, then we *should* assign them equal initial probabilities. Notice that these initial probabilities are assigned (perhaps *discovered* would be more appropriate) *a posteriori*. We *know* certain events are equally probable; that is why we say they are. This contrasts sharply with the principle of the logical theorists who say that certain events may be regarded as equally probable *because* they do not have contrary evidence. The physical theorist bases his initial probabilities on the *information* he has obtained by empirical investigation. The logical theorist bases his initial probabilities on his *lack* of information. While the particular values obtained by each theory might be identical, the *bases* of the assignments are quite distinct.

Given the Physical Principle of Indifference and physical ranges, then, we would proceed to obtain initial probabilities by applying the principle directly to *state descriptions*. Since this procedure and its problems are similar to those discussed under the logical range theory, we shall not take them up again here.

Before we leave the physical range theory, it is worthwhile and convenient to mention the so-called **propensity theory** which was introduced by the philosopher Karl Popper. Popper claims that when we utter such sentences as, say,

The probability of tossing a head with a fair coin is 0.5.

we mean that a particular part of the physical universe, namely our *experimental arrangement*, is such that it has a *tendency, disposition,* or *propensity* to produce the event of a head turning up about one-half of the time.

If we think of an experimental arrangement as a set of physical ranges with certain propensities, then we have a rough intuitive idea of the propensity theory. Instead of talking about ranges of physical *possibilities*, we would talk about ranges of physical *propensities*. Instead of measuring ranges of possibilities, we would measure ranges of propensities. The only difference, then, between a propensity theory of measuring probabilities and a physical range theory would be the difference between physical *propensities* and physical *possibilities—whatever that difference is*.

Alternatively, we might ignore the problem of what physical propensities *are*, or are *like*, and concentrate on the actual *frequencies* of the occurrences of certain events. The frequencies would be regarded as direct manifestations of propensities or tendencies in certain experimental arrangements. With this view (which seems to be nearer to Popper's), probabilities in the sense of propensities are measured by relative frequencies. Whether or not there is a *significant* difference between this view of the propensity interpretation and the frequency theories we are going to discuss is an open question.

ii) Frequency theories. We shall consider two types of frequency theories, one involving sequences with a finite number of elements and the other involving sequences with an infinite number of elements.

iia) According to the **finite frequency theory** of measuring probabilities which has been advocated by Bertrand Russell, we measure the probability of an event in three steps: 1. Select a relevant sequence of repetitive events and count its members. 2. Count the number of cases in that sequence which are "favorable" to the event whose probability is to be measured. 3. The ratio of the number of "favorable" cases to the total number of events in the selected sequence is the required numerical value. This ratio is the *relative frequency* of the occurrence of "favorable" cases in some sequences of events. It is the frequency of "favorable" cases relative to the selected sequence.

There are two main differences between this theory and the classical theory. The first has already been emphasized. Here we obtain numerical values *not* by considering mere logical possibilities but by *observing* some physical system. The second important difference is the introduction of the idea of a *sequence* of *repetitive events*. An event is called **repetitive** if it is repeatable an unlimited number of times; e.g., the appearance of a head on the toss of a certain coin, producing a defective machine, drawing a ball from a barrel (with replacement), catching a fish, shooting a duck, hitting a baseball, etc. Strictly speaking, we should say that repetitive events are nothing more than *kinds, types,* or *sorts* of events. It is the *kind* or *type* that recurs, not any particular event. You cannot, for instance, make *the very same hit* on your second turn at bat that you made on your first turn. But you can make *another hit;* i.e., you can repeat the *type* of performance but not the *particular* performance. A particular performance is an event which is not repeatable and it may, therefore, be called a **unique** event; e.g., the appearance of a head on the *next* toss of a certain coin, the birth of Fabian, drawing the very *first* ball from a barrel, shooting the *third* duck to fly over your barn, hitting three homeruns in one game for the first time, the death of Teddy Roosevelt, etc. The distinguishing characteristic of *unique* events is that they occur *only* once. The distinguishing characteristic of *repetitive* (strictly, *kinds, types,* or *sorts* of) events is that they *may* occur more than once. A **sequence** of repetitive events is an aggregate of such events. As far as the finite frequency theory is concerned, only *finite* sequences are considered.

EXAMPLE 1

What is the probability of tossing a three with a fair die?

Solution. To measure the probability of tossing a three with a fair die, we begin by *tossing the die* a number of times. Each toss of the die is a member of a *sequence* of tosses which is called a **reference class;** the reference class is nothing more than a special kind of *sample space.* It always has a *finite* number of members. The *original* or *initially given* reference classes are still called 'universes of discourse'. If, for example, a die is tossed six times then we have a sequence (or a reference class, or a universe of discourse) with six events. Each time the face with three dots turns up, we have a "favorable" case; e.g., if we toss only one three in six times, we have one "favorable" case. The measure of the probability of throwing a three with a fair die, then, is simply the ratio of the number of "favorable" cases to the total number of events in the reference class. In the present case, we might have a probability of $\frac{1}{6}$.

EXAMPLE 2

Rodney Rotgut produced 100 jugs of homemade whiskey. He sold 90 of them at $1.00 a jug and the others at $.50. What is the probability of selling a jug of Rotgut's whiskey for $1.00?

Solution. Our reference class consists of the sequence of 100 *sales*. There are 90 "favorable" cases in this class; i.e., 90 jugs were sold at $1.00 each. Hence $\frac{90}{100}$ or 90 percent of the jugs sold at $1.00. Thus, the probability of selling a jug of Rotgut's whiskey for $1.00 is 0.9.

EXAMPLE 3

Suppose you are picking apples from a tree in the dark. After your basket is full, you bring it into the barn and examine its contents. Table 5.31 is a summary of what you find.

	Wormy	Nonwormy
Red apples	20	30
Green apples	10	40

TABLE 5.31

Before venturing up the tree again, you are interested in finding the following probabilities:

a)   The probability of picking a red apple.
b)   The probability of picking a wormy apple.
c)   The probability that any green apple picked will be wormy.
d)   The probability that any nonwormy apple picked will be red.

Solution. To begin with, you have a sequence of 100 *picks*. To determine the number of times you picked a red apple, find the *sum* of the entries on the *line* following 'red apples'. You picked 50 red apples. Hence, the answer to a) is: The probability of picking a red apple is $\frac{50}{100}$ or 0.5. To determine the number of wormy apples picked, find the *sum* of entries in the *column* below 'wormy'. You picked 30 wormy apples. Hence, the answer to b) is: The probability of picking a wormy apple is $\frac{30}{100}$ or 0.3.

Here c) and d) both involve *conditional* probabilities. In c) we are given the special condition that a *green* apple has been picked, and we want to know the probability that it is wormy. Our *new sample space*, then, is the sequence consisting of only 50 *green* apples. To determine the number of green apples which are wormy, simply read the entry in the lower left corner of the table. You picked 10 green apples with worms. Hence, the ratio of the number of green *and* wormy apples to the number of green apples is $\frac{10}{50}$; i.e., $\frac{10}{50}$ or 20 percent of all the green apples picked are wormy. Thus, the answer to c) is: The probability that any green apple picked will be wormy is 0.2.

To determine the probability that any nonwormy apple picked will be red, begin by finding the total number of nonwormy apples; i.e., find the sum of the entries in the column below 'nonwormy'. Our *conditional sample space* contains 70 nonwormy apples. Exactly 30 of these are red. Hence, the ratio of the number of nonwormy *and* red apples to the total number of nonwormy apples is $\frac{30}{70}$. Thus, the probability that any nonwormy apple picked will be red is $\frac{3}{7}$ or about 0.43.

iib)   According to the **limiting frequency theory** of measuring probabilities which has been developed by Richard von Mises, we measure the probability of an event in three steps: 1. Select a relevant *random* sequence of events. 2. Determine the *limit* of the relative frequency of "favorable" cases in this sequence. 3. That *limit* is the required numerical value.

There are two main differences between this *limiting* frequency theory and the *finite* frequency theory. First, here we are concerned with sequences which are infinitely long. If we tried to *count* all the members in such sequences, we would never finish counting. Second, we are concerned with *limiting* values of relative frequencies in such sequences, not merely with a finite number of events. The first of these novelties requires no explanation, but the second does. More precisely, we must begin with an explanation of the ideas of a *limit* and a *random* sequence.

Suppose a coin is tossed 10 times with the following outcomes.

$$H \quad H \quad T \quad H \quad T \quad H \quad T \quad H \quad T \quad T$$

The '*H*'s and '*T*'s are short for 'heads' and 'tails', respectively. After each toss we may determine the *proportion* of heads up to that point. The fractions below each '*H*' and '*T*' indicate these proportions.

H	H	T	H	T	H	T	H	T	T
1/1	2/2	2/3	3/4	3/5	4/6	4/7	5/8	5/9	5/10

After four tosses, $\frac{3}{4}$ of the events in the sequence are "favorable". After seven tosses, $\frac{4}{7}$ of the events are "favorable". At the end of our experiment, the ratio of "favorable" cases to the total number of events in the sequence is $\frac{5}{10}$. As we increased the number of members in this sequence, the proportion of heads approached $\frac{1}{2}$. If the proportion of heads continues to approach $\frac{1}{2}$ as the length of the sequence is increased indefinitely, then we say that the *limit* of the relative frequency of heads in this sequence is $\frac{1}{2}$. Similarly, if the length of the sequence is increased indefinitely and the proportion of heads approaches $\frac{3}{4}$ or $\frac{5}{6}$, then we say that the *limit* of the relative frequency of heads in this sequence is $\frac{3}{4}$ or $\frac{5}{6}$, respectively. In either of these latter two cases, we would say that the coin was not fair. Quite generally, then, we may define the limit of a sequence of such fractions as follows. The **limit** of a sequence of fractions is a number which is such that after a certain place in the sequence has been reached, all the fractions in the sequence are very close to it. To make this phrase "very close" more precise, we may say that given *any* small number e, it is possible to find a place in the sequence after which all the fractions lie between the limit L and e (i.e., between $L - e$ and $L + e$). Any sequence which has a limit is called **convergent. Divergent** sequences have no limits. If a sequence *is* convergent then "in the long run" the procedure we have just described will find it.

The second notion that must be explained is that of *randomness*. Suppose the following sequence is continued indefinitely.

(A) $H \quad T \quad H \quad T \quad H \quad T \quad H \quad T \quad H \quad T \quad \ldots$

The limit of the relative frequency of '*H*'s in this sequence is $\frac{1}{2}$. In *this* respect, there may be no difference between this sequence (A) and the following.

(B)   *T   H   H   H   T   H   T   H   T   T   . . .*

However, while the *limit* of the relative frequency of heads in both of these sequences may be the same, the *order* of the sequences is quite different. The '*H*'s' and '*T*'s' are distributed in a *regular* fashion in (A); i.e., every '*H*' is followed by a '*T*' and vice versa. But in (B) the '*H*'s' and '*T*'s' are distributed in an *irregular* fashion; i.e., sometimes an '*H*' is followed by a '*T*', sometimes it is followed by two '*T*'s', sometimes it is followed by another '*H*', etc. The '*H*'s' and '*T*'s' in the latter sequence are supposed to illustrate the beginning of a sequence of randomly distributed '*H*'s' and '*T*'s'; i.e., a sequence of '*H*'s' and '*T*'s' such that *no one knows or could know what is coming next.*

Two conditions have been used to define random distributions. A sufficient condition of randomness called 'insensitivity to place selection' was introduced by von Mises. A necessary condition of randomness called 'freedom from aftereffects' was introduced by Karl Popper. We shall use the former stronger condition in our definition of 'random sequences'.

Insensitivity to Place Selection: Each of the two sequences (A) and (B) illustrated above contains the first 10 members of an infinitely long sequence. In (A), the first member of the sequence is a head, the second is a tail, the third a head, etc. In other words, we could describe the order of (A) by saying that the *first place* in the sequence is occupied by a head, the second place is occupied by a tail, the third place by a head, etc. Now, if we selected every member of the sequence (A) occupying an *even* place, we would have a sequence of *tails* made up of the tail in the second place, the tail in the fourth place, the tail in the sixth place, etc. That is to say, we would have constructed a *subsequence* according to the following *rule of place selection:* Select all even-placed members of the original sequence. The limit of the relative frequency of '*H*'s' in the subsequence is 0. Applying this same rule to (B), we have the following subsequence.

(B′)   *H   H   H   H   T   · · ·*
             1/1   2/2   3/3   4/4   4/5

As the fractions beneath the letters show, the limit of the relative frequency of '*H*'s' in this subsequence is *not* $\frac{1}{2}$, but $\frac{4}{5}$. Other rules of place selection might select every odd-placed member of the original sequence, every third place, every fourth place, etc.

If a sequence is such that events are distributed in it in such a way that the limit of the relative frequency of the events in a *subsequence* constructed according to *any* rule of place selection (subject to three conditions mentioned below) is the same as the limit of the relative frequency of the events in the original sequence, then the latter is said to be **insensitive to place selection.** Sequences which are insensitive to place selection are **random** sequences; i.e., they are sequences of randomly distributed events.

The three conditions put on rules of place selection are that a) they must make no reference to any event or attribute whose probability is being determined; b) they must be applicable to a whole sequence no matter how long it is extended; and c) they must be specified *before* observing the sequence. Thus, if we happened to be interested in deciding whether or not '*H*'s' are randomly distributed in a sequence of '*H*'s' and '*T*'s', then, according to a), acceptable rules of place selection would not make *any* references to '*H*'s'. A rule which selected only the *first two* members of a sequence would be rejected by b) because it does not apply to the whole sequence. Again, if we made up our rules *after* observing the sequence, then if we had the time, energy, and ingenuity, we could always make up a rule to construct a *subsequence* in which the limit of the relative frequency of certain events in it *differed* from the limit in the *original* sequence. Hence, according to c), only rules which are specified *before* observing the sequence are acceptable.

Freedom from Aftereffect: Consider the following sequence (C).

(C)   *H H H T H T T T H T H H H T T H T T T H* ...

The limit of the relative frequency of '*H*'s' in this sequence is $\frac{1}{2}$. If we formed a subsequence by selecting every member of (C) which is *immediately preceded* by a '*T*', we would find the following.

(C1)   *H T T H H T H T T H* ...

The limit of the relative frequency of '*H*' in (C1) is also $\frac{1}{2}$. Again, if we formed a subsequence by selecting every member of (C) which is immediately preceded by '*H T H*', we would obtain the following.

(C2)   *T H*

The limit of the relative frequency of '*H*' in (C2) is $\frac{1}{2}$. Similarly, selecting every member which is immediately preceded by '*H H H T*', we find a subsequence in which the limit of the relative frequency of '*H*' is $\frac{1}{2}$.

If a sequence is such that events are distributed in it in such a way that the limit of the relative frequency of the events in a *subsequence* constructed by selecting the events immediately following *any* group of predecessors is the *same* as the limit of the relative frequency of the events in the original sequence, then the latter is said to be **free from aftereffect.** According to Popper, then, sequences which are free from aftereffect may be called 'random sequences'; i.e., they are sequences of randomly distributed events. Since, as we mentioned above and as G. H. von Wright has demonstrated, *freedom from aftereffect* is only a *necessary* condition of randomness, we are not using it in our definition of 'random sequences'. The fact that it is a *weaker* condition than *insensitivity to place selection* may be seen by noticing that a rule for the selection of members with certain predecessors is nothing more than a *special sort* of rule of place selection; i.e., Popper's condition is included in von Mises' condition. Consider two examples of probability measurements with the limiting frequency theory.

EXAMPLE 4

The Hangitall Company produces about 4000 coat hangers a week. The quality control department claims that about 5 percent of the hangers made every week are defective. What is the probability that any hanger produced by the Hangitall Company is defective?

Solution. We have a theoretically unlimited sequence of *hangers produced* by Hangitall, and we know that week after week about 5 percent of them are defective. We suppose the defective hangers are randomly distributed and that the limit of the relative frequency of defective hangers produced by Hangitall is 0.05. Hence, the probability that any hanger produced by the Hangitall Company is defective is 0.05.

EXAMPLE 5

A certain baseball player has a lifetime batting average of 0.282. What is the probability that he will make a hit?

Solution. We have a theoretically unlimited sequence of *times at bat.* We suppose that the hits are randomly distributed in this sequence and that the limit of the relative frequency of hits is roughly 0.28. Hence, the probability that the given baseball player will make a hit is 0.28.

c)   SOME ADVANTAGES AND DISADVANTAGES OF THE PHYSICAL INTERPRETATION

There are two main advantages of the physical interpretation. The first one reveals an immediate superiority *over* the logical interpretation. The *first* advantage of the physical interpretation is the resolution of Alfred Ayer's problem of the equal correctness of all nonself-contradictory probability sentences. On the logical interpretation, such sentences are analytic and, therefore, one is as good as another. Hence, there is no reason to prefer probability sentences involving *all* available relevant evidence over those involving only *initially* given evidence. However, the physical interpretation provides quite different options. On this interpretation, probability sentences are never logically true (analytic) or logically false (self-contradictory). They are factual (or empirical, or synthetic) sentences which may be *corrected* or *improved* by further investigation. Hence, there is an excellent reason to prefer probability sentences involving *all* available relevant evidence over those involving only initially given evidence; namely, the former *could* be more accurate.

The *second* advantage of the physical interpretation is that it satisfies the *intuitive belief* of many people that probability sentences are *about* physical phenomena. Many people believe that when we utter a probability sentence, we *mean* to be saying something about some part of the physical universe. Hence, any interpretation which does not meet this requirement is intuitively unsatisfactory for these people. Certainly such sentences as

The probability of tossing a head with this fair coin is 0.5.

seem to be analogous to

The temperature of the room is 70°F.
The weight of the stone is 14 pounds.
The length of the bridge is 100 feet.

Each of these sentences seems to be *about* some property of the physical universe. Most people would reject any interpretation of the latter three sentences which had the result that the sentences were not *about* physical phenomena but *about* logical possibilities or psychological attitudes. Similarly, there are many people who would reject any interpretation of probability sentences which have the same result. The fact, then, that the physical interpretation does not have this result contributes to its intuitive satisfactoriness and must be considered a major advantage.

There are two main disadvantages of the physical interpretation. The *first* disadvantage is that sentences about physical probabilities are *not available prior to observation* to be used to appraise predictions and actual frequencies. For example, recall the case of the lottery which Otto believed he would win though he had a ticket with an *a priori* probability of $\frac{1}{1000}$ of being drawn. Our appraisal of Otto's prediction *seemed* quite legitimate, but if the logical interpretation is given up in favor of the physical one, such an appraisal would be completely without foundation. On the physical view, *prior* to observation we have no reason at all to assign any event any probability. Hence, on this view, we must abandon *a priori* appraisals of predictions. Again, suppose Otto won roughly 50 percent of the lotteries in which he bought only one ticket. Given this information and the physical interpretation, we have no good reason to *suspect* foul play. We have certain events occurring with a certain frequency and, for all we know, that frequency is just as it should be; i.e., for all we know, the lotteries are not "fixed". Again, then, while the *prior* appraisal of this frequency *seemed* legitimate, such appraisals must be abandoned when the physical interpretation is adopted. On the physical interpretation, logical possibilities are simply useless for the assessment of predictions and actual frequencies.

The *second* disadvantage of the physical interpretation is that *either* a problem of the proper application of the Physical Principle of Indifference *or* a problem of the proper selection of reference classes must be faced. If either a physical range or (one view of) a propensity theory is used to measure probabilities, then one must decide whether the physical principle is to be applied to state descriptions or to structure descriptions. This is basically the same problem that logical theorists face. On the other hand, if a frequency theory is used to measure probabilities, then one must decide how to select proper reference classes. This problem is frequently overlooked, but it is as serious as the other. Consider the following example.

Suppose it is given that

1)   The probability of '*H given A*' is *x*.
2)   The probability of '*H, given A and B*' is *y*. ($x \neq y$)

Each of these sentences gives the probability of '*H*' relative to a different reference class. But which sentence should we accept? Which is the most accurate? Most people would say that we should prefer sentence 2) because that involves all our available evidence or, as Hans Reichenbach says, "the narrowest class for which reliable statistics can be compiled". Unfortunately this answer is not (as Reichenbach recognized) always helpful. There are cases in which 1) would be preferred to 2). For example, suppose it is known that

1′)   The probability that Roger will receive an 'F' on a math exam *given* his past performance on such exams is *x*.
2′)   The probability that Roger will receive an 'F' on a math exam, *given* his past performance on such exams *and* his past performance on music exams is *y*. ($x \neq y$)

This time 1′) would be accepted as a more accurate or reliable estimate of Roger's performance on a forthcoming math exam than 2′). It is clear, then, that the problem of the proper selection of reference classes is not solved by the "narrowest class" rule. Moreover, in the absence of some plausible solution to this problem, the choice of proper reference classes remains somewhat arbitrary.

Before closing this discussion of the physical interpretation, we must mention the problem which relative frequency theories have with *unique* events. You recall that such theories require sequences of events to begin with; i.e., the universe of discourse for such theories is always a sequence of *repetitive* events. Hence, in the absence of such a sequence, it is logically impossible to measure the probability of any event. Now, unique events are by definition events which are not repetitive. Hence, a crucial question arises for those who wish to measure probabilities using some sort of frequency theory; namely, How can we measure the probability of unique events? For example, how can we measure the probability of the death of George Washington in 1799? There are two alternatives. In the first place, the frequentist may simply deny that his theory is *applicable* to unique events and ignore them completely. Whether or not they have measurable probabilities on some other theory, he may say that they surely do not have measurable probabilities in any frequency sense. Hence, they are beside the point. On the other hand, the frequentist may consider the problem of assigning probabilities to unique events a serious challenge and attempt to meet it somehow. Hans Reichenbach's theory of the "weight of hypotheses" is just such an attempt and it will be discussed in detail in Chapter 8. Whatever the outcome of this problem of unique events, it must be emphasized that it is *not* a problem for the physical interpretation in general. It is a problem for those who wish to *measure* probabilities using some sort of frequency theory. Advocates of the physical interpretation who employ some sort of physical range or propensity theory of measuring probabilities do not have any particular problem with unique events. (Or, if they do have this problem, then it is shared by *every* other theory given *any* interpretation.)

Review problems for Sec. 5.3.

1. What is meant by 'the physical interpretation of probability sentences'?

2. What is the difference between a physical range and a logical range?

3. What is the Physical Principle of Indifference, and exactly how does it differ from the (logical) Principle of Indifference?

4. Describe the propensity theory of measuring probabilities.

5. Explain the difference between repetitive and unique events.

6. What is a reference class?

7. How is the probability of an event measured on the finite frequency theory?

Use the finite frequency theory to answer the following.

8. While I was walking down the street one bright and sunny day, I came across a great big box floating in the bay. I pulled it in and opened it up, and much to my surprise I drew out three jugs of wine, six salamis, four loaves of bread, two bags of potato chips, and five jars of pickles. Find the probability of drawing out a

a) salami

b) loaf of bread

c) jug of wine

d) jar of pickles

e) bag of potato chips

f) jug of wine *or* a bag of potato chips

g) jar of pickles *or* a loaf of bread

h) salami *or* a loaf of bread

9. A certain used-car salesman recorded the following *sales* for last year.

	1960	1961	1962	1963	Total
Fords	30	40	40	20	130
Plymouths	20	10	30	40	100
Chryslers	20	10	30	30	90
Buicks	10	30	20	20	80
Total	80	90	120	110	400

On the basis of this information, what is the probability of selling a

a) Plymouth
b) Buick
c) 1962 car
d) 1963 car
e) 1960 Ford
f) 1961 Chrysler
g) 1962 Buick
h) Buick *or* a Ford

i) Chrysler *or* a Ford
j) Ford *given* that it is a 1960 car
k) Buick *given* a 1963 car
l) Plymouth *given* a 1961 car
m) 1960 car *given* that it is a Chrysler
n) 1962 car *given* a Ford
o) 1961 car *given* a Buick

10. A young man bought a box of assorted stamps from a retired philatelist. The first 140 stamps drawn from the box were distributed as follows.

	One-cent	Two-cent	Five-cent	Airmail	Total
Canadian	10	2	3	5	20
Spanish	2	10	1	9	22
French	3	7	6	7	23
German	3	5	9	10	27
Indian	5	4	8	3	20
Japanese	15	3	4	6	28
Total	38	31	31	40	140

What is the probability of drawing out a stamp which is

a) Indian
b) French
c) Japanese
d) Spanish two-cent
e) Japanese airmail
f) German five-cent
g) Indian one-cent
h) worth five cents
i) worth one cent
j) Canadian *or* Indian
k) French *or* Spanish
l) German *or* Japanese *or* Indian
m) Canadian one-cent *or* German two-cent

n) French airmail *or* Spanish one-cent
o) German five-cent *or* Indian two-cent
p) French *given* that it is airmail
q) Japanese *given* one-cent
r) Canadian *given* two-cent
s) five-cent *given* Spanish
t) two-cent *given* German
u) one- *or* two-cent, *given* French
v) airmail *or* five-cent, *given* Indian
w) two-cent *or* five-cent, *given* Spanish
x) Canadian *or* German, *given* airmail
y) Indian *or* Japanese, *given* one-cent
z) French *or* Spanish, *given* five-cent

11. What are the two main differences between the limiting frequency and the finite frequency theories?

12. Give an informal definition of 'the limit of a sequence'.

13. What is the difference between convergent and divergent sequences?

14. What is a rule of place selection?

15. Explain the condition of insensitivity to place selection. How is it related to randomness?

16. Explain the condition of freedom from aftereffect. How is it related to randomness?

17. What is one main advantage of the physical interpretation of probability sentences?

18. What is one objection to the physical interpretation? What, if any, reply might be offered to this objection?

19. What is one disadvantage of any frequency theory of measuring probabilities? What, if any, reply might be offered to it?

5.4 The psychological interpretation

a) THE PROBLEM OF MEANING

As we suggested earlier, according to the psychological interpretation, 'probability' is interpreted as a *psychological attitude* toward the occurrence or nonoccurrence of certain events. Probability sentences are about *actual* degrees of *belief* or *credibility*. According to those who defend this interpretation, people are supposed to have various discernible *belief-states* ranging from complete certainty to total skepticism. Sometimes we say we *know* that such and such is the case; i.e., we *feel certain* that it is the case. Sometimes we say we *believe very strongly* that such and such is the case. Sometimes our belief is not quite so strong. Sometimes we have serious doubts, etc. For example, we know (if we know *anything*) that we were born; we believe very strongly that we shall survive our fiftieth birthday; we believe somewhat less strongly that we shall survive our seventieth birthday; we have serious doubts about surviving our ninetieth birthday; and we do not believe we shall be around to celebrate our one hundred and tenth birthday. Although you might believe more or less strongly about any of the events mentioned here (e.g., you may have serious doubts about surviving your seventieth birthday), none of these *belief* sentences sounds peculiar *as* a belief sentence. People do, as a matter of fact, express themselves *as if* they had various discernible *belief-states* or *actual degrees of belief* or *degrees of credibility*.

Those who adopt the psychological interpretation, then, assume that probability sentences are *about* the same things that belief sentences are about. Hence, to say that a certain event is probable is to say that someone believes it will occur. To say that it is more probable that Mr. Clean is right than that Mr. Dirty is right is to say that someone would sooner believe Mr. Clean than Mr. Dirty. To say that it is highly probable that it will rain is to say that someone strongly believes that it will rain. No attempt is made to answer the question, '*Why* does someone have this or that belief?' Logical theorists generally insist that if an answer to this question were sought, the *logical* foundations of the interpretation would be revealed; and physical theorists usually claim, on the contrary, that its *physical* foundations would show up. While it is surely an important and interesting question to raise, it may be ignored entirely without disastrous consequences. There is no logical absurdity involved in the view that probability sentences are about actual belief-states *whatever* the causes of the latter or whatever sort of evidence led to the latter. At any rate, this is where the psychological theorist begins.

b)   The Problem of Measurement

Granting, then, that probabilities are to be determined by and based on psychological considerations alone, the question again arises, *How do we obtain initial numerical probabilities?* According to the **personal odds theory** introduced by Frank P. Ramsey, we measure the probability of an event in two steps: 1. Determine the highest odds a rational person would be willing to offer in a bet on the event in question. 2. If the odds in favor of the event are m to n ($m:n$), then the probability of the event is $m/(m + n)$. The numerical values obtained by this method are usually called **personal probabilities.** The reason for the name 'personal odds theory' is apparent; i.e., the numerical values are derived from personal odds. Because the fraction $m/(m + n)$ is called a 'betting-quotient', this method of measuring probabilities is often referred to as 'the betting-quotient theory'.

Two assumptions must be noted immediately. In the first place, it is assumed that a person's *betting behavior* is a direct reflection or indication of his degrees of *belief*. If, for example, a person is willing to give *very high odds* in a bet on the occurrence of some event, then it is assumed that he *believes very strongly* that the event will occur. In the second place, contemporary defenders (e.g., Leonard J. Savage) of this or more sophisticated personal odds theories assume that the rational person referred to in step 1. should be a *slightly* "idealized" person; i.e., he is a person who never bets foolishly or capriciously. In particular, he does not place his bets in such a way that it is impossible for him to win. This is about as far as our "idealization" may be pushed, since it is *actual* degrees of belief we are interested in measuring, *not ideal* ones. John G. Kemeny has shown that if a person's betting behavior is such that the odds he is willing to give yield probabilities which are consistent with the principles of the calculus of probability, then it *is* possible for him to win; i.e., he is a sufficiently "rational" bettor and his betting-quotients are "fair".

Example 1

A certain rational bettor is willing to give odds of 3 to 1 in favor of the Red Sox in their next game. What is the probability that the Red Sox will win?

Solution. The odds in favor of the Red Sox are $m:n$, which is $3:1$. Hence, the probability that the Red Sox will win is $m/(m + n) = 3/(3 + 1) = \frac{3}{4}$.

Example 2

The owner of a certain racetrack is willing to give you odds of 100 to 1 *against* your horse coming in first. What probability is he assigning to the event of your horse coming in first?

Solution. If the owner of the track is willing to give you odds of 100 to 1 *against* your horse coming in first, then, as far as he is concerned, the probability that your horse will *not* come in first is $m/(m + n) = 100/(100 + 1) = \frac{100}{101}$. We may consider the two events, that of your horse coming in first and that of your horse not coming in first, as the only two members of our universe of discourse. The *sum* of probabilities of all the events in a universe of discourse is 1. Hence, to find the probability that your horse *will* come in first, we simply subtract $\frac{100}{101}$ from 1; i.e., the probability that the owner is assigning to the event of your horse coming in first is $\frac{1}{101}$.

Example 3

Suppose Clarence is only willing to make an *even* bet on some event. What is the probability of that event?

Solution. Clarence is not giving any odds at all. Hence, $m:n$ equals $1:1$. So the probability of the event in question is $1/(1 + 1) = \frac{1}{2}$.

c)   Some Advantages and Disadvantages of the Psychological Interpretation.

There are four main advantages of the psychological interpretation. *First*, no Principle of Indifference is required; *second*, probability sentences are empirically testable. The first point needs no explanation. With respect to the second, it must only be emphasized that the testability of probability sentences is contingent upon the assumption that degrees of belief are in complete agreement with betting behavior. While the latter is publicly observable, the former is not. Hence, the assumption is crucial for this second advantage.

The third advantage of this interpretation is identical to the second advantage of the logical interpretation and it reveals a superiority of the psychological interpretation over the physical one. The *third* advantage is that sentences about psychological probabilities are available *prior to observation* to be used in the appraisal of predictions and actual frequencies. Enough has already been said about the use of probability sentences for both purposes. All that must be added is that, *unlike* probability sentences in the logical interpretation, probability sentences in the psychological interpretation *have* predictive force. For example, on the latter interpretation

The probability that a six will turn up is $\frac{1}{6}$.

is a claim about the odds a person will or will not be willing to give in a bet on the occurrence of a six. Hence, both kinds of probability sentences may be used in appraisals, but only the latter has predictive force.

The *fourth* advantage of the psychological interpretation is its agreement with ordinary ways of talking about probabilities. We have already seen that people express themselves as if they had various recognizable belief-states and that it is generally assumed that there is a close relation between these states and probability. The psychological interpretation is only a short step from these familiar facts of life. The assumed *proximity* between belief-states and probability becomes an *identity*. To the man on the street, this must be considered a major advantage.

There are two main disadvantages of the psychological interpretation. In the *first* place, according to the psychological interpretation, the probability of an event may be radically altered if someone simply *changes his mind*. For example, if some rational bettor feels extremely confident that a coin is going to turn up heads, we would have to say the probability of tossing a head is, say, 0.9. If he suddenly changes his mind, the probability of this event might drop considerably, say, to 0.2. As long as he does not violate any of the conditions of the probability calculus and does not bet in such a way that he *cannot* win, we would have to accept his initial probability assignments. Hence, this interpretation permits much more variation of initial probabilities than most people would be willing to grant. Furthermore, this extreme variability implies a *second* disadvantage: There might be an unalterable disagreement about the probability of some hypothesis (say, some scientific theory or law) either because the initial probability assigned to it by one rational bettor differs radically from that assigned to it by another or because the same person vacillates among a number of possible values. Hence, although this interpretation provides an objective basis (i.e., a publicly testable one), it *might not* provide a *stable* one.

Review problems for Sec. 5.4.

1. What is the meaning of 'the psychological interpretation of probability sentences'?

2. How are probabilities obtained from personal odds?
   Using the personal odds theory of measuring probabilities, answer the following.

3. Lawrence is willing to give odds of 4 to 1 in favor of Arabia becoming a modern nation. What is the probability that Arabia will become a modern nation according to Lawrence? What is the probability that it will not become a modern nation?

4. Bishop Harold would give odds of 1 million to 1 that God exists. According to the bishop, what is the probability that God exists?

5. A certain bookmaker offers odds in favor of the first of each of the pairs of teams listed below.

	Teams	Odds		Teams	Odds
a)	Florida vs. Georgia	5:4	k)	Maine vs. Vermont	9:8
b)	N. Carolina vs. Alabama	1:6	l)	Harvard vs. Brown	6:4
c)	Miss. vs. Tenn.	3:2	m)	Yale vs. Dartmouth	5:1
d)	S.M.U. vs. Texas	7:9	n)	Ohio State vs. Mich.	10:9
e)	L.S.U. vs. Vanderbilt	10:4	o)	Purdue vs. Notre Dame	2:10
f)	Md. vs. Penn. State	3:5	p)	Illinois vs. Wisconsin	4:7
g)	V.P.I. vs. R.P.I.	4:2	q)	Indiana vs. Minn.	3:8
h)	Navy vs. N.Y.U.	6:2	r)	U.C.L.A. vs. U.S.C.	12:10
i)	Army vs. Colgate	8:3	s)	Stanford vs. Washington	2:8
j)	Cornell vs. Columbia	2:2	t)	Oregon vs. Montana	5:9

According to the bookmaker, what is the probability of the first of each of these pairs of teams winning?

6. What are two advantages of the psychological interpretation of probability sentences?

7. What is one objection to the psychological interpretation? What, if any, reply might be offered to this objection?

Suggestions for further reading related to Chapter 5.

Barker, S. F., *Induction and Hypothesis, A Study of the Logic of Confirmation.* Ithaca, N.Y.: Cornell University Press, 1962, Chapters 1–4.

Carnap, Rudolf, *The Logical Foundations of Probability.* Chicago: University of Chicago Press, 1950, Chapters 1, 2, and 4.

Foster, Marguerite H., and Martin, Michael L., eds., *Probability, Confirmation and Simplicity.* New York: The Odyssey Press, Inc., 1966, Parts I and II.

Kneale, William, *Probability and Induction.* Oxford: The Clarendon Press, 1952, Parts I and III.

Kyburg, Henry E. Jr., *Probability and the Logic of Rational Belief.* Middletown, Conn.: Wesleyan University Press, 1961, Part I.

Mises, Richard von, *Probability, Statistics and Truth*, Trans. by Hilda Geiringer. London: George Allen and Unwin Ltd., 1957, first and third lectures.

Nagel, Ernest, *Principles of the Theory of Probability.* Chicago: Universtiy of Chicago Press, 1958.

Pap, Arthur, *An Introduction to the Philosophy of Science.* New York: Free Press of Glencoe Inc., 1962, Part Three.

Chapter

6

The Calculus of Probability

In this chapter we shall consider the third of our four basic problems. The question is, *What principles are used to calculate with initially given probabilities to obtain others?* We shall answer this question by introducing some of the fundamental principles of the calculus of probability. These principles may be presented in the form of an uninterpreted axiomatic system with rigorous derivations of theorems from a handful of postulates. On the other hand, the principles may be introduced in a fairly informal fashion with examples and indications of the status of certain principles in relation to others. The latter procedure will be followed here. By the time we reach the end of the section, the reader should have a fair working knowledge of these principles as well as some idea of the status of each of them as postulates, theorems, or definitions.

6.1 Multiplication principles

To begin with, we are given a universe of discourse abbreviated by 'U' with a finite number n of discrete elements. Each element in U has associated with it a real number in the interval from 0 to 1 inclusive called a 'probability-value'. If 'A' represents any element whatsoever and

$$P(A)$$

is used to abbreviate the phrase

the probability-value of the element represented by 'A'

or, briefly, (but less accurately)

the probability of 'A'

we may express our first postulate thus:

(1) $P(A) \geq 0.$

To keep our discussion as general as possible, we shall let 'A' as well as 'B', 'C', 'D', and 'E' be interpreted as sentences, propositions, terms, classes, events, attributes, etc. Such versatile variables will be called **element variables.** They are place holders for unspecified elements. Some typical interpretations of 'A' would be

            (the sentence) 'A head will turn up.'
            (the proposition) that a head will turn up
            (the term) 'heads'
            (the class of) heads
            (the event of) a head turning up.

Expression (1) is our first example of a *probability sentence schema.* It becomes a probability sentence when 'A' is replaced by some appropriate element. When the expression '$P(A)$' is appropriately replaced by a *number*, namely 0, a fraction, or 1, expression (1) becomes an ordinary sentence saying that a certain real number is greater than or equal to 0.

Our second postulate is that the probability of the whole universe of discourse is 1; i.e.,

(2) $P(U) = 1.$

Because, according to (1), probability-values must be greater than or equal to 0 and, according to (2), they must be less than or equal to 1, it follows that they must be real numbers in the interval from 0 to 1, inclusive; i.e.,

$$0 \leq P(A) \leq 1.$$

Since a universe of discourse is nothing but the sum total of its constituent elements, we may rewrite (2) in a somewhat longer form. If

$$E_1, E_2, \ldots, E_n$$

are all the elements in U, according to (1) and (2),

$$P(E_1) + P(E_2) + \cdots + P(E_n) = 1.$$

That is, according to (1) and (2), each element has a probability-value and the sum total of these probabilities is 1.

EXAMPLE 1

Suppose U consists of the six faces of a fair die. Each face is an element with a probability, say, of $\frac{1}{6}$. The sum of the six probabilities is 1.

EXAMPLE 2

Suppose U is a group of five candidates in a beauty contest. Perhaps each candidate has a *different* probability of winning; e.g.,

Candidate	Probability of Winning
one	0.05
two	0.35
three	0.20
four	0.30
five	0.10
Total	1.00

But the sum of these probabilities is 1.

The third postulate is called the

General Multiplication Principle: If 'A' and 'B' represent any two elements, then the probability of 'A *and* B' equals the product of the probability of either one and the probability of the other *given* that one. That is,

$$P(A \text{ and } B) = P(A) \times P(A, B) = P(B) \times P(B, A).$$

This expression may be abbreviated by eliminating '*and*' in favor of a dot '·' and dropping the multiplication sign '×'. Hence, the *General Multiplication Principle* may be expressed thus:

(3) $P(A \cdot B) = P(A)P(A, B) = P(B)P(B, A).$

It must *not* be assumed that '*and*' or the dot which abbreviates it is a sentential operator. 'A' and 'B' represent *elements* which may or may not be *sentences*. Hence, we cannot assume that the expression '$A \cdot B$' always represents a sentential function and that the dot represents a sentential operator. If the elements represented by

'*A*' and '*B*' happen to be, say, *classes* then '*A*·*B*' represents the *intersection* of two classes. The **intersection** of two classes is the class consisting of everything that is a member of *both* classes. For examples, the intersection of the class of women and the class of doctors is the class of women doctors; the intersection of the classes of males and students is the class of male students; the intersection of the classes of Canadians and generals is the class of Canadian generals; etc. In most texts '*A* ∩ *B*' (read '*A cap B*') is used to abbreviate the phrase 'the intersection of the classes *A* and *B*'.

As (3) suggests, '*A*·*B*' is *commutative*; i.e., the *order* of the elements is irrelevant. 'And' is also *associative*; i.e., the *grouping* of three or more elements is irrelevant; e.g., '*A*·(*B*·*C*)' is equivalent to '(*A*·*B*)·*C*'.

We have already distinguished initial or absolute probability from conditional or relative probability. (See Sec. 5.2, b: i.) The expressions

$$P(A, B) \quad \text{and} \quad P(B, A)$$

are usually called 'conditional probabilities'. The left-hand expression may be read

a)   The probability '*from A to B*'.
b)   The probability of '*B given A*'.
c)   The probability of '*B relative to A*'.

In contrast, the expressions

$$P(A) \quad \text{and} \quad P(B)$$

are usually called 'initial probabilities'. [In most texts the *given* element is written *after* the other element; e.g., '*P*(*B*, *A*)' is short for a)–c) above. This convention has the advantage of spatially locating the elements in the abbreviation just as they are located in the ordinary English phrases, as in b) and c). We are writing the *given* element *first* because by the time a student reaches Part Two he is used to putting things that are *given* (premises) first.]

EXAMPLE 3

The probability of a female customer entering a certain shop is 0.2. Once a female is in the shop, however, the probability that something will be sold is 0.6. What is the probability that a female customer will enter the shop *and* that something will be sold?

Solution. Let *P*(*A*) be the probability of a female customer entering the shop; i.e.,

$$P(A) = 0.2.$$

Let *P*(*B*) be the probability of selling something in the shop. The probability that something will be sold *given* a female customer in the shop will be

$$P(A, B) = 0.6.$$

Thus, the probability that a female customer will enter the shop *and* that something will be sold is

$$P(A \cdot B) = P(A)P(A, B)$$
$$= (0.2)(0.6)$$
$$= 0.12.$$

EXAMPLE 4

If Filmore carries the ball the probability of a long gain is 0.8. But the quarter-back does not think it is fair to overwork Filmore, so the latter carries the ball only 40 percent of the time. What is the probability that Filmore will carry the ball *and* that he will make a long gain?

Solution. Let $P(A)$ be the probability that Filmore will carry the ball; so

$$P(A) = 0.4.$$

The probability of a long gain is $P(B)$. Hence, the probability of a long gain *if* Filmore carries the ball is

$$P(A, B) = 0.8.$$

Therefore, the probability that there will be a long gain *with* Filmore carrying the ball is

$$P(A \cdot B) = P(A)P(A, B)$$
$$= (0.4)(0.8)$$
$$= 0.32.$$

EXAMPLE 5

If Claude stays up all night studying, it is an even bet that he will pass his chemistry examination. However, the chances of Claude staying up all night studying are 1 in 20. What is the probability that Claude will stay up all night studying *and* that he will pass his chemistry examination?

Solution. Let $P(A)$ be the probability that Claude will stay up all night; thus

$$P(A) = \tfrac{1}{20} = 0.05.$$

The probability that Claude will pass is $P(B)$. Hence, $P(A, B)$ is the conditional probability of Claude's passing the examination provided that he stays up all night studying. Since this is an even bet, we may suppose

$$P(A, B) = 0.5.$$

Hence, the probability that Claude will stay up all night studying *and* pass his chemistry examination is

$$P(A \cdot B) = P(A)P(A, B)$$
$$= (0.05)(0.5)$$
$$= 0.025.$$

The General Multiplication Principle is easily generalized to obtain the probability of more than two elements. For example, the probability of '*A and B and C*' is

$$P(A \cdot B \cdot C) = P(A)P(A, B)P(A \cdot B, C).$$

(To simplify our notation, we are not grouping elements by two's; e.g., we have just written '$P(A \cdot B \cdot C)$' instead of the more accurate '$P[(A \cdot B) \cdot C]$'.) That is, following (3), the probability of three elements is simply the product of the probability of the first *and* the second (given the first) *and* the third (given both the first and the second). The probability of '*A and B and C and D*' is

$$P(A \cdot B \cdot C \cdot D) = P(A)P(A, B)P(A \cdot B, C)P(A \cdot B \cdot C, D).$$

If the probability of an element (represented by) '*B*' equals the probability of '*B given A*', then '*A*' and '*B*' are said to be **independent.** That is, '*A*' and '*B*' are independent if and only if

(4) $P(B) = P(A, B).$

If '*A*' and '*B*' are independent then '*B*' makes as little difference to '*A*' as '*A*' does to '*B*'. So (4) could just as well have been expressed

$$P(A) = P(B, A).$$

Elements which are independent of one another are, as far as their probabilities are concerned, irrelevant to one another. Hence, (4) is frequently used as a *definition* of irrelevance; i.e., of the irrelevance of any element '*A*' to any other element '*B*'. It follows, then, that '*A*' is generally *defined* as relevant to '*B*' provided that the probability of '*B*' does not equal the probability of '*B given A*'; i.e., '*A*' is **relevant** to '*B*' if and only if

$$P(B) > P(A, B) \quad or \quad P(B) < P(A, B).$$

If (the elements represented by) '*A*' and '*B*' are independent, then we may substitute '$P(B)$' for '$P(A, B)$' in the General Multiplication Principle (3). This substitution yields the

Special Multiplication Principle: If '*A*' and '*B*' are independent then the probability of '*A and B*' equals the product of the probability of '*A*' and the probability of '*B*'. That is, if '*A*' and '*B*' are independent

(5) $P(A \cdot B) = P(A)P(B).$

EXAMPLE 6

Suppose two fair coins are tossed. What is the probability that both will land with heads facing up?

Solution. The coin tosses are independent of one another. If $P(A)$ is the probability of a head on the first coin and $P(B)$ is the probability of a head on the second coin, then, assuming that

$$P(A) = 0.5 = P(B),$$

we have by (5)

$$P(A \cdot B) = P(A)P(B)$$
$$= (0.5)(0.5)$$
$$= 0.25.$$

EXAMPLE 7

Fritz owns two wristwatches. The probability that one will break is 0.1, and the probability that the other will break is 0.9. What is the probability that both watches will break?

Solution. The watches work independently of one another. Hence, if we let $P(A)$ be the probability that the first one will break and $P(B)$ the probability that the second one will break, then the probability that both watches will break is

$$P(A \cdot B) = P(A)P(B)$$
$$= (0.1)(0.9)$$
$$= 0.09.$$

The Special Multiplication Principle is easily generalized to obtain the probability of more than two elements. For example, if '*A*' and '*B*' and '*C*' are independent, the probability of '*A and B and C*' is

$$P(A \cdot B \cdot C) = P(A)P(B)P(C).$$

Quite generally, if

$$E_1, E_2, \ldots, E_n$$

are n independent elements, then

$$P(E_1 \cdot E_2 \cdot \ \cdots \ \cdot E_n) = P(E_1)P(E_2) \ \cdots \ P(E_n).$$

The General Multiplication Principle (3) is fruitful in another way. If both sides of

$$P(A \cdot B) = P(A)P(A, B)$$

are divided by $P(A)$, we find

(6) $$P(A, B) = \frac{P(A \cdot B)}{P(A)}.$$

If $P(A)$ does not equal 0, then equation (6) provides a definition of 'conditional probability'; i.e., of the probability of any element 'B' relative to any other element 'A'. If $P(A) = 0$ then '$P(A, B)$' is undefined. We could, of course, *introduce* a definition of conditional probability such as (6) and derive the General Multiplication Principle by *multiplying* both sides of (6) by $P(A)$. But here we have proceeded in the opposite direction; we *postulated* the General Multiplication Principle and derived a definition of conditional probability from it. There is no significant difference in the two approaches.

We have already measured conditional probabilities by simply counting possibilities. Consider an application of (6).

EXAMPLE 8

Suppose a fair die is tossed and a face with an odd number of dots on it turns up. What is the probability that the face with five dots has turned up?

Solution. Let $P(A)$ be the probability that a face with an odd number of dots has turned up. Since the die is fair,

$$P(A) = \tfrac{1}{2}.$$

If $P(B)$ is the probability that the face with five dots has turned up, then $P(A \cdot B)$ is the probability of an odd face *with* exactly five dots turning up. Hence,

$$P(A \cdot B) = \tfrac{1}{6}.$$

The probability that the odd face which has turned up is *also* a face with five dots is

$$P(A, B) = \frac{P(A \cdot B)}{P(A)} = \frac{\tfrac{1}{6}}{\tfrac{1}{2}} = \frac{1}{3}.$$

Review problems for Sec. 6.1.

1. Define the following
    a) probability-value
    b) element variable
    c) intersection

2. What is '$P(A)$' short for?

3. Express the first postulate (1) in ordinary language and with symbols.

4. Express the second postulate (2) in ordinary language and with symbols.

5. Suppose a certain universe of discourse U contains exactly three elements represented by 'A', 'B', and 'C', then fill in the following blanks.

   a) $P(A)$ _____ $P($_____$) +$ _____$(C) =$ _____
   b) $P($_____$) = 1$
   c) $P(A)$ _____ 0
   d)   If $P(A) = \frac{1}{2}$ and $P(B) = \frac{1}{4}$ then $P(C) =$ _____.
   e)   If $P(B) = \frac{1}{8}$ and $P(C) = \frac{2}{8}$ then $P(A) =$ _____.
   f) 1 _____ $P(B)$

6. Express the General Multiplication Principle (3) in ordinary language and with symbols.

7. Express the following in symbolic notation.

   a)   the probability of 'C'   e)   the probability of 'A and B, given C'
   b)   the probability of 'C given A'   f)   the probability of 'C, given A and B'
   c)   the probability of 'C and B'   g)   the probability of 'A and B, given C and D'
   d)   the probability of 'A and B and C'   h)   the probability of 'D, given A and B and C'

In the following problems and in *all* future sections, either the *classical*, the *finite frequency*, or the *personal odds* theories will be used to obtain initial probabilities. The context or general statement of each problem will suggest the appropriate theory.

8. If Sophie runs out of glue, the odds in favor of her borrowing from Liz are 4 to 1. The odds in favor of Sophie running out of glue are 3 to 2. On the basis of these odds (and the General Multiplication Principle), what is the probability that Sophie will *both* run out of glue *and* borrow from Liz?

9. Given a choice between the electric chair and hanging, 90 percent of the condemned men in a certain prison prefer the chair. Only 5 percent of the men in the prison are given a choice in this matter. What is the probability of a prisoner *both* receiving a choice between the electric chair and hanging *and* preferring the chair?

10. The probability of a soldier receiving a letter at a certain post is 0.8. If a soldier does get a letter, the probability that it is from the Secretary of Defense is 0.002. What is the probability that a soldier at the post will get a letter *and* that it will come from the Secretary of Defense?

11. The probability of Wilfred's ticket being drawn in the plant lottery is 0.001. The probability that Wilfred will quit his job if his ticket is drawn is 0.4. What is the probability that Wilfred's ticket will be drawn *and* that he will quit his job?

12. The chances of a certain tube burning out are 1 in 6. If it does burn out, the chances of receiving static are 5 in 6. What is the probability that the tube will burn out *and* static will be received?

13. About 20 percent of the customers in Lou's diner order eggs for lunch. If someone orders eggs, the chances of his ordering ham are 6 in 10. The probability that a customer who has ordered ham and eggs will order fried potatoes is 0.7. What is the probability that a customer in Lou's diner will order ham *and* eggs *and* fried potatoes for lunch?

14. The probability of Mary marrying Harry is 0.4. If Mary marries Harry, the probability of Barry burying Larry is 0.3. If Mary marries Harry and Barry buries Larry, then the probability of Terry tarrying is 0.6. What is the probability of Mary marrying Harry *and* Barry burying Larry *and* Terry tarrying?

15. Suppose U consists of the three elements 'A', 'B', and 'C', then fill in the blanks.

   a) $P(A \cdot \underline{\hspace{1cm}}) = P(\underline{\hspace{1cm}})P(A, C)$

   b) $P(C \cdot B) = P(C)P(\underline{\hspace{1cm}})$

   c) $P(A \cdot \underline{\hspace{1cm}} \cdot C) = P(\underline{\hspace{1cm}})P(A, \underline{\hspace{1cm}}) \underline{\hspace{1cm}} (A \cdot B, \underline{\hspace{1cm}})$

   d) $P(A, \underline{\hspace{1cm}}) = \dfrac{P(\underline{\hspace{1cm}} \cdot C)}{P(\underline{\hspace{1cm}})}$

   e) $P(A \cdot B, C) = \dfrac{P[(\underline{\hspace{1cm}} \cdot B) \cdot \underline{\hspace{1cm}}]}{P(\underline{\hspace{1cm}})}$

16. Define the following using ordinary language and symbolic notation.

   a) 'A' and 'B' are independent.

   b) 'A' is irrelevant to 'B'.

   c) 'A' is relevant to 'B'.

17. The probability that Mabel will wear her red coat is 0.6. The probability that she will wear her black shoes is 0.4. What is the probability that Mabel will wear her red coat *and* her black shoes?

18. About 50 percent of the lawyers in town are good speakers. Only 25 percent of the lawyers in town are good painters. What is the probability that a lawyer in town is both a good speaker *and* a good painter?

19. In a certain army 2 percent of the men are generals, 30 percent have good conduct medals, and 12 percent are married. What is the probability of a man in this army being a married general with a good conduct medal?

20. Suppose one man in six are in love, one man in eight are poets, four men in nine are happily employed, and six men in seven are courteous, what is the probability that a man is a courteous happily employed poet who is in love?

6.2   Addition principles

The fourth *postulate* we have to consider is called the

General Addition Principle: If 'A' and 'B' represent any two elements, the probability of '*either A or B, or both*' equals the sum of the probability of 'A' and the probability of '*B*' *minus* the probability of '*both A and B*'. Using the wedge '∨' to abbreviate '*either . . . or . . . , or both*', the *General Addition Principle* may be expressed thus:

(7) $P(A \lor B) = P(A) + P(B) - P(A \cdot B).$

As in the case of '*and*', it must *not* be assumed that '*either . . . or . . . , or both*' or the wedge which abbreviates it is a sentential operator. '*A*' and '*B*' represent elements which may or may not be *sentences*. Hence, we cannot assume that the expression '*A ∨ B*' always represents a sentential function and that the wedge represents a sentential operator. If the elements represented by '*A*' and '*B*' happen to be, say, classes then '*A ∨ B*' represents the *union* of two classes. The **union** of two classes is the class consisting of everything that is a member of *either* one *or* both classes. For examples, the union of the class of women and the class of doctors is the class of individuals who are either women or doctors, or both; the union of the classes of males and students is the class of individuals who are either males or students, or both; the union of the classes of Canadians and generals is the class of individuals who are either Canadians or generals, or both; etc. In most texts '*A ∪ B*' (read '*A cup B*') is used to abbreviate the phrase 'the union of the classes *A* and *B*'.

The wedge is *commutative* and *associative*. Hence, '*A ∨ B*' is equivalent to '*B ∨ A*', and '*A ∨ (B ∨ C)*' is equivalent to '*(A ∨ B) ∨ C*'. Hereafter the '*or both*' will be understood but not written.

Whenever '*A*' and '*B*' appear *together*, '*A*' appears and '*B*' appears. Hence, if $P(A \cdot B)$ is not subtracted from $P(A) + P(B)$ in (7), then the probability of '*A · B*' is being counted *twice*. An example will make the situation clearer.

EXAMPLE 1

Suppose '*A*' and '*B*' represent two classes of individuals, say, men and policemen. The classes may be diagramed by overlapping rectangles.

We may use the number of individuals (represented by 'X's') in each class as a measure of its probability. Thus

$$P(A) = \tfrac{12}{20} = P(B)$$

and

$$P(A \cdot B) = \tfrac{4}{20}.$$

If we compute the probability of '$A \lor B$' *without* subtracting $P(A \cdot B)$, we find

$$P(A \lor B) = P(A) + P(B)$$
$$= (\tfrac{12}{20}) + (\tfrac{12}{20})$$
$$= \tfrac{24}{20} \quad \text{(absurd)}.$$

This result violates our second postulate and is patently absurd because the numerator is greater than the total number of individuals in our universe of discourse. We obtained this result because we counted the four 'X's' in the center rectangle *twice*. We counted each of these 'X's' when we measured the probability of 'A' and we counted them again when we measured the probability of 'B'. Hence, if we subtract the probability of 'A *and* B' from the result above, we shall in effect be counting the 'X's' in the center rectangle only *once*. The probability of 'A *and* B' is $\tfrac{4}{20}$. Thus,

$$P(A \lor B) = P(A) + P(B) - P(A \cdot B)$$
$$= (\tfrac{12}{20}) + (\tfrac{12}{20}) - (\tfrac{4}{20})$$
$$= \tfrac{10}{10} = 1.$$

EXAMPLE 2

Forty percent of all the citizens in a certain town are college graduates. Twenty percent of all the citizens in the town are mechanics. If the probability that any citizen is *both* a college graduate *and* a mechanic is 0.05, what is the probability that any citizen we meet is *either* a college graduate *or* a mechanic?

Solution. Let $P(A) = 0.4$ be the probability of meeting a college graduate and $P(B) = 0.2$ the probability of meeting a mechanic. Hence, the probability of meeting *either* a college graduate *or* a mechanic is

$$P(A \lor B) = P(A) + P(B) - P(A \cdot B)$$
$$= (0.4) + (0.2) - (0.05)$$
$$= 0.55.$$

EXAMPLE 3

What is the probability of tossing *either* a six *or* a three with a fair die?

Solution. The probability of tossing a six with a fair die is $P(A) = \tfrac{1}{6}$. Similarly, the probability of tossing a three with such a die is $P(B) = \tfrac{1}{6}$. Clearly *both* the six *and* the three cannot appear together. Hence, $P(A \cdot B) = 0$. Thus, the probability of tossing *either* a six *or* a three with a fair die is

$$P(A \lor B) = P(A) + P(B) - P(A \cdot B)$$
$$= (\tfrac{1}{6}) + (\tfrac{1}{6}) - 0$$
$$= \tfrac{1}{3}.$$

The General Addition Principle may be generalized to obtain the probability of at least one of more than two elements. For example, the probability of '*either A or B or C*' is

$$P(A \lor B \lor C) = P(A) + P(B) + P(C) - P(A \cdot B)$$
$$- P(A \cdot C) - P(B \cdot C) + P(A \cdot B \cdot C).$$

In the formula above, $P(A \cdot B \cdot C)$ is *added* because when we subtract $P(A \cdot B)$, $P(A \cdot C)$, and $P(B \cdot C)$ from the initial sum, exactly $P(A \cdot B \cdot C)$ is subtracted *twice*. To verify this remark, consider the following Venn diagram. Each of the circles represents a class containing five individuals.

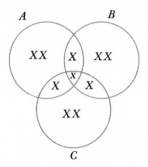

Using the number of individuals in each part of the diagram as a measure of probability, we have

$$P(A) = P(B) = P(C) = \tfrac{5}{10}$$
$$P(A \cdot B) = P(A \cdot C) = P(B \cdot C) = \tfrac{2}{10}$$
$$P(A \cdot B \cdot C) = \tfrac{1}{10}.$$

Thus, the expanded General Addition Principle *without* the addition of $P(A \cdot B \cdot C)$ yields

$$P(A \lor B \lor C) = (\tfrac{5}{10}) + (\tfrac{5}{10}) + (\tfrac{5}{10}) - (\tfrac{2}{10}) - (\tfrac{2}{10}) - (\tfrac{2}{10})$$
$$= \tfrac{9}{10}.$$

That is exactly $\tfrac{1}{10} = P(A \cdot B \cdot C)$ less than it should be since

$$P(A \lor B \lor C) = P(U) = 1.$$

Hence, $P(A \cdot B \cdot C)$ must be added to the expanded General Addition Principle.

In Example 3 we considered two *events* which could not occur at the same time. If the side of the die with six dots turned up then the side with three dots could not turn up. When *events* are related in such a way that the occurrence of one *excludes* the occurrence of the other, they are called 'mutually exclusive'. We shall define a *more general* but analogous notion of mutually exclusive *elements* thus: '*A*' and '*B*' represent **mutually exclusive elements** if '*A and B*' is impossible (in any sense of this word; e.g., logically impossible, physically impossible, technically impossible, etc.) If the elements represented by '*A*' and '*B*' are mutually exclusive then

(8) $P(A \cdot B) = 0.$

Applying (8) to the General Addition Principle (7), we may derive the

Special Addition Principle: If '*A*' and '*B*' are mutually exclusive, the probability of '*either A or B*' is the sum of the probability of '*A*' and the probability of '*B*'; i.e., if '*A*' and '*B*' are mutually exclusive,

(9) $(A \lor B) = P(A) + P(B).$

Example 4

There is a probability of 0.5 that Hilton Holton will become a brain surgeon and a probability of 0.2 that he will become a shoe salesman. Assuming that he cannot do both, what is the probability that Hilton Holton will become *either* a brain surgeon *or* a shoe salesman?

Solution. We have assumed the two vocations are mutually exclusive. Hence, if $P(A) = 0.5$ is the probability that Hilton Holton will become a brain surgeon and $P(B) = 0.2$ is the probability that he will become a shoe salesman, then the probability that he will become *either* a brain surgeon *or* a shoe salesman is

$$P(A \lor B) = P(A) + P(B)$$
$$= (0.5) + (0.2)$$
$$= 0.7.$$

Example 5

Fifty percent of the outlaws in Ghouls Gulch try to avoid the sheriff by escaping through the pass. Only 3 percent of them try to avoid the sheriff by climbing over the mountain. What is the probability that an outlaw will *either* try to escape through the pass *or* climb over the mountain?

Solution. Let $P(A) = 0.5$ be the probability that an outlaw will try to escape through the pass, and $P(B) = 0.03$ be the probability that he will climb over the mountain. Hence, the probability that an outlaw will *either* try to escape through the pass *or* climb over the mountain is

$$P(A \lor B) = P(A) + P(B)$$
$$= (0.5) + (0.03)$$
$$= 0.53.$$

The Special Addition Principle is easily generalized to obtain the probability of exactly one of more than two elements. For example, if '*A*', '*B*', and '*C*' are mutually exclusive, the probability of '*either A or B or C*' is

$$P(A \lor B \lor C) = P(A) + P(B) + P(C).$$

Quite generally, if

$$E_1, E_2, \ldots, E_n$$

are *n* mutually exclusive elements, then

$$P(E_1 \lor E_2 \lor \cdots \lor E_n) = P(E_1) + P(E_2) + \cdots + P(E_n).$$

In Sec. 2.4 we introduced the notion of *complementary terms.* Complementary terms denote classes of things that are mutually exclusive and exhaustive in any universe of discourse; e.g., *everything* is *either* a man *or* a nonman, and nothing is *both.* We frequently have to consider *elements* which are not only mutually exclusive but exhaustive of a given universe. For examples, we might be interested in determining the probability of a *sentence* and its *negation*; we might be interested in determining the probability of the occurrence or nonoccurrence of some *event*; the appearance or nonappearance of some *attribute*; etc. We shall use the term **complementary elements** to designate any elements that are *both* mutually exclusive and exhaustive in any given universe of discourse. Following our practice in Sec. 2.4, we shall abbreviate the phrase

the complement of 'A'

by

$$\overline{A}.$$

Then we may summarize our discussion of complementary elements thus: '*A*' and '*B*' represent complementary elements if and only if they are mutually exclusive and

$$A + B = U.$$

Since '*B*' represents the complement of '*A*', we may rewrite the expression above

$$A + \overline{A} = U.$$

Because '*A*' and '*$\overline{A}$*' are mutually exclusive,

(10) $P(A \cdot \overline{A}) = 0.$

Since they are exhaustive,

(11) $P(A \lor \overline{A}) = 1 = P(U).$

Ignoring '$P(U)$' in (11), we may apply the Special Addition Principle to it to obtain

(12) $P(A) + P(\overline{A}) = 1.$

This principle (12) is merely a special case of the formula for n elements which we derived earlier. Subtracting $P(A)$ from both sides of (12), we find

(13) $P(\overline{A}) = 1 - P(A).$

Expression (13) may be called the **Complement Principle.** It provides a definition of 'the probability of the *complement* of A'.

EXAMPLE 6

The odds in favor of Norton's selling his Buick this year are 2 to 1. What is the probability that Norton will *not* sell his car this year?

Solution. Given the odds in favor of Norton's selling his Buick, we shall assume that the probability that he will sell is $P(A) = \frac{2}{3}$. The probability that he will *not* sell must be

$$P(\overline{A}) = 1 - P(A)$$
$$= \tfrac{1}{3}.$$

EXAMPLE 7

Exactly 66 percent of the girls in a certain sorority are blonds. What is the probability that any girl chosen in this sorority is *not* a blond?

Solution. Let $P(A) = 0.66$ be the probability of choosing a blond girl in the sorority. Then the probability that any girl chosen in the sorority is *not* a blond is

$$P(\overline{A}) = 1 - P(A)$$
$$= 0.34.$$

Review problems for Sec. 6.2.

1. Express the General Addition Principle (7) in ordinary language and with symbols.

2. Make up an example to illustrate the need for the subtraction of $P(A \cdot B)$ from $P(A) + P(B)$ in the General Addition Principle.

3. Express the following in symbolic notation.

     a)   the probability of 'A *or* B'
     b)   the probability of 'A *or* B, *given* C'
     c)   the probability of 'A *or* B, *given* C *and* D'
     d)   the probability of 'A *or* B *or* C'

4. Thirty percent of the members of a fraternity are undertakers and 60 percent are dentists. If the probability of a dentist in this fraternity being an undertaker is 0.01, what is the probability of a member being *either* an undertaker *or* a dentist?

5. The probability of having a flat tire on this road is 0.25. The probability of breaking your fan belt is 0.05. The chances of both hardships occurring together are 1 in 1000. What is the probability of *either* a flat tire *or* a broken fan belt?

6. The probability of a history exam Tuesday is $\frac{1}{3}$ and the probability of a geology exam is also $\frac{1}{5}$. If the chances of having two exams in one day are 1 in 10, what is the probability of *either* a history *or* a geology exam Tuesday?

7. Half of the metaphysicians in the world write poetry and a fourth of them play the bongo drums. Only 10 percent of the metaphysical poets play bongo drums. What is the probability that a metaphysician *either* writes poetry *or* plays the drums?

8. When Joe leaves the house, the probability that he will forget his wallet is 0.4, that he will forget his handkerchief is 0.16, that he will forget his keys is 0.24, that he will forget his tie is 0.06, and that he will forget his manners is 0.02. Suppose these events are mutually exclusive, what is the probability that Joe will forget either his wallet *or* his handkerchief *or* his keys *or* his tie *or* his manners?

9. Fill in the blanks.
   a) $P(A) + P(\overline{A}) =$ _____
   b) $P(A \lor B \lor C) = P(\underline{\quad}) + P(B) +$ _____ $- P(A \cdot B) - P(\underline{\quad}) -$
      $P(B \cdot C) +$ _____
   c) $P(\overline{A}) =$ _____
   d) If A and B are mutually exclusive then $P(A \cdot B) =$ _____.
   e) If A and B are mutually exclusive then $P(A \lor \underline{\quad}) =$ _____ $+ P(B)$.

10. If the probability that Smith is a Hungarian Gypsy is put at 0.4, what is the probability that Smith is not a Hungarian Gypsy? What is the probability that Smith both is and is not a Hungarian Gypsy? That he either is or is not one?

11. What is *wrong* with each of the following?
    a) If A and B are independent then $P(A) > P(B, A)$.
    b) The following initial probabilities are assigned to three mutually exclusive and exhaustive events: $P(A) = \frac{1}{8}$, $P(B) = \frac{3}{4}$, $P(C) = \frac{1}{2}$.
    c) $P(A \lor B) = P(A) + P(B)$
    d) $P(A, B) = [P(A \cdot B)]/P(B)$
    e) $P(A \cdot B) > P(A)$

12. Three men are shooting at a target. The probability of the first man hitting it is $P(A) = 0.2$, of the second hitting it is $P(B) = 0.3$, and of the third hitting it is $P(C) = 0.15$. What is the probability that
    a) All three will miss the target?
    b) The first man will miss it?

   c)   Either the first *or* the third man will hit it?

   d)   Either the first *or* the second man will hit it?

   e)   The second *and* third man will hit it?

13.   If $P(A) = 0.12$, $P(A \lor B) = 0.44$, and $P(B) = 0.38$, what is the value of $P(A \cdot B)$?

14.   If $P(A \cdot B) = 0.21$, $P(A \lor B) = 0.69$, and $P(A) = 0.6$, what is $P(B)$?

15.   If $P(A \lor B) = 0.75$, $P(B) = 0.7$, and $P(A \cdot B) = 0.15$, what is $P(A)$?

16.   If $P(A) = 0.2$ and $P(A \cdot B) = 0.03$, what is $P(A, B)$?

17.   If $P(A, B) = 0.3$ and $P(A \cdot B) = 0.21$, what is $P(A)$?

18.   Given $P(A \lor B \lor C) = 0.58$, $P(C) = 0.06$, and $P(A) = 0.4$, what is $P(B)$?

19.   Given $P(B) = 0.2$, $P(A \lor B \lor C \lor D) = 0.77$, $P(C) = 0.08$, and $P(D) = 0.4$, what is $P(A)$?

20.   If $P(A \cdot B) = \frac{1}{6}$ and $P(A, B) = \frac{1}{3}$, what is $P(A)$?

21.   If $P(A) = \frac{5}{9}$ and $P(A, B) = \frac{27}{40}$, what is $P(A \cdot B)$?

22.   If $P(A \cdot B) = \frac{2}{7}$ and $P(A, B) = \frac{1}{3}$, what is $P(A)$?

23.   Make up examples to illustrate the following.

   a)   General Multiplication Principle   e)   mutually exclusive hypotheses

   b)   independent hypotheses   f)   Special Addition Principle

   c)   Special Multiplication Principle   g)   Complement Principle

   d)   General Addition Principle

24.   What is the *union* of two classes?

6.3 Bayes's theorem

Two years after the death of the Reverend Thomas Bayes in 1761, his "Essay Towards Solving a Problem in the Doctrine of Chances" was published in the *Philosophical transactions of the Royal Society*. The essay contained the famous *Principle of Inverse Probability* or what is now known as *Bayes's theorem*. After introducing an essential part of Bayes's theorem in the form of another principle, we shall investigate Bayes's theorem in detail.

The *Principle of Total Probability* (sometimes called the 'Rule of Elimination') is an essential part of Bayes's theorem and a direct consequence of some of the principles already introduced.

The **Principle of Total Probability** says that given a set of mutually exclusive and exhaustive elements represented by '$E_1, E_2, \ldots, E_n$' each of whose probability is greater than zero, the probability of 'A' equals the sum of the probabilities of

'$E_1 \cdot A$, $E_2 \cdot A$, . . . , $E_n \cdot A$'. Let us consider this more carefully. We are given a set of mutually exclusive and exhaustive elements; i.e.,

$$E_1 \vee E_2 \vee \cdots \vee E_n.$$

We are interested in determining the probability of some element 'A'. In view of what is already given, we know that 'A' must appear with one of the elements above; i.e., we know that

$$(E_1 \cdot A) \vee (E_2 \cdot A) \vee \cdots \vee (E_n \cdot A)$$

are our only possibilities. Hence, the probability of 'A' equals the probability of '$E_1 \cdot A$ *or* $E_2 \cdot A$ *or* . . . *or* $E_n \cdot A$'; i.e.,

$$(14) \qquad P(A) = P[(E_1 \cdot A) \vee (E_2 \cdot A) \vee \cdots \vee (E_n \cdot A)]$$
$$= P(E_1 \cdot A) + P(E_2 \cdot A) + \cdots + P(E_n \cdot A).$$

The long expression on the right side of this equation may be abbreviated with the help of the standard sign of summation, the Greek capital letter sigma 'Σ'. Instead of the long expression, we may write

$$\Sigma P(E_i \cdot A) \qquad (i = 1, 2, \ldots, n),$$

which means exactly the same thing.

EXAMPLE 1

Either it will rain or not. If it rains the probability of a flood is 0.8. If it does not rain the probability of a flood is 0.2. Suppose the probability of rain is 0.7, what is the probability of a flood?

Solution. The following diagram may help clarify our situation in this example.

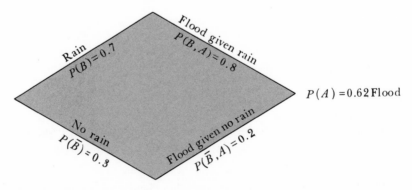

The diagram shows exactly what we are given and what we must eliminate. We have the probability of rain, no rain, a flood given rain, and a flood given no rain.

We want to know the probability of a flood *all by itself*. (The answer is already included in the diagram.) We may obtain this probability by *eliminating*, as it were, the other elements 'B' and '$\bar{B}$'. Hence, the alternative name 'Rule of Elimination' is fairly descriptive.

Let $P(B) = 0.7$ be the probability that it will rain. So $P(\bar{B}) = 1 - P(B) = 0.3$ is the probability that it will not rain. $P(B, A) = 0.8$ is the probability of a flood *given* rain and $P(\bar{B}, A) = 0.2$ is the probability of a flood *given no* rain. Hence, according to the Principle of Total Probability (14), the probability of a flood is

$$P(A) = P(B \cdot A) + P(\bar{B} \cdot A)$$
$$= P(B)P(B, A) + P(\bar{B})P(\bar{B}, A)$$
$$= (0.7)(0.8) + (0.3)(0.2)$$
$$= 0.62.$$

EXAMPLE 2

The probability that Melvin will pass his zoology test is 0.3. If he passes the test, the probability that he will be elected president of his class is 0.8. If he fails, the probability that he will be elected is 0.5. What is the probability that Melvin will be elected president of his class?

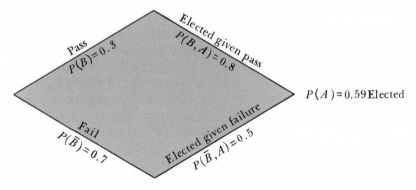

The elements 'B' and '$\bar{B}$' are eliminated as it were to obtain $P(A)$.

If the probability that Melvin will pass his zoology test is $P(B) = 0.3$, then the probability that he will *not* pass is $P(\bar{B}) = 1 - P(B) = 0.7$. The probability that Melvin will be elected president of his class *if* he passes is $P(B, A) = 0.8$. If he fails his test, the probability that he will be elected is $P(\bar{B}, A) = 0.5$. Hence, the probability that Melvin will be elected president of his class is

$$P(A) = P(B \cdot A) + P(\bar{B} \cdot A)$$
$$= P(B)P(B, A) + P(\bar{B})P(\bar{B}, A)$$
$$= (0.3)(0.8) + (0.7)(0.5)$$
$$= 0.59.$$

EXAMPLE 3

Suppose a particular football team, say the Lions, is 3 yards away from the opponent's goal line. The players have one of three mutually exclusive and exhaustive options; namely, they can attempt a forward pass, a run, or a field goal. The probabilities for each of these options are as follows:

$$\text{Probability of passing } = P(B) = 0.3.$$
$$\text{Probability of running } = P(C) = 0.5.$$
$$\text{Probability of kicking } = P(D) = 0.2.$$

The probabilities of scoring *given* the alternatives above are

$$\text{Scoring given pass } = P(B, A) = 0.4.$$
$$\text{Scoring given run } = P(C, A) = 0.6.$$
$$\text{Scoring given kick } = P(D, A) = 0.7.$$

The ball has not been put in play yet, and what is required is the probability that the Lions will score; i.e., $P(A)$.

Solution. A diagram of our situation this time would show three paths leading to the probability in question.

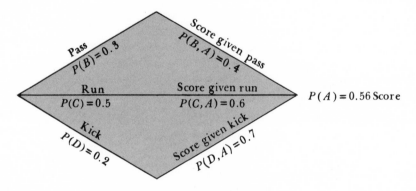

The Lions can score (represented by) 'A' *either with* a pass 'B' *or with* a run 'C' *or with* a kick 'D'. Hence

$$P(A) = P[(B \cdot A) \vee (C \cdot A) \vee (D \cdot A)]$$
$$= P(B \cdot A) + P(C \cdot A) + P(D \cdot A)$$
$$= P(B)P(B, A) + P(C)P(C, A) + P(D)P(D, A)$$
$$= (0.3)(0.4) + (0.5)(0.6) + (0.2)(0.7)$$
$$= (0.12) + (0.30) + (0.14)$$
$$= 0.56.$$

Thus, *prior* to putting the ball in play, we may say that the probability of the Lion's scoring is $P(A) = 0.56$.

According to **Bayes's theorem,** given a set of mutually exclusive and exhaustive elements represented by 'E_1, E_2, . . . , E_n,' each of whose probabilities is greater than zero, the probability of any one of these elements 'E_0 *given* A' is the ratio of the probability of '$E_0 \cdot A$' to the sum of the probabilities '$E_1 \cdot A$, $E_2 \cdot A$, . . . , $E_n \cdot A$'. Let us consider this mouthful more carefully, especially in its relation to the Principle of Total Probability. Again we are given a set of mutually exclusive and exhaustive elements

$$E_1 \lor E_2 \lor \cdots \lor E_n.$$

We are also given 'A'; i.e., we are not seeking the probability of 'A', but we already know that one of the following has appeared:

$$(E_1 \cdot A) \lor (E_2 \cdot A) \lor \cdots \lor (E_n \cdot A).$$

Bayes's theorem is used to determine the probability of any element 'E_0 *given* A'. It tells us that this probability is the ratio of the probability of '$E_0 \cdot A$' to the sum of the probabilities of '$E_1 \cdot A$, $E_2 \cdot A$, . . . , $E_n \cdot A$'. That is,

(15) $$P(A, E_0) = \frac{P(E_0 \cdot A)}{\Sigma P(E_i \cdot A)}$$

$$= \frac{P(E_0)P(E_0, A)}{\Sigma P(E_i)P(E_i, A)} \qquad (i = 1, 2, \ldots, n).$$

Notice that this principle is a direct consequence of familiar principles. According to the definition of conditional probability (6), if $P(A) \neq 0$

$$P(A, E_0) = \frac{P(A \cdot E_0)}{P(A)}.$$

According to the General Multiplication Principle (3), we may substitute for the *numerator* on the right side of this equation '$P(E_0)P(E_0, A)$'. That gives us

$$P(A, E_0) = \frac{P(E_0)P(E_0, A)}{P(A)}.$$

The Principle of Total Probability allows us to substitute '$\Sigma P(E_i \cdot A)$' $(i = 1, 2, \ldots, n)$ for '$P(A)$'. Hence, we obtain Bayes's theorem or (15). Bayes's theorem, then, is nothing but a special way of writing the definition of conditional probability (6). Hence, the latter is often called 'Bayes's theorem' too.

The expression '$P(E_0, A)$' is called the **likelihood** of 'E_0 *relative to* A'. It is nothing more than the *conditional probability* of 'A *relative to* E_0'. The left side of Bayes's theorem (15) is referred to as an **inverse** probability in contrast to all the probabilities on the right side, which are called **forward** probabilities. These latter two names are simply convenient labels for the various expressions appearing in the theorem and they are only applicable in reference to it; i.e., apart from their positions in the theorem, it is meaningless to call '$P(A, E_0)$' an 'inverse' probability or '$P(E_0, A)$' a 'forward' one.

The descriptive force of the alternative name of (15), namely '*The Principle of Inverse Probability*', is now apparent. This principle tells us how to obtain inverse probabilities from forward ones. Bayes's theorem has also been called "the rule for the probability of a cause" and "the rule for the probability of hypotheses". These names and some other interesting facts about the theorem will be explained with the help of some examples.

EXAMPLE 4

Prior to his examination, we suppose the probability that Malcolm is a cheater is $P(B) = 0.2$. If he cheats, the probability that he will pass is $P(B, A) = 0.8$. If he does not cheat, the probability that he will pass is $P(\overline{B}, A) = 0.4$. The fact is that Malcolm has passed his examination. The question is, What is the probability that he is a cheater?

Solution. We are given two paths leading to Malcolm's passing.

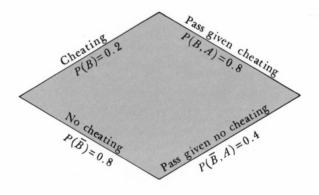

We know that Malcolm passed, but what we would like to know is the probability that he cheated *given* the fact that he passed; i.e., we want to find $P(A, B)$. Applying Bayes's Theorem, we have

$$P(A, B) = \frac{P(B \cdot A)}{P(B \cdot A) + P(\overline{B} \cdot A)}$$

$$= \frac{P(B)P(B, A)}{P(B)P(B, A) + P(\overline{B})P(\overline{B}, A)}$$

$$= \frac{(0.2)(0.8)}{(0.2)(0.8) + (0.8)(0.4)}$$

$$= 0.33.$$

After the results of the examination are obtained (i.e., *given* Malcolm's passing), the probability that Malcolm is a cheater is $P(A, B) = 0.33$. This is *greater* than the probability we initially assigned to Malcolm's being a cheater. Hence, we have "learned something" from the examination, namely, that we cannot trust Malcolm as much as we originally supposed.

EXAMPLE 5

Prior to meeting Zigler on the street, we suppose the probability that he had strawberries for breakfast is $P(B) = 0.5$. When Zigler eats strawberries for breakfast, the probability that he will have an upset stomach is $P(B, A) = 0.2$. When he does not eat strawberries for breakfast, the probability that he will have an upset stomach is $P(\overline{B}, A) = 0.3$. We happen to meet Zigler on the street and we find that he has an upset stomach. What is the probability that he had strawberries for breakfast?

Solution. We are interested in the probability that Zigler had strawberries for breakfast *given* the fact that he now has an upset stomach; i.e., we are seeking $P(A, B)$. Bayes's theorem yields

$$P(A, B) = \frac{P(B)P(B, A)}{P(B)P(B, A) + P(\overline{B})P(\overline{B}, A)}$$

$$= \frac{(0.5)(0.2)}{(0.5)(0.2) + (0.5)(0.3)}$$

$$= 0.4.$$

If Zigler's upset stomach is regarded as an *effect* which may be *caused* by his eating strawberries, the descriptive sense of the name "rule for the probability of a cause" is apparent. *Given* an *effect*, Bayes's theorem was used to determine the probability of a particular *cause*. If we interpret '*B*' as the *hypothesis*

Zigler ate strawberries for breakfast.

then Bayes's theorem may be regarded as a "rule for the probability of a hypothesis". *Given* a particular *event* (Zigler's upset stomach), the theorem may be used to determine the probability of a particular explanatory hypothesis. The probability of this explanatory hypothesis is 0.4. Finally, if the *explanatory function* of the hypothesis is emphasized, Bayes's theorem may be regarded as a rule for the probability of an explanation.

One of the outstanding features of Bayes's theorem, perhaps *the* outstanding feature, is its sensitivity to *new* evidence. Suppose, for example, we discover that Zigler *also* has hives. The *likelihood* of his eating strawberries *given both* an upset stomach *and* hives is $P(B, A \cdot C) = 0.7$, while the *likelihood* of his *not* eating strawberries given these two facts is $P(\overline{B}, A \cdot C) = 0.4$. Bayes's theorem now yields

$$P(A \cdot C, B) = \frac{P(B)P(B, A \cdot C)}{P(B)P(B, A \cdot C) + P(\overline{B})P(\overline{B}, A \cdot C)}$$

$$= \frac{(0.5)(0.7)}{(0.5)(0.7) + (0.5)(0.4)}$$

$$= 0.64.$$

Hence, the probability that Zigler ate strawberries for breakfast *given* the fact that he has *both* an upset stomach *and* hives is $P(A \cdot C, B) = 0.64$. The new evidence, then, has increased the conditional probability of 'B', however this element variable is interpreted. Some other evidence 'D' might increase this probability even more, or it might decrease it.

Notice that we are definitely not receiving something for nothing. Bayes's theorem is applicable *provided that* we can assign a "reasonable" *prior* probability $P(B)$ *and* that this probability is not so small that the effect of any amount of evidence will be negligible. As we have seen, the first proviso may face serious philosophic problems. To elucidate the point of the second proviso, suppose $P(B) = 0.00001$ (so $P(\overline{B}) = 0.99999$). If everything else remains the same,

$$P(A \cdot C, B) = 0.000017.$$

Hence, the smaller $P(B)$ becomes, the more difficult it becomes to obtain a conditional probability of 'B' which is significantly different from $P(B)$. In the extreme case in which $P(B) = 0$, Bayes's theorem is entirely useless. If $P(B)$ is "reasonable" however, then the conditional (or inverse, or posterior) probability of 'B' increases or decreases as the *likelihood* of 'B' increases or decreases.

EXAMPLE 6

A certain scientist has three mutually exclusive hypotheses to account for the occurrence of some phenomena 'A'. One of these hypotheses must be correct. Since he is the sole author of one of them, 'B', he assigns it a higher initial *personal* probability than the others. The complete assignments of prior probabilities and likelihoods are as follows.

$$P(B) = 0.5 \qquad P(B, A) = 0.2$$
$$P(C) = 0.3 \qquad P(C, A) = 0.4$$
$$P(D) = 0.2 \qquad P(D, A) = 0.7$$

Find

a)   the probability of 'B given A'
b)   the probability of 'C given A'
c)   the probability of 'D given A'

Solution. According to Bayes's theorem, we have

$$P(A, B) = \frac{P(B)P(B, A)}{P(B)P(B, A) + P(C)P(C, A) + P(D)P(D, A)}.$$

Substituting numerical values for letters,

$$P(A, B) = \frac{(0.5)(0.2)}{(0.5)(0.2) + (0.3)(0.4) + (0.2)(0.7)}$$

$$= \frac{0.10}{0.36} = 0.28.$$

Hence, the answer to a) is

$$P(A, B) = 0.28.$$

The answer to b) is

$$P(A, C) = \frac{P(C)P(C, A)}{0.36} = \frac{(0.3)(0.4)}{0.36} = 0.33.$$

And the answer to c) is

$$P(A, D) = \frac{P(D)P(D, A)}{0.36} = \frac{(0.2)(0.7)}{0.36} = 0.39.$$

Notice that although the favored hypothesis 'B' had the highest initial probability, its conditional probability on 'A' is lower than the conditional probabilities of the other two hypotheses. This supports the view of defenders of the psychological interpretation who claim that the effect of "reasonable" initial probabilities tends to become negligible as more reliable conditional probabilities are obtained. It will be worthwhile to pursue this claim a bit further.

Suppose our scientist discovers some new data 'E' that his hypotheses must explain; i.e., now he has 'A *and* E' to account for. Instead of using Bayes's theorem with the problematic initial probabilities $P(B)$, $P(C)$, and $P(D)$, he can build upon the recently obtained conditional probabilities $P(A, B)$, $P(A, C)$, and $P(A, D)$. That is, *his second experiment begins where his first experiment ended.* He has

$$P(A, B) = 0.28 \qquad P(B, A \cdot E) = 0.4$$
$$P(A, C) = 0.33 \qquad P(C, A \cdot E) = 0.8$$
$$P(A, D) = 0.39 \qquad P(D, A \cdot E) = 0.5$$

The new likelihoods were obtained (like the old ones) from some other experiments. Bayes's theorem yields the following new probabilities:

$$P(A \cdot E, B) = \frac{P(B)P(B, A \cdot E)}{P(B)P(B, A \cdot E) + P(C)P(C, A \cdot E) + P(D)P(D, A \cdot E)}$$

$$= \frac{(0.28)(0.4)}{(0.28)(0.4) + (0.33)(0.8) + (0.39)(0.5)}$$

$$= \frac{0.11}{0.57} = 0.19.$$

and

$$P(A \cdot E, C) = \frac{P(C)P(C, A \cdot E)}{0.57} = \frac{(0.33)(0.8)}{0.57} = 0.46$$

and

$$P(A \cdot E, D) = \frac{P(D)P(D, A \cdot E)}{0.57} = \frac{(0.39)(0.5)}{0.57} = 0.35.$$

These results again illustrate the fact that even if the prior probability of a hypothesis is overrated, as our information increases, the effect of the overrating becomes negligible. '*B*' was overrated to begin with, but further experiments have shown that it is the least probable of the three hypotheses under consideration. Moreover, as things now stand (i.e., after our second experiment), the conditional probability of '*C*' is higher than that of either of its competitors. Hence, from the first to the second experiment, the relative status of '*C*' and '*D*' has changed. A glance at the new *likelihoods* of '*C*' and '*D*' would have been sufficient to see that the relative status of these two hypotheses had changed. Bayes's theorem was required to *measure* their new probabilities. The method (which we have just illustrated) of beginning with more or less "reasonable" *personal probabilities* and building upon these (by means of Bayes's theorem) with probabilities obtained from empirical investigations is known as **the method of Bayesian inference.**

Review problems for Sec. 6.3.

1. Express the Principle of Total Probability in ordinary language and in symbolic notation.

2. Express the following without using the sign 'Σ'.
   a) ΣB_i $(i = 1, 2, 3)$
   b) $\Sigma B_i \cdot A$ $(i = 1, 2, \ldots, 6)$
   c) $\Sigma (A \vee B)_i$ $(i = 1, 2, 3, 4)$
   d) $\Sigma (A_i \cdot B)$ $(i = 1, 2, \ldots, n)$

3. The probability that we shall burn coal in our new furnace is $P(B) = 0.2$ and the probability that we shall burn wood is $P(\overline{B}) = 0.8$. If we burn coal, the chances are 8 in 10 that our heating bills will exceed our budget; and if we burn wood these chances drop to 6 in 10. What is the probability that our heating bills will exceed our budget?

4. The probability that Junior carries stones in his pocket is $P(B) = 0.5$ and the probability that he does not carry stones in his pocket is $P(\overline{B}) = 0.5$. If Junior carries stones in his pocket, the probability that there is a hole in his pocket is $P(B, A) = 0.9$.

If he does not carry stones in his pocket, the probability of a hole is $P(\overline{B}, A) = 0.4$. What is the probability that there is a hole in Junior's pocket?

5. Thirty percent of the senior class gifts in past years have been paintings, 60 percent have been statues, and 10 percent have been large photographs. If the senior gift is a painting, the probability that the class will have to borrow some extra money is $P(B, A) = 0.7$. If the gift is a statue, the probability that they will have to borrow is $P(C, A) = 0.6$. If the gift is a large photograph, the probability that they will have to borrow is $P(D, A) = 0.3$. What is the probability that the senior class will have to borrow some extra money?

6. The odds in favor of having cake tonight are 4 to 6. The odds in favor of having pie are 3 to 7, and these are also the odds in favor of ice cream. If we have cake there is a probability of $P(B, A) = 0.7$ that Hans will behave. This is also the probability that Hans will behave *if* we have ice cream; i.e., $P(D, A) = 0.7$. If we have pie the probability that Hans will behave is $P(C, A) = 0.5$. What is the probability that Hans will behave?

7. The probability that Dean took an overdose of sleeping pills is $P(B) = 0.02$, that he overworked himself is $P(C) = 0.2$, and that he overindulged in the sauce is $P(D) = 0.78$. If Dean took an overdose of sleeping pills, the probability that he will collapse is 0.6. If he overworked himself the probability that he will collapse is 0.5; and if he overindulged in the sauce the probability that he will collapse is 0.4. What is the probability that Dean will collapse?

8. Given

$$P(B) = P(C) = P(D) = P(E) = 0.25$$
$$P(B, A) = 0.2 \qquad P(C, A) = 0.7$$
$$P(D, A) = 0.1 \qquad P(E, A) = 0.8,$$

find $P(A)$.

9. If $P(B) = 0.5 = P(\overline{B})$, $P(B, A) = 0.4$, and $P(A) = 0.5$, what is the value of $P(\overline{B}, A)$?

10. If $P(B, A) = 0.9$, $P(\overline{B}, A) = 0.6$, $P(A) = 0.69$, and $P(B) = 0.3$, what is $P(\overline{B})$?

11. If $P(C, A) = 0.4$, $P(D, A) = 0.3$, $P(B) = 0.3$, $P(C) = 0.2$, $P(D) = 0.5$, and $P(A) = 0.41$, what is $P(B, A)$?

12. What is the value of $P(B)$ when $P(A) = 0.7$, $P(\overline{B}) = 0.4$, $P(B, A) = 0.7 = P(\overline{B}, A)$?

13. Why is the Principle of Total Probability sometimes referred to as the 'Rule of Elimination'?

14. Express Bayes's theorem in ordinary language and in symbolic notation.

15. How is the Principle of Total Probability related to Bayes's theorem?

16. How is Bayes's theorem related to the definition of conditional probability (6)?

17. How is the phrase "the *likelihood* of '*B relative to A*'" expressed symbolically?

18. How are *inverse* probabilities distinguished from *forward* probabilities in Bayes's theorem?

19. Why is Bayes's theorem sometimes referred to as the 'Principle of Inverse Probability'?

20. The probability that there is a spy among us is $P(B) = 0.6$. If there is a spy among us the probability that the enemy will obtain the secret documents is $P(B, A) = 0.7$. The probability that the enemy will find the secret documents if there is no spy among us is $P(\overline{B}, A) = 0.2$. Given that the enemy has the documents, what is the probability that there is a spy among us?

21. The chances of Silvester the cat playing in this room are 7 in 10. If Silvester was not playing in the room then the chances of the goldfish disappearing are about 1 in 10. With Silvester in the room, the chances of the goldfish disappearing are about 8 in 10. Given the missing goldfish, what is the probability that Silvester was playing in the room?

22. It is an even bet that Ted was in charge of the meeting. If he was in charge of the meeting then the probability of a change in policy is 0.7. The probability of a change in policy without Ted in charge is 0.4. Relative to our information that there has been a change in policy, find the probability that

    a) Ted was in charge of the meeting.
    b) Ted was not in charge of the meeting.

23. The probability that Floyd flew is 0.3, that he took the train is 0.5, and that he boarded the bus is 0.2. If Floyd flew then the probability that he would arrive Wednesday is 0.6. If he took the train the probability that he would arrive Wednesday is 0.7; and if he boarded the bus the probability that he would arrive Wednesday is 0.4. Given that he arrived Wednesday, find the probability that

    a) Floyd flew.
    b) He took a train.
    c) He boarded the bus.

24. The probability of Bentley joining the army is 0.6. The probability of his joining the navy is 0.2, and that is also the probability of his joining the marines. If Bentley joined the army then the probability that he would be in Germany now is 0.7. If he joined the navy the probability that he would be in Germany now is 0.2. In the marines, the probability of his being in Germany would be 0.5. Given that Bentley is in Germany now, find the probability that

    a) He joined the army.
    b) He joined the navy.
    c) He joined the marines.

25. The probability that Phil drove is 0.5, that Fred drove is 0.3, and that Fritz drove is 0.2. When Phil drives, the probability of an accident is 0.2. When Fred drives, the probability of an accident is 0.6, and when Fritz drives, the probability of an

accident is 0.7. We have just been informed that there has been an accident and we would like to have the probability that

a) Phil drove.
b) Fred drove.
c) Fritz drove.

26. Given

$$P(B) = 0.4 \qquad P(B, A) = 0.7$$
$$P(C) = 0.3 \qquad P(C, A) = 0.6$$
$$P(D) = 0.2 \qquad P(D, A) = 0.8$$
$$P(E) = 0.1 \qquad P(E, A) = 0.5$$

find

a) $P(B \cdot A)$ e) $P(A, B)$
b) $P(C \cdot A)$ f) $P(A, C)$
c) $P(D \cdot A)$ g) $P(A, D)$
d) $P(E \cdot A)$ h) $P(A, E)$

27. Why is Bayes's theorem sometimes referred to as

a) 'the rule for the probability of a cause'
b) 'the rule for the probability of a hypothesis'

28. What is the method of Bayesian inference?

29. Make up an example of the method of Bayesian inference.

6.4 Rules of succession

The principles presented in Secs. 6.1–6.3 are accepted by almost everyone and they may be found in most "practical" introductions to the theory of probability. The rules of succession that are presented in this section are a bit problematic and are frequently omitted from introductory texts. They are included here primarily because of their philosophic interest. Their proofs are omitted because they involve more mathematics than readers of this text are supposed to have.

Laplace's rule of succession says that if it is equally probable that any individual (person, place, or thing) will have a certain property represented by 'F' and if m of n observed individuals have this property, the probability that the *next* individual observed will have F is

$$\frac{m + 1}{n + 2}.$$

EXAMPLE 1

We are drawing balls from a bag containing black and white balls. After each draw, we *replace* the ball. If 8 of the first 10 drawn are white, what is the probability that the *next* ball drawn will be white?

Solution. Laplace's rule of succession yields

$$\frac{m+1}{n+2} = \frac{8+1}{10+2} = \frac{3}{4}.$$

EXAMPLE 2

We are visiting a foreign country and discover that 999 out of 1000 people observed are wearing sweaters. (Presumably the chances of anyone wearing or not wearing a sweater are equal.) What is the probability that the *next* person observed will be wearing a sweater?

Solution. According to Laplace's rule of succession, we have

$$\frac{m+1}{n+2} = \frac{999+1}{1000+2} = \frac{500}{501}.$$

As the solution to this problem suggests, Laplace's rule yields values approaching unity as m/n approaches unity.

A corollary of Laplace's rule says that if it is equally probable that any individual will have a certain property represented by 'F' and if m of n observed individuals have this property, the probability that the *next* n' individuals will have F is

$$\frac{m+1}{n+n'+1}.$$

EXAMPLE 3

We are picking peaches from a tree and find that 12 out of 15 picked so far are wormy. What is the probability that the *next* 6 picked will be wormy?

Solution. The corollary of Laplace's rule of succession yields

$$\frac{m+1}{n+n'+1} = \frac{12+1}{15+6+1} = \frac{13}{22}.$$

EXAMPLE 4

Out of 99 safety pins produced by a certain machine, only 10 were defective. What is the probability that the *next* 5000 will *not* be defective?

Solution. The corollary of Laplace's rule yields

$$\frac{m+1}{n+n'+1} = \frac{89+1}{99+5000+1} = \frac{9}{510}.$$

If m/n remains stable, the corollary to Laplace's rule yields values approaching 0 as n' approaches infinity. Since the data on which the predictions are made are *not* increasing, but the scope of the predictions *is* increasing, one would expect the predictions to become increasingly uncertain. Laplace's corollary completely agrees with this expectation. .

One of the standard objections to Laplace's rule of succession is that it allows one to obtain probabilities from *complete ignorance*. If we are given no data at all (i.e., $m = 0$ and $n = 0$), the probability that the *next* individual observed will have *any* property is $\frac{1}{2}$. This, of course, should have been expected from any rule of probability bearing the name of the greatest of all classical theorists. It is a direct consequence of the Principle of Indifference; i.e., it is a consequence of the *a priori* assumption of equal initial probabilities. Nothing further needs to be said about this. What is worse, however, is that the rule leads to probability values greater than unity. To illustrate this point, consider the following case.

We have a bag of balls from which three are drawn. The first ball drawn is red; the second ball drawn is white; and the third drawn is blue. According to Laplace's rule, the probability that the *next* ball drawn will be red is

$$\frac{m+1}{n+2} = \frac{1+1}{3+2} = \frac{2}{5}.$$

Similarly, the probability that the *next* ball drawn will be white is $\frac{2}{5}$, as is the probability that the *next* ball drawn will be blue. Since the balls and drawings are independent of one another, the Special Addition Principle tells us that the probability of drawing *either* a red ball *or* a white ball *or* a blue ball is

$$\tfrac{2}{5} + \tfrac{2}{5} + \tfrac{2}{5} = \tfrac{6}{5}.$$

This result is absurd and violates our first postulate. Since it is a consequence of Laplace's rule of succession, the latter is unacceptable.

Two methods have been suggested to avoid these objections. The simplest way to avoid the objections is to abandon the "normalizing factor" $\frac{1}{2}$ from Laplace's rule. The result of this move has been called (by Carnap) the **straight rule**: If m of n individuals are observed to have a certain property represented by 'F' and this is *all* the information we have about these individuals, the probability that the *next* individual observed will have F is m/n. Some writers have applied the name 'straight rule' to the two types of frequency theories considered in Sec. 5.3. Both of the latter theories have been referred to as 'rules for induction by enumeration'. Hence, the rule just presented has also been called a 'rule for induction by enumeration'. There is surely enough similarity between this rule and the two frequency theories to apply the same name to all three. But in this text the name 'straight rule' will be reserved for the rule presented above, a rule which may be distinguished from the two frequency theories by the fact that it is only applicable to *unique individuals* or *unique sets of individuals* in a sequence (e.g., the very *next* event, the *next* 10 trials, etc.) Following W. E. Johnson, we may call such nondemonstrative inferences from an observed sequence of individuals to a *particular* member or to *particular* members of that sequence an **eduction.** Thus, we may say that all the rules of succession presented in this section are *eductive rules.* Nondemonstrative inference rules involving *indefinite* members (e.g., *a* head turning up, *an* ace appearing, *a* man dying before his ninetieth birthday, etc.) or *all* members (e.g., *all* basketball players are over 6 feet tall, *all* men die before reaching 120 years of age, etc.) of sequences will be called **inductive** rules and the inferences themselves, **inductions.** Until we reached this section, the only nondemonstrative inferences we considered were *inductive.*

Those who advocate the straight rule are more cautious than Laplace. If no observations have been made (i.e., $m = n = 0$) and we have no other relevant information, then, according to the straight rule, *nothing* can be said about the probability that the *next* (first) individuals observed will have the property represented by '*F*', whatever that property is. Nevertheless, it has been protested that defenders of this rule seem extremely bold when, after observing one individual out of one with F and completely lacking other relevant information, they assert that the probability that the *next* (second) individual observed will have F is 1. Those who raise this objection seem to reason as follows. Whenever a probability of unity is assigned to an event, most people assume that it is "practically speaking" certain that the event will occur. That is, the chances of its not occurring are so small that they may be ignored. If such attitudes are adopted toward events with such probabilities, then on the basis of a single observation and with no other relevant information the value yielded by the straight rule is *extravagant.* This argument is convincing only insofar as people *are* actually misled by a probability value based *solely* on a single observation. Given only a single observation with no other relevant information, however, it is difficult to imagine many people being extraordinarily impressed with *any* probability assignment.

An alternative method of salvaging Laplace's rule of succession has been suggested by Carnap. In our discussion of the logical range theory, we found it useful to distinguish primitive properties from other properties. Given a universe of coin tosses with two (ordinary) properties, that of being a head and that of being a tail, we *defined* the latter in terms of the former. We called the property of being a head a 'primitive property' simply because it was the property in terms of which the other property (being a tail) was defined. Every property (primitive or not) in a universe of discourse has a predicate coordinated with it which is used to refer to it; e.g., we use the predicate 'is a head' to refer to the fact that a coin has the property of being a head. Primitive properties may be said to have **primitive predicates** coordinated with them. (Carnap originally stipulated that primitive predicates must be logically independent, but J. G. Kemeny showed that this restriction may be abandoned if some additional postulates are introduced. The details of these moves will not be considered here.) A conjunction of *all* primitive predicates (or the negations of some or all of them) in a language is called a **predicate expression.** For example, consider a simple little world of coin tosses with the *single* primitive property of being a head. We shall have one primitive predicate to refer to this property, namely 'is a head'. In a world with r primitive predicates, there are exactly $k = 2^r$ predicate expressions. (We always assume the number of primitive predicates *equals* the number of primitive properties.) For the little world under consideration, we have $k = 2^r = 2^1 = 2$. They are

Predicate Expressions ($k = 2$)
_____
is a head

is not a head

It must be emphasized that predicate expressions are *quite different* from state descriptions in three important respects. a) State descriptions are *sentences*; predicate expressions are merely *parts* of sentences. b) The name of every individual in the given universe of discourse *must* appear in *every* state description as the subject of some conjunct; individual names usually do not occur at all in predicate expressions and *never* occur as the subject of some conjunct. (If a predicate expression *had* a subject prefixed to it, the result would be a *sentence*.) c) When we count the number of state descriptions 2^{nr} in a universe, we must consider the number of individuals n *and* the number of primitive predicates r; when we count the number of predicate expressions k, we must consider *only* the number of primitive predicates. All these distinctions are fundamental. Hence, the idea of predicate expressions should be regarded as an additional tool for our analysis.

We suppose, then, that any individual in this little world may be completely described (for our purposes) by attributing to it one of the properties referred to by the expressions above. If we assign every predicate expression a number w, called the *width* of that expression, then Carnap's revised rule of succession may be specified as follows. If m of n individuals are observed to have a certain property represented by 'F' and if the predicate coordinated with this property has a width of w, the probability that the *next* individual observed will have F is

$$\frac{m + w}{n + k},$$

where $k = 2^r$ and there are r primitive predicates. Carnap calls (a somewhat more rigorously specified version of) this rule, the **singular predictive inference rule.** In the simplest cases (the *only* kind we shall consider) $w = 1$.

In the extreme case of a world small enough to be described by a *single* primitive predicate, the singular predictive inference rule becomes indistinguishable from Laplace's rule of succession; i.e., we have

$$\frac{m + w}{n + k} = \frac{m + 1}{n + 2}.$$

Hence, while our simple little world was useful to explain the various parts of Carnap's rule, it will not suffice to show the difference in the numerical values yielded by the two rules, a difference that may easily be enormous. The following examples will elucidate Carnap's rule and provide a comparison of it with Laplace's *and* the straight rule.

EXAMPLE 5

Consider the case of a man drawing balls from a barrel with replacement (i.e., he replaces each ball drawn out). He has drawn three red balls, two white, two blue, two black, and one green. The question is, What is the probability that the very *next* ball he draws will be red?

Solution. To solve this problem with the help of the singular predictive inference rule, we begin by determining the number of primitive predicates k. We can distinguish five primitive properties, namely, the five colors red, white, blue, black, and green. We have a primitive predicate for each one. Hence, the total number of predicate expressions for this universe of discourse is $k = 2^r = 2^5 = 32$. According to Carnap's rule, the required probability is

$$\frac{m + w}{n + k} = \frac{3 + 1}{10 + 32} = \frac{2}{21}.$$

Laplace's rule yields

$$\frac{m + 1}{n + 2} = \frac{1}{3}.$$

The extremely "cautious" straight rule yields $m/n = \frac{3}{10}$.

Notice that the reason Carnap's rule yields a value so much lower than the values yielded by the other rules is that Carnap's rule takes account of certain *logical possibilities* which the other rules ignore. There are many different kinds of nonred balls and, therefore, many different *ways* for a nonred ball to appear. Carnap's rule is designed to be "sensitive" to these different possibilities; the other rules are not. Carnap's rule takes full account of *frequencies* in the empirical factor 'm/n' and *logical possibilities* in the logical factor 'w/k'. Laplace's rule takes full account of frequencies in the empirical factor 'm/n' but only a limited account of logical possibilities in the logical factor '$\frac{1}{2}$'. The straight rule only takes full account of frequencies. While we cannot decide here what one's rules of succession *ought* to take account of, certain more or less unsatisfactory consequences have been indicated for Laplace's and the straight rule. The following example reveals an infelicity in Carnap's rule

EXAMPLE 6

Suppose a man is drawing balls from a barrel with replacement. He draws 1 red ball out of 12. Moreover each of the 12 balls has a different color. What is the probability that the *next* ball he draws will be red?

Solution. We begin by determining the number of predicate expressions for this universe. There are 12 primitive predicates. Hence $k = 2^{12} = 4096$. According to the singular predictive inference rule, the probability that the *next* ball drawn will be red is

$$\frac{m + w}{n + k} = \frac{1 + 1}{12 + 4096} = \frac{2}{4108} = 0.00005.$$

There is an enormous difference between this result and the 0.14 yielded by Laplace's rule or the 0.08 yielded by the straight rule. Apart from the fact that 0.00005 seems to be an implausible value to assign to the probability in question, the example suggests that in some situations or for some universes of discourse the logical factor 'w/k' might be so *small* that the affect of almost any amount of empirical data would be negligible. This may be intuitively satisfactory to anyone who advocates the *logical* interpretation, but to someone looking for a rule which somehow *balanced* the significance of logical and empirical information, the result seems a bit one-sided.

Review problems for Sec. 6.4.

1. What is Laplace's rule of succession?

    Use Laplace's rule to solve the next three problems.

2. If $\frac{3}{4}$ of the ranchers you have seen at a meeting are corn growers, what is the probability that the *next* rancher you see will be a corn grower?

3. Exactly $\frac{9}{10}$ of the football players who have been injured this year have weighed over 220 pounds. What is the probability that the next football player who is injured will weigh over 220 pounds?

4. Two-thirds of those who have left our prison have returned. What is the probability that the next person who leaves our prison will return? What is the probability that he will not return?

    Use Laplace's corollary to solve the next three problems.

5. If 45 out of the last 60 people to cross the bridge have been from Ontario, what is the probability that the next 100 people who cross the bridge will be from Ontario?

6. Exactly $\frac{19}{25}$ of the teenagers who have come to the beach have driven their own cars. What is the probability that the next 2000 who come will drive their own cars?

7. All 10 of the observed inhabitants of a certain village have been nearsighted. What is the probability that the next 5000 observed will be nearsighted?

8. What is one objection to Laplace's rule of succession? What reply, if any, might be offered to it?

9. What is the straight rule?

10. What is one objection to the straight rule, and what, if any, reply might be offered to it?

11. How is induction by enumeration related to the straight rule and frequency theories?

12. What is the difference between an induction and an eduction?

13. What is a predicate expression?

14. Identify three ways in which predicate expressions differ from state descriptions.

15. What is Carnap's singular predictive inference rule?

16. Why are 'm/n' and 'w/k' in Carnap's rule referred to as the 'empirical factor' and the 'logical factor', respectively?

17. In terms of logical and empirical factors, how do the three rules of succession differ? Use the singular predictive inference rule to solve the following.

18. A bag is full of balls colored red, blue, green, or yellow. If $\frac{5}{8}$ of the balls drawn from the bag with replacement are red, what is the probability that the *next* ball drawn will be red? (*Note:* $k = 2^r = 2^4$.)

19. Given another bag with similarly colored balls and $\frac{1}{3}$ of those drawn out red, what is the probability that the next ball drawn will be red? What is the probability that the next ball drawn will not be red? (*Note:* Use the Complement Principle for the latter *or* else Carnap's rule with '$1 - (w/k)$' instead of 'w/k'.)

20. Given a third bag with similarly colored balls and six out of six drawn red, what is the probability that the next ball drawn will be red?

21. Suppose you are given a box of tickets numbered from 1 to 6. If three out of the first eight drawn with replacement have the number 2 on them, what is the probability that the next ticket drawn will have a 2 on it?

22. Given another box of similarly numbered tickets and $\frac{1}{3}$ of those drawn out with the number 4 on them, what is the probability that the next ticket drawn will have a 4 on it? What is the probability that the next ticket drawn will not have a 4 on it?

23. Given a third box of similarly numbered tickets and $\frac{4}{5}$ drawn with the number 6 on them, what is the probability that the next ticket drawn will have a 6 on it? What is the probability that the next ticket drawn will not have a 6 on it?

Comprehensive review questions for Chapter 6.

1. The probability of my son becoming a pianist is 0.25. The probability of his becoming a jazz pianist is 0.19. Given the fact that he has become a pianist, what is the probability that he plays jazz?

2. Aunt Lil will either buy Jed *only* a shirt or a tie or a pair of socks. The probability that she will buy him a shirt is 0.3 and that is also the probability that she will buy

him a tie. The probability that she will buy him a pair of socks is 0.2. What is the probability that she will buy him *either* a shirt *or* a tie *or* a pair of socks? What is the probability that she will buy him a tie *or* a pair of socks?

3. The chances of Radcliff finding the book he needs are 4 in 10. If he finds the book the probability that he will write an acceptable term paper is 0.8. If he does not find the book the probability that he will write an acceptable paper is 0.3. Find the probability that he will

   a) find the book *and* write an acceptable paper
   b) not find the book *and* write an acceptable paper
   c) write an acceptable paper

4. Forty percent of the men in our family are mailmen and 30 percent of them have flatfeet. If the probability of a man in our family being a flat-footed mailman is 0.15, what is the probability of one being *either* flat-footed *or* a mailman?

5. If Ginger ate the candy the probability that she would be sick now is 0.7. If she did not eat the candy the probability that she would be sick now is 0.3. The probability that Ginger ate the candy is 0.6. Find the probability that

   a) Ginger ate the candy *and* is sick.
   b) Ginger did not eat the candy *and* is sick.
   c) Ginger ate the candy *given* that she is sick.
   d) Ginger did not eat the candy *given* that she is sick.

6. The probability of meeting a representative from Illinois is 0.03; New York, 0.2; Texas, 0.16; Michigan, 0.4; and Kansas, 0.13. Find the probability of meeting a representative from

   a) Illinois *or* New York
   b) Illinois *or* Michigan
   c) Texas *or* Kansas
   d) Texas *or* Illinois
   e) Texas *or* Michigan *or* New York
   f) New York *or* Illinois *or* Kansas
   g) Michigan *or* Kansas *or* Illinois
   h) Illinois *or* New York *or* Texas *or* Michigan
   i) Kansas *or* Michigan *or* New York *or* Illinois
   j) at least one of the five states.

7. Given

$$P(B) = P(C) = P(D) = P(E) = P(F) = 0.2$$

$$P(B, A) = 0.5 \qquad P(E, A) = 0.8$$

$$P(C, A) = 0.6 \qquad P(F, A) = 0.9$$

$$P(D, A) = 0.7$$

   find

   a) $P(A)$
   b) $P(B \cdot A)$
   c) $P(C \cdot A)$
   d) $P(D \cdot A)$
   e) $P(E \cdot A)$
   f) $P(F \cdot A)$
   g) $P(A, B)$
   h) $P(A, C)$
   i) $P(A, D)$
   j) $P(A, E)$
   k) $P(A, F)$

Suggestions for further reading related to Chapter 6.

Feller, William, *An Introduction to Probability Theory and Its Applications*. New York: John Wiley & Sons, Inc., 1957, Chapters 1 and 5.

Gnedenko, B. V., and Khinchin, A. YA, *An Elementary Introduction to the Theory of Probability*, Trans. by W. R. Stahl. San Francisco, Calif.: W. H. Freeman & Co., Publishers, 1961, Chapters 1–4.

Goldberg, Samuel, *Probability*, An introduction. Englewood Cliffs, N. J.: Prentice-Hall, Inc., 1960, Chapters 1 and 2.

Kolmogorov, A. N., *Foundations of the Theory of Probability*. New York: Chelsea Publishing Co., 1956, Chapter 1.

Mosteller, Frederick, Rourke, Robert E. K., and Thomas, George B., Jr., *Probability With Statistical Applications*. Reading, Mass.: Addison-Wesley Publishing Co., Inc., 1961, Chapters 3 and 4.

Reichenbach, Hans, *The Theory of Probability*, Trans. by Ernest H. Hutton and Maria Reichenbach. Berkeley, Calif.: University of California Press, 1949, Chapter 3.

Thorp, Edward O, *Elementary Probability*. New York: John Wiley & Sons, Inc., 1966, Chapters 1 and 2.

Chapter

7

Distributions

We have talked about distributions of many different kinds of things; e.g., the distribution of heads in a sequence of coin tosses, the distribution of test grades, the distribution of wormy apples in a sequence of picks, the distribution of red balls in a box, the distribution of customers in certain stores, etc. In this chapter we shall introduce standard methods of summarizing distributions, methods of constructing certain kinds of distributions (the principles of permutations and combinations), and two especially important types of distributions (the binomial and normal distributions). Along the way we shall consider a few more principles of the calculus of probability.

7.1 Distribution summaries

Suppose a class of 30 students is given an arithmetic test and the scores are arranged in descending order from the highest score 30 to the lowest score 3.

30	28	26	24	24	23	22	21	20	20
20	20	20	20	18	17	16	16	15	15
14	14	13	13	11	10	9	8	6	5

30 Test Scores

Figure 7.11

Figure 7.11 may be regarded as a *picture* of the results of the arithmetic test. Since every one of the scores is recorded, the *accuracy* of this picture cannot be questioned. But it is not an easy picture to remember and it is not a very suggestive picture. Just looking at it, it is difficult to know if the class did well or poorly. What is required is a method of *summarizing* the information in Figure 7.11, a method which would provide a more lucid (less complicated) and suggestive picture. Such summaries of collections of numbers will be called **distribution summaries** (because they are merely summaries of distributions). Many writers (especially statisticians) refer to them as 'statistical summaries'. The increased lucidity and suggestiveness obtained by distribution summaries will not be a gift. We shall have to give up some *details*, and this is tantamount to suppressing a certain amount of *information* and *accuracy*. In this respect distribution summaries are no different from any other summaries. The formal science whose subject matter consists of the various kinds and techniques of constructing such summaries is called **descriptive statistics.**

The most widely used type of distribution summary records the *frequencies* with which various *classes* of numbers appear; it is called a **frequency distribution.** For example, consider Figure 7.12.

Class Interval	Class Frequency
30–27	2
26–23	4
22–19	8
18–15	6
14–11	5
10–7	3
6–3	2

Frequency Distribution of Scores

Figure 7.12

The 30 *scores* of Figure 7.11 have been divided neatly into the seven *classes* listed in the column under "class interval". The seven classes are distinguished from one another by their upper and lower class limits. The **upper class limit** of a class is the maximum value allowed to any member of that class; e.g., the highest value (score) allowed to a member of our second class (second line) is 26. Any score above 26 becomes *by definition* a member of the first class. The **lower class limit** of a class is the minimum value allowed to any member of that class; e.g., the lowest value allowed to a member of our first class is 27. Any score below 27 is *by definition* eliminated from the first class.

The **class interval** is the difference between the lower class limits of two successive classes; e.g., the difference between 27 and the very next lower class limit 23 is 4. All the class intervals in Figure 7.12 are the same length. It is not necessary to have equal class intervals for every class but it is usually convenient. Similarly, it was not necessary to construct seven classes with intervals of length 4. We might have constructed only two classes with intervals of length 15 or three classes with intervals of length 10. We used seven classes with intervals of length 4 because that seemed to provide a more lucid and suggestive summary. It is generally the case that the *data* to be classified and the immediate *purposes* of the classification "favor" certain groupings rather than others.

Each appearance of a *number* belonging to one of the seven classes is regarded as an appearance of the *class* itself. Hence, the numbers listed in the right-hand column are called **class frequencies.** For example, a score of *either* 30 *or* 29 *or* 28 *or* 27 appeared twice (30 and 28); hence, '2' is entered in the class frequency column opposite the class interval '30–27'. Four numbers in the interval from 26 to 23 inclusive appeared (26, 24, 24, 13). Hence, '4' is entered in the class frequency column opposite the class interval '26–23'.

An alternative method of summarizing data involves the use of graphs. For example, the information contained in Figure 7.12 might be summarized as in Figure 7.13.

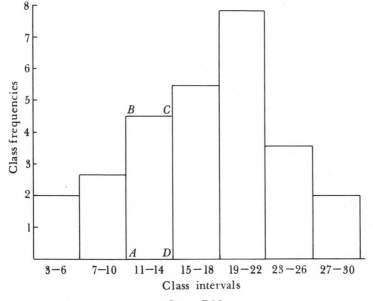

Figure 7.13

In this figure the class intervals are represented on a horizontal scale and the class frequencies are represented on a vertical scale. This method of summarizing data is called a **histogram.** Each rectangle, then, represents one of our seven classes; e.g., $A\ B\ C\ D$ represents the class of five scores (11, 13, 13, 14, 14) in the interval from 11 to 14 inclusive. If we had constructed only two classes with intervals of length 15, our corresponding histogram would have had only two tall rectangles; three classes with intervals of length 10 would have become a histogram with three rectangles.

Class marks or **class midpoints** are the midpoints between upper and lower class limits. Hence, to find the class mark of any class, we add its class limits and divide by 2; e.g., the class mark of our first class is

$$\frac{30 + 27}{2} = 28.5.$$

The class mark of the class represented by the rectangle $ABCD$ above is

$$\frac{11 + 14}{2} = 12.5.$$

Class marks are used for the alternative method of summarizing data shown in Figure 7.14.

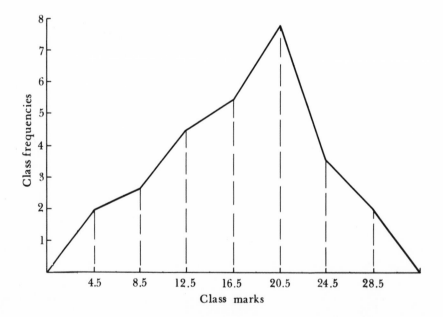

Figure 7.14

The single-line graph presented in Figure 7.14 is called a **frequency polygon.** Instead of indicating class intervals along the horizontal line, we used class marks. The upper part of the polygon is constructed by drawing a line connecting each of the midpoints of the tops of the rectangles in the histogram of Figure 7.13.

These three types of distribution summaries (frequency distributions, histograms, and frequency polygons) are more or less equally accurate, lucid, and suggestive. They certainly do not *exhaust* the class of such accurate, lucid, and suggestive summaries. We might, for example, represent the data by little human figures or stars or crosses, etc. There is practically no limit to the kinds of pictorial representations we might use. On the other hand, there are *shorter* types of summaries available which involve only one or two numbers. Such summaries exchange a *maximum* amount of *detail* for a minimum *description* of the given data. They might not be as accurate as the types of summaries we have already considered but, as we shall see, they *may* be as lucid and suggestive.

Suppose a class of 11 students is given a chemistry test and the scores are recorded as follows.

$$30 \quad 26 \quad 24 \quad 24 \quad 24 \quad 21 \quad 20 \quad 15 \quad 13 \quad 12 \quad 11$$

Eleven Test Scores

Figure 7.15

One short and simple way to summarize the results in Figure 7.15 is to give the "average" score. There are, however, three different numbers that might be considered the "average" score. The **arithmetic mean** (or **mean**) of a set of n numbers is the sum of these numbers divided by n. Using the Greek lowercase letter 'μ' (pronounced '*mu*') to abbreviate 'the arithmetic mean', the mean value of the numbers $X_1, X_2, \ldots, X_n$ is

$$\mu = \frac{X_1 + X_2 + \cdots + X_n}{n} = \frac{\sum X_i}{n} \qquad (i = 1, 2, \ldots, n).$$

The mean of the scores recorded in Figure 7.15 is

$$\mu = \frac{30 + 26 + \cdots + 11}{11} = 20.$$

Although our problems will only involve finding *population* means, it should be mentioned that statisticians usually use '$\overline{X}$' to represent the mean of a *sample* drawn from some population and 'μ' to represent the mean of the whole population.

The **median** of a set of n numbers is the *value* of the middle number when the whole set is arranged in descending order from the highest value to the lowest. The median of the scores recorded in Figure 7.15 is 21 since there are exactly five scores above and below it. If *n* happens to be an *even* number, the median is the mean of the middle two; e.g., the median of the numbers

$$10 \quad 8 \quad 6 \quad 4 \quad 3 \quad 1$$

is

$$\frac{6 + 4}{2} = 5.$$

The **mode** of a set of *n* numbers is the value that occurs most frequently; e.g., the mode of the set of numbers in Figure 7.15 is 24. The *modal* height of adult male pigeons is the most common height for these birds. The *modal* income of doctors is the most common income for doctors.

The mean, median, and mode are *single number* statistical summaries. They are usually referred to as **measures of central tendency** because in one way or another they indicate the tendency of data to cluster about this or that value. They have maximum brevity and they can be seriously misleading. For example, suppose a king reports that his five generals (all of whom are equally deserving) should not complain about their salaries because they are "averaging" $10,000 a year. If they have a *mean* salary of $10,000 but the distribution looks like this,

$$\$46,000 \quad \$1000 \quad \$1000 \quad \$1000 \quad \$1000,$$

then four generals have plenty to complain about. In this case, either the *median* or the *mode* $1000 would have been a more accurate summary of their situation. Again, suppose the following distribution of test scores is summarized by reporting that the average score is 60.

$$1 \quad 3 \quad 3 \quad 3 \quad 3 \quad 4 \quad 60 \quad 90 \quad 94 \quad 94 \quad 94 \quad 94 \quad 97$$

The *median is* 60, but this is hardly an accurate summary of the 13 scores. Most people either scored very low, 3, or very high, 94. Hence, it would be misleading to report a mode of 3 *or* of 94. To be precise, we should say the distribution has *two* modes or is **bimodal** about 3 and 94. So-called "memory courses" frequently yield distributions of test scores which are bimodal in character, because those who memorize the material have no trouble at all and those who fail to memorize the material are completely lost.

Distribution *summaries* may be used to determine initial probabilities in much the same way that the distributions themselves are used. The primary difference between using a summary of the data and using the whole collection is that the former may permit fewer judgements than the latter. For example, we could not make as many probability judgments given the frequency polygon in Figure 7.14 as we could given the complete collection of data in Figure 7.11. Using the complete collection, we might judge that the probability of a score of, say, 24 on similar tests is $\frac{2}{15}$. Such a judgment completely escapes the data provided by the frequency polygon. Nevertheless, a number of initial probabilities are preserved by most summaries. The formal science whose subject matter consists of the various kinds and techniques of making inferences from such summaries is called **statistical inference.**

EXAMPLE 1

Suppose a similar arithmetic test is going to be given to the class of students whose previous scores are summarized in Figure 7.12. What is the probability of a student obtaining a score between 18 and 15 inclusive?

Solution. Since 6 out of 30 students received scores in this interval, we would judge that the probability of a student scoring between 18 and 15 inclusive is $\frac{6}{30}$ or $\frac{1}{5}$.

EXAMPLE 2

Under exactly the same conditions as Example 1, what is the probability that a student will score *either* above 27 *or* below 7?

Solution. Since 2 students scored above 27 and 2 scored below 7, the probability that a student will score *either* above 27 *or* below 7 is $\frac{2}{15}$.

EXAMPLE 3

Under the same conditions, what is the probability that a student will score below 23 but above 14?

Solution. Scores below 23 and above 14 fall into the two classes, 22–19 and 18–15. There are 14 students in these classes. Hence, the probability that a student will score below 23 but above 14 is $\frac{7}{15}$.

Review problems for Sec. 7.1.

1. Construct a frequency distribution for the following collection of freshmen weights using the classes 110–114, 115–119, . . . , 130–134.

112	113	114	115	116	116	116	118	120	121
122	122	122	122	122	123	123	123	124	124
125	126	126	127	127	128	128	129	132	133

Using the frequency distribution constructed for Prob. 1, answer the following.

2. What are the five lower class limits?

3. What is the class interval of all five classes?

4. What are the class marks for these five classes?

5. Find the mean, median, and modal weights of the whole collection.

6. Find the mean, median, and modal weights of the class 115–119.

7. Construct a histogram and a frequency polygon for the 30 weights.

8. What is the probability that a freshman picked at random from this group weighs

    a) 116   d) from 110 to 114
    b) 122   e) either 127 *or* 123
    c) from 125 to 129   f) either 124 *or* 126 *or* 127
    pounds?

9. Given the information that the freshman picked belongs to the class 120–124, what is the probability that he weighs

    a) 122   d) 120 *or* 122
    b) 123   e) 122 *or* 123
    c) 124   f) 121 *or* 124
    pounds?

10. What is a measure of central tendency?

11. Make up a set of five numbers whose mean and median both equal 10.

12. Make up a set of five numbers whose mode and median both equal 5.

13. Suppose you are considering a new job and you are told that the mean salary of people in your class is $6000 a year. Would this information be more or less useful to you than the modal salary? Explain your answer.

14. Construct a frequency distribution for the following collection of test scores using the classes 0–9, 10–19, . . . , 90–99.

4	12	17	21	22	25	28	30	31	31
32	36	37	39	40	40	41	42	43	43
43	43	47	50	51	52	53	54	55	56
58	59	62	63	64	65	65	65	66	68
72	74	74	75	79	82	85	88	96	98

    Using the frequency distribution constructed for Prob. 14, answer the following.

15. What are the five upper class limits immediately following 9?

16. What is the class interval of all 10 classes?

17. Find the mean, median, and modal scores of the following classes.

    a) 20–29   c) 40–49
    b) 30–39   d) 70–79

18. Construct a histogram and a frequency polygon for the 50 scores.

19. If each of the 50 scores is written on a small piece of paper and put in a box, what is the probability of drawing out a paper (with replacement) with a score of

    a) 31
    b) 43
    c) 65
    d) 74 *or* 85
    e) 40 *or* 43
    f) 36 *or* 65 *or* 88

20. Find the probability of drawing out a paper with a score in the class

    a) 50–59
    b) 60–69
    c) 80–89
    d) 20–29 *or* 40–49
    e) 0–9 *or* 90–99
    f) 10–19 *or* 30–39 *or* 60–69

21. Given the information that a score drawn belongs to the class 40–49, what is the probability that it is

    a) 40
    b) 43
    c) 40 *or* 47
    d) 40 *or* 42 *or* 43

7.2   Variety and Chebyshev's theorem

Distribution summaries usually involve at least two numbers (not, however, two modal values as in the example above). It is customary to summarize a distribution by indicating not only its central tendency but also its variety. Statistical measures used to indicate the amount of variety in a set of data are called **measures of variety.** In many cases even a crude indication of the amount of variety in some data may correct a misleading description of central tendency. For example, given the information that the *mean* salary of five generals is $10,000 *and* the additional information that the salaries range from $46,000 to $1000, we would immediately sense something peculiar. Technically the **range** of a set of numbers is the difference between the largest and the smallest numbers in the set. The range of the generals' salaries is

$$\$46{,}000 - \$1000 = \$45{,}000.$$

If this range were *smaller*, say $1000, the five salaries would have been *more nearly alike.*

The range of a set of numbers is a very crude measure of variety. It can be extremely misleading. In the case of our five generals, for example, there is indeed a great *difference* between the largest and smallest salaries, but there is *not* a great deal of *variety* in the salaries. Four out of five are exactly the same. The two most reliable (i.e., least liable to be misleading) and frequently used measures of variety are the *variance* and the *standard deviation*. We shall consider each in turn.

Suppose two groups, I and II, of 10 children are given a spelling test and the scores obtained are listed in the first two columns of Figure 7.21.

I. Scores	II Scores	I. D	II. D	I. D^2	II. D^2
$\mu = 5$	$\mu = 4$	$\mu - X$	$\mu - X$	$(\mu - X)^2$	$(\mu - X)^2$
6	3	-1	1	1	1
8	1	-3	3	9	9
4	7	1	-3	1	9
9	3	-4	1	16	1
7	6	-2	-2	4	4
3	5	2	-1	4	1
2	3	3	1	9	1
5	6	0	-2	0	4
1	4	4	0	16	0
5	2	0	2	0	4
50	40			60	34

$$\sigma^2 = \frac{\Sigma\,(\mu - X)^2}{n} \qquad \text{I. } \sigma^2 = 6 \qquad \text{II. } \sigma^2 = 3.4$$

Results of Spelling Test

Figure 7.21

The mean score μ of each group is written immediately above each of the first two columns. The **deviation** D of any score from the *mean* of its group is the difference between the mean and that score; i.e., for any score X, its deviation D from the mean μ is

$$D = \mu - X.$$

The deviations from the mean of each of the scores of groups I and II are recorded under I. D (third column) and II. D (fourth column), respectively; e.g., the second number, -3, in the third column is obtained by subtracting the second number, 8, in the first column from the mean 5 of group I.

The *squares* of the deviations D^2 of each of the scores of groups I and II are recorded under I. D^2 (fifth column) and II. D^2 (sixth column), respectively; e.g., the second number, 9, in the fifth column is obtained by squaring the second number, -3, in the third column.

The *mean* of a set of squares of deviations from some population mean is called a **population variance**. The 'population variance' is abbreviated by the lowercase Greek letter sigma, squared; i.e.,

$$\sigma^2 = \frac{\Sigma\,(\mu - X_i)^2}{n} \qquad (i = 1, 2, \ldots, n).$$

For example, to find the variance of group I, we add the squares of the deviations listed under I. D^2 (column five) and divide by $n = 10$; i.e.,

$$\text{I} \quad \sigma^2 = \frac{\Sigma\,(\mu - X)^2}{n} = \frac{60}{10} = 6.$$

The *square root* of the population variance is called the **population standard deviation**; i.e.,

$$\sigma = \sqrt{\frac{\Sigma\,(\mu - X)^2}{n}}.$$

The standard deviation of group I is

$$\sigma = \sqrt{6} = 2.45.$$

Since it is easier to compute the variance of a set of numbers than the standard deviation and since they are equally reliable measures of variety, we shall usually employ the former: *the greater the variance, the greater the variety.* The variance of group I is 6 and this is greater than the variance of group II, which is 3.4. Hence, group I must have a greater variety of scores. Inspecting the first column of Figure 7.21, we find every number from 1 to 9 with only one number, 5, recurring. In the second column the numbers 8 and 9 do not occur at all, and both 3 and 6 recur. Group I, then, evidently does have more variety than group II. Of course, if we were only interested in deciding which group had more variety, we might just *count* differences and similarities as we have just done. The advantages of the variance are that the variance is a *unique measure* of variety and that it is mechanically obtainable even when the data consists of large numbers *of* large numbers.

Consider another example. Twenty salesmen are divided into two groups, A and B, and the number of sales each man makes in a week are recorded in Figure 7.22. We are interested in determining which group has the greater variety of success. We shall use the variety of *sales* made by each member of a group as a measure of the variety of *success* of that group. The former will be measured by the *variance.*

To begin with, we find the *mean* of each group. The mean of groups A and B is the same,

$$\text{A}\mu = \frac{\Sigma\,X_i}{n} = \frac{200}{10} = 20 = \text{B}\mu \qquad (i = 1, 2, \ldots, n).$$

The *deviations* of each man's sales from the mean of his group are listed in the third and fourth columns. Each of these deviations is *squared* and the results are recorded in the fifth and sixth columns. The *mean of the squared deviations* from the mean of each group is the *variance* of that group. Hence, the variance of group A is

$$\text{A}\sigma^2 = \frac{\Sigma\,(\mu - X)^2}{n} = \frac{354}{10} = 35.4.$$

A. sales	B. sales	A. D	B D	A. D^2	B. D^2
$\mu = 20$	$\mu = 20$	$\mu - X$	$\mu - X$	$(\mu - X)^2$	$(\mu - X)^2$
20	15	0	5	0	25
14	14	6	6	36	36
13	28	7	-8	49	64
19	22	1	-2	1	4
24	21	-4	-1	16	1
12	17	8	3	64	9
26	30	-6	-10	36	100
30	15	-10	5	100	25
16	18	4	2	16	4
26	20	-6	0	36	0
200	200			354	268

Results of One Week of Sales

Figure 7.22

This is greater than the variance of group B,

$$B\sigma^2 = \frac{\Sigma \, (\mu - X)^2}{n} = \frac{268}{10} = 26.8.$$

Similarly, the standard deviation of group A,

$$A\sigma = \sqrt{35.4} = 5.95,$$

is greater than the standard deviation of group B,

$$B\sigma = \sqrt{26.8} = 5.18.$$

Hence, using either the variance or its square root, the standard deviation, as a measure of variety, we find that group A has more variety than group B.

The steps leading to the population variance and the population standard deviation of a set of n numbers may be summarized as follows.

a) Find the mean.

b) Find the deviation of each number from the mean.

c) Find the square of each deviation.

d) The mean of the squared deviations is the population variance.

e) The square root of the population variance is the population standard deviation.

In each of the examples above we were given a distribution summary of a whole *population* rather than merely a summary of a *sample* taken from that population. We defined 'population variance' and 'population standard deviation', but we did not define 'sample variance' and 'sample standard deviation'. The former definitions will suffice for the problems we have to consider, but it is worthwhile to mention that they *differ* from the latter. The **sample variance** of a *sample* with n members is

$$s^2 = \frac{\Sigma \, (\overline{X} - X)^2}{n - 1}$$

and the **sample standard deviation** is

$$s = \sqrt{\frac{\Sigma \, (\overline{X} - X)^2}{n - 1}}.$$

The reason we define the sample variance and standard deviation using $n - 1$ in the denominators instead of n is that the given definitions provide better (i.e., unbiased) *estimates* of the population variance and standard deviation than definitions with n in the denominators. A similar adjustment is *not* required in the formula defining the *mean* of a population or sample. Given a sample with n members, the *sample* mean

$$\frac{\Sigma \, X_i}{n} \qquad (i = 1, 2, \ldots, n)$$

is an unbiased estimate of the *population* mean from which the sample is drawn.

Measures of central tendency and variety are not only useful for statistical *summaries*, they may also play an important role in certain *inferences*. To illustrate this fact, we shall introduce a principle which was first proved by the Russian mathematician P. L. Chebyshev in the middle of the nineteenth century. According to

Chebyshev's Theorem: Given *any* distribution of data, *at least* the fraction $1 - (1/n^2)$ of it lies within n standard deviations of the mean. For example, suppose $n = 2$. Then, according to Chebyshev's Theorem, *at least* $1 - (\frac{1}{4}) = 75$ percent of *any* distribution lies within 2 standard deviations of the mean. At least $1 - (\frac{1}{9}) = 88.8$ percent of *any* distribution lies within 3 standard deviations of the mean, etc. With the help of Chebyshev's theorem, given a sample or population mean and standard deviation, we can answer questions about the probability of selecting a certain datum from a certain population. Consider the following examples.

EXAMPLE 1

The mean income of a certain population of men is $110 per week and the standard deviation is $20. What is the probability that any man selected at random from this population earns more than $70 but less than $150 per week?

Solution. According to Chebyshev's theorem, we may say that *at least* 75 percent of the salaries are between $70 and $150 per week; i.e., at least 75 percent are within 2 standard deviations of the mean. Hence, we may say that the probability that any man selected at random from this population earns more than $70 but less than $150 per week is *at least* 0.75.

EXAMPLE 2

What is the probability that a man selected from the same population earns *more* than $210 per week?

Solution. The salary of a man earning $210 per week is 5 standard deviations above the mean. According to Chebyshev's theorem, *at most* 4 percent of the population is in that group. Hence, we may say that the probability that a man selected from the same population earns more than $210 per week is *at most* 0.4.

EXAMPLE 3

The mean number of presents Omar has received on each of his birthdays is 6 and the standard deviation is 2. What is the probability that Omar received 26 presents on some birthday?

Solution. In order for Omar to have received 26 presents on some birthday, he he would have had to exceed the mean by 10 standard deviations. The chances of this happening are *at most* 1 in 100. Hence, the probability that Omar received 26 presents on some birthday is at most 0.01.

Review problems for Sec. 7.2.

1. Define the following.

    a) range (of a set of data)
    b) population variance
    c) population standard deviation

2. For the following test scores, find the population

    a) mean   d) range
    b) median   e) variance
    c) mode   f) standard deviation

    1 3 5 6 6 6 7 8 9 9

3. Suppose one of the students who took the test (Prob. 2) happens to see the scores without knowing which is his. What is the probability that his score was

    a) 6
    b) 9
    c) 5 *or* 6 *or* 9

4. For the following IQ scores, find the population

    a) mean
    b) median
    c) mode

    d) range
    e) variance
    f) standard deviation

          106   110   112   115   120   122   123   123   123   126

5. What is the probability that a student whose IQ score is among the 10 above is 123?

6. Suppose the following two sets of numbers represent the heights of two groups of students.

             Group I: 55   55   60   63   66   67   68   68   69   69
             Group II: 52   55   58   59   59   60   60   60   68   69

    Find the population

    a) range of Group I
    b) range of Group II
    c) variance of Group I

    d) variance of Group II
    e) with more variety

7. Find the population mean, range, and variance of the following sets of numbers.

    a) 16   18   19   20   22
    b) 32   33   34   40   43   46
    c) 3   6   7   9   12   14   14   15
    d) 61   62   65   65   66   67   68   70   70

8. What is Chebyshev's theorem?

9. According to Chebyshev's theorem, at least what fraction of a distribution of numbers lies within n standard deviations of the mean when n equals

    a) 2
    b) 3
    c) 4
    d) 5

    e) 6
    f) 8
    g) 10
    h) 15

10. According to Chebyshev's theorem, at least what percentage lies within n standard deviations of the mean when n equals

    a) 2
    b) 3
    c) 4
    d) 5

    e) 6
    f) 8
    g) 10
    h) 15

11. The mean attendance for Monday nights at a certain theatre is 400 and the standard deviation is 25. What, *at least*, is the probability of having a crowd of from

    a) 300 to 500
    b) 350 to 450
    c) 200 to 600

    on a Monday night?

12. At Peter's Poultry House the mean number of chicken dinners sold on Sundays is 200 and the standard deviation is 15. *At most*, what is the probability of selling over 350 chicken dinners at Peter's Poultry House on a Sunday?

13. It takes Russell 22 minutes on the average to drive to work, with a standard deviation of 6 minutes. If Russell leaves home exactly 40 minutes before he is due at work, what is the probability that he will be late? If he leaves home exactly 52 minutes before he is due at work, what is the probability that he will be late?

14. Suppose the mean of a set of test scores is 75 and the standard deviation is 4. A teacher is going to give five different marks, namely, A, B, C, D, and E. Find the

   a) lower class limit of class A if it equals the mean μ plus 6 standard deviations σ, i.e., $\mu + 6\sigma$
   b) upper class limit of B $= \mu + 6\sigma - 1$
   c) lower class limit of B $= \mu + 2\sigma + 1$
   d) upper class limit of C $= \mu + 2\sigma$
   e) lower class limit of C $= \mu - 2\sigma$
   f) upper class limit of D $= \mu - 2\sigma - 1$
   g) lower class limit of D $= \mu - 6\sigma + 1$
   h) upper class limit of E $= \mu - 6\sigma$
   i) the probability of a student receiving either an A *or* an E
   j) the probability of a student receiving a C

7.3   Permutations and combinations

If you had to rank three candidates, Alice, Barbara, and Carol, for Homecoming Queen so there would be a queen and a first and second attendant, how many different ways could you do it? Suppose you begin by picking the queen. You have three choices which may be illustrated as follows.

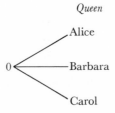

Queen

After deciding who should be queen, you must pick a first attendant. Since one girl has already been eliminated, there are only two choices left for first attendant. Continuing our illustration, we have

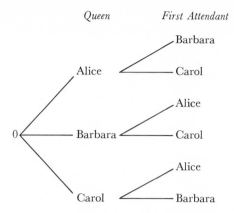

Proceeding in this fashion, by the time you reach the second attendant, you have only one candidate left. Hence, you have nothing to decide at all. The complete "picture" of the various ways of ranking the candidates looks like this.

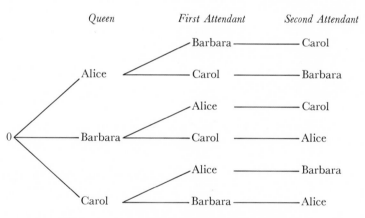

Tree Diagram for Permutations of Three Things All Together

Figure 7.31

The diagram in Figure 7.31 is called a **tree diagram.** It shows clearly that there are six possible rankings of the three candidates; i.e., there are six possible paths leading from 0 to a second attendant. Using '*A*', '*B*', and '*C*' to abbreviate 'Alice', 'Barbara', and 'Carol', respectively, the six arrangements are

$$A\ B\ C$$
$$A\ C\ B$$
$$B\ A\ C$$
$$B\ C\ A$$
$$C\ A\ B$$
$$C\ B\ A$$

When we count the number of ways candidates may be *ranked* for some position, *order* is important. It is one thing to choose Alice for queen and Barbara for first attendant, and quite another to choose Barbara for queen and Alice for first attendant. Any arrangement of things in which *order is important* is called a **permutation.** Other examples of permutations are the arrangements of letters in words, the arrangements of numbers on license plates, social security numbers, selective service numbers, sequences of courses (e.g., arithmetic, algebra, calculus), etc. Permutations may be contrasted with **combinations** or arrangements of things in which *order is not important.* Examples of combinations are arrangements of bottles or cans in a six-pack, eggs or oranges or apples, etc. in a carton, people seated in a bus, bricks in a wall, etc. Usually a cursory examination is sufficient to decide whether the problem is one of permutations or combinations.

The question,

How many different ways can you *rank* three candidates?

is an instance of the more general question,

How many *permutations* can be formed with three
different objects taken all together?

The answer to these questions is six.

The question,

How many *combinations* can be formed with
three different objects taken all together?

has a very different answer. Only *one combination* can be formed with three different objects taken all together because the *order* of the objects is irrelevant; e.g., each of the *six* permutations of '*A*', '*B*', and '*C*' involves only *one* combination of letters.

Permutations and combinations are nothing more than special kinds of *distributions.* If Alice wanted to know the *chances* of her becoming queen and her best friend Barbara becoming first attendant, she could use the information we have just obtained. After all, she is interested in the probability of a particular *permutation*, a probability which a classical theorist would suppose is $\frac{1}{6}$. This simple case illustrates an important fact, namely that knowledge of permutations and/or combinations can be useful for determining initital probabilities. The present section will introduce some of the basic principles of permutations and combinations.

If we had five candidates to rank, the tree diagram would have been pretty monstrous. We would have had five first choices, four choices after each one of those, three choices after one of the four, etc. Fortunately, we can dispense with the tree diagram and proceed immediately to the

First Principle of Permutations: The number of permutations of n different objects taken all together is the continued product of all the whole numbers from n to 1. The continued product of all the whole numbers from n to 1 is called **n factorial** and is abbreviated by '$n!$'. Thus,

$$n! = n \times (n - 1) \times (n - 2) \times \cdots \times 3 \times 2 \times 1.$$

Letting $0! = 1$, examples of the above are

$$1! = 1(0!) = 1$$
$$3! = 3 \times 2 \times 1 = 6$$
$$5! = 5 \times 4 \times 3 \times 2 \times 1 = 120.$$

Using '$_nP_n$' to abbreviate 'the number of permutations of n different objects taken n at a time', we may express the First Principle of Permutations thus:

(1) $_nP_n = n!.$

The formula (1) has no generally accepted name, but the one we are using seems appropriate. This is true of the other principles of combinations and permutations [i.e., (1)–(5)].

EXAMPLE 1

How many permutations can be formed from the letters in the word 'four'?

Solution. There are four letters in the word 'four'. Hence, according to the First Principle of Permutations, the number of Permutations of four letters taken four at a time is

$$_nP_n = {_4P_4} = 4! = 4 \times 3 \times 2 \times 1 = 24.$$

EXAMPLE 2

A comedian's act consists of eight jokes. How many different ways can he perform his act?

Solution. Assume that each permutation of his jokes is a slightly different act. The number of permutations of eight jokes taken eight at a time is

$$_nP_n = n! = 8! = 8 \times 7 \times 6 \times 5 \times 4 \times 3 \times 2 \times 1 = 40,320.$$

The **Second Principle of Permutations** we have to consider is this: The number of permutations of n different objects taken k at a time without repetitions is the continued product of all the whole numbers from n to $n - k + 1$. Using '$_nP_k$' to abbreviate 'the number of permutations of n different objects taken k at a time without repetitions', we may express the Second Principle of Permutations thus:

(2) $_nP_k = n \times (n-1) \times (n-2) \times \cdots \times (n-k+1)$

or

(3) $_nP_k = \dfrac{n!}{(n-k)!}.$

EXAMPLE 3

A president and vice-president are going to be elected from four members of a local club. How many different pairs of officers can be chosen?

Solution. What is required is the number of permutations of four different objects taken two at a time without repetitions. According to the Second Principle of Permutations in the form (2), this is the continued product of all the whole numbers from $n = 4$ to the *last term*

$$(n-k+1) = 3 = n - (k-1)$$

or

$$4 \times 3 = 12.$$

Applying the shorter form (3) of the second principle, we have

$$_nP_k = \frac{n!}{(n-k)!} = \frac{4!}{2!} = \frac{4 \times 3 \times 2 \times 1}{2 \times 1} = 12.$$

EXAMPLE 4

How many permutations can be formed from the first nine letters of the alphabet taking five at a time without repetitions.

Solution. According to the Second Principle of Permutations in form (2), the answer is the continued product of all the whole numbers from $n = 9$ to

$$n - k + 1 = 5$$

or

$$_nP_k = 9 \times 8 \times 7 \times 6 \times 5 = 15{,}120.$$

Applying the second principle in form (3), we have

$$_nP_k = \frac{n!}{(n-k)!} = \frac{9!}{4!} = \frac{9 \times 8 \times 7 \times 6 \times 5 \times 4 \times 3 \times 2 \times 1}{4 \times 3 \times 2 \times 1} = 15{,}120.$$

EXAMPLE 5

How many different 3-letter words can be formed from a 26-letter alphabet without repetitions? (Count any permutation as a word.)

Solution. The number of permutations of 26 letters taken 3 at a time without repetitions is by (3)

$$_nP_k = \frac{n!}{(n-k)!} = \frac{26!}{23!} = 26 \times 25 \times 24 = 15{,}600.$$

Or, applying formula (2), since

$$(n - k + 1) = 24,$$

we have

$$_nP_k = 26 \times 25 \times 24 = 15{,}600.$$

It has already been noted that *order* is *irrelevant* for *combinations* and that the number of combinations of three different objects taken all together is *one*. Using '$_nC_n$' or '$\binom{n}{n}$' to abbreviate 'the number of combinations of n different objects taken n at a time', we have *for all n*

(4) $\qquad _nC_n = 1 = \binom{n}{n}.$

Call this (4) the

First Principle of Combinations. It is quite trivial and easily distinguished from the First Principle of Permutations.

The **Second Principle of Combinations** is this: The number of combinations of n different objects taken k at a time is

(5) $\qquad _nC_k = \binom{n}{k} = \frac{n!}{(n-k)!\,k!}.$

This principle (5) is a direct consequence of familiar facts. You know that $_nC_k$ represents the number of combinations of n objects taken k at a time. That is, $_nC_k$ represents a certain number of "k-sized" combinations or combinations with exactly k objects. According to the First Principle of Permutations, k objects yield $k!$ permutations. Hence, the product of the number of combinations $_nC_k$ and the number of permutations $k!$ yielded by each of these "k-sized" combinations is the total number of *permutations* of n objects taken k at a time. In symbols,

$$_nC_k \times k! = _nP_k = \frac{n!}{(n-k)!}.$$

Dividing by $k!$, we find

$$_nC_k = \frac{n!}{(n-k)!\,k!}$$

which is just the Second Principle of Combinations (5).

EXAMPLE 6

How many combinations can be formed from four objects, say a, b, c, d, taken two at a time?

Solution. According to the Second Principle of Combinations, the answer to this question is

$$_nC_k = \frac{n!}{(n-k)!k!} = \frac{4 \times 3 \times 2 \times 1}{(3 \times 1)(2 \times 1)} = 6.$$

It will be instructive to compare this result with the number of *permutations* of the four objects taken two at a time. We have

$$_nP_k = \frac{n!}{(n-k)!} = \frac{4!}{2!} = \frac{4 \times 3 \times 2 \times 1}{2 \times 1} = 12.$$

The twelve permutations are as follows.

$$
\begin{array}{cccccc}
ab & ac & ad & bc & bd & cd \\
ba & ca & da & cb & db & dc
\end{array}
$$

Dividing the total number of permutations of n objects taken k at a time by $k!$ for the case at hand means dividing 12 by 2. The result is illustrated by *either* of the two *rows* of six *combinations* above.

EXAMPLE 7

A coach has seven runners from which he must choose a four-man relay team. How many different teams can he pick?

Solution. Applying the Second Principle of Combinations (5), we find that the number of four-man relay teams that can be formed from seven runners is

$$_nC_k = \frac{n!}{(n-k)!k!} = \frac{7!}{(3!)(4!)} = \frac{7 \times 6 \times 5 \times 4 \times 3 \times 2 \times 1}{(3 \times 2 \times 1)(4 \times 3 \times 2 \times 1)} = 35.$$

EXAMPLE 8

The caretaker of a small cemetery has 14 plots to look after. If he attends to 6 plots every day, how much variety can he get out of his job?

Solution. We assume that every new combination adds a little variety to the job. The number of combinations of 14 objects taken 6 at a time is

$$_nC_k = \frac{n!}{(n-k)!k!} = \frac{14!}{(8!)(6!)} = 3003.$$

It might not be such a boring job after all!

As the last example suggests, the task of counting combinations can be laborious. It is significantly simplified by a table of numbers invented by one of the most distinguished mathematicians of Europe, Blaise Pascal, around 1650. It is known as **Pascal's triangle** and is illustrated in Figure 7.32.

k	0	1	2	3	4	5	6	7	8	9	10	11	12	13	14	15
n																
0	1															
1	1	1														
2	1	2	1													
3	1	3	3	1												
4	1	4	6	4	1											
5	1	5	10	10	5	1										
6	1	6	15	20	15	6	1									
7	1	7	21	35	35	21	7	1								
8	1	8	28	56	70	56	28	8	1							
9	1	9	36	84	126	126	84	36	9	1						
10	1	10	45	120	210	252	210	120	45	10	1					
11	1	11	55	165	330	462	462	330	165	55	11	1				
12	1	12	66	220	495	792	924	792	495	220	66	12	1			
13	1	13	78	286	715	1287	1716	1716	1287	715	286	78	13	1		
14	1	14	91	364	1001	2002	3003	3432	3003	2002	1001	364	91	14	1	
15	1	15	105	455	1365	3003	5005	6435	6435	5005	3003	1365	455	105	15	1

Pascal's Triangle for $_nC_k$, $0 \le k \le n \le 15$.

Figure 7.32

The triangle is constructed in the following fashion. We begin with a column of $n + 1$ '1's'. In Figure 7.32 we have 16 '1's' in column 0. Column 1 begins with '1' in row 1. (*Note: not* row 0.) Each additional entry in this column is the sum of the number immediately above it and the number immediately to the left of that one. For example, the second entry '2' in column 1 is the sum of the 1 above it and the 1 to the left of that; the third entry '3' is the sum of 2 and 1; the fourth entry '4' is the sum of 3 and 1; etc. Column 2 begins with '1' in row 2. Each additional entry in this column is the sum of the number above it and the number to the left of that one; e.g., the entry '28' in row 8 is the sum of 21 and 7. Column 3 begins with '1' in row 3, etc.

While the construction of the triangle is slightly tedious, it has the advantage of being almost entirely mechanical. The application of Pascal's triangle to combinatorial problems is equally simple. The number of combinations of n objects taken k at a time equals the entry of the nth row and the kth column. For examples, the number of combinations of 4 objects taken 2 at a time equals the entry at row 4, column 2, namely, 6; the number of combinations of 7 objects taken 4 at a time equals the entry at row 7, column 4, which is 35; the number of combinations of 14 objects taken 6 at a time equals the entry at row 14, column 6; i.e., 3003. All these answers agree with those obtained with the Second Principle of Combinations.

Review problems for Sec. 7.3.

1. What is the difference between a permutation and a combination?

2. What is the First Principle of Permutations?

3. What does 'n factorial' mean?

4. Express the following in symbolic notation.

    a) the number of permutations of n different objects taken all together (two ways)
    b) the number of permutations of n different objects taken k at a time
    c) the number of permutations of six different objects taken two at a time

5. In how many ways can six people wait in line?

6. In how many ways can a boy arrange his 10 books on a shelf?

7. A president, vice-president, and secretary are to be chosen from five candidates. How many different sets of three officers can be formed?

8. Counting any arrangement of letters as a word, how many

    a) two-letter   c) four-letter
    b) three-letter   d) five-letter

    words can be formed from the letters in 'simpleton'?

9. Suppose the letters in 'simpleton' are written on little slips of paper and put into a hat. What are the chances of drawing out *without replacement*

    a) two letters spelling 'to'   e) four letters spelling 'pint'
    b) two letters spelling *either* 'to' *or* 'in'   f) five letters spelling 'notes'
    c) three letters spelling 'ten'   g) six letters spelling 'pistol'
    d) three letters spelling 'ten' *or* 'imp'

10. A group of shoppers is asked to pick the top three shaving creams from eight contenders and to rank those picked first, second, and third. How many different "top three" rankings can be formed?

11. Using *only* the five integers 1, 2, 3, 4, and 5, how many different four-numbered license numbers can be formed?

12. Suppose there are four roads between Dullsville and Stagnant City. If someone is going to make a return trip from the former to the latter *without* taking the same road both ways, how many different ways can the trip be made?

13. How many
    a) three-letter   c) five-letter
    b) four-letter   d) six-letter

    words can be formed from the letters in 'superman'?

14. Suppose the letters in 'superman' are written separately on little slips of paper and put into a hat. What is the probability of drawing out without replacement
    a) two letters spelling 'an'
    b) two letters spelling *either* 'an' *or* 'up' *or* 'me'
    c) three letters spelling 'man'
    d) three letters spelling 'man' *or* 'use'

15. How many combinations can be formed from n objects taken all together?

16. Express the following in symbolic notation *in two ways*.
    a) the number of combinations of n different objects taken n at a time
    b) the number of combinations of n different objects taken k at a time
    c) the number of combinations of 6 different objects taken 3 at a time

17. What is the Second Principle of Combinations?

    Use the Second Principle of Combinations to answer the next six questions.

18. Suppose a police department has 12 detectives to send out in pairs. How many different pairs can be formed?

19. In his junior year a student can choose any 5 of 15 different courses. How many different combinations can he form?

20. A veterinarian wants to cage nine dogs, three in a cage. How many different combinations can he form?

21. A collector can afford to buy 7 of 14 different antiques. How many different collections can he buy?

22. A certain manufacturer produces 37 different kinds of soup. If you have 3 different soups a week, how many combinations can you form?

23. Junior has 20 chemicals in his new chemistry set. If he always mixes exactly 5 at a time, how many different combinations can he make?

24. How is Pascal's triangle constructed?

25. How is Pascal's triangle related to the Second Principle of Combinations?

26. Use Pascal's triangle to find
    a) $_5C_2$ d) $_{12}C_8$
    b) $_7C_4$ e) $_{13}C_6$
    c) $_{11}C_3$ f) $_{15}C_{13}$

27. Suppose three of the dogs referred to in Prob. 20 are brothers and three of them are sisters. What is the probability that three brothers will end up in the same cage? (*Note:* The dogs are taken out of the whole group one at a time without replacement.) What is the probability that *either* three brothers *or* three sisters will end up in the same cage?

28. Suppose the detectives in Prob. 18 are distributed as follows.

> 4 first-year men
>
> 3 second-year men
>
> 3 third-year men
>
> 2 fourth-year men

What is the probability that

a)   two first-year men

b)   two second-year men

c)   two fourth-year men

will be sent out together?

7.4   Binomial and normal distributions

Consider a set of independent tosses of a fair coin. The initial probability of a head turning up is r and the initial probability of a tail turning up is $s = 1 - r$. The question is, What is the probability of obtaining k heads *and* $n - k$ tails *in* n *tosses?* Since the probability of a head is r, the probability of k heads is r^k (by the Special Multiplication Principle). Similarly, since the probability of a tail is $s = 1 - r$, the probability of $n - k$ tails is s^{n-k} or $(1 - r)^{n-k}$. Hence, the probability of k heads *and* $n - k$ tails is the product of $r^k s^{n-k}$. This is *part* of the answer we are seeking. We still have not found the probability of k heads and $n - k$ tails *in* n *tosses.* We know, however, that there are as many ways to obtain k heads and $n - k$ tails in n tosses as there are combinations of n objects taken k at a time; i.e., in n tosses there are ${}_nC_k$ combinations of k heads and $n - k$ tails. And it was just shown that the probability of each of these combinations is $r^k s^{n-k}$. Hence, the probability of obtaining k heads *and* $n - k$ tails *in* n *tosses* is the product of ${}_nC_k$ and $r^k s^{n-k}$; i.e.,

$$ {}_nC_k \, r^k s^{n-k} = \binom{n}{k} r^k s^{n-k}. $$

Quite generally, given a set of independent experiments with two possible outcomes, say success and failure, whose probabilities are r and $s = 1 - r$, respectively, the probability of k success *and* $n - k$ failures *in* n *experiments* is

(1) $$ {}_nC_k \, r^k s^{n-k} = \binom{n}{k} r^k s^{n-k}. $$

This formula (1) is the formula for a very important kind of distribution known as **the binomial distribution.** It represents the kth term of the expansion of the binomial $(r + s)^n$ (counting from 0 from right to left). The binomial distribution may be regarded as the distribution of the probabilities (frequencies) of two kinds of things, successes and failures, in a certain number of experiments, or simply as the distribution of two kinds of things in a certain number of experiments. The *formula* for the binomial distribution is another principle which may be used to calculate probabilities from other probabilities.

EXAMPLE 1

What is the probability of obtaining three heads and one tail in four tosses of a fair coin?

Solution. The probability of a head turning up is $r = 0.5 = s$, which is the probability of a tail turning up. Substituting in the formula for the binominal distribution (1), we have

$$\binom{n}{k} r^k s^{n-k} = \binom{4}{3} (0.5)^3 (0.5)^1 = (4)(0.125)(0.5) = 0.25.$$

EXAMPLE 2

Willie has to take eight independent tests in different subjects as part of the entrance requirements for some college. On any given test Willie has about a 40 percent chance of passing. What is the probability that Willie will pass exactly five of the eight tests?

Solution. Willie's chance of success on any test is $r = 0.4$. Hence, his chance of failure is $s = 1 - 0.4 = 0.6$. The probability that he will have five successes and three failures in eight independent tests is

$$\binom{n}{k} r^k s^{n-k} = \binom{8}{5} (0.4)^5 (0.6)^3 = (56)(0.01024)(0.216) = 0.124.$$

EXAMPLE 3

Twelve boys were invited to Zelda's party. The odds in favor of any one of them failing to show up are about 1 to 4. If exactly half of them fail to show up there will be just enough beer for everyone. What is the probability that there will be just enough beer for everyone?

Solution. We suppose that the probability of a boy's failing to show up is $r = \frac{1}{5}$. Hence, the probability of a boy's showing up is $s = \frac{4}{5}$. The probability that there will be just enough beer for everyone equals the probability that exactly 6 of 12 boys will fail to show up for the party. According to the formula for the binomial distribution, this is

$$\binom{n}{k} r^k s^{n-k} = \binom{12}{6} (0.2)^6 (0.8)^6 = (924)(0.000064)(0.262144) = 0.016.$$

A consequence of the binomial distribution which should be mentioned, though it cannot be investigated in detail here, was introduced in James Bernoulli's *Ars Conjectandi* (1713). According to **Bernoulli's theorem** or the **Law of Large Numbers,** if the probability of success on an experiment is r and m/n successes have been observed, then, as n approaches infinity, the probability that the difference between m/n and r will be very small approaches unity. Here "very small" may be understood as less than *any* small number e. In a slightly more compact form, the law may be expressed thus: Given an experiment with a probability of success r and m/n observed successes, as n approaches infinity, the probability that $|m/n - r| < e$ approaches unity, where e is any small number. Some people have suggested that the Law of Large Numbers tends to make the limiting frequency theory more plausible, since if the law is applicable to any physical phenomena (e.g., sequences of coin tosses or die tosses) there must *be* limiting frequencies.

As n increases, the distribution represented by the expansion of the binomial $(r + s)^n$ approaches the so-called *normal* distribution. Expansions of the binomial $(r + s)^n$ are easily constructed by ordinary multiplication or by applying the following **binomial rule** or **binomial theorem:** a) The first (left-hand) term in the expansion is r^n; b) the second term is $nr^{n-1}s$; c) in succeeding terms the powers of r decrease by 1; d) the coefficient of any term is the product of the coefficient of the preceding term and the power of r in that term, divided by one more than the power of s in that term. (Or, the coefficients of the terms correspond to the numbers in the nth row of Pascal's triangle.)

EXAMPLE 4

Expand $(r + s)^2$.

Solution. The first term is r^2. The second term is $nr^{n-1}s = 2rs$. The next term is the result of decreasing the power of r in the second term by 1 (which eliminates r, since $r^{1-1} = 1$), increasing the power of s by 1 (which gives us $s^{1+1} = s^2$), and dividing 2×1 (the product of the coefficient of the preceding term and the power of r in that term) by 2 (one more than the power of r in that term). Hence,

$$(r + s)^2 = r^2 + 2rs + s^2.$$

Notice that the coefficients

$$1 \quad 2 \quad 1$$

correspond to the numbers in row 2 of Pascal's triangle.

EXAMPLE 5

Expand $(r + s)^3$.

Solution. The first term is r^3. The second term is $nr^{n-1}s = 3r^2s$. The next term's *coefficient* is $3 \times \frac{2}{2} = 3$. Hence, the next term is $3r^{n-2}s^{1+1} = 3rs^2$. The final term is s^3. Thus,

$$(r + s)^3 = r^3 + 3r^2s + 3rs^2 + s^3.$$

Again, the coefficients

$$1 \quad 3 \quad 3 \quad 1$$

correspond to the numbers in row 3 of Pascal's triangle.

The primary reason the binominal expansion has been introduced is that as n increases, the distribution represented by the expansion approaches the *normal* distribution. Consider, for example, the expansion of $(r + s)^6$; i.e.,

$$r^6 + 6r^5s + 15r^4s^2 + 20r^3s^3 + 15r^2s^4 + 6rs^5 + s^6.$$

A frequency polygon of the seven classes represented in this expression is given in Figure 7.41.

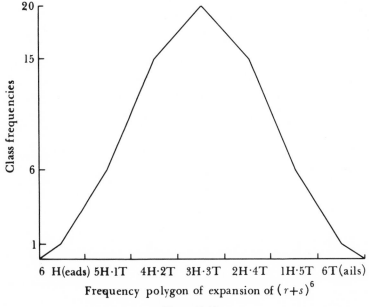

Frequency polygon of expansion of $(r+s)^6$

Figure 7.41

Inspection of this figure (and perhaps Pascal's triangle) may suggest that as n approaches infinity, the frequency *polygon* representing the expansion of $(r + s)$ *tends* to become a *smooth curve*. This is indeed the case. As n increases, the number of *terms* and *coefficients* of these terms increase. The straight lines connecting the various classes approach (without ever becoming) a smooth *continuous normal* curve. The **normal distribution curve,** then, may be regarded as the unattainable *limiting form* of the frequency polygon for the distribution resulting from the expansion of the binomial expression $(r + s)^n$.

The normal curve was first investigated by Abraham De Moivre around 1730. It was called the 'normal curve of errors' for many years because the distribution of errors of measurement may frequently be represented by it. But it is much more than a curve of errors. The heights and weights of biological species are normally distributed. The lengths of seashells of the same species, the lengths of tobacco leaves, the number of kernels on an ear of corn, the weights of hens' eggs, and the number of pigs per litter are all *normally* distributed. Psychological characteristics revealed by IQ scores and college aptitude and achievement tests are also normally distributed. The main characteristics of the Normal Distribution Curve are as follows.

a)   It is *symmetrical* about its mean; i.e., if a line is drawn from the x axis at the mean to the highest point of the curve, it divides the curve into two identical parts.

b)   It is *asymptotic* to the x axis; i.e., it comes nearer and nearer to the x axis but never reaches it.

c)   The total area between the curve and the x axis is exactly 1.

d)   Certain proportions of the area under the curve lie within specifiable distances from the mean. In particular, about

   i)   68 percent of the area under the curve lies within 1 standard deviation of the mean.

   ii)   95 percent lies within 2 standard deviations of the mean.

   iii)   99 percent lies within 3 standard deviations of the mean.

These properties are illustrated in Figure 7.42.

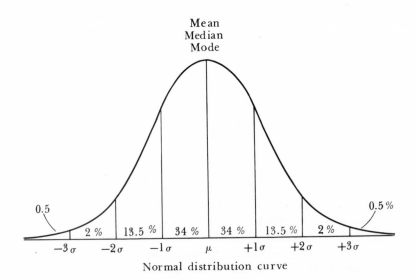

Normal distribution curve

We have already seen that it is possible to determine the probability of selecting a certain datum from *any* kind of distribution, given Chebyshev's theorem and a sample or population mean and standard deviation. The same possibility exists for *normal* distributions. The only difference is that we are able to make more precise judgments with a distribution which is known to be normal than with one about which we know nothing.

EXAMPLE 6

The results of a freshman algebra test were normally distributed with a mean of 64 and a standard deviation of 6. What is the probability that a student picked at random from the class scored above 58 but below 70?

Solution. A score in the interval between 58 and 70 is within 1 standard deviation of the mean. About 68 percent of the scores are in that interval. Hence, we may say that the probability that a student picked at random from the class scored above 58 but below 70 is 0.68.

EXAMPLE 7

We know that the heights of adult men are normally distributed with a mean of about 68 inches and a standard deviation of about an inch. What is the probability that your neighbor (who happens to be an adult man) is between 66 and 70 inches tall?

Solution. The heights of about 95 percent of the adult male population lie within 2 standard deviations of the mean. Hence, we may say that there is a probability of 0.95 that your neighbor's height is somewhere between 66 and 70 inches.

EXAMPLE 8

Floyd scored between 1 and 2 standard deviations below the mean on his College Aptitude Test. Before he took the test, how probable would we have estimated such a score?

Solution. About 13.5 percent of those who take such tests score between 1 and 2 standard deviations below the mean. Hence, we would have estimated the probability of Floyd's score at about 0.14.

With the help of ready-made tables indicating the areas under the normal curve at intervals of 0.1, statisticians are able to make much more precise and rapid probability judgments. Unfortunately, *that* story must be left to someone else.

Review problems for Sec. 7.4.

1. What is the formula for the binomial distribution?

2. Given $r = \frac{1}{2} = s$, find the value of

$$\binom{n}{k} r^k s^{n-k}$$

when $\binom{n}{k}$ equals

a) $_2C_1$ d) $_4C_2$

b) $_3C_2$ e) $_5C_3$

c) $_4C_1$ f) $_5C_4$

3. What is the probability of obtaining two heads and three tails in five tosses of a fair coin?

4. Suppose you are drawing balls from a barrel (with replacement) which contains $\frac{1}{3}$ white and $\frac{2}{3}$ black (i.e., $r = \frac{1}{3}$ and $s = \frac{2}{3}$). What is the probability of drawing two white balls and four black in six draws?

5. If the probability of making a profit on any stock you buy is 0.75 and the probability of a loss is 0.25, what is the probability of making a profit on exactly three of seven stocks and losing on the other four?

6. A certain drug has favorable effects on 80 percent of the patients who receive it and unfavorable effects on the other 20 percent. If the drug is given to eight patients, what is the probability that it will have a favorable effect on six and an unfavorable effect on the others?

7. The probability of the Tigers winning a game is 0.7 and the probability of a loss is 0.3. What is the probability that in nine games they will win five and lose four?

8. What is Bernoulli's theorem or the Law of Large Numbers?

9. What is the binomial theorem?

10. Expand the following.

a) $(r + s)^4$

b) $(r + s)^5$

c) $(r + s)^7$

11. Using Pascal's triangle, find the coefficients of the expansion of $(r + s)^n$ when n equals

a) 9

b) 12

12. Find the first three terms of the expansions of

  a) $(r + s)^{30}$
  b) $(r + s)^{100}$
  c) $(r + s)^{1000}$

13. What are the main characteristics of the normal distribution curve?

14. How is the expansion of the binomial $(r + s)^n$ related to the normal curve?

Use Figure 7.42 to answer the following five questions.

15. A drunken shepherd has spent most of the night counting his sheep over and over. On the basis of his repeated counts, he believes the mean number of sheep in his flock is 53 and the standard deviation is 3. What is the probability that he has

  a) from 50 to 56
  b) from 56 to 59
  c) from 44 to 47
  sheep?

16. A time-study man has calculated that the mean number of hours required to produce a certain product is 26 and the standard deviation is 2. Find the probability of taking

  a) more than 32
  b) from 26 to 24
  c) from 24 to 30

  hours to produce the product.

17. For every 1000 items produced by a certain machine the mean number of defects is 30 and the standard deviation is 4. In any set of 1000 items, what is the probability of

  a) less than 18
  b) from 18 to 34

  defects?

18. A general knows that on the average 100 men will be lost out of every 500 sent ashore. If the standard deviation is 20, what is the probability that if 500 men are sent ashore

  a) more than 160
  b) from 80 to 120

  will be lost?

19. In a certain area in the city on the average 10 out of every 80 youths are delinquents. If the standard deviation is 3, what is the probability that in any group of 80 youths selected from this area there will be

  a) from 16 to 19
  b) less than 1 or more than 19

  delinquents?

Suggestions for further reading related to Chapter 7.

Bryant, Edward C., *Statistical Analysis*. New York: McGraw-Hill Book Company, 1966, Chapters 1–4.

Dixon, Wilfrid J., and Massey, Frank J., Jr., *Introduction to Statistical Analysis*. New York: McGraw-Hill Book Company, 1957, Chapters 2–6.

Fisher, Ronald A., *Statistical Methods for Research Workers*. London: Oliver & Boyd Ltd., 1958, Chapter 3.

Hammond, Kenneth R., and Householder, James E., *Introduction to the Statistical Method*. New York: Alfred A. Knopf, Inc., 1962, Chapters 3 and 4.

Li, Jerome C. R., *Statistical Inference I*. Ann Arbor, Mich.: Edward Brothers, Inc., 1964, Chapters 2–5.

Mosteller, Frederick, Rourke, Robert E. K., and Thomas, George B., Jr., *Probability with Statistical Applications*. Reading, Mass.: Addison-Wesley Publishing Co., 1961, Chapters 2, 5, and 7.

> Rules and particular inferences alike are justified
> by being brought into agreement with each other.
> A rule is amended if it yields an inference we are
> unwilling to accept; an inference is rejected if it
> violates a rule we are unwilling to amend.
>
> *Nelson Goodman*

Chapter

8

Acceptance Rules

8.1 Probability and weight

We have considered three of the four problems around which our discussion of nondemonstrative inference has been organized, namely, the problems of the meaning of probability sentences, the measurement of probabilities, and the calculation of new probabilities from initially given ones. The problem before us now is, *How may probabilities be used to determine the acceptability of hypotheses and courses of action?* It has already been pointed out (in Sec. 5.1) that sometimes probabilities are practically decisive in judgments about acceptability and that sometimes probabilities are entirely irrelevant. We shall also investigate cases which fall between these extremes. No doubt some writers (e.g., Carnap) would insist that the principles introduced in this chapter belong to "applied" rather than "theoretical inductive logic" or to the "methodology of induction" rather than "inductive logic" proper. As long as there is no confusion about the nature of the problem before us, these names would seem to be as good as any other.

Acceptance rules are, as we indicated at the beginning of Part Two, nothing more than rules or principles which prescribe the acceptance of a certain hypothesis or course of action *given* certain premises or situations. *Note:* They do *not* tell us that a certain hypothesis or course of action *is implied by or follows from* certain premisses. That is what demonstrative *inference* rules do. Nondemonstrative *acceptance* rules only tell us that given certain premisses or situations, certain hypotheses or courses of action are *acceptable* or *more or less acceptable* or *acceptable to a certain degree*. Here, 'to accept' means roughly to regard as relatively unproblematic; i.e., unproblematic relative to some given evidence, situation, purposes, etc. No one has developed a plausible method of measuring the *degree* of acceptability of a hypothesis or course of action, so nothing further will be said about quantitative acceptance rules. The rules we shall consider are *either qualitative*, in the sense that they specify acceptable hypotheses or courses of action without making any comparison with others, *or comparative*, in the sense that they specify acceptable hypotheses or courses of action by making a comparison with others.

Any interpretation of a valid argument schema is a valid argument. In the method of natural deduction introduced in Chapters 3 and 4, we *validated* or *justified* demonstrative inferences by citing appropriate *inference* rules. Similarly, any interpretation of an *n*-valid argument schema is an *n*-valid argument, and in this chapter we shall *n-validate* or *justify* nondemonstrative inferences by citing appropriate *acceptance* rules.

An acceptance rule which *explicitly* takes account of the gains or losses involved in the acceptance of a hypothesis or course of action is called **utilitarian.** Most utilitarian rules have been designed to apply to situations involving the selection of acceptable courses of *action*. Examples of utilitarian rules are: Accept that course of action which minimizes the maximum possible loss; accept that course of action which has the maximum estimated utility. These and others will be explained in detail later.

An acceptance rule which does not *explicitly* take account of the gains or losses involved in the acceptance of a hypothesis or course of action is called **nonutilitarian.** All nonutilitarian rules seem to have been designed to apply to situations involving the selection of acceptable hypotheses (objects of belief) rather than acceptable courses of action. Examples of nonutilitarian rules are: Accept that hypothesis which has the maximum probability; accept that hypothesis which has the maximum likelihood. These and others will be explained in detail in this and the next section.

It *may* be the case that all acceptance rules take gains or losses into consideration *somehow*. This seems very likely. But they do not all make this consideration *explicit* and it is on this fact that our distinction is based. Similarly, it may be the case that all acceptance rules are "essentially" concerned with courses of *action*. This seems less likely. But they do not all make this concern *explicit* and this fact makes our distinction between accepting a hypothesis and accepting a course of action *prima facie* legitimate, though others might be more helpful.

The problem of selecting an appropriate *inference* rule to validate a given demonstrative inference can usually be solved (at the level at which we are working) by merely matching certain shapes or patterns against others. That is to say, we are frequently able to *see* in the literal sense of this word that this or that particular argument is patterned after this or that schema and that, therefore, the former may be validated by citing this or that rule. Unfortunately, as we shall see shortly, the selection of appropriate *acceptance* rules is usually more complicated. We usually have to compare numerical values (probabilities, likelihoods, utilities, etc.), and when utilitarian rules are involved, we have to carefully appraise our attitudes or feelings in order to select the "most appropriate of all rules" for a given situation. A considerable amount of ambiguity may be eliminated from our presentation of rules and illustrations if we make the (somewhat artificial) assumption that the *given* information is the *only* information available for any particular problem; i.e., for one reason or another *all other things are either equal or irrelevant*. Even with this proviso, however, much more must be left to common sense, intuition, and good fortune than most of us prefer.

In the rest of this section and in the next section we shall consider six non-utilitarian rules. The four that are introduced in this section make some sort of probability decisive in determining acceptability. The two that are introduced in the next section are only indirectly related to probability.

Rule of high probability: Accept that (relevant) hypothesis which has a high probability. As this rule is stated, it is vague because the word 'high' is vague. In place of 'high probability' we might have substituted 'a probability greater than 0.95' or 'a probability greater than 0.99', etc. This would have given us a more precise rule, but it would also have been restrictive for our purposes. We may assume that a 'high probability' means either of those more precise locutions, as well as others which are equally precise with perhaps slightly different numerical values. The rule is nonutilitarian since it does not involve any explicit reference to gains or losses, and it is qualitative in the sense that it prescribes the acceptance of certain hypotheses without appealing in any way to other hypotheses. Consider two simple examples of the application of this rule.

EXAMPLE 1

On the basis of all available evidence it is highly probable that a man named 'Napoleon Bonaparte' was born in 1769 and died in 1821. A historian asserts that Napoleon Bonaparte lived through the turn of the eighteenth century. Is this an acceptable claim?

Solution. The available evidence provides the following premiss.

> It is highly probable that Napoleon Bonaparte lived through the turn of the eighteenth century.

Given that premiss, the rule of high probability *n-validates, justifies,* or makes the inference to the hypothesis (conclusion)

> Napoleon Bonaparte lived through the turn of the eighteenth century.

acceptable.

EXAMPLE 2

Suppose the probability that you will survive the day is 0.99999. Is the hypothesis that you will survive the day acceptable?

Solution. On the basis of all available evidence, we may assert the following premiss.

There is a high probability that you will survive the day.

Given that premiss, the inference to the hypothesis (conclusion)

You will survive the day.

is *n*-valid (acceptable, or justified) according to the rule of high probability.

Sometimes false hypotheses are unwittingly accepted, and true hypotheses are rejected. Following the statisticians Jerzy Neyman and Egon Pearson, the rejection of a true hypothesis is usually referred to as a **type I error** and the acceptance of a false hypothesis is usually called a **type II error.** (The Neyman-Pearson acceptance rules are more precise and powerful, and they involve more technicalities than any of the rules we shall consider here.)

One of the main disadvantages of the rule of high probability is that it is only applicable when there is a relevant hypothesis which has a *high* probability. To illustrate this limitation, consider the following case. Suppose you are lost in a forest and you decide that the probability of finding your way home by moving forward is 0.2; by moving in the opposite direction, 0.2; by moving to the left, 0.4; and by moving to the right, 0.2. You have, then, four hypotheses to consider; namely,

a)   You will find your way home by moving forward.
b)   You will find your way home by moving in the opposite direction.
c)   You will find your way home by moving to the left.
d)   You will find your way home by moving to the right.

You imagine that these hypotheses are mutually exclusive and exhaustive; i.e., for one reason or another there are no other alternatives. None of them has a high probability. Hence, none of them would be acceptable according to the rule of high probability. But, on the basis of the information given, c) is at least *more acceptable* than all the others. Given the situation which we have roughly outlined and these four hypotheses, c) is "the best bet". Though it is not too attractive on its own, it is nevertheless comparatively attractive; i.e., it is comparatively acceptable or more acceptable than the others. This shows that the rule of high probability must be supplemented by the following comparative rule.

Rule of maximum probability: Accept that hypothesis which has the maximum probability (of all those considered). The point of this rule should be fairly clear in view of the example we have just considered. The rule is applicable to situations in which probabilities may be assigned to the various alternative hypotheses, but none of the probabilities are high (in the sense of the first rule). If none of the probabilities is higher than the others then the rule is inapplicable. If several have the same probability and this is higher than that of the others, these are equally acceptable and more acceptable than the others.

EXAMPLE 3

Seven people take part in the production of a certain item. The probabilities of each of them making a mistake are as follows.

Person	Probability of Mistake
1	0.02
2	0.3
3	0.2
4	0.03
5	0.1
6	0.12
7	0.23

But someone *did* make a mistake. Using the rule of maximum probability, *rank* the seven hypotheses naming the guilty party in terms of acceptability.

Solution. The seven hypotheses are

> Person 1 made a mistake.
> Person 2 made a mistake.
> .
>
> .
>
> .
>
> Person 7 made a mistake.

According to the rule of maximum probability, the hypothesis that person 2 made a mistake is more acceptable than any of the others. The complete ranking of suspects is person 2 first, then persons 7, 3, 6, 5, 4, and 1. Thus, the hypothesis that person 6 made a mistake is more acceptable than the hypothesis that person 4 made a mistake, and so on.

In order for a hypothesis to be pronounced 'acceptable' or 'more acceptable' than some others according to the rules above, it is necessary for the hypothesis to have some kind of probability. We have already seen, however, that frequency theorists have difficulty assigning probabilities to unique events and, therefore, to the hypotheses describing these events. Hence, they would have difficulty applying these rules. The problem becomes particularly acute when we consider certain unquestionably acceptable laws of nature. For example, on the basis of all available evidence, the hypothesis

> Sugar is soluble.

is clearly acceptable. But it is highly probable in a frequency sense? The hypothesis does not describe any sort of repetitive event, so it is difficult to see how the frequency theory of measuring probabilities could be applicable to this case at all. According to Hans Reichenbach, strictly speaking, such a hypothesis cannot be assigned a probability in the frequency sense. Reichenbach has suggested a method of assigning such hypotheses a "weight", however, and on the basis of such "weights" we may formulate acceptance rules similar to those we have just considered.

Rule of high weight: Accept that hypothesis which has a high weight. We measure the weight of a hypothesis in two steps: a) Derive predictions from the hypothesis; b) the *limit* of the relative frequency of successful predictions in the total sequence of derived predictions is the required value. The **weight of a hypothesis,** then, is nothing more than the limit of the relative frequency of successful predictions based on that hypothesis. Or, to put it a slightly different way, the weight of a hypothesis is equal to the probability (in the limiting frequency sense) of making a successful prediction with that hypothesis. For the vague phrase 'high weight' we may again substitute a more precise one such as 'weight greater than 0.95' or 'weight greater than 0.99'.

Although this rule does not mention probability at all, it is clear that any sentence about weights will satisfy the principles of the calculus of probability. This must be the case since weights are nothing more than probabilities measured by limiting frequencies. Hence, it is fair to say that as far as this rule is concerned, probabilities still play a decisive role in determining acceptability. Moreover, the rule is nonutilitarian and qualitative just like the rule of high probability.

Example 4

How is the rule of high weight used to show that the hypothesis

Sugar is soluble.

is acceptable?

Solution. To measure the weight of the hypothesis, we must derive predictions from it. In order to derive predictions from it, we must introduce some *test conditions.* The test conditions *plus* the hypothesis will yield predictions. Thus, we might argue as follows:

If

sugar is soluble   (hypothesis)

and

a lump of sugar is dropped into a glass of water   (test condition)

then

the lump of sugar will dissolve.   (prediction)

Each time a lump of sugar *does* dissolve, we say the hypothesis (plus the test conditions) has yielded a successful prediction. Each time a lump of sugar does not dissolve, we say the hypothesis (plus the test conditions) has yielded an unsuccessful prediction. (The question of whether the hypothesis *or* the test conditions *or* both produced the failure is crucial for an investigator, and often difficult to answer.) For the particular hypothesis we are considering, the limit of the relative frequency of successful predictions in the total sequence of derived predictions is 1. Hence, the weight of the hypothesis is 1. Thus, according to the rule of high weight, the hypothesis

Sugar is soluble.

must be pronounced 'acceptable.'

EXAMPLE 5

Use the rule of high weight to show that the hypothesis

Socrates had a pug nose.

is acceptable.

Solution. To determine the weight of this historical hypothesis, we must derive predictions from it. Hence, we might argue as follows.

If

Socrates had a pug nose   (hypothesis)

and

someone knew Socrates and
happened to describe his nose   (test condition)

then

it was described as a pug nose.   (prediction)

Each time Socrates' nose was described as a pug nose by someone who knew him, we say the hypothesis has yielded a successful prediction. Each time Socrates' nose was described as nonpug, we say the hypothesis has yielded an unsuccessful prediction. As it happens, everyone who knew Socrates and left posterity any description of his nose recorded its pugness in one way or another. Hence, the limit of the relative frequency of successful predictions based on the hypothesis that Socrates had a pug nose (plus the test conditions) is 1. Thus, the weight of this hypothesis is 1 and, according to the rule of high weight, the hypothesis is acceptable.

Just as the rule of high probability is restricted to situations in which some relevant hypothesis has such a probability, so the rule of high weight is restricted to situations in which some relevant hypothesis has such a weight. Thus, what is required is a comparative rule like the

Rule of maximum weight: Accept that hypothesis which has the maximum weight of all those considered. This rule is analogous to the rule of maximum probability and it is applicable in similar circumstances. That is, there are cases in which none of the hypotheses under consideration has a high weight, but some have higher weights than others. In such cases the most acceptable hypothesis is the one with the maximum weight. If none of them has a higher weight than the others then the rule is just inapplicable. If several have the same weight and it is higher than that of the others, the former are equally acceptable and more acceptable than the others.

EXAMPLE 6

Suppose you are lost in the forest again (it happens!). This time you have the same four hypotheses, namely, to go forward, backward, to the left, or to the right, but *no* probabilities. How is the rule of maximum weight applicable?

Solution. Each of the hypotheses may be used to determine a weight. For example, consider a),

You will find your way home by moving forward.

If a) is true and you proceed forward then after a certain length of time, say a half hour, you will be noticing certain familiar landmarks. You proceed forward, then, and keep a rough record of familiar and unfamiliar landmarks. The limit of the relative frequency of familiar landmarks recorded is the weight of the hypothesis under consideration. If this procedure is followed for each hypothesis (perhaps lengthening the time of search in one direction after each indecisive investigation of the whole set of hypotheses) then a set of weights will be obtained to which the rule of high weight may be applied.

Review problems for Sec. 8.1.

1. Define the following.
    a)   acceptance rule
    b)   type I error
    c)   type II error

2. What is the difference between utilitarian and nonutilitarian acceptance rules?

3. State the following rules.

    a)   high probability   c)   high weight
    b)   maximum probability   d)   maximum weight

    Identify the rule that is being applied in each of the next five problems.

4. If that hypothesis is accepted we have only 1 chance in 20 of making a mistake. So let us accept it.

5. When you compare the ratio of successful to total predictions made with both hypotheses, it becomes apparent that the former is more acceptable.

6. Of course it is not very probable, but it is more probable than all the others and that makes it our best bet right now.

7. Most of the consequences we have derived from that hypothesis have turned out false. Even though we have nothing better, we cannot accept it.

8. When its probability reaches 0.99, we just accept it and go on to another problem.

9. How is the *weight* of a hypothesis measured?

10. Do you think the introduction of the concept of weight solves the frequency theorist's problem with unique events? Explain your answer.

8.2 Likelihood and least squares

You recall that we defined "the likelihood of '*A given B*'" as the probability of '*B given A*'. We shall not introduce a new operator to express this relation symbolically. Instead we shall just stipulate that

$$P(A, B)$$

may be considered as an abbreviation of the phrases

the probability of '*B given A*'

(and its equivalents) or

the likelihood of '*A given B*'

(and its equivalents).

Since 'likelihood' is defined in terms of (conditional) probability, there is some justification for calling any rules involving likelihoods 'probabilistic rules'. There is an important difference between likelihoods and probabilities, however, a difference which has been regarded (by the twentieth-century statistician R. A. Fisher) and is *here* regarded as sufficient to withhold the name 'probability' from likelihoods. The difference is this: Likelihoods violate the second postulate of the calculus of probability because the sum of two or more likelihoods may be greater than 1. A glance at Examples 2, 3, 4, and 5 in our discussion of total probability and Bayes's theorem will illustrate this fact. While the sum of the probabilities of '*B*' and '*B̄*' must be 1, the sum of the likelihoods of '*B given A*' and '*B̄ given A*' may be greater than 1. We might, following Reichenbach, refer to these values greater than 1 as 'unbounded probabilities'; but since we have insisted that probabilities must satisfy the principles of the probability calculus, it seems better to adopt Fisher's view. The rule which Fisher suggested is called the 'method of maximum likelihood'. It is more sophisticated than the one we are going to introduce, but the latter is suggested by and similar to the former. Our rule is called the

Rule of maximum likelihood: Accept that hypothesis which has the maximum likelihood of all those considered. This rule is strictly analogous to the rules of maximum probability and weight. It is nonutilitarian and comparative. To apply it, we simply determine the likelihoods of the available hypotheses and accept the most *likely* one of the lot. Its major advantage is that it does not require any *a priori* assignment of initial probabilities. (This is also the major advantage of Fisher's method of maximum likelihood.) This will be apparent in the examples that follow.

Example 1

You shot a moose. The chances of finding it if it falls in its tracks are 9 in 10. The chances of finding it if it does not fall immediately are 6 in 10. You found it and are interested in determining which of the following hypotheses is more acceptable:

It fell immediately.
It did not fall immediately.

Solution. You do not have the initial or conditional probabilities of these hypotheses. If you assigned personal or logical *initial* probabilities to them (say, 0.5 each) then you could use Bayes's theorem to calculate the conditional probability of each of them *given* the information that you found the moose. But you do not want to make any *a priori* probability judgments. The rule of maximum likelihood presents an attractive option. Since the *likelihood* of the hypothesis that the moose fell immediately relative to the information that you found it is *greater* than the *likelihood* of the hypothesis that the moose did not fall immediately relative to that information, the former is more acceptable.

Example 2

If Moore is lecturing the probability of a full house is 0.7. If Russell is lecturing the probability of a full house is 0.9; and if Broad is lecturing the probability of a full house is 0.8. Given the information that the house is full, which of the following hypotheses seems to offer the most acceptable *explanation*?

Moore is lecturing.
Russell is lecturing.
Broad is lecturing.

Solution. Without making any *a priori* probability assignments, we may apply the rule of maximum likelihood to the given data to determine the most acceptable of the available hypotheses. It is most *likely* that Russell is lecturing. Hence, the hypothesis that Russell is lecturing seems to offer the most acceptable explanation for the full house.

EXAMPLE 3

It is known that Lyndon shot an old man and we are attempting to find an acceptable explanation. We have four hypotheses.

> Lyndon was angry with the old man.
> Lyndon was robbing the man.
> Lyndon was satisfying some gang's admission requirement.
> Lyndon was mentally deranged.

Using the relative frequency interpretation, we have found that the probability that Lyndon would shoot an old man in anger is 0.1; that he would shoot an old man while robbing him, 0.2; that he would shoot an old man to satisfy the requirement of some gang, 0.4; and that he would shoot an old man as a result of being mentally deranged, 0.2. Which hypothesis should we accept?

Solution. According to the rule of maximum likelihood, we should accept the hypothesis that Lyndon shot the old man in order to satisfy some gang's admission requirement. We accept this hypothesis because no other available hypothesis makes the event which occurred (i.e., Lyndon's shooting the old man) as probable. Or, to put it a slightly different way, *given* this hypothesis, the event which occurred is more probable than it is given any of our other hypotheses. Hence, this hypothesis provides the most acceptable explanation of the event.

The next rule we have to consider was introduced in 1795 by the German mathematician and astronomer Karl Friedrich Gauss. It is particularly applicable in situations in which a number of conflicting measurements of a certain object or phenomenon have been obtained and you are trying to *estimate* the real value on the basis of this data. That is, it is designed primarily to determine the *most acceptable estimate* of this value.

Estimates are peculiar objects of belief. If a car raced by you and you were asked to estimate its speed, you might say, "Seventy miles an hour". This may be your estimate, but it is merely an abbreviation of the object of your belief. You *believe that* the car was going 70 miles an hour, or you *believe that* 70 miles an hour is an acceptable estimate of the car's speed. The object of your belief is not just a rate of speed but a *hypothesis that* the car was traveling at this or that rate. Gauss's rule may be used to determine the most acceptable estimate, but we must then turn this estimate into a proper object of belief by formulating a suitable hypothesis. Let us begin our exposition with an example.

Suppose you have been trying to determine the length of time required to roll a stone down the entire length of some long and slightly inclined plane under certain normal conditions. You have performed the experiment (i.e., rolled a stone down the plane) three times and obtained the following different values: 18 minutes, 20 minutes, and 25 minutes. The question is, Given this data, what is the most acceptable estimate of the real length of time required to roll the stone down the entire length of the plane under normal conditions?

You have at least four plausible values to consider, namely 18 minutes, 20 minutes, 25 minutes, and the *mean* of these three, 21 minutes. Now, the most acceptable estimate we *could* make is one that is identical with the real value. The farther away from that value our estimate is, the less acceptable it is. If the real value is *estimated* at 18 minutes and it happens to *be*, say, 20 minutes, then we have errored by -2 minutes. If we estimate the real value at 25 minutes and it happens to be 20 minutes, then we have made a *larger error* of $+5$ minutes. The latter estimate is farther from the real value (or, farther from the *truth*) and is, therefore, less acceptable than the former. What is required, then, is a rule designed to select that estimate which has the *smallest error*. This is what Gauss's rule is designed to do.

If the real value we are trying to measure is estimated at o, then $x - o$ is the *size of the error made* when the measurement obtained for that value is x. If we have obtained n different measurements $x_1, x_2, \ldots, x_n$ then

$$(x_1 - o) + (x_2 - o) + \cdots + (x_n - o)$$

or

$$\Sigma (x_i - o) \qquad (i = 1, 2, \ldots, n)$$

represents the *sum* of the *errors* made in each measurement. These errors may be positive, negative, or zero depending on whether our *measurement* is larger than, smaller than, or identical to our *estimate* of the real value. To remove any negative values, each of these errors is *squared*. Thus,

$$(x_1 - o)^2 + (x_2 - o)^2 + \cdots + (x_n - o)^2$$

or

$$\Sigma (x_i - o)^2 \qquad (i = 1, 2, \ldots, n)$$

represents the *sum* of the *squared errors* made when the real value is estimated at o and a number of conflicting measurements $x_1, x_2, \ldots, x_n$ have been obtained for that value.

If we made m estimates $o_1, o_2, \ldots, o_m$ of the real value then we would have a set of m *sums* of squared errors, i.e.,

$$\Sigma (x_i - o_1)^2, \Sigma (x_i - o_2)^2, \ldots, \Sigma (x_i - o_m)^2 \qquad (i = 1, 2, \ldots, n).$$

Or, more succinctly, we would have

$$\Sigma \, (x_i - o_j)^2 \qquad (i = 1, 2, \ldots, n)$$
$$(j = 1, 2, \ldots, m).$$

The rule Gauss suggested to select the most acceptable estimate from this set is called the

Method of least squares: Accept that estimate which has the minimum sum of squared errors. Hence, if, for example,

$$\Sigma \, (x_i - o_1)^2 \qquad (i = 1, 2, \ldots, n)$$

is *less* than

$$\Sigma \, (x_i - o_2)^2 \qquad (i = 1, 2, \ldots, n)$$

then o_1 is a more acceptable estimate of the real value than o_2.

This rule is clearly comparative and nonutilitarian. It rests on two fairly reasonable assumptions: a) positive errors are as likely as negative errors; b) the size and probability of an error are *inversely* related. Both of these assumptions are supported by the fact (which we have already noticed in Sec. 7.4) that errors are *frequently normally* distributed. If a situation arises in which an investigator is known to be reckless or overly cautious or prejudiced one way or another then it would be a mistake to apply this rule. In the absence of such anomalies, however, the method of least squares is a useful acceptance rule.

EXAMPLE 4

Use the method of least squares to choose the most acceptable estimate of the length of time required to roll a stone down a given plane given the three measurements, 18 minutes, 20 minutes, and 25 minutes.

Solution. We shall make our selection from the four estimates already suggested, namely 18, 20, 25, and (the *mean* of these three) 21 minutes. Taking the 18-minute estimate first, we have the following sum of squared errors.

$$(x_1 - o_1)^2 + (x_2 - o_1)^2 + (x_3 - o_1)^2.$$

Substituting in this formula, we have

$$(18 - 18)^2 + (20 - 18)^2 + (25 - 18)^2$$

or

$$(0)^2 + (-2)^2 + (-7)^2 = 53.$$

The other three estimates yield the following sums of squared errors.

$$(18 - 20)^2 + (20 - 20)^2 + (25 - 20)^2 = 29$$
$$(18 - 25)^2 + (20 - 25)^2 + (25 - 25)^2 = 74$$
$$(18 - 21)^2 + (20 - 21)^2 + (25 - 21)^2 = 26.$$

According to the method of least squares, then, on the basis of the available information the most acceptable estimate of the length of time required to roll a stone down the given plane is 21 minutes (i.e., because the *sum* of the squared errors made when the real value is estimated at 21 is *smaller* than it is with any other available estimate).

Example 5

Morton found a new fishing hole. On the first day he caught 8 large fish. On the next second day he caught 6, on the third day 5 and on the last day 9. He plans to go fishing one day next week. What is the most acceptable estimate he can make of the number of fish he will catch?

Solution. Morton does not have any probabilities, weights, or likelihoods to apply directly, but he does have the method of least squares. He considers five estimates, namely, 8, 6, 5, 9, and (the *mean* of these four) 7 fish. Then he determines the sums of the squared errors for each estimate.

$$(8 - 8)^2 + (6 - 8)^2 + (5 - 8)^2 + (9 - 8)^2 = 14$$
$$(8 - 6)^2 + (6 - 6)^2 + (5 - 6)^2 + (9 - 6)^2 = 14$$
$$(8 - 5)^2 + (6 - 5)^2 + (5 - 5)^2 + (9 - 5)^2 = 26$$
$$(8 - 9)^2 + (6 - 9)^2 + (5 - 9)^2 + (9 - 9)^2 = 26$$
$$(8 - 7)^2 + (6 - 7)^2 + (5 - 7)^2 + (9 - 7)^2 = 10.$$

According to the method of least squares, then, the most acceptable estimate of the number of fish Morton will catch one day next week is 7.

Example 6

Five investigators measured the probability of a certain type of plastic resisting the impact of a shotgun blast. Each one came up with a different answer. The first one said the plastic had a 50:50 chance of *not* shattering; the second figured it had 6 chances in 10 of not shattering; the third figured 7 in 10; the fourth, 8 in 10; and the fifth, 9 in 10. What is the most acceptable estimate of the probability of the plastic resisting the impact of a shotgun blast?

Solution. Applying the method of least squares to this problem, we would have at least five plausible estimates, namely, the five probabilities already determined. Their *mean* is identical to the third investigator's probability, 0.7, so this value seems to have a good chance of being the most acceptable estimate. The sums of the squared errors for the five estimates are as follows.

Estimate	Squared Error Sum
0.5	0.3
0.6	0.15
0.7	0.1
0.8	0.15
0.9	0.30

The most acceptable estimate of the probability of the plastic resisting the impact of a shotgun blast is 0.7, since it yields the minimum squared error sum.

Review problems for Sec. 8.2.

1. How is "the likelihood of '*C given D*' " defined?

2. What reason would anyone have for withholding the name 'probability' from likelihood?

3. Express the following in symbolic notation.

   a) the likelihood of '*A, given B and C*'
   b) the likelihood of '*A and B, given C*'
   c) the likelihood of '*A or B or C, given D*'
   d) the likelihood of '*C or D, given A and B*'

4. What is the rule of maximum likelihood?

5. The results of a history examination are posted as follows for a class of 60 students.

	A	B	C	D	E	Total
Freshmen	0	2	4	5	4	15
Sophomores	1	2	5	3	3	14
Juniors	1	3	5	4	2	15
Seniors	2	4	6	4	0	16
Total	4	11	20	16	9	60

A student is picked at random from the class, and it is required to find the *likelihood* that he is a

a) freshman *given* that his grade is *B*
b) freshman *given* that his grade is *D or E*
c) junior *given* that his grade is *A*
d) junior *given* that his grade is *A or C*
e) junior *or* senior, *given* that his grade is *A*
f) junior *or* senior, *given* that his grade is *E*
g) junior *or* sophomore, *given* that his grade is *B*
h) junior *or* sophomore, *given* that his grade is *D or E*

    i)   sophomore *or* freshman, *given* that his grade is *A or B or C*

    j)   sophomore *or* freshman, *given* that his grade is *D*

    k) senior *or* freshman, *given* that his grade is *A or D*

6. What is the method of least squares?

7. Find the sum of the squared errors for the following estimated values and measurements.

	Estimated Value		*Measurements*			
a)	18	15	16	17	18	19
b)	34	30	32	34	35	35
c)	51	47	48	48	53	53
d)	106	103	104	106	106	107
e)	73	68	72	72	73	74

Use the method of least squares to answer the following questions.

8. Beatrice has had six weekly quizzes in sociology with the following scores: 58, 63, 60, 64, 59, and 62. She estimates that her next score will be 62. Find the sum of the squared errors when the score is estimated at

    a)   61

    b)   62

    c)   Which estimate is more acceptable?

9. A truck driver is estimating the number of service stops required between New York and Dallas, Texas. The number of stops required for the last six trips were 27, 27, 26, 29, 28, and 28. Find the sum of the squared errors when the number of stops is estimated at

    a)   27

    b)   28

    c)   Which estimate is more acceptable?

10. A fighter's weight has varied repeatedly for 6 weeks as follows: 134, 140, 139, 135, 138, and 142 pounds. Find the sum of the squared errors when his present weight is estimated at

    a)   137 pounds

    b)   139

    c)   Which estimate is more acceptable?

11. The manager of a local telephone company has three estimates of the number of long distance calls that will be made Saturday, namely 201, 202, and 203. The last nine Saturdays have had the following numbers of calls: 199, 202, 200, 204, 203, 201, 202, 202, and 200. Find the sum of the squared errors when the number of calls is estimated at

    a)   201   c)   203

    b)   202   d)   Which estimate is most acceptable?

8.3   Minimax and minimin

All the rules that will be introduced in the remaining sections of this chapter are comparative and utilitarian. Each of them is designed to select a *course of action* only after considering the *alternatives* and the *gains and losses* involved in any selection.

Suppose a friend offers to find you a blind date for a dance Saturday night. You immediately have two options. You can accept the offer or reject it. If you accept it and she (or he) is wonderful then you will be very happy. If you accept it and she (or he) is miserable then you will be miserable. Of course, you could reject it. But if you reject it and she (or he) is wonderful then you will "kick yourself" for turning it down. As far as you can tell, however, you would rather have to kick yourself than face a miserable evening. If you reject it and she (or he) is miserable then you will not be overjoyed (because you will be home alone when you might have been out dancing), but you will not "kick yourself" or be miserable either. We may summarize these four possibilities thus.

States of Nature

	She (or he) is wonderful.	She (or he) is miserable.
Accept offer	You will be very happy. (1)	You will be miserable. (4)
Reject offer	You will "kick yourself". (3)	You will not be overjoyed. (2)

Courses of Action (vertical label at left)

A Payoff Matrix

The relevant possible **courses of action** are the *acts* that might be performed or the *decisions* that might be made in a given situation. These are listed vertically in the left-hand column, and it is assumed that the list is made up of *mutually exclusive* and *exhaustive* options. The person(s) who must perform the acts or make the decisions will be called the **decision maker(s)**. The relevant possible **states of nature** may be regarded as events (in the broad sense of this term) whose occurrence or nonoccurrence will affect the results of the course of action followed by the decision maker. These are listed horizontally across the top of the brackets. It is assumed that this list is also made up of *mutually exclusive* and *exhaustive* items.

If the decision maker knows exactly which state of nature obtains or will obtain when he accepts a given course of action, we say he is operating under **conditions of certainty.** If *every* relevant state of nature is assigned a probability (or weight, or likelihood), we say he is operating under **conditions of risk.** If *none* or only *some* of the payoffs are assigned probabilities, we say he is operating under **conditions of uncertainty.**

The **payoffs** are gains or losses attached to each course of action *and* state of nature. They are listed within the brackets. The whole tabular summary is called a **payoff matrix** (plural, 'matrices'). Many writers use the more general term 'values' instead of 'payoffs'. Others prefer the more classical term 'utilities'; e.g., as in Sec. 8.7. We are using 'payoffs' because it seems more descriptive; i.e., the things designated by this term are rewards or punishments received as a result of certain human *actions*.

Notice that each of the four payoffs has a number in parentheses beside it. These **payoff numbers** represent the *preference order* or *rank order* or *comparative status* of the payoffs for the decision maker. For example, your first preference is (1), to be very happy. This is ranked over (2), being not overjoyed. The latter is preferred to (3), "kicking yourself", and that is better than (4), being miserable. A matrix may contain more or less than four different payoff numbers. For example, if someone ranks every possible payoff *the same*, then only *one* number, say (1), will appear in the matrix beside each payoff. If there are four payoffs but three of them are ranked *the same below* the fourth, then the matrix will have (1) beside the preferred payoff and (2) beside *each* of the other three. If there are *n* different payoffs and someone is able to distinguish *n* different levels of preference, then there will be *n* different numbers beside the payoffs, and so on. Usually the context or statement of the problem makes the preference order obvious, so the payoff numbers are superfluous. But in cases in which the options are not particularly clear, these numbers are an aid to the reader's intuition. They are also useful in illustrating general points schematically.

The question is, On the basis of the information summarized in the payoff matrix, what is the most acceptable course of action? Since no probabilities (or weights, or likelihoods) are given, the decision maker is operating under conditions of *uncertainty*. This will be the typical situation for this and the next three sections where six more or less plausible rules will be introduced which have been designed especially for just such circumstances. To begin with, consider the acceptance rule suggested by the American mathematician Abraham Wald and known as

Minimax loss: Accept that course of action which allows the smallest maximum possible loss. The application of this rule involves two steps. a) For each possible course of action, determine the *worst* thing that can happen; i.e., determine the maximum possible loss for each alternative. b) Then accept that course of action which allows the *smallest* maximum possible loss. For example, the maximum loss you could suffer as a result of *accepting* your friend's offer is an evening of misery, while the maximum loss you could suffer as a result of *rejecting* his offer is having to "kick yourself". You believe that the latter loss is not as serious as the former. Hence, according to the minimax loss rule, the most acceptable course of action for you is to *reject* his offer.

EXAMPLE 1

You are driving along on a toll road and you notice that you have about a quarter of a tank of gasoline. There is a service station immediately in view, but you would rather not stop now. You visualize the following payoff matrix.

	Find out later that you had enough already.	Find out later that you did not have enough.
Stop now for gas	You would feel foolish. (3)	You would be very pleased. (1)
Do not stop now	You would feel lucky. (2)	You would "kick yourself all over". (4)

What is the best course of action?

Solution. The *worst* thing that can happen if you stop now is that you may end up feeling foolish. If you do not stop now, however, you *could* end up "kicking yourself all over the place". The latter possibility is more distasteful than the former. Therefore, according to the minimax loss rule, the best course of action is to stop for gasoline right now (because that involves the smallest maximum loss).

EXAMPLE 2

Hoyle is thinking about selling his house this year and has heard that its value may increase by next year. He imagines the following payoff matrix.

	Values increase	Values do not increase
Sell now	Lose $2000. (3)	No loss. (1)
Sell next year	No loss. (1)	Lose $1200. (2)

What course of action is most acceptable for Hoyle?

Solution. Notice that the payoff numbers range from (1) to (3) and that (1) is assigned to both occurrences of 'No loss' in the matrix. This means that only three *levels* of preference are recognized and that two payoffs occupy the same (first) level. If Hoyle sells now and values increase, he loses $2000. The maximum loss he can incur if he sells next year is $1200. Hence, according to the minimax loss rule, the most acceptable course of action for Hoyle is to sell his house next year.

The minimax loss rule has been referred to as "a pessimist's rule" because it requires special attention to be given to unpleasant outcomes. A *slightly* more "optimistic" rule would be

Minimin loss: Accept that course of action which allows the smallest minimum possible loss. It is still "pessimistic" in the sense that it directs our attention to unpleasant outcomes. But it is a bit "optimistic" because it recommends the selection of a course of action which *may allow* a maximum loss; i.e., the course of action which has the minimum loss in one state of nature may also have the maximum loss in another state of nature, but this rule ignores the latter entirely. The two steps involved in the application of the minimin loss rule are

a) determine the minimum possible losses for each course of action. b) Then accept that course which has the *smallest* minimum possible loss.

EXAMPLE 3

A friend of yours seems to be in need of some extra cash. Because he is a friend, you feel obliged to help him. You doubt that he will repay anything lent to him, and you imagine you have the following payoff matrix.

	He accepts your offer.	He rejects your offer.
Offer $10.00	You will be happy to help but troubled about losing the $10.00. (1)	You will be happy about keeping your money but insulted by his attitude toward your offer. (2)
Offer $30.00	You will be less happy to help and more troubled about losing $30.00. (2)	You will be happier about keeping your money but insulted by his attitude toward your offer. (2)

What is your most acceptable course of action.

Solution. As far as you can tell, the prospect of losing $30.00 to your friend if he accepts your offer is as unbearable as his insulting attitude if he rejects it. Hence, the *maximum* possible displeasure yielded by each course of action is the same. But if you offer your friend $10.00, you *might* lose less than the maximum. You might suffer the very *minimum* amount of possible displeasure in the given situation. This is precisely the course of action recommended by the minimin loss rule; i.e., your most acceptable course of action is to offer your friend $10.00 (because that allows the smallest minimum possible loss).

EXAMPLE 4

Ronald is not much of a gambler but he has been invited to play poker with some local "sharks". He finds himself with the following payoff matrix.

	The sharks are kind.	The sharks are unkind.
Play	Lose about $5.00. (2)	Lose about $50.00 (3)
Do not play	Nothing lost. (1)	Nothing lost. (1)

What is Ronald's best course of action?

Solution. To apply the minimin loss rule, Ronald begins by determining the minimum possible loss for each course of action. The minimum possible loss if he plays is about $5.00; while if he does not play he cannot lose anything. Hence, according to the minimin loss rule, the best course of action for Ronald is not to play poker with the "sharks".

Ronald's payoff matrix is unlike any of those considered thus far, for whatever happens as a result of his *not* playing is better than (preferred to) anything that could happen as a result of his playing. A course of action which yields payoffs that are *worse* than those yielded by some other course of action given *any* state of nature is said to be **dominated** by that other course of action. Thus, for Ronald, playing is dominated by *not* playing. Since a course of action which is dominated by another will never be accepted (as long as the other is available), such alternatives may be eliminated from consideration. For Ronald's case this means that after determining the relative values of each of the payoffs, one course of action should be eliminated immediately. The *only* acceptable course of action for Ronald is not to play poker with the "sharks".

It is important to notice now that no principle has been given to help one decide whether the minimax or the minimin loss rule *should* be applied. Sometimes this presents no problem because both rules prescribe the very same course of action; e.g., as in Example 4. But frequently the rules prescribe opposite courses of action given the same states of nature, payoffs, and preference rankings; e.g., as in Example 1. Hence, a principle of application for each of these acceptance rules *seems* to be required, but *there is no such principle*. As long as the information required by each rule is given, either rule may be employed. If someone believes maximum possible losses may be ignored in favor of minimum possible losses then he may use the minimin loss rule. *Given his attitude* toward possible losses, the minimin loss rule will select the most acceptable course of action *for him* or for a person with such an attitude. Neither rule can prescribe the most acceptable courses of action for everyone, but both rules do prescribe the most acceptable courses of action for some people. If you are particularly "pessimistic" usually or in some special situation you may apply the minimax loss rule. If you are "not quite as pessimistic" you may apply the minimin loss rule. The rule will prescribe a course of action that is acceptable *given* one or the other of these two *attitudes*. Your own common sense, intuition, and good fortune will have to prescribe *the most acceptable attitude*.

Similar remarks are applicable to *all* utilitarian acceptance rules. In a given situation the rules select an acceptable course of action or hypothesis *relative to* some particular set of *attitudes* or *judgments of value*. *One* reason why there are so many different utilitarian rules is that there are many different views about what is especially important or valuable in general and in special situations.

Review problems for Sec. 8.3.

1. Explain the following.
   a) conditions of certainty
   b) conditions of risk
   c) conditions of uncertainty

2. Describe the various parts of a payoff matrix.

3. When is a course of action dominated by another?

4. What is the minimax loss rule?

Apply the minimax loss rule to the following problems to determine the most acceptable course of action in each case.

5. A man is trying to decide whether or not he should believe in the existence of God. He imagines the following payoff matrix.

	God exists.	God does not exist.
Believe	Go to heaven. (1)	Have dissatisfaction of a false belief. (3)
Disbelieve	Go to hell. (4)	Have satisfaction of a true disbelief. (2)

Should he believe or not?

6. The Chicago Bears are deep in their own territory and it is fourth down with 3 yards to go for a first down. The quarterback is trying to decide whether he should punt the ball or run. His matrix is as follows.

	Play succeeds.	Play fails.
Punt	Lose ball but out of danger. (2)	Lose ball and still in danger. (3)
Run	Keep ball and earn first down. (1)	Lose ball and face more danger. (4)

Should he punt or not?

7. Julius is considering taking out fire insurance on his house. He visualizes the following matrix.

	Fire	No fire
Insure	Lose $2000. (3)	Lose $60.00. (2)
Do not insure	Lose $12,000. (4)	No loss. (1)

Should he insure or not?

8. Suppose 'A_1' and 'A_2' are abbreviations for 'the first course of action' and 'the second course of action', respectively, and 'S_1' and 'S_2' are short for 'the first state of nature' and 'the second state of nature', respectively. Is A_1 or A_2 more acceptable?

	S_1	S_2	S_3
A_1	(1)	(2)	(3)
A_2	(4)	(5)	(2)

9. Which course of action is most acceptable?

$$
\begin{array}{c}
 & S_1 & S_2 & S_3 \\
A_1 & \left[(5) \right. & (3) & \left. (2) \right] \\
A_2 & (6) & (1) & (4) \\
A_3 & (3) & (4) & (2)
\end{array}
$$

10. Which course of action is most acceptable?

$$
\begin{array}{c}
 & S_1 & S_2 & S_3 \\
A_1 & \left[(7) \right. & (5) & \left. (3) \right] \\
A_2 & (8) & (4) & (3) \\
A_3 & (1) & (2) & (4) \\
A_4 & (2) & (7) & (6)
\end{array}
$$

11. What is the minimin loss rule?

Apply the minimin loss rule to the following.

12. JoJo is trying to decide whether or not he should escape from prison to see his girl-friend. He figures he has the following payoff matrix.

	She's waiting.	She's gone.
Escape	Be hunted but happy. (1)	Be hunted and bitter. (4)
Do not escape	Be comfortable but sad. (3)	Be comfortable and satisfied. (2)

Should he escape or not?

13. Which of the courses of action recorded in the matrix for Prob. 9 is most acceptable?

14. Which of the courses of action recorded in the matrix for Prob. 10 is most acceptable?

8.4 Maximin and maximax

If the last two rules were appropriately referred to as more or less "pessimistic" then the two we are about to consider should be regarded as more or less "optimistic". The last two directed attention to losses. The two we are going to consider in this section direct attention to gains. The first of these two is a bit less "optimistic" than the second. It is called

Maximin gain: Accept that course of action which allows the largest minimum possible gain. The application of this rule involves two steps. a) For each possible course of action, determine the *least* possible gain; i.e., determine the minimum possible gain for each alternative. b) Then accept that course of action which allows the *largest* minimum possible gain.

EXAMPLE 1

Herbie has an important ball game to play on Saturday afternoon and wants to have a date for a party Friday night. He is thinking about bringing one of two very nice girls, namely Lucy, who enjoys dancing, or Julie, who can take it or leave it. He does not know if there will be dancing at the party and would rather not have to sit around talking to Lucy all night. He has the following payoff matrix.

	There will be dancing at the party.	There will not be dancing at the party.
Bring Lucy	Have fun and get tired. (2)	Have less fun but get less tired. (3)
Bring Julie	Have less fun and get tired. (4)	Have fun and get less tired. (1)

What course of action should Herbie follow?

Solution. The evening is bound to be pretty enjoyable with either Lucy or Julie, but Herbie does not want to get too tired because he wants to be fresh for the ball game. To apply maximin gain, he first decides that the least amount of pleasure he can have in Lucy's hands is to have a little less fun without getting tired. With Julie he could have the same amount of fun but he would get tired. Hence, the maximin gain rule prescribes bringing Lucy to the party (because this course of action allows the largest minimum possible gain).

EXAMPLE 2

Big Billie the basketball star has been approached by some gangster to "shave" points (i.e., score less) in Saturday's game. He will be paid according to the number of points he "shaves" and whether his team wins or loses. Big Billie's coach wants him to score as much as possible and will reward him accordingly. Big Billie finds himself faced with the following payoff matrix.

	We win.	We lose.
"Shave" points	Make $300.00 (3)	Make $500.00 (1)
Score plenty	Make $400.00 (2)	Make $200.00 (4)

What is the more acceptable course of action for Big Billie?

Solution. If Big Billie "shaves" points the minimum possible gain he can make is $300.00. If he scores plenty the minimum possible gain he can make is $200.00. Therefore, the maximin gain rule prescribes "shaving" points, since that course of action allows the largest minimum possible gain.

EXAMPLE 3

Hutchins is a poor student who has lost interest in school and failed to attend quite a few lectures. Final exams are drawing near and he is wondering if it would be worthwhile to start attending all lectures. He imagines he has the following payoff matrix.

	He has learned enough on his own.	He has not learned enough on his own.
Attend all lectures	Pass all six courses. (1)	Pass four courses. (3)
Continue to skip lectures	Pass five courses. (2)	Pass three courses. (4)

What is the best course of action for Hutchins?

Solution. The minimum possible gain Hutchins faces if he attends all lectures is passing four courses. The minimum possible gain he faces if he continues to skip lectures is passing three courses. According to the maximin gain rule, then, the best course of action for Hutchins is to attend all lectures (because that allows the largest minimum possible gain).

Because the maximin gain rule directs attention to *gains*, it has been regarded as more "optimistic" than either the minimax or minimin loss rules. But because it concentrates on *minimum* gains it is a bit more "pessimistic" than

Maximax gain: Accept that course of action which allows the largest maximum possible gain. The application of this rule again involves two steps. a) For each possible course of action, determine the *greatest* possible gain; i.e., determine the maximum possible gain for each alternative. b) Then accept that course of action which allows the *largest* maximum possible gain. Consider the following examples.

EXAMPLE 4

Roy Restless is very disturbed by one of the dean's policies. He is thinking about organizing a mass demonstration against the policy, but he has the suspicion that plans for a change might be under way already. He knows that although other people would like a change, many people are opposed to any sort of mass demonstration. He has the following payoff matrix.

	Plans for a change are already being considered.	No plans for a change are being considered.
Organize a demonstration	Policy will be changed and enemies will be made. (2)	Policy will not be changed and enemies will be made. (4)
Do not organize a demonstration	Policy will be changed and no enemies will be made. (1)	Policy will not be changed and no enemies will be made. (3)

What is the most acceptable course of action for Roy?

Solution. The maximum gain Roy faces if he organizes a demonstration is a change in the policy and the creation of some enemies. The most he can gain if he does *not* organize a demonstration is possibly a change in policy *and* certainly no more enemies. The latter payoff is preferred to the former. Hence, the maximax gain rule recommends no demonstration (because that has the largest maximum possible gain).

EXAMPLE 5

Salvatore Savethajunc is trying to decide whether or not he should refinish an old pine cabinet. He knows that some people will pay more for it if it is refinished and that others will pay more for it with the original finish. He would like to sell it as soon as possible and make as much as possible in the deal, but he does not know which type of customer will be stopping in his shop in the near future. He figures he has the following payoff matrix.

	A customer will come in looking for a refinished cabinet.	A customer will come in looking for a cabinet with the original finish.
Refinish it	Make about $350.00. (1)	Make about $100.00. (3)
Do not refinish it	Make about $50.00. (4)	Make about $300.00. (2)

What is the best course of action for Salvatore?

Solution. The maximum possible gain for Salvatore if he refinishes the cabinet is about $350.00. If he does not refinish it he could gain at most $300.00. Hence, applying the maximax gain rule, the best course of action for Salvatore is to refinish the cabinet (because that allows the largest maximum gain).

Review problems for Sec. 8.4.

1. What is the maximin gain rule?
   Apply the maximin gain rule to the following.

2. Heinz is doing fine on his test until he reaches the last section. At that point he begins to wonder if he should copy Frank's answers. He visualizes the following matrix.

	Frank studied.	Frank did not study.
Copy	Make about 20 points. (1)	Make about 5 points. (3)
Do not copy	Make about 10 points. (2)	Make about 10 points. (2)

   Should he copy or not?

3. Dennis has a date with his girlfriend's best friend. He would like to kiss her, but he is afraid of the consequences. In particular, he considers the following possibilities.

	His girlfriend hears about everything.	His girlfriend does not hear about everything.
Kiss her	Have fun but lose girlfriend. (2)	Have fun and keep girlfriend. (1)
Do not kiss her	Keep girlfriend but have less fun. (3)	Keep girlfriend but have less fun. (3)

Should he kiss her or not?

4. Is A_1 or A_2 more acceptable?

$$
\begin{array}{c c c c}
 & S_1 & S_2 & S_3 \\
A_1 & (3) & (2) & (4) \\
A_2 & (4) & (1) & (5)
\end{array}
$$

5. Given the following matrix of gains:

$$
\begin{array}{c c c c c}
 & S_1 & S_2 & S_3 & S_4 \\
A_1 & (6) & (7) & (1) & (2) \\
A_2 & (5) & (4) & (3) & (6) \\
A_3 & (4) & (1) & (5) & (9) \\
A_4 & (2) & (8) & (3) & (7)
\end{array}
$$

a)   Select the most acceptable course of action.

b)   Is A_1 or A_4 more acceptable?

c)   Rank the four courses of action in order of acceptability, beginning with the most acceptable.

6. What is the maximax gain rule?

Apply the maximax gain rule to the following.

7. When David meets Goliath, he imagines the following matrix.

	Goliath is too much.	Goliath can be beaten.
Fight	Become a dead hero. (3)	Become a live hero. (1)
Run	Become a live coward. (2)	Become a live coward. (2)

What should David do?

8. Which course of action recorded in the matrix for Prob. 4 is more acceptable?

9. Rank the four courses of action given in Prob. 5 in order of acceptability beginning with the most acceptable.

8.5   Minimax regret

A leading statistician and defender of the personal odds theory of measuring probabilities, L. J. Savage, has argued that the last four rules introduced (minimax and minimin loss and maximin and maximax gain) fail to capture an essential aspect of human decision making. According to Savage, using these rules, someone might be forced into accepting a course of action which he would later come to regret. There is nothing startling about the fact that someone might regret having done this or that (although someone thoroughly committed to a certain view of the world and to a rule consistent with that view should have little or no regrets about his actions), but the idea of designing an acceptance rule to minimize (maximum) regret has been extremely fruitful. In this section we shall present the type of objection Savage raises against the last four rules and then consider his alternative.

To illustrate the infelicity Savage finds in the minimax loss rule, consider the following case.

CASE 1

A banker is thinking about withdrawing his support from a local farmer who seems to be fighting a lost cause to save his farm. He figures he has the following payoff matrix.

	There will be a good crop this year.	There will not be a good crop this year.
Withdraw support now	Lose about $99. (2)	Lose about $99. (2)
Do not withdraw support now	Lose about $1. (1)	Lose about $100. (3)

If the banker applies the minimax loss rule then he will withdraw support now, because that course of action allows the smallest maximum possible loss of $99. But Savage would argue, because the banker *could* lose so much less if he does not withdraw support now *and* there is a good crop, it seems more plausible *not* to withdraw support. That is, if the banker withdraws support now *and* there is a good crop, then he will *regret* having taken this course of action. Hence, it would be wiser to take the other course.

Similar objections may be raised against the other three rules, but consider only the following objection to the maximin gain rule.

CASE 2

The same banker is thinking about withdrawing his support from another farmer, but in this case he has the following payoff matrix.

	There will be a good crop this year.	There will not be a good crop this year.
Withdraw support now	Gain about $2. (2)	Gain about $2. (2)
Do not withdraw support now	Gain about $100. (1)	Gain about $1. (3)

If the banker applies the maximin gain rule then he will withdraw support now, because that course of action allows the largest minimum possible gain of $2. But again Savage would argue that because the banker *could* gain so much more if he does not withdraw support now *and* there is a good crop, it seems more plausible *not* to withdraw support. That is, if the banker withdraws support now *and* there is a good crop, then he will *regret* having taken this course of action. Hence, it would be wiser to pursue the other course.

The acceptance rule Savage suggested avoids objections like those we have just considered. It is called

Minimax regret: Accept that course of action which allows the smallest maximum possible regret. The application of this rule requires four steps. a) Determine a relevant payoff matrix of gains or losses. b) Determine a regret matrix based on this payoff matrix. c) Find the maximum possible regret attached to each relevant course of action. d) Then accept that course of action which allows the *smallest* maximum possible regret.

The amount of **regret** involved in any *payoff* in some state of nature is equal to the difference between that payoff and the most preferred payoff possible for that state of nature. Schematically we may illustrate this as follows. Suppose someone has a matrix of payoffs ranked thus.

$$\begin{array}{c c c} & S_1 & S_2 \\ A_1 & \begin{bmatrix} (2) & (3) \\ A_2 & (1) & (4) \end{bmatrix} \end{array}$$

Then his **regret matrix** or tabular summary of the amount of regret involved in every payoff in the matrix above looks like this.

$$\begin{array}{c c c} & S_1 & S_2 \\ A_1 & \begin{bmatrix} \text{Regret. } (2) & \text{No regret. } (1) \\ A_2 & \text{No regret. } (1) & \text{Regret. } (2) \end{bmatrix} \end{array}$$

If he takes A_1 and S_2 occurs then he will have *no* regret because the payoff attached to A_1 *and* S_2 is the most preferred payoff possible in S_2. On the other hand, if he takes A_2 and S_2 occurs then he will have something to regret because the payoff attached to A_2 *and* S_2 is *not* the most preferred payoff possible in S_2. Similarly, A_1 involves some regret *if* S_1 occurs, but A_2 does not involve any regret if S_1 occurs. He does not know whether S_1 or S_2 will occur, but he does know whether or not he will have something to regret for having chosen A_1 or A_2.

Let us see what happens when the minimax regret rule is applied to the banker's problem in Case 1. His payoff matrix may be abbreviated thus.

$$\begin{array}{c c c} & S_1 & S_2 \\ A_1 & \begin{bmatrix} \text{Lose about \$99. } (2) & \text{Lose about \$99. } (2) \\ A_2 & \text{Lose about \$1. } (1) & \text{Lose about \$100. } (3) \end{bmatrix} \end{array}$$

So his regret matrix looks like this.

$$\begin{array}{c c c} & S_1 & S_2 \\ A_1 & \begin{bmatrix} \text{Regret worth about ``\$98''. } (3) & \text{No regret. } (1) \\ A_2 & \text{No regret. } (1) & \text{Regret worth about ``\$1''. } (2) \end{bmatrix} \end{array}$$

(The double quotation marks are put around '$98' and '$1' because we are using these monetary measures in a peculiar way, namely, as *rough* measures of regret. Sometimes other convenient and rough measures are used. We do not have an official or standard measure of this feeling.) The minimax regret rule prescribes A_2 (i.e., *not* withdrawing support now), because that allows the *smallest* maximum possible regret. This agrees with Savage's intuition (and many others!) exactly.

Apply the minimax regret rule to the banker's problem in Case 2. His payoff matrix may be abbreviated thus.

$$
\begin{array}{c}
 \qquad\qquad S_1 \qquad\qquad\qquad\qquad S_2 \\
\begin{array}{cl}
A_1 & \left[\begin{array}{ll} \text{Gain about \$2. (2)} & \text{Gain about \$2. (2)} \\ \text{Gain about \$100. (1)} & \text{Gain about \$1. (3)} \end{array}\right] \\
A_2 &
\end{array}
\end{array}
$$

So his regret matrix looks like this.

$$
\begin{array}{c}
 \qquad\qquad S_1 \qquad\qquad\qquad\qquad\qquad S_2 \\
\begin{array}{cl}
A_1 & \left[\begin{array}{ll} \text{Regret worth about "\$98". (3)} & \text{No regret. (1)} \\ \text{No regret. (1)} & \text{Regret worth about "\$1". (2)} \end{array}\right] \\
A_2 &
\end{array}
\end{array}
$$

The minimax regret rule again prescribes A_2 (i.e., *not* withdrawing support now), which agrees with Savage's intuition.

It is clear then that the minimax regret rule does capture one of the essential aspects of human decision making which is missed by the four rules previously introduced. Consider one final example.

A student is in his junior year of college and thinking about changing his major course of study to either chemistry or mathematics. He knows that he is bound to lose some credits in the switch, but he is more troubled by the possibility that the required courses may become too difficult for him. He has figured out the following payoff matrix.

	It will be too difficult.	It will not be too difficult.
Change to mathematics	Lose about 7 credits. (3)	Lose about 5 credits. (1)
Change to chemistry	Lose about 9 credits. (4)	Lose about 4 credits. (2)

From this he obtains the following regret matrix.

	It will be too difficult.	It will not be too difficult.
Change to mathematics	No regret. (1)	Regret worth about "1 credit". (2)
Change to chemistry	Regret worth about "2 credits". (3)	No regret. (1)

Applying the minimax regret rule, he decides to change to mathematics, because that allows the smallest maximum possible regret.

Review problems for Sec. 8.5.

1. What is the minimax regret rule?

2. How is the 'regret' involved in any payoff defined?
   Apply the minimax regret rule to the following.

3. Girard is in a hurry to reach home after a hard day at the office. He can take the Freeway or Washington Avenue. He can make better time on the Freeway unless he meets the crowd coming out of the ball game. He imagines he has the following payoff matrix.

	He will meet the crowd.	He will not meet the crowd.
Use Freeway	Take 50 minutes to reach home. (4)	Take 10 minutes to reach home. (1)
Use Washington Avenue	Take 23 minutes to reach home. (3)	Take 20 minutes to reach home. (2)

   Which road should Girard take?

4. The coach of a professional baseball team is trying to decide whether or not he should send a certain rookie back to the minor league. He has the following payoff matrix.

	Rookie will improve.	Rookie will not improve.
Keep him	Lose about $5000. (2)	Lose about $8000. (3)
Send him back	Lose about $10,000. (4)	Lose about $2000. (1)

   Should the coach keep him or send him back?

5. Select the most acceptable course of action for the following.

   a) Sec. 8.3, Example 2   d) Sec. 8.4, Example 2
   b) Sec. 8.3, Example 4   e) Sec. 8.4, Example 3
   c) Sec. 8.3, Prob. 7   f) Sec. 8.4, Example 5

8.6   Hurwicz' rule

The final acceptance rule we have to consider for decision makers operating under conditions of uncertainty was introduced by Leonid Hurwicz in 1951. We will call it

Hurwicz' rule: Accept that course of action which has the maximum optimism-weighted value. The application of this rule involves two steps. a) Determine the optimism-weighted value of each relevant course of action. b) Then accept that course of action with the largest optimism-weighted value.

To determine the optimism-weighted value of a course of action A, begin by assigning *personal* probabilities of z to the *most* preferred *payoff* and $1 - z$ to the *least* preferred *payoff* possible with A. The probability z is called your (or the decision maker's) **index of optimism.** It represents the odds you would be willing to give in a bet that you will obtain the most preferred payoff possible with A if you accept that course of action. If M is the maximum possible gain and m is the minimum possible gain obtainable with A then $zM + (1 - z)m$ is the **optimism-weighted value** of that course of action. Consider the following examples.

EXAMPLE 1

Butch is short of cash and thinking about borrowing some from either Fred or Ned. Fred and Ned will be more or less generous depending on whether or not they were recently promoted. Butch begins, then, with the following payoff matrix.

	They were promoted.	They were not promoted.
Ask Fred	Receive about \$10.00. (1)	Receive about \$3.00. (4)
Ask Ned	Receive about \$6.00. (2)	Receive about \$5.00. (3)

If Butch's index of optimism is $z = 0.3$ what is the most acceptable course of action for him?

Solution. Since Butch's index of optimism is $z = 0.3$, he figures the probability that he will receive the maximum loan from either Fred or Ned is 0.3. That makes the probability that he will receive the minimum loan from either friend $1 - z = 0.7$. So the optimism-weighted value of asking Fred for a loan is

$$(0.3)(10) + (0.7)(3) = 5.1.$$

Since this is *less* than

$$(0.3)(6) + (0.7)(5) = 5.3,$$

the optimism-weighted value of asking Ned for a loan, Hurwicz' rule prescribes the latter course of action. That is, Butch should ask Ned for a loan because that has the largest optimism-weighted value.

EXAMPLE 2

A captain is trying to decide which of two tactics to employ against the enemy. He knows his position is such that either tactic must result in substantial gains. But he also knows that the enemy has recently made one or the other of two important moves and that each of these has a different effect. He has calculated the following payoff matrix.

	The enemy made move I.	The enemy made move II.
Employ first tactic	Capture about 200 men. (2)	Capture about 100 men. (4)
Employ second tactic	Capture about 150 men. (3)	Capture about 300 men. (1)

The captain's index of optimism is $z = 0.6$. What is his best course of action?

Solution. Given the index of optimism $z = 0.6$, we must multiply the *most* preferred payoff possible with the first tactic by 0.6 and the *least* preferred payoff possible with this tactic by $1 - z = 0.4$. The sum of these two products is

$$(0.6)(200) + (0.4)(100) = 160.$$

This is the optimism-weighted value of employing the first tactic. Similarly, the optimism-weighted value of employing the second tactic is

$$(0.4)(15) + (0.6)(300) = 240.$$

Hurwicz' rule prescribes employing the second tactic, because that has the largest optimism-weighted value. Notice that the probability $z = 0.6$ *changed columns* as it were in this example. This is possible because this probability is assigned to *payoffs, not* to states of nature.

EXAMPLE 3

A medical missionary has had eight patients brought to him with roughly the same symptoms. He believes they have one of two different diseases. He must decide to apply one of two treatments, and his payoff matrix looks like this.

	They have disease *S*.	They have disease *S'*.
Use treatment *A*	Cure six. (2)	Cure five. (3)
Use treatment *A'*	Cure eight. (1)	Cure two. (4)

Given an index of optimism $z = 0.8$, what is the most acceptable course of action for the missionary?

Solution. The optimism-weighted value of using treatment *A* is

$$(0.8)(6) + (0.2)(5) = 5.8.$$

Because this is *less* than

$$(0.8)(8) + (0.2)(2) = 6.8,$$

the optimism-weighted value of using treatment *A'*, Hurwicz' rule prescribes the latter course of action.

If a decision maker has an index of optimism of 1, then the application of Hurwicz' rule is tantamount to the application of the maximax gain rule. We may illustrate this schematically as follows. Suppose we are given

$$
\begin{array}{cc}
 & S_1 \quad S_2 \\
\begin{array}{c} A_1 \\ A_2 \end{array} & \begin{bmatrix} (1) & (4) \\ (2) & (3) \end{bmatrix}
\end{array}
$$

If $z = 1$ then the optimism-weighted value of A_1 becomes

$$(1)(1) + (0)(4) = (1);$$

i.e., it becomes identical with the *most* preferred payoff possible with A_1. Similarly, the optimism-weighted value of A_2 becomes

$$(1)(2) + (0)(3) = (2),$$

which is the *most* preferred payoff possible with A_2. Choosing between these two payoffs is tantamount to choosing between the maximum possible gains of each course of action. Thus, Hurwicz' rule reduces to the maximax gain rule when $z = 1$.

If a decision maker has an index of optimism of 0, then the application of Hurwicz' rule is tantamount to the application of the minimax loss rule. This may also be illustrated with the schema above. If $z = 0$ then the optimism-weighted value of A_1 becomes

$$(0)(1) + (1)(4) = (4),$$

which is identical with the least preferred payoff possible with A_1. The optimism-weighted value of A_2 becomes

$$(0)(2) + (1)(3) = (3),$$

which is the *least* preferred payoff possible with A_2. Choosing between these two payoffs is tantamount to choosing between the maximum possible losses of each course of action. Thus, Hurwicz' rule reduces to the minimax loss rule when $z = 0$.

Review problems for Sec. 8.6.

1. Define the following.

    a) Hurwicz' rule
    b) index of optimism
    c) optimism-weighted value

    Apply Hurwicz' rule to the following.

2. A doctor has from 6 months to 1 year to live and 10 patients to cure. He would like to cure as many patients as possible and he imagines he has the following matrix.

$$
\begin{array}{ccc}
 & \text{Live 1 year.} & \text{Live 6 months.} \\
\text{Try to cure all 10} & \left[\text{Cure 10. (1)}\right. & \left.\text{Cure 2. (4)}\right] \\
\text{Try to cure only 5} & \left[\text{Cure 5. (2)}\right. & \left.\text{Cure 4. (3)}\right]
\end{array}
$$

Find the optimism-weighted value of

a) trying to cure all 10,
b) trying to cure only 5,

when the doctor's index of optimism is $z = 0.4$.

c) Which course of action is more acceptable?

3. From Prob. 2, find the optimism-weighted value of

a) trying to cure all 10,
b) trying to cure only 5,

when the doctor's index of optimism is $z = 0.2$.

c) Which course of action is more acceptable?

4. An Indian chief is trying to decide whether he should attack the settlers now or wait for reinforcements. He does not know if the settlers have repeating rifles or not, and he believes he has the following possibilities.

$$
\begin{array}{ccc}
 & \begin{array}{c}\text{Settlers have repeating} \\ \text{rifles.}\end{array} & \begin{array}{c}\text{Settlers do not have} \\ \text{repeating rifles.}\end{array} \\
\text{Wait} & \left[\text{Kill about 30 settlers. (3)}\right. & \left.\text{Kill about 50 settlers. (1)}\right] \\
\text{Attack} & \left[\text{Kill about 20 settlers. (4)}\right. & \left.\text{Kill about 40 settlers. (2)}\right]
\end{array}
$$

Find the optimism-weighted value of

a) waiting for reinforcements
b) attacking now

when the chief's index of optimism is $z = 0.6$.

c) Which course of action is more acceptable?

5. From Prob. 4, find the optimism-weighted value of
a) waiting for reinforcements
b) attacking now

when the chief's index of optimism is $z = 0.7$.

c) Which course of action is more acceptable?

6. A farmer has two brands of fertilizer to use which respond differently to different weather conditions. He has the following matrix.

$$
\begin{array}{ccc}
 & \text{Cold weather coming} & \text{Hot weather coming} \\
\text{Use } x & \left[\text{Produce 100 bushels. (1)}\right. & \left.\text{Produce 80 bushels. (3)}\right] \\
\text{Use } y & \left[\text{Produce 70 bushels. (4)}\right. & \left.\text{Produce 90 bushels. (2)}\right]
\end{array}
$$

Find the optimism-weighted value of

a)   using brand x

b)   using brand y

when the farmer's index of optimism is $z = 0.3$.

c)   Which course of action is more acceptable?

7.   From Prob. 6 find the optimism-weighted value of

a)   using brand x

b)   using brand y

when the farmer's index of optimism is $z = 0.7$.

c)   Which course of action is more acceptable?

8.   Find the optimism-weighted value of
a)   "shaving" points
b)   scoring plenty

given the matrix in Sec. 8.4, Example 2 and $z = 0.4$.

c)   Which course of action is more acceptable?

9.   From Prob. 8, find the optimism-weighted value of
a)   "shaving" points
b)   scoring plenty

when $z = 0.9$.

c)   Which course of action is more acceptable?

10.   Find the optimism-weighted value of

a)   attending all lectures
b)   continuing to skip lectures

given the matrix in Sec. 8.4, Example 3 and $z = 0.3$.

c)   Which course of action is more acceptable?

8.7   Laplace and expected utility

The two rules that will be introduced in this section are designed for a decision maker operating under conditions of *risk;* i.e., some kind of probability (weight, or likelihood) is assigned to *every* state of nature. Unlike the six rules we have just considered which only allow certain maximum and/or minimum payoffs to affect the final prescription, these rules allow *every* payoff to have some affect on this prescription. The first one employs Laplace's Principle of Indifference and will be called the

Laplace utility rule: Accept that course of action which has the maximum Laplace utility. The application of this rule involves two steps. a) Determine the Laplace utility of each relevant course of action. b) Then accept that course of action with the largest Laplace utility. To determine the Laplace utility of a course of action A, begin by assigning probabilities of $1/n$ to *each* of the n payoffs possible with A. If U_i ($i = 1, 2, \ldots, n$) is the utility (or value to the decision maker) of the ith payoff possible with A, then

$$\frac{1}{n} U_1 + \frac{1}{n} U_2 + \cdots + \frac{1}{n} U_n$$

or

$$\frac{U_1 + U_2 + \cdots + U_n}{n}$$

is the **Laplace utility** of that course of action. Consider the following examples.

EXAMPLE 1

You are on your way to your friend's house in the country. You want to take one of two shortcuts, but you have heard that one of them is being repaired. You have the following payoff matrix.

	The road is being repaired.	The road is not being repaired.
Try the first short cut	Save 4 miles. (3)	Save 6 miles. (1)
Try the second short cut	Save 3 miles. (4)	Save 5 miles. (2)

According to the Laplace utility rule, which shortcut should you try?

Solution. Since $n = 2$, the Laplace utility of the first shortcut is

$$\frac{4 + 6}{2} = 5.$$

The Laplace utility of the second shortcut is

$$\frac{3 + 5}{2} = 4.$$

Hence, the Laplace utility rule prescribes trying the first shortcut (because that has the largest Laplace utility).

EXAMPLE 2

An innkeeper has to stock a fresh supply of clams for the weekend special. He does not know if it will be a busy weekend and imagines that he has the following payoff matrix.

	It will be a busy weekend.	It will not be a busy weekend.
Stock 100 clams	Make $30.00. (1)	Make $10.00. (3)
Stock 50 clams	Make $15.00. (2)	Make $10.00. (3)

What is the best course of action for the innkeeper?

Solution. Since $n = 2$, and the Laplace utility of stocking 100 clams

$$\frac{30 + 10}{2} = 20$$

is *larger* than the Laplace utility of stocking 50 clams

$$\frac{15 + 10}{2} = 12.5,$$

the former course of action should be followed.

EXAMPLE 3

A quarterback believes the situation calls for either a pass or a run. The opponents have been using four-, five-, and six-man lines, and he figures he has the following payoff matrix.

	They use a four-man line.	They use a five-man line.	They use a six-man line.
Pass	Gain 5 yards. (4)	Gain 7 yards. (2)	Gain 15 yards. (1)
Run	Gain 7 yards. (2)	Gain 6 yards. (3)	Gain 4 yards. (5)

According to the Laplace utility rule, what is his most acceptable course of action?

Solution. Since $n = 3$, the Laplace utility of passing is

$$\frac{5 + 7 + 15}{3} = 9.$$

This is greater than the Laplace utility of running,

$$\frac{7 + 6 + 4}{3} = 5.7.$$

Hence, according to the Laplace utility rule, the most acceptable course of action is a pass.

The second rule we have to consider for decision makers operating under conditions of *risk* allows us to avoid any application of the Principle of Indifference. It will be called the

Expected utility rule: Accept that course of action which has the maximum expected utility. The application of this rule involves two steps. a) Determine the expected utility of each relevant course of action. b) Then accept that course of action with the largest expected utility.

To determine the expected utility of a course of action A, begin by assigning (some kind of) probabilities (weights, or likelihoods) to *each* of the payoffs possible with A. If U_i and p_i $(i = 1, 2, \ldots, n)$ are the utility and probability (weight, or likelihood), respectively, of the ith payoff possible with A, then

$$p_1 U_1 + p_2 U_2 + \cdots + p_n U_n$$

or

$$\Sigma\, p_i U_i \qquad (i = 1, 2, \ldots, n)$$

is the **expected utility** of that course of action.

EXAMPLE 4

A basketball coach is trying to decide whether he should play Marinelli or Kregenow at center. He believes there is a probability of 0.8 that the opponents will play a zone defense and a probability of 0.2 that they will defend man to man. He figures he has the following payoff matrix.

	They will play a zone.	They will play man to man.
Kregenow plays center	He will score 22 points. (2)	He will score 16 points. (4)
Marinelli plays center	He will score 20 points. (3)	He will score 23 points. (1)

According to the expected utility rule, what is the coach's best course of action?

Solution. Applying the given probabilities, we find the expected utility of playing Kregenow at center is

$$(0.8)(22) + (0.2)(16) = 20.8.$$

The expected utility of playing Marinelli at center is

$$(0.8)(20) + (0.2)(23) = 20.6.$$

Hence, the best course of action for the coach is to play Kregenow at center, because that has the largest expected utility.

EXAMPLE 5

Mother Fletcher is sending her two sons to town to buy groceries. She always lets one son hold the money. Sheldon, her oldest son, does not drink much but he does not know much either. Duncan, her youngest son, knows quite a bit more, but he also drinks quite a bit more. She figures that the probability of finding a bar open this time is about 0.9, and she visualizes the following payoff matrix.

	The boys will find an open bar.	The boys will not find an open bar.
Let Sheldon carry the money	Save $15.00. (3)	Save $20.00. (2)
Let Duncan carry the money	Save $10.00. (4)	Save $30.00. (1)

What is the best course of action for Mother Fletcher?

Solution. The expected utility of letting Sheldon carry the money is

$$(0.9)(15) + (0.1)(20) = 15.5.$$

This is greater than the expected utility of letting Duncan carry the money,

$$(0.9)(10) + (0.1)(30) = 12.$$

Hence, the best course of action for Mother Fletcher is to let Sheldon carry the money. (*Moral:* A slow sober Sheldon is more reliable than a drunken Duncan.)

EXAMPLE 6

Rocco is thinking about selling newspapers Sunday. He has heard that the Daily News sells exceptionally well when there are floods or revolutions, and the Tribune does well when there are murders or floods. He calculates the following payoff matrix.

	There will be many murders.	There will be many floods.	There will be many revolutions.
Sell Tribune	Sell 100 papers. (1)	Sell 80 papers. (3)	Sell 60 papers. (5)
Sell Daily News	Sell 70 papers. (4)	Sell 100 papers. (1)	Sell 90 papers. (2)

If he assigns personal probabilities of 0.2 to the first, 0.5 to the second, and 0.3 to the third state of nature, what is Rocco's best course of action?

Solution. The expected utility of selling the Tribune on Sunday is

$$(0.2)(100) + (0.5)(80) + (0.3)(60) = 78.$$

Since this is *smaller* than the expected utility of selling the Daily News on Sunday,

$$(0.2)(70) + (0.5)(100) + (0.3)(90) = 91,$$

the latter is Rocco's best course of action.

Review problems for Sec. 8.7.

1. What is the Laplace utility rule?

    Apply the Laplace utility rule to the following.

2. Find the Laplace utility of
    a) asking Fred
    b) asking Ned

    given the matrix in Sec. 8.6, Example 1.

    c) Which course of action is more acceptable?

3. Find the Laplace utility of
    a) employing the first tactic
    b) employing the second tactic

    given the matrix in Sec. 8.6, Example 2.

    c) Which course of action is more acceptable?

4. Find the Laplace utility of
    a) using treatment A
    b) using treatment A'

    given the matrix in Sec. 8.6, Example 3.

    c) Which course of action is more acceptable?

5. A local store owner is trying to beat his competitors by stocking one of two types of beer for a forthcoming convention. He does not know whether the meeting involves mathematicians, philosophers, or historians. His matrix looks like this.

	Mathematician's convention	Philosopher's convention	Historian's convention
Stock A	Sell about 40 cases. (6)	Sell about 80 cases. (2)	Sell about 60 cases. (4)
Stock B	Sell about 50 cases. (5)	Sell about 90 cases. (1)	Sell about 70 cases. (3)

Find the Laplace utility of
a) stocking A
b) stocking B
c) Which course of action is more acceptable?

6. A farmer is thinking about testing one of two new fertilizers on his tomato plants. He knows the plants can respond in three different ways and that his payoff matrix is as follows.

	Response *A*	Response *B*	Response *C*
Use brand *x*	Four tomatoes per plant. (2)	Three tomatoes per plant. (3)	Five tomatoes per plant. (1)
Use brand *y*	Three tomatoes per plant. (3)	Four tomatoes per plant. (2)	Two tomatoes per plant. (4)

Find the Laplace utility of

a)   using brand *x*
b)   using brand *y*
c)   Which course of action is more acceptable?

7.   A psychologist believes he is able to assign numerical values to the utilities of certain courses of action and states of nature as follows.

$$
\begin{array}{ccc}
 & S_1 & S_2 & S_3 \\
A_1 & 19\ (2) & 16\ (4) & 13\ (6) \\
A_2 & 20\ (1) & 14\ (5) & 17\ (3)
\end{array}
$$

Find the Laplace utility of

a) A_1
b) A_2

c)   Which course of action is more acceptable?

8.   What is the expected utility rule?
Apply the expected utility rule to the following.

9.   Find the expected utility of
a)   asking Fred
b)   asking Ned

given the matrix in Sec. 8.6, Example 1 and a probability of 0.6 that they were promoted.

c)   Which course of action is more acceptable?

10.   Find the expected utility of

a)   employing the first tactic
b)   employing the second tactic

given the matrix in Sec. 8.6, Example 2 and a probability of 0.3 that the enemy made move I.

c)   Which course of action is more acceptable?

11.   Find the expected utility of
a)   using treatment *A*
b)   using treatment *A'*

given the matrix in Sec. 8.6, Example 3 and a weight of 0.2 that they have disease *S*.

c)   Which course of action is more acceptable?

12. Find the expected utility of

    a) stocking A

    b) stocking B

given the matrix in Prob. 5 and a probability of 0.2 for a mathematician's convention, 0.5 for a philosopher's convention, and 0.3 for a historian's convention.

    c) Which course of action is more acceptable?

13. Find the expected utility of

    a) using brand x

    b) using brand y

given the matrix in Prob. 6, a probability of 0.5 for response A, 0.4 for B, and 0.1 for C.

    c) Which course of action is more acceptable?

14. Find the expected utility of

    a) A_1

    b) A_2

given the matrix in Prob. 7 and a probability of 0.6 for S_1, 0.3 for S_2, and 0.1 for S_3.

    c) Which course of action is more acceptable?

Suggestions for further reading related to Chapter 8.

Braybrooke, David, and Lindblom, Charles E., *A Strategy of Decision*. New York: Free Press of Glencoe, Inc., 1963, Parts One to Three.

Bross, Irwin D., *Design for Decision*. New York: The Macmillan Co., 1953.

Carnap, Rudolf, *Logical Foundations of Probability*. Chicago: University of Chicago Press, 1950, Sections 50 and 51.

Gore, William J., and Dyson, J. W. (eds.), *The Making of Decisions*, A reader in Administrative Behavior. New York: Free Press of Glencoe, Inc., 1964.

Jeffrey, Richard C., *The Logic of Decision*. New York: McGraw-Hill Book Company, 1965.

Levi, Isaac, "On the Seriousness of Mistakes," *Philosophy of Science*. January, 1962.

Luce, R. Duncan, and Raiffa, Howard, *Games and Decisions*. New York: John Wiley & Sons, Inc., 1964, Chapters 1, 2, 13, and 14.

Thrall, R. M., Coombs, C. H., and Davis, R. L., *Decision Processes*. New York: John Wiley & Sons, Inc., 1960.

Chapter

9

Causality, Analogy, and Plausibility

We have completed our investigation of the four problems around which our discussion of nondemonstrative inference has been organized. The topics introduced in this chapter belong to the same subject but, for one reason or another, could not be integrated into previous chapters.

9.1 Mill's canons

It used to be a maxim of natural philosophy that every event has a cause. The task of the natural philosopher (or the philosopher of nature) was to find as many causal connections in the world as possible. Nowadays we do not hear about the maxim very often, though most people seem to assume that it is true. Whether or not the maxim is true, it is worthwhile to ask if there are any distinguishing characteristics by means of which one might identify causally connected events. An affirmative answer to this question was given by the early nineteenth-century British astronomer and philosopher John Herschel. Herschel designed five rules or canons of induction which were supposed to be helpful in distinguishing *causally* related events from *casually* related ones. The five canons were popularized by John Stuart Mill in his *System of Logic* (1843). Mill regarded them as useful aids for a scientific investigator. They do not constitute infallible rules for the identification of causal connections, but they do offer more or less plausible suggestions about *where, when,* and *how* one might expect to find such connections. Because the *third* canon is merely the joint application of the first two and the *fourth* (the canon of residues) is a special case of the second, we shall not consider either the third or fourth canons.

To begin with, we must introduce a few new terms that will be useful in our presentation. Let us use the letters from '*A*' to '*E*' to represent unspecified distinct events.

$$\overline{A}$$

will be used as an abbreviation of the phrase

the absence of the event represented by '*A*'.

We shall say that an event represented by '*A*' is **sufficient** for (or a **sufficient condition** of) an event represented by '*E*' if and only if, under any circumstances, the former is always followed by the latter. That is, the very fact that (some event represented by) '*A*' is the case assures us that (some other event represented by) '*E*' will be the case no matter what happens. For examples,

> Failing to pass a final examination is sufficient for failing (some) courses.
>
> Strenuous exercise is sufficient for fatigue.
>
> Having one's head cut off is sufficient for one's dying.

We shall say that an event represented by '*A*' is **necessary** for (or a **necessary condition** of) an event represented by '*E*' if and only if, under any circumstances, '$\overline{A}$' is always followed by '$\overline{E}$'. That is, the very fact that '$\overline{A}$' is the case assures us that '$\overline{E}$' will be the case no matter what happens. For examples,

> Gasoline is necessary for the running of my automobile.
>
> The ability to read is necessary for one to earn a college degree.
>
> Oxygen is necessary for human life.

If an event represented by '*A*' is sufficient for another event represented by '*E*' then the latter is necessary for the former, and vice versa. For examples,

> Failing (some) courses is a necessary condition of failing some examinations.

Fatigue is a necessary condition of strenuous exercise.

One's dying is a necessary condition of having one's head cut off.

We shall say that an event represented by '*A*' is **causally connected** to another event represented by '*E*' if and only if '*A*' is *either* necessary *or* sufficient for '*E*'. Hence, all the last nine examples above may be regarded as illustrations of causally connected events. We shall say that '*A*' **causes** '*E*' if and only if '*A*' is *both* necessary *and* sufficient for '*E*'. That is, the very fact that '*A*' is the case assures us that '*E*' will be the case *and* the very fact that '$\overline{A}$' is the case assures us that '$\overline{E}$' will be the case no matter what happens. Some typical examples are

Lowering the temperature of water below 0°C at standard atmospheric pressure causes the water to freeze.

Laceration of an artery of a living human being causes profuse bleeding.

A poor undergraduate academic record causes the rejection of some graduate school applicants.

Notice that each of these examples might be regarded as *incomplete* in the sense that, strictly speaking, many more *necessary* conditions *could* be mentioned. For example, consider the case of the laceration of an artery. If we asked, say, a physicist what causes the profuse bleeding following the severing of an artery, he might quote some laws concerning the flow of liquids with a certain density through tubes constructed of a certain substance and having a certain length, breadth, shape, etc. A surgeon might tell us that it is the action of the heart pumping about 75 cubic centimeters per beat which causes the terrific release of blood. A layman might say it is caused by a sharp instrument, and so on. The physicist, surgeon, and layman would all be citing necessary conditions, and these are surely part of the set of events that constitute the *cause* of the profuse bleeding.

The apparent incompleteness of our examples of causes is fairly typical. It is usually possible to continue to name necessary conditions for the occurrence of any event (depending, of course, on the generality of the conditions and on the particular event selected). But for certain *purposes* or relative to certain *interests* a number of necessary conditions may be beside the point. For example, to illustrate our definition of '*A* causes *E*', the short illustrations offered above seem adequate. In a physics textbook the physicist's remarks suggested above would have to be greatly elaborated. In short, the completeness or incompleteness of an illustration depends to a large extent on the purposes at hand.

Given these preliminary definitions, we may proceed to Mill's canons. The first is called

The canon of agreement: If it is known that an event represented by '*A*' always precedes another event represented by '*E*' (and there is no reason to suspect that '*A*' is *not* causally connected to '*E*'), regard the two events as causally connected. We may illustrate the canon of agreement as follows.

$$A \ B \text{ precedes } E$$
$$A \ C \text{ precedes } E$$
$$\underline{A \ D \text{ precedes } E}$$
$$A \text{ is causally connected to } E$$

The parenthetical expression does not appear in this schema or in most statements of Mill's canons, but it is obviously important. Without it students (and even instructors) tend to treat the canons as historically interesting but practically silly comments about causality. Indeed, without the *assumption* appearing in the parentheses, that is just about what the canons *are*. To keep the illustrations as simple as possible, however, this assumption is not represented. Moreover, to keep the statements of other canons as brief as possible, hereafter the assumption will be omitted altogether. But it *must not* be forgotten.

Example 1

Monday Bruce eats eggs and ham for breakfast, and later he breaks out in a rash. Tuesday Bruce eats eggs and bacon for breakfast and breaks out in a rash. Wednesday Bruce eats eggs and pancakes for breakfast and again breaks out in a rash. (He has no reason to suspect that his eating eggs is not causally connected to his rash.) Hence, the canon of agreement tells him that he may regard his eating eggs as causally connected to his rash.

Example 2

Monday Hughes whistles and winks at his secretary, and he is slapped. Tuesday Hughes whistles and smiles at his secretary and is slapped. Wednesday Hughes whistles and pinches his secretary and is again slapped. The canon of agreement tells him that he may regard his whistling at his secretary as causally connected to his being slapped.

 Mill's second canon is called

The canon of difference: If it is known that an event represented by '*A*' always precedes an event represented by '*E*' *and* that '$\bar{A}$' always precedes '$\bar{E}$', regard the former event as the cause of the latter. Schematically we have

$$A \ B \text{ precedes } E$$
$$A \ C \text{ precedes } E$$
$$A \ D \text{ precedes } E$$
$$\bar{A} \ B \text{ precedes } \bar{E}$$
$$\bar{A} \ C \text{ precedes } \bar{E}$$
$$\underline{\bar{A} \ D \text{ precedes } \bar{E}}$$
$$A \text{ causes } E$$

EXAMPLE 3

When John holds his breath and raises his arm, his face becomes red. When John holds his breath and blinks his eyes, his face becomes red. When John holds his breath and ties his shoe, his face becomes red. When John breaths normally and raises his arm, blinks his eyes, or ties his shoe, his face does not become red. Hence, the canon of difference tells us that we may regard John's holding his breath as the cause of his face becoming red.

EXAMPLE 4

When a lump of sugar is put into a cup of water and the cup is placed on the floor, the sugar dissolves. When a lump of sugar is put into a cup of water and the cup is covered, the sugar dissolves. When sugar is put into a cup of water and the cup is placed beside an open window, the sugar still dissolves. When a lump of sugar is put into a dry cup, however, and the cup is placed on the floor, covered, or placed beside an open window, the sugar does not dissolve. Hence, the canon of difference tells us that putting the sugar into the water causes the sugar to dissolve.

The canon of difference comes very close to our definition of '*A* causes *E*' since it takes account of both necessity and sufficiency. It is employed in one way or another by nearly all experimenters. If, for example, we want to decide whether or not a new drug will have a certain effect, then we apply the drug to a group of individuals (e.g., rats, cats, people, etc.) in certain circumstances and withhold it from a similar group. The group from which the drug is withheld is called a **control group.** The group to which the drug is applied is called an **experimental group.** If certain effects always appear in the presence of the drug (in the experimental group) and never appear in its absence (in the control group) then the drug may be regarded as the cause of those effects. Of course, if we have some reason to suspect that the drug is not the cause of those effects, we must take that into consideration, and we can never eliminate the possibility of *hidden causes*. Neither of these provisos, however, seriously limits the usefulness of the canon of difference.

The final canon (Mill's fifth) we have to consider is called

The canon of concomitant variations: If it is known that whenever an event represented by '*A*' varies, then another event represented by '*E*' also varies, regard the two events as causally connected. This canon is applicable to events which not only admit of *presence or absence* but also of *degrees of change or variation*.

EXAMPLE 5

The *faster* you walk, the sooner your muscles become stiff. Hence, the canon of concomitant variations tells us that there is a causal connection between the rapidity of your gait and the rapidity with which your muscles become stiff.

EXAMPLE 6

The more Charlie Brown studies, the better grades he receives. According to the canon of concomitant variations, we may say that there is a causal connection between Charlie's studying and his grades.

When it is possible to *measure* the events under consideration, it is frequently convenient to illustrate the results on a graph of dots called a **scatter diagram.** For example, suppose you are blowing up a balloon and measuring its diameter after each blow. The scatter diagram illustrating the relation between the number of blows and the size of the balloon's diameter might look like Figure 9.11.

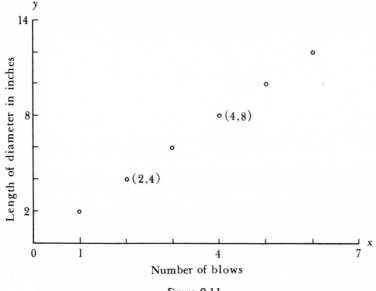

Figure 9.11

Here the length of the balloon's diameter in inches is measured on the vertical *y* axis and the number of blows is recorded on the horizontal *x* axis. The balloon's diameter increases 2 inches with each blow. In the expression '(2, 4)' in the diagram, 2 is the value of *x* or the number of blows and 4 is the value of *y* or the length of the balloon's diameter in inches. Here '(4, 8)' tells us that four blows makes the diameter 8 inches. Quite generally, '(*a, b*)' tells us that when the value of *x* is *a*, the value of *y* is *b*.

If a line were drawn through the dots in Figure 9.11, it would be perfectly straight and slope upward from left to right. In such cases we would say there is a **perfect positive correlation** between the events under consideration. That is, the events represented on the *y* axis vary *directly* with events represented on the *x* axis. For the case at hand we would say that there is a perfect positive correlation between the number of blows and the width of the balloon's diameter or that the width of the balloon's diameter varies directly with the number of blows.

Sometimes, when a line is drawn through the dots in a scatter diagram, it is straight but slopes downward from left to right. In such cases we say there is a **perfect negative correlation** between the events under consideration. That is, the events represented on the *y* axis vary *inversely* with events represented on the *x* axis. For example, Figure 9.12 illustrates a perfect negative correlation between the length of a cigar and the number of puffs taken from it.

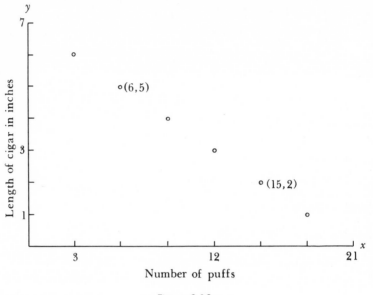

Figure 9.12

This time, as the values of *x* *increase*, the values of *y* *decrease*. The expression '(6, 5)' in the diagram tells us that when 6 puffs have been taken from the cigar, it is 5 inches long. Then '(15, 2)' tells us that after 15 puffs have been taken, the cigar is only 2 inches long, and so on.

Figure 9.13 is a scatter diagram for two events which have no *correlation* at all, say, the number of flowers in front of the homes of 10 men and the men's IQ's.

Scatter diagrams are useful supplements to Mill's canon of concomitant variations, but they are by no means the last word. Statisticians have developed numerical measures of correlation called **correlation coefficients** which are much more "sensitive" than the naked eye. Unfortunately, however, these are beyond the scope of our present investigation.

Before closing our discussion of Mill's canons and correlations, in general, it should be emphasized that it is quite possible to have a high (positive or negative) correlation between causally *unrelated* events. For example, it is possible to have a high correlation between IQ scores and the number of flowers in front of homes, although the two things are causally unrelated. It is not possible, however, to

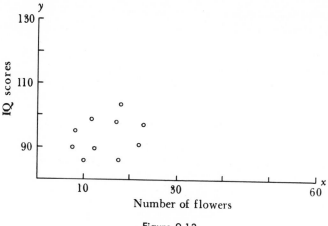

Figure 9.13

have a low correlation between two things that are causally connected. A low correlation between two things is a good reason for believing that they are *not* causally connected.

Review problems for Sec. 9.1.

1. Explain the following.
   a) An event represented by '*A*' is *sufficient* for another event represented by '*E*'.
   b) An event represented by '*A*' is *necessary* for another event represented by '*E*'.
   c) An event represented by '*A*' is *causally connected* to another event represented by '*E*'.
   d) An event represented by '*A*' *causes* another event represented by '*E*'.

2. If (an event represented by) '*A*' is sufficient for '*E*', what relation does '*E*' have to '*A*'?

   Decide whether the canon of agreement or the canon of difference is employed in each of the following five questions.

3. She was fine until the spider walked across her plate. Then she screamed. I guess the spider must have made her scream.

4. We had 30 children from broken homes and with low IQ's living in Area B and they all had trouble with the police. Another 30 children with similar IQ's and broken homes in Area A did not have any trouble with the police. Until someone comes up with a better hypothesis, we are assuming that there is something about Area B that causes delinquency.

5. Charlie had steak, peas, potatoes, coffee, and apple pie for dinner, and shortly after that he had terrible pains in his stomach. Luke had ham, peas, rice, tea, and cherry pie for dinner, but he had severe stomach pains too. I bet it was the peas that caused the stomach trouble.

6. She had a fever but no swelling. About 15 minutes after I gave her a shot of penicillin, her hands and feet began to swell. I imagine the penicillin had that effect.

7. They are both leaders but they have little else in common. Tom is big, strong, fairly bright, and mean. Dick is small, weak, pretty stupid, but also very mean. I would hate to say that their meanness makes them leaders, but I don't know what else we could say.

8. What is the canon of concomitant variations?

9. Construct a scatter diagram for the following data and decide whether salary and rent changes are positively or negatively correlated. (The correlations need not be perfect.)

Salary	Rent
$3500	$52
5600	70
4200	59
6300	76
4900	64

10. A certain factory has been trying to hire someone for a certain position for over a year. Without changing the salary, they have continued to drop the number of hours required. Construct a scatter diagram for the following data and decide whether the number of hours are correlated negatively or positively with the number of applicants.

Hours	Applicants
54	12
35	37
50	14
42	24
46	18
38	30

11. Given the sales data recorded below, construct scatter diagrams and decide whether there is a perfect positive, perfect negative, or no correlation between the items in the following pairs

a) hot dogs and jars of mustard   d) hamburgers and jars of mustard
b) hot dogs and hamburgers   e) potato chips and jars of mustard
c) hot dogs and potato chips

April	Hot Dogs	Hamburgers	Potato Chips	Jars of Mustard
1	60	60	75	2
2	15	90	135	$\frac{1}{2}$
3	135	10	105	$4\frac{1}{2}$
4	90	40	30	3
5	75	50	120	$2\frac{1}{2}$
6	30	80	45	1
7	105	30	15	$3\frac{1}{2}$
8	45	70	90	$1\frac{1}{2}$
9	120	20	60	4

9.2 Analogy

The word 'analogy' comes from the Greek 'analogia' which means identity of proportion. Nowadays we say that there is an **analogy** between two things when there is some similarity or resemblance between them. The former, identity of proportion, is a special case of the latter, similarity or resemblance. In an **argument by analogy,** one argues that because certain things are similar in certain respects, they are probably similar in certain others too. The argument usually takes one of two different forms, both of which shall be introduced below.

a) ANALOGOUS RELATIONS

We are all familiar with mathematical arguments based on identities of proportion. For example, given

$$4 \text{ is to } 2 \text{ as } 8 \text{ is to } 4$$

or, for short,

$$4:2 = 8:4$$

and that

$$4 \text{ is twice } 2,$$

we would conclude *with certainty* that

$$8 \text{ is twice } 4.$$

More generally, given

$$a:b = c:d$$

and, say,

$$a > b \quad \text{or} \quad a = b \quad \text{or} \quad a = \frac{b}{2} \quad \text{or} \quad a = nb,$$

we would conclude *with certainty* that

$$c > d \quad \text{or} \quad c = d \quad \text{or} \quad c = \frac{d}{2} \quad \text{or} \quad c = nd.$$

Such arguments are demonstrative and valid. Schematically, they may be represented as follows.

Whatever relation a has to b, c has to d.
a has relation R to b.
c has R to d.

Here the first premiss tells us that *every* relation *a* has to *b*, *c* has to *d*. The second premiss *identifies* one of the relations *R* that *a* has to *b*. Hence, we may conclude with certainty that *c* has *R* to *d*.

The nondemonstrative argument by analogy which is based on analogous relations may be regarded as a *weakened* form of the schema above. Instead of '*whatever*', we have '*some*' or '*most*' or, when we are fortunate, '*a certain percentage r*'. Schematically, the **argument by analogy based on analogous relations** looks like this.

> Some (or most, or a certain percentage *r*) of the relations
> *a* has to *b*, *c* has to *d*.
> *a* has relation *R* to *b*.
> It is probable (more probable than not, or probable to
> a degree *r*) that *c* has *R* to *d*.

There are two closely related points to be noted immediately about this schema. In the *first* place, the conclusion (without the probabilistic qualifying phrases) could not be *derived* from the premisses; i.e., the argument is not valid. The first premiss tells us that some (most, or a certain percentage *r*) of the relations that *a* has to *b*, *c* also has to *d*. The second premiss identifies *one* of the relations *R* that *a* has to *b*. *R may or may not* be a relation that *c* has to *d*. Hence, we cannot conclude with certainty that *c* has *R* to *d*.

In the *second* place, however, it does seem to be the case that the given premisses make the conclusion more or less probable and, therefore, more or less acceptable. Let us consider this claim more carefully.

Any similarity of relations (or properties) between couples (or individuals) is called a **positive analogy.** Any dissimilarity of relations (or properties) between couples (or individuals) is called a **negative analogy.** The simplest way to obtain a numerical measure of the probability of the conclusion of an analogical argument is to use the *ratio* of the number of *positive* analogies to the *total* number of (positive and negative) analogies in some relevant universe of discourse. The details of this move might be worked out along the lines of any of the theories of measuring probabilities considered in Chapter 5. Needless to say, the problems and options introduced in that chapter will have to be faced again. For example, most people would agree that the universe of discourse employed in most problems would not include *every* analogy between two individuals (or couples). If we are comparing performances on, say, spelling or arithmetic tests there would be little point in including information about hair and eye coloring or height and weight. Similarly, if we are comparing political or religious attitudes, information about attitudes toward certain fruits and vegetables might be irrelevant, and so on. As we learned in Chapter 5, however, there is no neat solution to the problem of the selection of an appropriate universe of discourse.

Rather than review the problems involved in the determination of numerical values, we shall simply assume for expository purposes that the ratio of the number of positive analogies to the total number of relevant analogies may be used as a measure of the probability of the conclusion of an analogical argument.

There are three cases to consider.

CASE 1

In the weakest case, it is only known that *some* or *at least one* relation *a* has to *b*, *c* has to *d* (and that *a* has *R* to *b*). We have no idea of the *proportion* of positive or negative relevant analogies involved. Hence, we make the *qualitative* judgment that it is probable that *c* has *R* to *d*.

CASE 2

It is known that *most* (or, perhaps, *few*) of the relevant relations *a* has to *b*, *c* has to *d* (and that *a* has *R* to *b*); i.e., we know that there is a high (low) proportion of positive analogies. That means there are *more* (*fewer*) *chances than not* that *c* has *R* to *d*. Therefore, we make the *comparative* judgment that it is more (less) probable than not that *c* has *R* to *d*.

CASE 3

We are fortunate enough to know the exact ratio *r* of the number of positive to total relevant analogies involved. So we made the *quantitative* judgment that there is a probability of degree *r* that *c* has *R* to *d*.

We are seldom in a position to make a quantitative judgment about the conclusion of an analogical argument. Usually we are faced with qualitative or comparative judgments and it is *hardly ever* clear which. In the typical case, a writer or speaker will simply say something like

$$a \text{ is to } b \text{ as } c \text{ is to } d$$

and the reader or listener is left completely in the dark as to just how many relevant relations *a* has to *b* that *c* has to *d*. In the typical case, then, we begin with a cautious qualitative judgment which may or may not be altered depending on whether or not more information is available.

EXAMPLE 1

Harry Truman was related to Franklin Roosevelt as Lyndon Johnson was related to John Kennedy. Johnson was vice president under Kennedy. Hence, it is probable that Truman was vice president under Roosevelt.

Here we are given no hint of the *proportion* of relevant *relations* shared by both couples. So we can only judge that the conclusion is *probable*.

EXAMPLE 2

Most of the relations Red China has to Albania, the Soviet Union has to Poland. Red China largely determines Albania's foreign policy. It is more probable than not that the Soviet Union largely determines Poland's foreign policy.

Here we are told that there are more chances than not that any relation Red China has to Albania, the Soviet Union has to Poland. So we can make the comparative judgment that the conclusion is *more probable than not*.

EXAMPLE 3

Suppose 75 percent of the relations Alice has to her mother, Alan has to his father. Alice is taller than her mother. There is a probability of 0.75 that Alan is taller than his father.

Here we are told the exact proportion of the relations shared by the two couples; i.e., we know the ratio of the number of positive to total relevant analogies involved. So we can make the quantitative judgment that the conclusion has a *degree of probability* of 0.75.

b) ANALOGOUS PROPERTIES

Frequently the idea of identity of proportion is abandoned entirely and the argument by analogy is based on *similarity of properties*. Schematically, the **argument by analogy based on analogous properties** looks like this.

> a has the properties $P_1, P_2, \ldots, P_n$.
> b has some (most, or a certain percentage r) of these properties.
> ────────────
> It is probable (more probable than not, or probable to a degree r) that b has P_i.

Here the first premiss tells us that a has a certain set of properties represented by '$P_1, P_2, \ldots, P_n$'. The second premiss tells us that some (most, or a certain percentage r) of these properties are possessed by b; i.e., it gives us some information regarding the positive analogies between a and b. 'P_i' represents one of the properties that a is known to have but b is *not* known to have. On the basis of the given premisses, however, we conclude that it is probable (more probable than not, or probable to a degree r) that b has the property represented by 'P_i'.

The limiting case of this form of analogical argument is the following trivially valid argument.

> a has the properties $P_1, P_2, \ldots, P_n$.
> b is identical to a.
> ────────────
> b has P_i.

Here the first premiss identifies the properties possessed by a. The second premiss identifies b with a; i.e., it tells us that a and b have the *same* properties. Hence, it follows with certainty that b has the property represented by 'P_i'.

EXAMPLE 4

The planet Earth has water, warmth, and living things. Mars has water and warmth. Hence, it is probable that Mars has living things.

Here we are given no hint of the *proportion* of *properties* shared by Earth and Mars; i.e., we are given no hint regarding the ratio of the number of positive to total relevant analogies between *a* and *b*. So we only judge that the conclusion is probable.

Example 5

Larry is like Barry in practically every relevant respect. Larry is anemic. Hence, it is more probable than not that Barry is anemic.

Here we are told that the ratio of positive to total relevant analogies between Larry and Barry is high. So we make the comparative judgment that the conclusion is more probable than not.

Example 6

In a recent series of tests we found that Floyd and Boyd scored alike 40 percent of the time. Floyd scored low on music appreciation. Hence, there is a probability of 0.4 that Boyd scored low on music appreciation.

This time we are given the exact ratio of the number of positive to total relevant analogies between the individuals in question. So we make the quantitative judgement that the conclusion has a degree of probability of 0.4.

Review problems for Sec. 9.2.

1. Define the following

    a) argument by analogy
    b) positive analogy
    c) negative analogy

2. Illustrate schematically an argument by analogy based on

    a) analogous relations
    b) analogous properties

3. How might positive and negative analogies be used to obtain probabilities?

4. Given

    i) Len is tall, dark, handsome, rich, and a good salesman.
    ii) Ben is tall, dark, handsome, and poor.

    Which, if any, of the following conclusions are warranted, which are not warranted, and why?

    a) It is probable that Ben is a good salesman.
    b) It is probable that Ben is happy.
    c) It is more probable than not that Ben is a good salesman.

5. List the positive and negative analogies given in the two premisses in Prob. 4.

6. In Prob. 4, how might someone justify assigning the conclusion that Ben is a good salesman a probability of 0.75?

7. In Prob. 4, if the second premiss is changed from ii) to

    ii′) Ben is tall, dark, ugly, and poor.

    does it become more or less probable that Ben is a good salesman? Why?

8. Given

    i) Jesus Christ is to some Christians as the Amida Buddha is to some Buddhists.
    ii) Jesus Christ protects Christians.

    Which, if any, of the following conclusions are warranted, which are not warranted, and why?

    a) It is more probable than not that the Amida Buddha protects Buddhists.
    b) The Amida Buddha protects Christians.
    c) It is probable that the Amida Buddha protects Buddhists.

9. If the first premiss of the argument in Prob. 8 is changed to

    i′) Most of the relations Jesus Christ has to Christians the Amida Buddha has to Buddhists.

    which of the three conclusions in Prob. 8 are warranted, which are not, and why?

10. Given

    i) Eighty percent of the properties possessed by generals are possessed by college administrators.
    ii) College administrators enjoy working on committees.

    Which, if any, of the following conclusions are warranted, which are not, and why?

    a) It is probable that generals have to sit on committees.
    b) It is more probable than not that generals enjoy working on committees.
    c) It is probable to a degree 0.8 that generals have to sit on committees.
    d) It is improbable that generals do not enjoy working on committees.
    e) It is probable to a degree 0.2 that generals do not enjoy working on committees.

9.3   Relative plausibility

In Chapter 5 we introduced the psychological interpretation of probability sentences and the personal odds theory of obtaining initial numerical probabilities. In this section we are going to introduce another theory of measuring probabilities within the psychological interpretation. Here, however, with the exception of the extreme values 0 and 1, we shall *not* be concerned with the problem of obtaining numerical values for probabilities; i.e., we shall not be concerned with a quantitative concept of probability. Instead we shall be considering the *increases and decreases* of probabilities under various conditions; i.e., we shall be concerned with a concept of probability that is essentially *comparative*. On the whole we shall be summarizing some results of the work of the contemporary mathematician Gÿorgy Polya.

To begin with, Polya notes (as we noted in Sec. 5.4) that people often talk as if they were able to distinguish various belief-states ranging from complete certainty to total scepticism. He claims, however, it is by no means obvious that such states can be measured with any precision and assigned significant numerical values. Furthermore, it is *not necessary* to obtain numerical values for probabilities. It is possible to gain considerable *insight into* and *justification for* more or less "standard" ways of thinking about nondemonstrative inferences *without* tackling the problem of obtaining initial numerical values. All that is required is a comparative notion of probability and the probability calculus.

Let us suppose, then, that we have a comparative concept of probability which, following Polya, we shall call **plausibility.** We shall assume that for most *pairs* of sentences we are able to decide whether one is more plausible than the other or whether they are equally plausible. If a sentence is known to be true, it is assigned a maximum plausibility value of 1. If a sentence is known to be false, it is assigned a minimum plausibility value of 0. Sentences which are not known to be true and not known to be false are assigned a *nondeterminable* plausibility value between 0 and 1. To abbreviate phrases like

$$\text{The } \textit{plausibility} \text{ of `}A\text{',}$$

Where 'A' typically represents some unspecified sentence, we shall use the familiar notation

$$P(A).$$

We may briefly summarize the characteristics of the notion of plausibility we are going to work with as follows.

    a)   If 'A' is known to represent a true sentence, $P(A) = 1$.

    b)   If 'A' is known to represent a false sentence, $P(A) = 0$.

    c)   If 'A' is not known to represent a true sentence and not known to represent a false sentence then $0 < P(A) < 1$.

    d)   For most sentences represented by 'A' and 'B', it is known that $P(A) = P(B)$, $P(A) > P(B)$, or $P(A) < P(B)$.

Polya claims that there are generally accepted nondemonstrative inference rules or *patterns of plausible inference* which may be justified by the principles of the calculus of probability. We shall present three of these rules and briefly review Polya's justifications for them.

According to the so-called

Fundamental pattern of plausible inference: If it is known that 'A' implies 'B' and it is later found that 'B' represents a true sentence, the plausibility of 'A' can *only* increase. Schematically, we may represent this pattern thus:

'*A*' implies '*B*'.

'*B*'s truth is later established.

'*A*'s' plausibility is increased.

EXAMPLE 1

Mother has the suspicion that Lulu ate the blueberries. She knows that if Lulu ate the blueberries, her tongue will be blue. She examines Lulu's tongue and finds that it *is* blue. Hence, the plausibility of her suspicion has been increased.

EXAMPLE 2

It seems plausible to suppose that the accidents occurring at a certain intersection are the result of an ambiguous set of traffic signs. If the signs are at fault, then when they are changed, the accident rate should drop. The signs are changed and the accident rate drops. So, the supposition of the causal connection between the accidents and the ambiguous set of traffic signs becomes more plausible.

EXAMPLE 3

A historian is interested in gathering evidence in support of his hypothesis that Bubbles wrote a certain play. He knows that if Bubbles wrote the play then there will be no Latin expressions in it. He later finds that it does not contain any Latin expressions. So, the plausibility of his hypothesis has been increased.

The fundamental pattern of plausible inference may be justified as follows. We are given a hypothesis represented by '*A*' with an initial plausibility between 0 and 1; i.e.,

$$(1) \qquad 0 < P(A) < 1.$$

We know that '*A*' *implies* '*B*' and that the initial plausibility of '*B*' is also between 0 and 1. Hence,

$$(2) \qquad P(A, B) = 1$$

and

$$(3) \qquad 0 < P(B) < 1.$$

Whether or not $P(B)$ is equal to, greater, or less than $P(A)$ is irrelevant. The question is: If we find that '*B*' represents a true sentence, how will this effect the plausibility of '*A*'? Or, how will the plausibility of '*A relative to B*' compare with the initial plausibility of '*A*'? Will

$$P(B, A)$$

be greater than, less than, or equal to

$$P(A)?$$

To answer this question, we recall that, according to the General Multiplication Principle,

$$P(A \cdot B) = P(B \cdot A)$$

and

(4) $\qquad P(A)P(A, B) = P(B)P(B, A).$

In view of (2) we may substitute '1' for '$P(A, B)$' in (4) to obtain

(5) $\qquad P(A) = P(B)P(B, A).$

In view of (3)

(6) $\quad P(B)P(B, A) < P(B, A).$

That is, the product of $P(B, A)$ *and* some fraction $P(B)$ must be *lower* than $P(B, A)$ itself. Hence, (5) and (6) together imply

(7) $\qquad P(A) < P(B, A).$

This, then, is the answer to our question: The plausibility of '*A given B*' must be higher than the initial plausibility of '*A*'. This is how Polya justifies the fundamental pattern of plausible inference.

The second and third rules we have to consider are consequences of equation (5). The *second* rule is: If $P(B, A)$ remains fixed, then $P(A)$ *varies* in the *same direction* as $P(B)$. That is, if it is known that '*A*' implies '*B*' and the plausibility of '*B*' increases, the plausibility of '*A*' can *only* increase. On the other hand, if it is known that '*A*' implies '*B*' and the plausibility of '*B*' decreases, the plausibility of '*A*' can *only* decrease.

Example 4

We are not sure that Agnes ate the steak, but we know that if she did, she went to church Friday. We discover new evidence supporting the hypothesis that she went to church Friday. Hence, the plausibility of the hypothesis that Agnes ate the steak has been increased.

Example 5

Originally it seemed hardly plausible to believe that Joe was clairvoyant, but no one doubted that if he was, he knew the Yankees would win the pennant. In view of what he later told us, it seemed more plausible to grant that he *did* know the Yankees would win the pennant. Therefore, the idea that Joe was clairvoyant was more plausible than we originally thought.

EXAMPLE 6

At first it seemed to be an even bet that Bilgewater bought the house. There was no doubt, however, that if he bought the house he needed a new car. After further investigation we found that it was very implausible to suppose he needed a new car. Hence, it became less plausible that he bought the house.

EXAMPLE 7

A priori we simply do not know whether or not Ibin Gabin is a dictator. If he is a dictator then he will be hated by most people. Our intelligence reports reveal that probably only a small percentage of the population hate him. Therefore, it seems less plausible to suppose that Ibin Gabin is a dictator.

If both sides of equation (5) are divided by $P(B)$

$$(8) \qquad \frac{P(A)}{P(B)} = P(B, A).$$

we obtain a *third* rule of plausible inference. Equation (8) tells us that the more *implausible* '*B*' is *before* its truth is determined, the greater will be the increase in the plausibility of '*A*' *after* '*B*'s' truth is determined. In other words, the increase in the plausibility of '*A*' *varies inversely* with the plausibility of '*B*' before its truth is known.

In symbols, if we are given (8) and

$$(9) \qquad P(A) \leqslant P(B) < 1,$$

then, as $P(B)$ decreases from 1 to $P(A)$, $P(B, A)$ increases from $P(A)$ to 1. The nearer $P(B)$ is to $P(A)$ before '*B*' is established, the nearer $P(B, A)$ must be to 1; hence, the *less* the establishment of '*B*' *can increase* $P(B, A)$. On the other hand, the farther $P(B)$ is from $P(A)$ before '*B*' is established, the farther $P(B, A)$ must be from 1; hence, the more the establishment of '*B*' *can increase* $P(B, A)$.

EXAMPLE 8

An archaeologist has a hunch that at a certain time a particular race of men lived in a certain area. He knows that if his hunch is correct there must be some artifacts and a cemetery nearby. He figures it is very easy to find something that could be considered a human artifact; e.g., if he finds a blunt stone he can say it was used as a hammer; if he finds a sharp stone he can say it was used as a knife; etc. But it is difficult to invent an ancient burial ground. After some searching, he does find some stones that might have been used as hammers. This increases the plausibility of his hunch slightly. Then he stumbles across an ancient tomb. According to equation (8), the latter discovery increases the plausibility of his hunch much more than the former.

EXAMPLE 9

On the basis of the information Doctor Quack received on the phone, he believes that the Prince has a certain disease, D. If the Prince has D then he will have two types of symptoms. The first type is typical of most diseases, but the second is peculiar to D. A thorough examination reveals that the Prince has both types of symptoms. Applying equation (8), Doctor Quack believes that his discovery that the Prince has the second type of symptoms increases the plausibility of his original diagnosis much more than the discovery that the Prince has the first type.

Review problems for Sec. 9.3.

1. What are the basic characteristics of Polya's concept of plausibility?

2. State the
   a) fundamental pattern
   b) second rule
   c) third rule
   of plausible inference.

3. Briefly reconstruct the justification for each of the rules above.

4. Suppose you are given an object that may or may not be a magnet, and you know that magnets attract iron. Later you find that the object does attract iron. Which, if any, of the following conclusions are warranted, which are not, and why?

   a) Some magnets attract iron.
   b) The plausibility of the hypothesis that the object is a magnet has been increased.
   c) The plausibility of the hypothesis that the object is a magnet is greater than the plausibility of the hypothesis that the substance attracted is iron.
   d) The plausibility of the hypothesis that the object is a magnet varies inversely with the plausibility that the substance attracted is iron.

5. Suppose you have been kidnapped. You do not know where you have been taken and you have been unable to unscramble any of the various sensations you have been receiving. You are only sure of the following.

   i)   If you are near the sea you will hear its roar.
   ii)   If you are in the mountains you will find it difficult to breathe.
   iii) If you are near the swamp you will hear frogs and crickets at night.

   After some careful observation you obtain the following information.

   iv)   It is plausible to suppose that the belches you heard came from a frog.
   v)   There is no doubt at all that you are finding it difficult to breathe.
   vi)   The idea that anything you have heard recently could be the roar of the sea is a bit less plausible than your supposition about the frogs.

Which, if any, of the following conclusions are warranted, which are not, and why?

a)   The plausibility of the hypothesis that you are near the swamp has been increased.

b)   The plausibility of the hypothesis that you are near the sea has been increased.

c)   It is more plausible to suppose that you are near the sea than that you are near the swamp.

d)   The hypothesis that you are in the mountains is highly plausible.

e)   If you hear crickets then the plausibility of the hypothesis that you are near the swamp will be increased.

f)   If it becomes a certainty that you do not hear the roar of the sea then the hypothesis that you are near the sea will be falsified.

6.   If, at the beginning of our investigation, we know that 'A' implies 'B_1' and 'B_2', and that $P(B_1) > P(B_2)$, will the plausibility of 'A' be increased more by the discovery that 'B_1' represents a true sentence *or* by the discovery that 'B_2' represents a true sentence? Why?

Suggestions for further reading related to Chapter 9.

Achinstein, Peter, "Variety and Analogy in Confirmation Theory", *Philosophy of Science*, July, 1963.

Carnap, Rudolf, "Variety, Analogy and Periodicity in Inductive Logic", *Philosophy of Science*, July, 1963.

Hesse, Mary B., *Models and Analogies in Science*. London: Sheed & Ward Ltd., 1963, Chapter 3.

Polya, G., *Patterns of Plausible Inference*. Princeton, N. J.: Princeton University Press, 1954, Chapters XIII and XV.

Shapere, Dudley, "Plausibility and Justification in the Development of Science", *The Journal of Philosophy*, October, 1966.

Skyrms, Brian, *Choice and Chance*, An Introduction to Inductive Logic. Belmont, Calif.: Dickenson Pub. Co., Inc., 1966, Chapter IV.

Wright, Georg Henrik von, *A Treatise on Induction and Probability*. Paterson, N. J.: Littlefield, Adams and Company, 1960, Chapter Four.

Truth will sooner come out from error
than from confusion.

Francis Bacon

Part

THREE

Informal

Principles

Chapter

10

Fallacies

A demonstrative argument schema is invalid if it may be given an interpretation such that its premisses are all true and its conclusion is false. Interpretations of such schemata are invalid demonstrative arguments, and the latter are called 'unsound'. Interpretations of valid demonstrative schemata that have at least one false premiss are also called 'unsound'.

An argument schema is nondemonstratively invalid, or *n*-invalid, if it may be given an interpretation such that its premisses are all true and its conclusion is not as acceptable as it is supposed (claimed, or alleged) to be. Interpretations of such schemata are *n*-invalid arguments. The latter as well as arguments that are *n*-valid (nondemonstratively valid) with at least one false premiss are also called 'unsound'.

The word 'fallacy' comes from the Latin '*fallere*' or '*fallacia*' meaning to deceive or deception, respectively. Today 'fallacy' is usually used to denote any erroneous inference. Occasionally it is used synonymously with 'falsehood'. In this text we are going to define a **fallacy** as any formal or informal *mistake* made in an argument.

If someone employs an argument that may be regarded as an interpretation of an invalid or *n*-invalid schema, we shall say that a **formal fallacy** has been committed; e.g., the fallacy of affirming the consequent, the fallacy of denying the antecedent, etc. If someone employs an argument that is *unsound whether or not* it involves a formal fallacy, we shall say that an **informal fallacy** has been committed; e.g., appealing to pity, authority, force, etc. We emphasize "*whether or not*" because a given argument may be *both* formally and informally fallacious, but *some* unsound arguments do not involve any formal fallacy. It should also be noted that a given argument may involve more than one informal fallacy.

Different logicians have suggested different classification of fallacies, and there is very little agreement about the number and kinds of subclasses required for an exhaustive division. From the point of view of *neatness*, it is indeed unfortunate that no satisfactory classification has been designed. But from the practical point of view (i.e., insofar as one is concerned *primarily* with the recognition of fallacies) such a classification is *unnecessary*. A great deal of constructive work can be done without such a classification.

In view of the comments in the last paragraph, it should be understood that the division of fallacies in this chapter is at best a fairly plausible and convenient one. More important perhaps, examine the following diagram which illustrates the symmetric classification of arguments presented in this text.

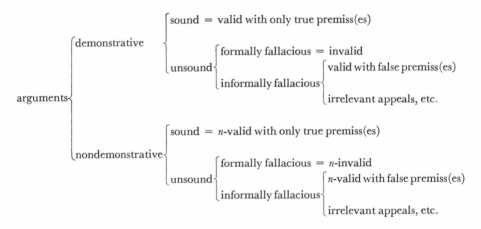

10.1   Fallacies of ambiguity

The ten fallacies considered in this section involve ambiguous or confused arguments and claims, so we have collected them under the name of **fallacies of ambiguity.** They are all informal fallacies.

a) *Begging the Question.* We seldom defend a view that we do not favor and we often assume that any view we favor is true. Hence, when we are constructing arguments in support of our views, it often happens that we simply *assume* the view we should be proving. When this happens, the fallacy of **begging the question** (*petitio principii*, i.e., assuming an inferior or less than self-evident principle) is committed. Question-begging arguments are *unsound* but *valid*; i.e., they do not involve any *formal* fallacy. They are unsound because in one way or another a question at issue is *assumed* rather than proved.

For example, consider the following arguments.

> If God does not exist, men should not worship.
> But men should worship.
> ———————————————
> God exists.

> If God does not exist, men should not believe everything that is written in the Bible.
> But men should believe everything that is written in the Bible.
> ————————————————————————————————
> God exists.

> The soul is simple because it is immortal.
> ————————————————————
> It must be immortal because it is simple.

Since the conclusion of the first two examples is that God exists, the existence of God is evidently the question at issue. The second premiss of the first argument asserts that men should worship. But men should worship only if God exists, since men are not obliged to worship nonentities. Hence, if the truth of this premiss is granted, then the question at issue is answered in favor of God's existence. That is, the argument only "proves" the existence of God *after* that existence is *assumed*; i.e., it is circular.

Similar remarks apply to the second argument. Its second premiss is true only if God exists, since men are not obliged to believe falsehoods and *one* of the assertions in the Bible is that God exists. Thus, if the truth of this premiss is granted, then the question at issue is again answered in favor of God's existence; i.e., the argument is circular.

The third argument is the most obvious of the three. The soul's simplicity is supposed to follow from its alleged immortality, and the latter is "proved" by appealing to the former. Hence, the simplicity of the soul is "proved" by this argument only *after* that simplicity is *assumed*.

b) *Complex Questions.* The fallacy of **complex** or **leading questions** is committed whenever a question is phrased so that it cannot be answered without granting a particular answer to some question at issue. For example, suppose the question at issue is whether or not Orville has *ever* gambled on Sundays? His mother-in-law raises the complex question, Are you still gambling on Sundays? Whether Orville answers "yes" or "no" to this question, he has apparently admitted that he *has* gambled on Sundays, and that was the question at issue.

Again suppose the question at issue is whether Alice should take a train or drive her father's car to New York. Her father raises the complex question, Will you be taking the 8:40 or the 10:30 train? No matter which alternative Alice chooses, the question at issue has already been answered for her.

Finally, the question at issue is much too often whether one should fix the old car or buy a new one. And typically the automobile dealer begins with the question, What sort of car were you looking for? As far as he is concerned, the real question at issue has already been answered. But the truth of the matter is that he has simply committed the fallacy of *complex questions.*

c) *Accident.* The fallacy of **accident** (*fallacia accidentis*) is committed when a generalization or general principle is improperly applied to a single instance. For example, it is generally true that children ought to obey their parents. If Johnny's parents are psychopaths, however, it would surely be a mistake to insist that the injunction applies to Johnny. That is to say, Johnny's "accidental" circumstances are such that the principle is inapplicable. Hence, one who applied the principle to Johnny's case would be committing a fallacy of *accident.*

Again, suppose a "loan shark" pointed out to his overdue debtor that a man ought to pay his debts and that insofar as he failed to pay his debts, he ought to expect punishment. Here is a perfectly good principle improperly applied. The principle should only be applied to legitimate creditors. If a man borrows money in good faith and is then confronted with the alternatives of paying an extraordinarily high interest rate or incurring, say, physical punishment, he is *not obliged* to meet either. If he has any moral obligation at all, it is to contact the police. Here the "loan shark" has committed the fallacy of *accident.*

The fallacy of *accident* is committed by lawyers, judges, and jurists who refuse to recognize mitigating circumstances when judging a person. Mitigating circumstances are, after all, accidents or additional elements in a situation which require special attention. When such elements are ignored, the "letter" of the law is apt to be served without serving its "spirit".

d) *Continuum.* The fallacy of the **continuum** is committed when it is argued that because there is a continuous distribution of differences between two extremes, there is no "real" difference. For example, it might be argued that because there is a continuous distribution of differences between good and evil, nothing is "really" good or evil. Since there is no abrupt and obvious dichotomy between good and evil, there is supposed to be no "real" dichotomy at all.

Similarly, it has been argued that there is no "real" difference between what we ordinarily call 'consciousness' and 'unconsciousness' because electroencephalogram patterns display more or less continuous changes. On this view, only dead people are completely unconscious. Whether or not it would be more profitable in the long run to adopt this rather extraordinary usage of the terms 'conscious' and 'unconscious', it is surely a fallacy to suppose that there are no important or "real" differences between the ordinary referents of these terms. The whole history of anesthesia sufficiently demonstrates this fact. Quite generally, then, whenever it is argued that extremes are unimportant or "unreal" because there is a whole *continuum* of differences between them, the fallacy of the *continuum* is committed.

e) *Composition.* The fallacy of **composition** is committed when it is argued that a property which is affirmed or denied of every part of some whole must be affirmed or denied of the whole. For example, one might argue that people are very small because people are made of cells and cells are very small. In this case, the property of being small is erroneously attributed to a whole organism *because* it is attributed to its constituent parts. Similarly, one might argue that that pipelines must be short because they are made of short segments; i.e., the property of being short is erroneously attributed to the whole line because it is attributed to each part of the line. Again, it might be argued that songs do not have melodies because they are made of individual notes which do not have melodies; i.e., the property of being melodious is withheld from whole songs because it is withheld from individual notes.

f) *Division.* The fallacy of **division** is committed when one argues that a property which is affirmed or denied of a *whole* must be affirmed or denied of each of its parts. For example, a philosopher might claim that subatomic particles must be intelligent because people are intelligent. (To which one is tempted to reply that some of them must be pregnant too because some women are pregnant.) Similarly, one might infer that every page of a book is heavy because the book is heavy, that every member of a team is good because the team is good, etc.

g) *Equivocation.* The fallacy of **equivocation** (*equivocatio* or *homonymia*) is committed when the double meaning of a term is played upon in a misleading or erroneous fashion. For example, suppose a philosopher claims that everything in the universe has some sort of experience because experience is nothing more than interaction, and everything in the universe interacts with something. Here the ambiguity of the term 'interaction' has lead to the peculiar view that, say, tables and chairs have experiences. Tables and chairs may be said to *interact* in the sense that a chair cannot occupy the very same place at the same time a table is occupying it; i.e., tables and chairs are not entirely independent with respect to their spatial locations. People might interact in this sense *or* in the sense that they may exchange ideas by communicating with one another. Ordinarily only this more or less conscious type of interaction is considered experience. The fallacy of *equivocation* has been committed by playing on these two different senses of *interaction*.

The terms 'independent' and 'dependent' are notoriously ambiguous. If someone informs you that Simon Butcher is independent, exactly what has he told you? Is he politically, religiously, economically, or socially independent? Is he a free thinker or a free lover? Is he a lover of free thinking or does he just think about loving freely? The fallacy of *equivocation* would be committed if someone began with a premiss attributing independence in one sense to Butcher and concluded from it that Butcher possessed independence in an entirely different sense. Similarly, one might *equivocate* on the term 'dependent' by fallaciously deriving, say, Butcher's economic dependence from his religious dependence.

h) *Amphiboly.* An **amphibolous** sentence is one that is ambiguous due to its peculiar structure. The fallacy of **amphiboly** (*fallacia amphibolia*) is committed when the amphibolous structure of a sentence is played upon in a misleading or erroneous fashion. Suppose, for example, you are in a restaurant and have just finished a delicious tossed salad. You call the manager to ask him what was in the dressing and who made it. The manager replies, "The chef tossed the salad with greasy hair tonic." Hopefully, he meant to say that the chef who uses greasy hair tonic tossed the salad. But he might have been suggesting the recipe for the dressing, namely greasy hair tonic. The fallacy of *amphiboly* is committed if one infers from the manager's reply that greasy hair tonic must have been used in the salad dressing.

Again, suppose someone advertises his automobile for sale with the following notice.

> For sale: 1964 Ford with automatic transmission,
> radio, heater, power brakes, power steering, and
> windshield wipers in good condition.

When you inspect the car, you find that the windshield wipers are the *only* accessories that are in good condition. When you charge the vendor with misrepresentation, he replies, "You misread the ad. Read it again." The ad was *amphibolous* and the vendor used it to commit the fallacy of *amphiboly*.

The attendant at a roulette wheel in an amusement park offered some naive spectators "ten bets for a dollar". Since this sounded like a bargain, the spectators gave him the dollar. After the first bet was made and lost, they began to make a second. But the attendant insisted that they had misunderstood him. "Ten bets for a dollar", he explained "meant ten bets for a dollar *each*". This is another instance of the fallacy of *amphiboly*.

i)   *Accent.*   Sometimes a sentence takes on different meanings as it is *accented* in different ways. The fallacy of **accent** (*fallacia accentus*) is committed when an improperly accented false or misleading sentence is inferred from a sentence which is true if properly accented. For example, someone might infer from the principle

> Men ought to be kind to strangers.

that *women* may treat strangers any old way and that both men and women may be mean to *friends*. Again, describing a football player who decided to sign a contract to play for another team, a coach said, "Oh, he's a good *football player*". While he was certainly that, the coach accented "football player" so we might infer fallaciously that he was *only* that or that, all things considered, he was not worth signing anyhow.

The practice of indicating that certain words are italicized in a quotation which were not emphasized in the original text is supposed to eliminate the fallacy of *accent* from written material. Thus if *rose* or *smell* is underlined in

> A rose by any other name would smell as sweet.

one might infer fallaciously that Shakespeare was concerned primarily with roses or smells. However, this claim was supposed to illustrate his feeling about the essential attributes of things and of the inessential relation between these attributes and their names.

j)   *Wrong Reason.*   If someone attacks some claim on the ground that it leads to contradictions, but in fact it is some *other* claim which is faulty, the fallacy of appealing to the **wrong reason** is committed. In Latin this is known as the fallacy of *non propter hoc;* i.e., literally, not because of *it.* As we have just suggested, this fallacy occurs in the context of a *reductio ad absurdum* type of argument. Some-one attempts to prove that a claim is unacceptable because it leads to contra-dictions. He lists a set of premisses including the dubious claim and derives a contradiction. The fallacy of *wrong reason* is committed if a contradiction may be inferred from the set of premisses *without* the dubious claim.

Suppose someone presents the following argument.

1.   If Leavitt communicates with the spirits of the departed then he deserves a promotion.
2.   He does not deserve a promotion, but he does communicate with the spirits of the departed.
3.   Leavitt has extrasensory perception.
C.   Leavitt deserves a promotion.

To prove that premiss 3 is false, an objector derives a contradiction from *all three* premisses. But a contradiction may be derived from the first two premisses alone, namely the following:

Leavitt both deserves a promotion and does not deserve a promotion.

Hence, the objector has committed the fallacy of *wrong reason;* i.e., premiss 3 has been rejected for the *wrong reason.*

Again, suppose the following argument is presented.

1.   Some lovers are not fighters.
2.   All soldiers are fighters.
3.   All lovers are soldiers.
4.   All soldiers are courageous.
C.   All lovers are fighters.

An objector claims that since the four premisses taken together lead to both C and its denial

Some lovers are not fighters.

premiss 4 must be rejected. However, the same contradiction may be derived from the first three premisses alone. Hence, premiss 4 has been rejected for the *wrong reason.*

Review problems for Sec. 10.1.

1. Define the following fallacies.

   a) begging the question   f) division
   b) complex questions   g) equivocation
   c) accident   h) amphiboly
   d) continuum   i) accent
   e) composition   j) wrong reason

2. Name and explain the type of fallacy suggested in the following.

   a) Alcoholic: Will my wife leave me?
       Psychiatrist: Men who drink more often than not lose their wives.
   b) There cannot be any real difference between science and art because the methods of each gradually shade into the other.
   c) Honey: What makes you think we have to buy a new radio?
       Sam: Because we have to listen to more spy stories.
       Honey: Why do we have to listen to more spy stories?
       Sam: Because we have to buy a new radio.
   d) Amateur: Isn't this drink something else?
       Professional: I'll say. It's *something* else!
   e) Mayor: In the first place, everyone knows we need a new fire engine. In the second place, we need a new ambulance. And finally, at least one person thinks we don't need a new fire engine.
       Alderman: If we accept those points we're committed to nonsense. Clearly we do not need an ambulance.
   f) Question: Did Klutz plan to murder Benz?
       Prosecutor: Mr. Klutz, what made you think your plan would work?
   g) Blondie: Was he mad because you spilled your coffee on him?
       Dagwood: Yes, he was.
       Blondie: Then you should have had him locked up like any other madman.
   h) That sorority must be beautiful, because every girl in it is beautiful.
   i) This is a free country, isn't it? So what's yours is mine.
   j) Ethel: All the elephants in the zoo would cover a whole tennis court.
       Fred: I didn't know they made elephants that big.
   k) Question: Why are there juvenile delinquents?
       Sociologist: There are juvenile delinquents because many juveniles break the law and the reason so many juveniles break the law is that they are juvenile delinquents.
   l) Mutt: I would like to see the old woman with the silver legs.
       Jeff: What makes you think anyone here has silver legs?
       Mutt: Because your ad said that a coffee table belonging to an old woman with silver legs was for sale.

m) People's motives come in all shades. So there aren't any purely good or purely evil motives.

n) Able: But I have already shown you that we may derive a contradiction from those premisses *without* my claim.

Baker: Right! So your claim must be rejected.

o) Is Berferd still sucking his thumb?

p) Prophet: The end of the world is coming next week.

Client: That's what you said last week.

Prophet: So, next week we shall see if I'm right. Right?

q) That team must be loaded with stars. They haven't lost a game yet.

r) I don't care if he did weigh three times as much as you. A good scout *always* tries to help. You should have jumped in and tried to save him.

s) I don't see how that team can lose. It's loaded with stars.

t) Certainly we need a new ball park if our children are going to be kept off the streets. If we do need a new ball park then we must borrow money from New York. So, because we have to borrow money from New York, it follows that we need a new ball park.

u) Priest: It is written, "Thou shalt not kill".

Accomplice: *I* didn't disobey the commandment. I paid someone else to do the killing.

3. Make up examples of each of the fallacies defined in Prob. 1.

10.2 Irrelevant appeals

One of the fallacies identified earliest by Aristotle was that of being ignorant of the question at issue (*ignoratio elenchi;* i.e., literally, ignorant refutations). A fallacy of **ignoratio elenchi** is committed when the *wrong point is proved* or when the conclusion established by some set of premisses is *irrelevant* to the point at issue. The present section has been entitled "irrelevant appeals" because in one way or another most instances of *ignoratio elenchi* turn out to be just that; i.e., irrelevant appeals. With the exception of hasty generalization, none of the fallacies presented has to involve a formal mistake; i.e., they are *informal* fallacies.

a) *Force.* The fallacy of making an irrelevant appeal to **force** (*argumentum ad baculum*) is committed when some kind of *force* or violence is used to bring about the acceptance of some view. Examples with which you are probably familiar include the following.

If I stepped out of bounds then I will take my ball and go home.
I did not step out of bounds.

Either I'm right or you don't take the car tonight.
I'm right.

If it's your move I'll quit.
It's my move.

In each of these cases, if the premisses prove anything, it is that some kind of *force* is going to be applied *unless* a certain view is accepted. Or, to put it in a slightly different way, a certain view is going to be accepted *or else*. But the threat of *force* or violence is beside the point. The question at issue, say, in the last example is *not* what happens if it's your move, but whose move it is. The appeal to *force* is, from a logical point of view, an irrelevant (though often persuasive) appeal.

b) *Pity*. The fallacy of introducing an irrelevant appeal to **pity** (*argumentum ad misericordiam*) is committed when one tries to persuade someone to accept a particular view by arousing his sympathy or compassion. For example, a defense attorney might try to persuade a jury that his client is innocent by listing *ad nauseum* the unfortunate consequences of a conviction; e.g., the client's wife would have to find a job and since she is a dumb but attractive woman, she would probably become a prostitute; the three children would be on the streets more often without anyone to watch them; no doubt the boy who has homosexual tendencies would become an overt homosexual; etc. In view of all these "facts" the attorney would argue that his client must be innocent. The appeal is tear-jerking but irrelevant.

Again, a student who missed practically every class and did nothing outside of class to master the material notified me that if he failed the course he would probably be drafted into the army. Others have been faced with losing their parent's support, being thrown out of school, losing their girls or their fraternity membership, etc. Even *after* the appeal to *pity* is explained to them, they come up with these howlers! But, of course, the question at issue in such cases is not what happens if the student fails, but whether or not he deserves to fail. The appeals to one's compassion are stimulating but irrelevant.

c) *Ignorance*. The fallacy of appealing to **ignorance** (*argumentum ad ignorantiam*) is committed when it is argued that the absence of evidence for (against) a claim *must* be counted as evidence against (for) it. For example, the failure to produce reliable evidence for (against) the existence of God might be used as evidence of his nonexistence (existence). The failure to disprove the existence of telepathy might be used as evidence for its existence. The failure of a person to think of a *better* course of action might be used as evidence that the present course is good. (All courses of action might be bad.)

Now, usually one who makes an assertion must assume the responsibility of defending it. If this responsibility or *burden of proof* is shifted to a critic, the fallacy of appealing to *ignorance* is committed. Suppose, for example, that Tillie claims it is impractical to send a man to Mars because the money that will be required for the project could be spent on urgently needed artificial kidneys. Billy claims that the trip to Mars is *not* impractical. When Tillie asks Billy for a reason for his view, Billy replies, "Prove that I'm wrong". Billy has passed the burden of proof back to Tillie. Tillie has already defended her claim and now Billy is requiring her to defend *his* claim by an *argumentum ad ignorantiam;* i.e., *his* claim is supposed to be true provided that Tillie is unable to refute it.

Sometimes the failure to produce evidence *for* a claim *should* be counted as evidence *against* it. For example, suppose someone says there is an elephant in your room. If you go to your room, look all around, and fail to find any evidence in support of this claim, you are justified in treating this lack of *supporting* evidence as *disconfirming* evidence; i.e., the failure to find evidence for the claim may be considered evidence for the *denial* of the claim. Such a move is justifiable because one can hardly fail to find evidence for the fact that an elephant is in his room *provided that* i) he looks for it and ii) it is there. Hence, the failure to find evidence that an elephant is there must be counted as evidence that *no* elephant is there. On the other hand, if someone claims that your room is full of air, the situation is quite different. Your room *is* full of air, but if you look around (i.e., as you might look around to find an elephant), you will not find any. Air is not the kind of thing you can find by just looking around. Hence, the fallacy of appealing to *ignorance* would be committed if someone argued that since the air cannot be seen, it must not exist. In short, then, the failure to find evidence for a claim should be counted as evidence against it *provided that* such evidence is ordinarily observable when it exists. If the evidence is ordinarily unobservable when it exists, then the failure to observe it cannot prove anything.

d) *Abusing the Man.* The fallacy of **abusing the man** (*argumentum ad hominem*) is committed when the defender of an issue is attacked instead of the issue itself. Suppose, for example, the only eyewitness to some crime happens to be an exconvict. Instead of denying the witness's testimony directly, the defense attorney tries to discredit it by discrediting its source, namely, the witness. He informs the jury that people who have been in prison have very little respect for such things as truth, justice, or the law; that about two-thirds of all exconvicts return to prison; that it is much easier to lie than it is to commit almost any crime; that, therefore, the likelihood that an exconvict is a liar is very high. In short, the argument of the defense attorney comes down to this

> Exconvicts are bad men.
> _____
> Whatever they say is false.

The argument is equally fallacious if the bad man happens to be a Communist, Fascist, slum landlord, sex pervert, etc. The evil that men do does not always effect their assertions.

Again, the fallacy of *abusing the man* might be committed by pointing out that a man's behavior is inconsistent with his claims; e.g.,

> He does not practice what he preaches.
> _____
> What he preaches is false.

> You would not want your sister to marry a Negro.
> _____
> Negroes are not as good as Caucasians.

In reply to the first argument, it might be noted that while it is true that a person ought to do good rather than evil, most people talk about it much more than they practice it. In reply to the second argument, it might be remarked that you would not want your sister to marry your brother (or your father or mother for that matter) but that does not prove that your brother is not as good as your sister.

e) *Popular Sentiments.* The fallacy of appealing to **popular sentiments** (*argumentum ad populum;* i.e., to the people) is committed when, in the absence of a plausible argument for some view, the *feelings* or *attitudes* of a group of people are appealed to to win acceptance. Suppose, for example, that a prosecutor is unable to prove that a defendant is guilty of treason. In the absence of genuine evidence, he proceeds to point out the evils of treason. He reminds the jury that anyone who would aid or comfort an enemy of his own country ought to be severely punished; that anyone who would sell out his own people belongs behind bars; that treason is a sin against God and country; that a jury which would acquit such a man would surely face the judgment of their consciences; etc. By skillfully tugging at the emotional heartstrings of the jury and by appealing to the *sentiments* of the people, the prosecutor may be able to have his view accepted.

Advertisers and salesmen often commit the fallacy of *popular sentiments.* One might even say with Willie Loman that "it comes with the territory". But what, after all, is the force of such arguments as the following?

> Our sewing machine is made in America by
> American engineers and technicians.
> Our sewing machine is well-made.

> I've been selling used cars on this corner
> for 20 years. My daddy sold cars on this
> corner and my granddaddy sold buggies on
> this corner. My little boy (bless his heart)
> sells newspapers on this corner.
> I would not defile the great heritage of
> this corner by selling you a substandard
> automobile.

> Knowledge is power. The wise man is a
> wealthy man. He who faces the modern
> world without an education enters the
> battle of life unarmed. Any man who does
> not guarantee his child the finest education
> that money can buy has neglected his
> God-given duty.
> This encyclopedia I am selling is a bargain.

In the first case the appeal is made to one's national patriotism, in the second to one's local patriotism and general respect for longevity of business establishments, and finally the appeal is made to the advantages of knowledge and the responsibilities of parenthood. These are appeals to *popular sentiments*.

f) *Authority.* Very early in our lives we are taught to respect authority. We learn to obey the rules of our parents, guardians, teachers, ministers, civil authorities, peer group organizations, etc. The fallacy of **appealing to authority** (*argumentum ad verecundiam*, literally, an argument to modesty) is committed when an appeal is made to one's modesty in the face of an alleged but illegitimate or pseudoauthority. The strength of a claim is not determined by the authority of its supporters, but by the *evidence* those supporters have adduced or *could* adduce.

In practice, the fallacy is usually committed in a fairly obvious fashion. Consider the vast number of movie stars and athletes that have been used to endorse everything from orange juice to airplanes. The advertiser never claims that the "star" is a recognized authority in the field, say, of citrus juices. It is not necessary. He knows that many people admire the "star" and that many will jump from 'the star is good' to 'the product is good'. And that is just the fallacious leap he is encouraging. Hence, both the advertiser (wittingly) and the consumer (unwittingly) commit the fallacy of appealing to authority.

The fallacy is not eliminated by the *kind* of products or people involved. The inferences from

Star X believes it.

to either

You need Upforever Garters.

or

You should contribute to the Community Chest.

are equally fallacious. You might call this the 'good guy fallacy'; i.e., Good guy X says that such and such is true, so it *is*.

The fallacy of appealing to authority is also committed when a reputable authority in one area is presented as an authority in an entirely different area. For example, one might argue that what Bertrand Russell has to say about religion is valuable because what he has said about mathematical logic is valuable or what the President has to say about foreign relations is reliable because what he has said about domestic relations is reliable.

We might be willing to accept, say, Russell's unproved claims about some issue related to mathematical logic, because in the past he has demonstrated competence in this area. His unsubstantiated claims in this area are like *promisory notes* with a very high cash value. It is highly probable that he can back up his claims here. But Russell's competence in religious matters, some would say, has not been demonstrated. In this area we do not know what his notes are worth. Hence, the appeal to Bertrand Russell as an authority on religion *because* he is an authority on mathematical logic is an appeal to an irrelevant authority.

g) *Straw Man.* The fallacy of attacking a **straw man** is committed when a weak *argument* for a view or an *implausible* statement of a view is attacked (usually successfully) instead of equally accessible stronger arguments or more plausible statements.

Consider the following implausible *statements* of some more or less widely held views. Darwin's theory of evolution boils down to the claim that some of your relatives are monkeys. The concept of God is that of an old man who dabbles in clay figures. The Christian view of eternal life is that when you leave this life you take up residence in another place which swings from cellar to ceiling from now on. These views are obviously farfetched and easily attacked. But they are caricatures of more profound views. They are *straw men*. They are, as the name suggests, cheap imitations of the "real thing". Hence, their refutation is irrelevant to the genuine article.

The *straw man* fallacy is often committed by attacking weak *arguments* for a view instead of easily accessible stronger ones. For example, it might be claimed that the *only* reason you should not steal from your neighbors is that years ago your parents taught you not to steal. Then, since your parents probably passed on what their parents passed on to them, etc., there just is not much of a reason for you not to steal. This argument is a *straw man*. There are a number of more plausible arguments against stealing than "You were taught not to steal"; e.g., stealing is morally wrong; thieves may be punished by fines, imprisonment, adverse public opinion, etc. The refutation of the *straw man* is an *ignoratio elenchi*.

h) *Hasty Generalization.* The fallacy of **hasty generalization** is committed when, after observing that a small number or a special sort of the members of some group have some property, it is inferred that the whole group has the property. To put it in the language of the statisticians, we might say it is an inference from a quantitatively (insufficiently large) or qualitatively (peculiarly selected) unrepresentative sample to a whole population. The fallacy is *formal* because an *n-invalid* schema is always involved. Consider the following examples of *hasty generalizations* from *quantitatively* unrepresentative samples. First, someone infers that all Italians eat spaghetti on Saturdays from the fact that his Italian neighbor eats spaghetti on Saturdays. Again, he infers that a silver lure will work on all bass because it worked on one. Finally, he decides that all Plymouths are defective automobiles because his Plymouth is defective. His error is apparent. He makes a judgment about a population containing thousands of individuals on the basis of his observation of one. Actually, it is fairly certain that his *generalization* would have been practically as *hasty* if he had a sample of, say, five or six. A mathematician or statistician could even give us a fairly precise estimate of its *degree* of hastiness (i.e., of its reliability or probable accuracy).

Examples of hasty *generalizations* from *qualitatively* unrepresentative samples might include the following. Someone infers that all the women in some hospital wear maternity dresses on the basis of his observation of some *pregnant* women in maternity dresses. He infers that everyone who stands on the corner of 9th Street and Hough Avenue begs, because some *panhandler* displays that sort of behavior. He supposes that everyone is interested in directing traffic, because he has observed a *policeman* directing traffic. In short, his error is that he makes a judgment about a large population on the basis of his observation of certain members of that population who have very *special positions* or who happen to be in extraordinary or *atypical situations.*

i) *Special Pleading.* The fallacy of **special pleading** is committed when, instead of presenting all the evidence or information one has about some view, one presents only a *special part* of it. More precisely, a *special pleader* presents only the information which is *favorable* to his own position. Hence, for example, a used-car salesman might describe the beautiful interior upholstery of an auto-mobile but fail to mention its defective transmission; i.e., he makes the case for his sales price as strong as possible by neglecting to mention any unfavorable information.

One who applies so-called universally applicable principles to everyone but himself is also a *special pleader.* For example, the history of higher education in America is full of cases in which men who had spent years advocating limited powers for college presidents began their *own* presidential careers by demanding complete autonomy for themselves. Similarly, at lower levels of administration we find that men who argue that deans should be subject to faculty review boards frequently resist the idea after they have become deans.

j) *Faulty Analogy.* Two things are said to be 'analogous' insofar as they are similar. Thus, a heart is analogous to a pump insofar as it is similar to a pump. An umbrella is analogous to a tree insofar as they are similar. There is an analogy between the supreme ruler of a state and the captain of a ship insofar as there is a similarity between the two. In an *argument by analogy*, one argues that because two things are analogous or similar in some respects, it is *likely* that they are similar in some other or others. Schematically, analogical arguments might be represented as follows:

> Object *a* has properties *P, Q, R, S,* and *T.*
> Object *b* has properties *P, Q, R, S.*
> It is likely that *b* also has *T.*

For example, consider the following:

> Object *a* has a brain, talks, writes, reads, and thinks.
> Object *b* has a brain, talks, writes, and reads.
> It is *likely* that *b* also thinks.

(For a more rigorous treatment of analogical arguments, see Sec. 9.2.) This sort of argument may be muddled in at least two ways. A fallacy of **faulty analogy** is committed if i) the conclusion of an analogical argument is supposed to be certain or ii) the analogous things have more *differences* than similarities. Let us consider each of these cases more carefully.

i) In the first place, a fallacy of *faulty analogy* is committed if one assumes that the conclusion of an analogical argument must be certain and not merely more or less acceptable. Analogical arguments are a type of nondemonstrative argument. Hence, by definition, their conclusions are only supposed to be more or less acceptable.

ii)   Frequently a *faulty analogy* occurs because two things which have some similarities have even *more* differences. Suppose, for instance, it is claimed that professional fighters are like racehorses. There are certain similarities between fighters and racehorses. The success of either is a function of their strength, training, spirit, and good fortune. But there are many more *important differences* which are apt to be disguised by this simile. For example, it might be supposed that fighters are insensitive to human problems, that they do not need friends, that they do not have hopes or dreams, that they may be "turned out to pasture" as it were when they are too old to compete, etc. In short, the needs of fighters are quite different from those of racehorses. Hence, one would be committing a serious fallacy of *faulty analogy* if one inferred on the basis of their similarities that, say, we have no more responsibility to fighters than we do to racehorses. Too often just this sort of inference has been made about professional athletes.

Review problems for Sec. 10.2.

1.   Define the following fallacies.

   a)   appeal to force   f)   abusing the man
   b)   appeal to pity   g)   straw man
   c)   appeal to ignorance   h)   hasty generalization
   d)   appeal to authority   i)   special pleading
   e)   popular sentiments   j)   faulty analogy

2.   Name and explain the type of fallacy suggested in the following.

   a)   Middle-class children don't need better schools. Only children from slum areas need them.
   b)   I've never seen God, and that's proof enough for me that he doesn't exist.
   c)   As far as I can see, the main argument for democracy is that Jefferson thought it was a good idea.
   d)   Women are like buses. So, one is as good as another.
   e)   If the army is so great, why aren't you in it?
   f)   Defense: Are you going to believe that this poor, ignorant, sickly, lonely, dirty, bewildered, frightened little girl could have planned to murder anyone?
   g)   Gestapo: I can't force you to remember. But I wonder if you know how an animal feels when it's being branded.
   h)   I don't see how you can call yourself a Texan and not contribute to the Save the Alamo Fund.

i) My Uncle Ralfe, the barber, says it's easy to have babies and that women who cry and moan during the delivery are just chickens.

j) Did you see that woman go through the red light? Man, women drivers are really pathetic.

k) Salesman: It's a smaller unit. It costs less to install. It looks better. What else can I say?

   Prospect: You forgot to mention the fact that it costs more to run.

l) Sure Christianity is convincing, if you think a guy could walk on water.

m) Attorney: Of course, if you want to believe the testimony of this alcoholic, this unstable reprobate, you may.

n) Abner: What makes you so sure that's Mammy's pipe?

   Daisy Mae: No one has proved that it's not.

o) Women grow up, but men are like little boys all their lives.

p) Student: When I'm lying in some muddy foxhole with trench foot, I'll remember how I got there. I ask you, sir, do I deserve that kind of suffering for failing a biology test?

q) Of course it's my turn. Or would you like a rap in the mouth?

r) What do you mean "Not all Negroes carry knives"? I saw one carrying a knife the other day.

s) According to the Right Reverend Rand, Zeke doesn't have polio and that's good enough for me.

t) What do you mean "Should we fight in Viet Nam"? You're an American aren't you?

3. Make up examples of each of the fallacies defined in Prob. 1.

Suggestions for further reading related to Chapter 10.

Bentham, Jeremy, *The Handbook of Political Fallacies*. New York: Harper & Row, Publishers, 1962.

Carney, James D., and Scheer, Richard K., *Fundamentals of Logic*. New York: The Macmillan Co., 1964, Chapters 1, 2, 4–6.

Fearnside, W. Ward, and Holther, William B., *Fallacy: The Counterfeit of Argument*. Englewood Cliffs, N. J.: Prentice-Hall, Inc., 1959.

Hepp, Maylon H., *Thinking Things Through*. New York: Charles Scribner's Sons, 1956, Chapters 3, 5, and 31.

Little, Winston W., Wilson, W. Harold, and Moore, W. Edgar, *Applied Logic*. Boston: Houghton Mifflin Co., 1955, Part One.

Michalos, Alex C., *Fallacies and Deceptions*. Englewood Cliffs, N.J.: Prentice-Hall, Inc., to be published in 1970.

Schipper, Edith Watson, and Schuh, Edward, *A First Course in Modern Logic*. New York: Holt, Rinehart and Winston, Inc., 1960, Chapters 5–9.

Thouless, Robert H., *How to Think Straight*. New York: Simon and Schuster, Inc., 1939.

Chapter

11

Definition

11.1 Purposes of definition

If you ask any schoolboy what a definition is, he can probably give you a fairly accurate answer. He would say, perhaps, that a definition is an explanation of the meaning of a word or that you define a word when you tell someone what it means. If you ask him for an example, he might point to his shoe and say "This is a shoe" or he might say "A shoe is something you wear over your sock".

Our hypothetical schoolboy is on the right track. In this chapter it is assumed that a **definition** *is* an explanation of the meaning of a *word*, though it will be shown in a) below that this may be disputed. Furthermore, it will be shown, as our schoolboy suggested, that there are many different methods of definition.

a) NOMINAL AND REAL DEFINITIONS

No doubt the *purpose* of some definitions is the explanation of the meaning of *words*. A definition that is supposed to explain what a *word means* is called a **nominal** definition; e.g.,

> 'Limp' means lacking firmness.
> 'Vino' means wine in Italian.
> A 'couple' means a pair.
> 'Obfuscate' means to confuse.

It would be a mistake, however, to assume that definitions serve only *one* purpose. Indeed there are practically an *unlimited* number of purposes that might be served by definitions; e.g., to eliminate or *create* ambiguity, to increase vocabulary, to teach a moral (religious, economic, or sociological, etc.) principle, to impress or deceive friends (enemies, employers, or strangers, etc.), to beg a question, to win a game, etc. Clearly, we cannot hope to consider all or even almost all the purposes of definitions. But there are *three* more (i.e., besides explaining the meaning of a word) which are so fundamental that one or another of them is *always* involved in *any* definition. These, then, merit special attention.

In any definition, the thing to be defined is called the **definiendum** and the thing that does the defining is called the **definiens.** In the examples in the last paragraph, 'limp' is a definiendum and 'lacking firmness' is a definiens; 'couple' is a definiendum and 'a pair' is a definiens; etc.

A definition which is supposed to explain what a *thing is* is called a **real** definition; e.g.,

An art museum is a building in which works of art are stored and exhibited.
A thief is a person who steals.
A triangle is a plane figure bounded by three straight lines.
A Canadian is a citizen of Canada.

Some people (especially philosophers) claim that *only words* can be defined, not things; i.e., that all definitions are nominal definitions or that there are no real definitions. Sometimes, as our hypothetical schoolboy suggested, the claim is made true by definition and alternative definitions are simply ignored. But frequently it is claimed or implied that there is something *wrong* with the very idea of a *real* definition. Real definition, the objection often runs, involves a search for the "essential nature" or "essence" of things. But *both* the meaning of the word 'essence' *and* the existence of "essences" remain problematic after more than 2000 years of debate. That is, nobody seems to know exactly what the word means, and *a fortiori* nobody seems to be able to prove that there are such things as "essences". Furthermore, it might be argued, when someone utters a sentence such as

A thief is a person who steals.

what he "really" means is that the word 'thief' means a person who steals. Hence, even if there are "essences" floating about somewhere, they are clearly *beside the point.* All we are "really" interested in are words and their meanings.

Neither of these objections to real definition is very convincing. In reply to the first, it must be insisted that some real definitions do *not* involve a search for "essences". The examples offered above do not involve any appeal to "essences", and such examples could easily be multiplied. In reply to the second, it should be noted that some people "really" make claims about *things* other than words. Nowadays, of course, words seem to occupy most of the philosophers' time. But there are lots of things in the world besides words and it seems slightly dogmatic to say that everyone who gives a *prima facie* real definition "really" intends to give a nominal one.

While the arguments against real definition seem much too weak to warrant the conclusion that there are no real definitions, it *does* simplify matters in a fairly innocuous way to *assume* that all definitions are nominal. This course seems to be followed by most writers (of logic texts) today and it will be followed here. Those definitions which seem to have for their *purpose* the explanation of *things* other than words will be interpreted as explanations of the meanings of *words*.

b) STIPULATIVE AND LEXICAL DEFINITIONS

Suppose that we have decided to explain the meaning of a word to someone, we then have the option of *establishing* a new definition or of *reporting* an already established one. That is, we must decide which of two *secondary* purposes we wish to achieve. We must decide whether we want to *stipulate* that a certain word will mean a certain thing (or that a certain word will mean the same as some other words) or *report* the fact that a certain word means a certain thing to some particular group of people (or that a certain word means the same as some other words to some particular group of people). Let us consider each of these secondary purposes more carefully.

When someone *assigns* a word a meaning or *announces* that, say, from now on in such and such circumstances a certain word is going to mean a certain thing or that a certain word is going to be synonymous with a certain other word or phrase, he is giving a **stipulative** definition. For examples,

> In this text 'sentence' means a declarative sentence.
> In this class the *Filipendula rubra* will be called the 'queen of the prairie'.
> In this game linemen are called 'horses'.

In each of these examples certain *circumstances* are specified in which the stipulations are supposed to hold. They hold in a certain text or a certain class or a certain game. We might have suggested temporal limits (e.g., for the next hour, this semester, for the rest of the night, etc.) or, perhaps, spacial limits (e.g., in this town, on this ship, on this mountain, etc.). The important point is that a stipulative definition is *usually* offered for this or that occasion, circumstance, or context and *not* for all time or for all occasions. Moreover, the *novelty* of a stipulative definition is usually *bound to* the announced context or circumstance. That is, a stipulative definition is always novel or *original* in *some* context, though it may not be completely original in a wider context. For example, the definition of a 'wild card' as a one-eyed jack might be new in some particular game, although other people had introduced the same stipulation in other games.

Such definitions might be appropriately called 'original' because, as we have just noted, they assign *new* meanings to words. Alternatively, they might be called 'legislative' or 'institutional' to suggest their *systemic* function; i.e., they are frequently required in the construction of formal systems such as legal codes and scientific theories. Again, we might refer to them as 'imperative definitions' to emphasize the fact that they are often intended as orders, demands, or commands. On the other hand, since they are frequently invitations or proposals to let certain words mean certain things, 'invitatory' or 'propositive definitions' might be appropriate. Again, they might be called 'coordinative' or 'interpretive definitions' because they are sometimes used to *coordinate* certain words with certain things or to *interpret* certain words as meaning certain things. ('Coordinative definition' is *usually* applied only to cases in which the *thing* coordinated with a word is a physical object; e.g., a small dot '.' might be coordinated with the word 'point'.) Any of these names would be adequate for our purposes, as long as it is remembered that the distinguishing characteristic of this sort of definition is the novel assignment of meaning to words in certain specified circumstances.

Insofar as stipulative definitions are *commands* or *proposals*, they cannot be true or false. The stipulative definition

(1)   In this game 'blox' shall mean a blue ox.

could not have a truth-value any more than the command

> Let 'blox' mean a blue ox in this game.

or the proposal

> Would you please let 'blox' mean a blue ox in this game?

Of course, if sentence (1) is taken as a *prediction* about the future meaning of 'blox' in some game then (1) must be true or false; i.e., (1) is true if 'blox' *does* mean a blue ox in the future and false if it does not. But if (1) *is* interpreted as a prediction, it is no longer a *stipulation*. As a stipulation, or more precisely, as a stipulative definition, (1) is neither true nor false.

As it was suggested above, a definition might serve an alternative *secondary* purpose. When someone *reports* the fact that a certain word means a certain thing (or that a certain word means the same as some other words) to some particular group of people, he is giving a **lexical** definition. For examples,

> 'Dyad' means a couple to English-speaking people in the
> twentieth century.
> 'Circus bees' mean body lice to the inmates of the
> prison in Joliet, Illinois in 1950.
> 'Tag' means day to twentieth-century Germans.

Insofar as lexical definitions are *factual reports* about the meaning of words for certain people, they must be true or false. For example, if 'dyad' does not mean a couple to *any* Englishmen or to any *twentieth-century* Englishmen, the definition offered of 'dyad' in the paragraph before this one is false. It does not follow, of course, that the truth-value of a lexical definition is always *known*. If someone claims that 'dyad' meant a couple to all of Aristotle's nephews, for instance, we might *never* be able to find out whether or not his claim is true.

Review problems for Sec. 11.1.

1. Define the following.
   a) nominal definition   d) lexical definition
   b) real definition   e) definiens
   c) stipulative definition f) definiendum

2. Identify the kind of definition illustrated in each of the sentences below.
   a) 'Fink' means an informer in the language of prison inmates in 1960.
   b) A *fink* is a person who reveals the secrets of other inmates.
   c) In this gang 'fink' means a dead man.
   d) A rumble is a fight between two or more street gangs.
   e) Street gangs call their battles with other gangs 'rumbles'.
   f) Let us call intra-gang battles, 'rumbles'.

3. Make up examples of each of the kinds of definitions distinguished in Prob. 1.

11.2 Methods of definition

In this section we shall consider eight methods of (nominal) definition. Since each of the methods might be used to serve a stipulative or a lexical *purpose*, we have sixteen kinds of definitions according to method and (secondary) purpose; e.g., stipulative synonymous, lexical synonymous, stipulative analysis, lexical analysis, etc.

a) Synonymous Definition

When someone defines a word by giving one or more *synonyms* for it, he gives a **synonymous** definition; e.g.,

> 'Dozen' means twelve.
> 'Lawyer' means attorney.
> 'Large' means big.

If it is *stipulated* that in such and such circumstances a certain word is synonymous with a certain other word, the definition is a **stipulative synonymous** one; e.g.,

> In this text 'statement' is synonymous with 'proposition'.
> In this course 'set' and 'class' are synonymous.

If it is *reported* that a certain word is synonymous with a certain other word for this or that group of people at such and such a time, the definition is **lexical synonymous;** e.g.,

> 'Dip' and 'pickpocket' are synonymous for the inmates of the prison at Joliet, Illinois in the twentieth century. 'Television' and 'idiot box' are synonymous for my children this year.

Since some words do not have synonyms, it is not always possible to give a synonymous definition of a word.

Abbreviative definitions are an important kind of synonymous definition. When someone introduces a short expression to stand in place of a longer one, he gives an **abbreviative** definition; e.g.,

> 'U. S. S. R.' means the Union of Soviet Socialist Republics.
> 'Y.M.B.A.' means the Young Men's Buddhist Association.

In a synonymous definition, the definiendum and definiens are *equivalent*; i.e., the meaning of a sentence in which either of the words occurs is not changed if the other is substituted for it. While some writers claim that the definiens and definiendum of *every* "good" definition must be equivalent, this requirement is not insisted upon here. Since words are sometimes defined by *things* which are not words and (logically) could not be equivalent to words, the equivalence requirement is too restrictive.

b)   DEFINITION BY ANALYSIS

When someone defines a word by giving an *analysis* of the thing designated by it, he gives a definition **by analysis.** The analysis is accomplished by finding a class to which the thing designated by the word belongs and then specifying the attribute or attributes which distinguish the given thing from all other members of that class. The larger class to which the thing designated by the word belongs is called its **genus.** The attribute or attributes which distinguish the thing from all other members of that genus are called its **differentiae** (singular, **differentia**). The differentiae are used to determine a smaller class which is included in the genus and called a **species.** For examples,

> A pentagon is a polygon (genus) with five sides (differentia).
> A man is an animal (genus) with rationality (differentia).
> An ibex is a goat (genus) that is wild *and* has large horns (differentiae).

Traditionally such definitions have been called 'definitions by *genus* and *differentiae*'. We are using the term 'definition by analysis' to contrast it with the next method to be introduced, namely, 'definition by synthesis'.

If it is *stipulated* that a thing which is designated by a certain word will be analyzed in a certain fashion, the definition is a **stipulative definition by analysis;** e.g.,

> In this game we shall say the quaterback is the player (genus) who calls the signals (differentia).

If it is *reported* that a thing which is designated by a certain word is analyzed in a certain fashion by a particular group of people at a particular time, the definition is a **lexical definition by analysis;** e.g.,

> To the inmates of the prison at Joliet, Illinois in the twentieth century, a butcher is a physician (genus) who works in a prison (differentia).

Hereafter we shall not give stipulative and lexical definitions after specifying the particular method under discussion.

Words that designate *unanalyzable* things cannot, of course, be defined by the method of analysis. For example, insofar as an ancient Greek might have considered the four "elements", earth, air, fire, and water, unanalyzable, the words 'earth', 'air', 'fire', and 'water' would have been *indefinable by analysis*. Similarly, because the twentieth-century British philosopher G. E. Moore believed that good is unanalyzable, he rejected every definition by analysis of 'good'. Since it frequently happens that words which are indefinable by one method are definable by some other method, the fact that a word is indefinable *by analysis* does not prove that it is *completely* indefinable.

c) DEFINITION BY SYNTHESIS

When someone defines a word by describing the *relations* of the thing designated by the word to other things, he gives a definition **by synthesis;** e.g.,

'Two' means the integer between one and three.
A vice-president is an officer whose rank is directly below that of a president.
A semifinal race is a race that immediately precedes the final one.

Such definitions might be called 'relational' because they define a word by *relating* the thing designated by it to some particular thing or group of things. Alternatively, they might be called 'locant' definitions to emphasize the fact that they define a word by *locating* it in a system of other words or by locating the thing designated in a system of things.

Causal or *genetic* definitions are an important species of definition by synthesis. When someone defines a word by describing the *genesis* or *cause* of the thing designated by the word, he gives a **causal** or **genetic** definition; e.g.,

> Pellagra is a noncontagious disease caused by deficient diet.
> Ice is the solid form of water which is produced by freezing.
> Static electricity is a type of electricity produced by friction.

Since it is always logically possible (i.e., not self-contradictory) to relate a thing to *something*, *every* word is theoretically definable by synthesis. Even *proper names* might be defined by synthesis; e.g., Pegasus is the mythological winged horse who arose out of the blood of Medusa after the latter was killed by Perseus.

d)   CONTEXTUAL DEFINITION

Almost all methods of definition proceed by first *mentioning* the word to be defined and then explaining it; e.g., we mention the word 'thief' and then explain it by saying that it means a person who steals.   In a **contextual** definition, how-ever, we explain the meaning of a word by *using* it in some phrase or sentence. In the most obvious sort of contextual definition, we begin by *using* the word we are interested in defining in some phrase or sentence; then that whole phrase or sentence is *mentioned* as a definiendum; e.g.,

> 'Stone A is *harder* than stone B' means that A can scratch
> B but B cannot scratch A.

Here the word we are interested in defining is 'harder'. (Alternatively, we could say that we are interested in defining the predicate 'is harder than'.) Hence, we begin by using the word in the sentence

> Stone A is *harder* than stone B.

Then, instead of just mentioning the word 'harder' as our definiendum (e.g., 'harder' means . . .), we mention the whole sentence in which 'harder' is used. Notice, incidentally, that while the definiens and definiendum of our definition are equivalent, the definiens is *not* equivalent to the *word* we are interested in defining; i.e., 'harder' *itself* is not equivalent to 'A can *scratch* B but B cannot scratch A'.

Consider another example,

> 'A has *authority* over B' means that A has the power to
> direct B's activity but B does not have the power to
> direct A's activity.

Here the word we are interested in defining is 'authority' (or, perhaps, the predi-cate 'has authority over'). Hence, we begin by *using* the word in the sentence

> A has authority over B.

Then, instead of mentioning the word 'authority' as our definiendum (e.g., 'authority' means . . .), we mention the whole sentence in which 'authority' is used.

Such definitions might be called 'implicative' because they explain the meaning of a word by implication, not by direct assertion; i.e., instead of explaining a word '*w*' by saying " '*w*' means . . . ", the word is used in a sentence which *implies* that '*w*' means such and such. Again, some authors have called this method of definition 'implicit' for roughly the same reason; i.e., the meaning of the word defined is not given explicitly but only *implicitly*. We can figure out the meaning of the word from the context in which it is used. Finally, this method of definition has been referred to as 'definition in use' to emphasize the fact that in it words are defined *in use*; i.e., words are defined by using them in sentences and explaining the latter.

Review problems for Sec. 11.2 (a–d)

1. Define the following.

a)	synonymous definition	f)	species
b)	abbreviative definition	g)	stipulative definition by analysis
c)	definition by analysis	h)	definition by synthesis
d)	genus	i)	causal definition
e)	differentia	j)	contextual definition

2. Define the following words by genus and differentia.

a)	squirrel	d)	Amazon
b)	square	e)	democracy
c)	camel	f)	bachelor

3. Identify the kind of definition illustrated in each of the sentences below.

    a) '*A* has the *same weight* as *B*' means that if *A* and *B* are put in the opposite pans of a balance, neither pan will be lower than the other.
    b) A *snack* is a small meal.
    c) 'Gamba' means leg in Italian.
    d) *Tetanus* is an infectious disease caused by the tetanus bacillus.
    e) 'S.C.' means South Carolina.
    f) A 'tight-end' is an end who plays about one foot away from the tackle.
    g) The *diagonals* of a square divide it into two right-angled isosceles triangles.
    h) A returned check is marked 'insufficient funds' when there is not enough money in the account to cover it.
    i) 'Damma' means law in Pali.
    j) 'etc.' means and so forth.

4. Make up examples of the following.

a)	stipulative definition by analysis	d)	real causal definition
b)	lexical contextual definition	e)	stipulative synonymous definition
c)	lexical abbreviative definition	f)	lexical definition by synthesis

e)   DENOTATIVE DEFINITION

A word *denotes* each and every *thing* to which it applies; e.g., the word 'horse' denotes each and every horse (Citation, Man-O-War, Silver, etc.). The *totality of things* denoted by a word is called its **denotation** or **extension;** e.g., Citation, Man-O-War, and Silver constitute *part* of the denotation or extension of the word 'horse'. A word *connotes* each and every *characteristic* anything must possess to be correctly denoted by that word; e.g., the word 'horse' connotes a solid-hoofed quadruped, etc. The *totality of characteristics* anything must possess to be correctly denoted by a word is called the word's **connotation** or **intension;** e.g., anything correctly denoted by the word 'horse' must be a solid-hoofed quad-ruped, etc.

Now, when someone defines a word by mentioning *part* or *all* of its denotation, he gives a **denotative** definition; e.g.,

> 'Criminal' means Al Capone, Jesse James, Jack the Ripper, and Lee Harvey Oswald.
> 'Painter' means Michelangelo, Renoir, Brueghel, Rembrandt, and Picasso.
> A rodent is a mouse, squirrel, rabbit, beaver, porcupine, or hamster.

To be a bit more precise, we might define the **extensional meaning** of a word as its denotation and then say that 'criminal' *extensionally means* Al Capone, Jesse James, Jack the Ripper, and Lee Harvey Oswald. Using the **intensional meaning** or connotation of the word, we might say 'criminal' *intensionally means* a person who breaks the law.

Such definitions might be called 'exemplificatory' or 'exemplifying' because they explain the meaning of a word by *mentioning examples* of the things or the types of thing denoted by it. Note that the things are *not presented* or *displayed* but only *mentioned.* This is the main difference between this method and the *ostensive* method to be considered next. Again, this kind of definition might be called 'enumerative' because it defines a word by *enumerating* part or all of the word's extension.

The primary advantage of giving a denotative definition is that it is usually easier to think of examples of things denoted by a word than it is to think of words to express its connotation. On the other hand, some words cannot be defined by this method at all; e.g., 'infinity'. Furthermore, examples are usually ambiguous. To get the point of an example, the learner must select just those characteristics *intended* to be illustrated and this may be an extremely complicated affair. Con-sider how often you have to ask people for the "point" of their examples or how often you are confronted with the questions, What's the point? What's that supposed to prove? In our example of 'criminal' above, for instance, the things mentioned might be used as examples of men, biped creatures, corpses, or Cauca-sians, etc. Indeed, if a learner was unfamiliar with the *activities* these men engaged in, he could not be expected to select the characteristic intended to be illustrated; i.e., the denotative method would be completely ineffective.

f) OSTENSIVE DEFINITION

When someone defines a word by *presenting* a thing denoted by it, he gives an **ostensive** definition. A thing denoted by a word may be *presented* in at least five different ways. i) It might happen that a word one is interested in defining denotes a thing which is already attracting the attention of some learner; i.e., the thing may be *presenting itself* as it were. For example, suppose a small child comes to you crying about the cut on his knee. You look at it and say "Cut!". By the time this scene has been repeated for the cut on his other knee, both hands, and his nose three or four times, he probably will have learned the meaning of the word 'cut'. To be more precise, we could say he will have learned part of the extensional meaning of the word 'cut' by the ostensive method of definition. ii) If the thing denoted by the word to be defined has not already attracted the attention of the learner, you might present it by *pointing to it* while uttering the word; e.g., you might point to the child's cut and say "Cut!". iii) A **demonstrative** word is one that indicates different things as it is used by different people, in different places, or at different times; e.g., 'I', 'me', 'us', 'here', 'now', 'there', 'this', 'that', 'today', 'yesterday'. Now, a thing denoted by a word might be presented by using a demonstrative word; e.g., you might say to the child "*That's* called a 'cut'." iv) A thing denoted by a word might be presented by using *both* demonstrative words and pointing; e.g., you might *point* to the child's cut and say "*That's* a cut". v) A thing denoted by a word might be presented by drawing a picture of it. [Here we are extending the meaning of the word 'present' to include things (pictures) which would ordinarily be called '*re*presentations'.]

As we noted in our discussion of denotative definition, the difference between it and ostensive definition is that the former involves *mentioning* a thing or things denoted by the word to be defined and the latter involves *presenting* something; e.g., the former might involve *mentioning*, say, Jesse James, while the latter might involve *presenting* him. It follows, then, that it might be possible to give a denotative definition of a word, but *im*possible to give an ostensive definition of it; e.g., we might mention God as a denotative definition of 'spirit', but we could not present him.

g) RULE-GIVING DEFINITION

When someone defines a word by giving a *rule* which explains its use, he gives a **rule-giving** definition; e.g.,

> 'I' is used by a speaker to refer to himself.
> 'And' is used to conjoin words, phrases, or sentences.
> 'Hurrah' is used to express extreme joy.

All words are used according to some rule, but because most words are *names* of some thing or things, their rules of application are usually not mentioned. When someone defines a word by indicating the thing or things it names, however, he is implying that the word's rule of use is that it is a name.

Such definitions might be called 'functional' because they explain the meaning of a word by describing its *function*. The logical operators introduced in Chapter 1 (i.e., 'and', 'or', 'not', 'if–then', etc.) are defined by this method. Indeed, the very word 'operator' suggests that the function of these words is not to *name* something but to *do* something else. All *demonstrative* words such as 'I' and 'now' are usually defined by rule-giving definitions.

h) OPERATIONAL DEFINITION

When someone defines a word by specifying that if certain operations are performed, then the word is applicable to a particular thing if and only if certain results are obtained, he gives an **operational** definition; e.g.,

> If a person is given a Stanford-Binet IQ test, then we say he is *mentally deficient* if and only if he scores below 70.
> If a 2-pound weight is put on one pan of a balance and another object is put on the other, then the object *weighs* 2 *pounds* if and only if neither of the pans is lower than the other.
> If a fair election is held, then candidate *A* is preferred to *B* if and only if *A* receives a majority of the votes.

Operational definitions have received a considerable amount of attention from scientists and philosophers interested in the methodology of science. Words without a clear operational meaning have been discredited and discarded. For example, since the time of Aristotle some biologists have talked about entelechies; i.e., the vital forces or directing principles of life and growth. But no one has been able to specify any test which might be performed to determine when an entelechy is present and when it is absent. Hence, the word is *operationally meaningless*.

Review problems for Sec. 11.2 (e–h)

1. Define the following.

    a) intension   e) connotation
    b) operational definition   f) denotative definition
    c) ostensive definition   g) intensional meaning
    d) extension   h) denotation

2. Arrange the following terms in order of increasing extension (i.e., from smallest to largest).

       halfback, athlete, slow right halfback, man, ballplayer, slow right
       halfback named 'Zilch', animal, football player, back, right halfback.

3.   Explain the following maxim: The extension and intension of terms are usually inversely related in size. (You may use examples.)

4.   Identify the kind of definition illustrated in each of the sentences below:

     a)   'Ocean' means the Atlantic and the Pacific.
     b)   If we drop it in water, then it is sugar if and only if it dissolves.
     c)   This is the letter 'A'.
     d)   Say 'Oh' when you are surprised.
     e)   A basketball team is a center, two guards, and two forwards.

5.   Make up examples of the following:

     a)   a word with a nonexistent denotation   c)   rule-giving definition
     b)   ostensive definition   d)   denotative definition

Suggestions for further reading related to Chapter 11.

Beardsley, Monroe C., *Practical Logic*. Englewood Cliffs, N. J.: Prentice-Hall, Inc., 1961, Chapters 2–6.

Black, Max, *Critical Thinking*. Englewood Cliffs, N. J.: Prentice-Hall, Inc., 1960, Chapters 9–11.

Leonard, Henry S., *Principles of Right Reason*. New York: Holt, Rinehart and Winston, Inc., 1957, Parts Two, Three, and Four.

Robinson, Richard, *Definition*. Oxford: The Clarendon Press, 1965.

Scriven, Michael, "Definitions, Explanations and Theories," in *Minnesota Studies in the Philosophy of Science*, eds. H. Feigl, M. Scriven, and G. Maxwell, vol. II, 1958.

Solutions to Representative Problems

Chapter 1

1.1

3. a) sentence; c) sentence; e) schema.

5. a) not truth-functional; c) truth-functional.

1.2

5. 2^N.

9. a) not wff; c) not wff; e) not wff.

1.3

1. a) $M \vee J$; c) $(M \cdot B) \vee (M \cdot -B)$.

2. a) $-(M \vee J)$;
c) $[-J \cdot (M \cdot B)] \cdot [(M \cdot B) \vee (M \cdot -B)]$;
e) $\{[-J \cdot (M \cdot B)] \cdot [(M \cdot B) \vee (M \cdot -B)]\} \vee -(J \cdot -B)$;

g) $-\{-[-(J \cdot -B)] \cdot [-J \cdot (M \cdot B)]\}$;
i) $-(M \vee J) \cdot \{[-J \cdot (M \cdot B)] \vee [(M \cdot B) \vee (M \cdot -B)]\}$.

4. a) t; c) f; e) t; g) t.

5. a) f; c) f; e) f; g) t; i) f.

6. f.   .

7. nothing.

8. f.

9. nothing.

10. t.

11. nothing.

1.4

4. a) $L \supset M$; c) $C \supset T$;
   e) $J \supset S$.

7. a) f; c) t; e) f.

9. a) t; c) t; e) f; g) t; i) t.

10. $-P \supset C$.

11. t.

12. t.

13. nothing.

14. t.

15. f.

16. nothing.

17. f.

1.5

2. 8, 4, 2, 1.

3. contingent.

4. a) contingent; c) contingent;

     e) tautologous; g) tautologous;
     i) contingent; k) tautologous.

6. a) tautologous; c) contingent;
    e) tautologous; g) tautologous.

1.6

3. a) f; c) t; e) t; g) t; i) f;
   k) f; m) f.

1.7

2. a) I; c) I; e) I; g) V;
   i) I.

3. a) valid

$$(K \cdot R) \supset -P$$
$$\underline{P}$$
$$-K \lor -R$$

c) invalid

$$A \supset (S \lor D)$$
$$\underline{-S}$$
$$-A$$

e) valid

$$-J \supset S$$
$$S \supset (F \lor T)$$
$$\underline{-T}$$
$$-S \lor F$$

g) invalid

R
$E \supset -M$
$\underline{-E \supset (J \vee -R)}$
$M \equiv -J$

i) valid

$R \cdot [P \cdot (B \cdot O)]$
$R \equiv (-B \cdot -P)$
$\underline{-O \supset B}$
$O \supset (P \cdot -R)$

4. a) I;   c) V;   e) I;   g) I.

Chapter 2

2.1

2. a) impossible;   c) Some men are not sad.   e)   All men are sad.

4. a) **E**;   c) **O**;   e) **E**;   g) **I**.

6. a) universal negative;   c) particular negative;   e) universal negative;   g) particular affirmative.

7. a) sentence;   c) schema;   e) schema.

2.2

2. a) All ice carriers are icemen.
    c) No persons are persons who like poor losers.
    e) All times when you are in doubt are times when you should punt.
    g) Some mermaids are slippery persons.
    i) All owls are wise birds.
    k) All persons who make mistakes and fail to correct them are persons who make a second mistake.
    m) No people you can cheat are cheaters.
    o) Some frogs are intelligent animals.
    q) All persons identical with Mancini are persons who study.
    s) Some persons are persons who stole my gal.

2.3

4. a) IV;   c) II;   e) II.

6. a) V;   c) V;   e) V.

7. a) V;   c) I;   e) V;   g) I;   i) V.

8. a) I;   c) NA;   e) I;   g) NA;   i) V.

2.4

1. a) $E\overline{T} = 0$;   c) $TD \neq 0$;
   e) $TY = 0$;   g) $EH \neq 0$;
   i) $VJ \neq 0$.

2. a) V;   c) V;   e) I;   g) V;
   i) V.

3. a) I;   c) V;   e) NA;   g) I;
   i) V.

4. a) valid
   All A are C.
   All U are A.
   All U are C.

c) valid
   Some O are T.
   All O are C.
   Some C are T.

e) valid
   No T are A.
   Some O are T.
   Some O are not A.

g) valid
   All B are N.
   Some B are A.
   Some A are N.

i) invalid
   Some G are not I.
   All D are G.
   Some D are I.

2.5

1. a) subject, predicate;
   c) subject;   e)   predicate;
   g) subject, predicate.

2. a) V;   c) Rules V, II, VI;
   e) Rule IV;   g)   Rule I, IV;
   i) Rule I.

3. a) V;   c) Rule II, VI;   e)   NA;
   g) Rule III;   i)   Rule V.

4. a) valid
   No O are Q.
   All T are O.
   No T are O.

c) valid
   Some G are not D.
   All G are T.
   Some T are not D.

e) invalid, Rule IV
   No B are A.
   Some E are B.
   Some E are A.

g) invalid, Rule V, VI
   Some L are R.
   Some L are not A.
   No A are R.

2.6

1. a) No H are A.
   Some D are A.
   All R are H.
   _____
   Some D are not H.
   Some R are not D.

   c) All N are A.
   All L are I.
   All I are E.
   Some N are L.
   _____
   Some L are A.
   Some A are I.
   Some E are A.

   e) Some A are O.
   All O are E.
   All A are C.
   All E are U.
   _____
   Some C are O.
   All O are U.
   Some C are U.

   g) No E are C.
   All W are H.
   All L are C.
   Some W are E.
   _____
   Some E are H.
   Some H are not C.
   Some H are not L.

   i) No E are U.
   Some O are R.
   All R are I.
   All I are U.
   All W are E.
   _____
   All R are U.
   No R are E.
   No R are W.
   Some O are not W.

2. a) All E are R.
   All R are O.
   Some E are L.
   All O are C.
   _____
   All R are C.
   All E are C.
   Some C are L.

   c) invalid

   e) All O are E.
   All A are X.
   No I are E.
   All X are I.
   _____
   All A are I.
   No I are O.
   No A are O.

   g) invalid

   h) invalid

   i) No H are C.
   All W are T.
   All B are I.
   Some W are H.
   All I are C.
   _____
   Some W are C.
   Some H are T.
   Some T are not C.
   Some T are not I.
   Some T are not B.

2.7

2. a) f; c) f; e) f; g) u;
    i) f; k) f; m) u; o) t;
    q) f; s) t; u) t; w) t.

3. a) Some persons who only die once
        are brave persons.
    c) Some stinking activities are think-
        ing activities.
    e) No perfect persons are men.

4. a) No persons identical with Kilroy
        are nondead persons.

c) All lovers are nonmad lovers.
e) All transient things are nonperma-
    nent things.

5. a) Some nonlazy animals are not
        nonsloths.
    c) Some nonrotten rodents are not
        nonfat rats.
    e) All nonpests are nontests.

6. a) f; c) f; e) t; g) t.

Chapter 3

3.1

2. a) 1. Given
        2.
        3. 2
        4. A, 3
        5.
        6. B
        7. add
    c) 1. Given
        2.
        3.
        4. 1, 2
        5. A, simp
        6. C, 5
        7. 3
        8. $-A$
    e) 1. D
        2.
        3.
        4. E, 3
        5. simp
        6. $-B$
        7. $C \equiv D$, 6
        8. 7, mt

g) 1.
    2.
    3.
    4. 2, simp
    5. $-B$
    6. simp
    7. E, 5
    8. 1
    9. $-F$, mt
i) 1.
    2.
    3.
    4. simp
    5. $A \equiv -B$, add
    6. C, D, cd
    7. 3
    8. 7, simp
    9. $D \lor -F$
    10. simp
    11. 10
k) 1. Given
    2.
    3. C, simp

4. 3, simp
5. $E \supset D$, 1, 4
6.
7. $E \supset D$
8.

m) 1. $-A \lor -B$
2. Given
3. $-A$
4.
5. $-A$, add
6. 5
7. $-C \lor -F$, cd
8.
9. $-F$
10. $-(-A \lor -B)$
11. add
12. 11, 5, elim

o) 1.
2.
3. 1, simp
4. A, 2, 3
5. $-A$, 1
6. 5, simp
7. B, elim
8. 7, 3, conj
9. $(B \cdot -C)$, 8, 6, conj
10. $-A, B$, 4, 9

i) 1. $(C \supset D) \supset [(D \supset E) \cdot (B \supset A)]$ Given
2. $(D \cdot B) \cdot (C \supset D)$ Given
3. $C \supset D$ 2, simp
4. $(D \supset E) \cdot (B \supset A)$ 1, 3, mp
5. $D \supset E$ 4, simp
6. $D \cdot B$ 2, simp
7. D 6, simp
8. E 5, 7, mp
9. $B \supset A$ 4, simp
10. B 6, simp
11. A 9, 10, mp
12. $E \cdot A$ 8, 11, conj

3. a) 1. $A \supset -(B \lor C)$ Given
2. B Given
3. $B \lor C$ 2, add
4. $-A$ 1, 3, mt

c) 1. $(A \lor -B) \supset C$ Given
2. $C \supset -(D \equiv E)$ Given
3. A Given
4. $A \lor -B$ 3, add
5. C 1, 4, mp
6. $-(D \equiv E)$ 2, 5, mp

e) 1. $B \supset (A \lor D)$ Given
2. $D \supset -(C \supset F)$ Given
3. $B \cdot -A$ Given
4. B 3, simp
5. $A \lor D$ 1, 4, mp
6. $-A$ 3, simp
7. D 5, 6, elim
8. $-(C \supset F)$ 2, 7, mp

g) 1. $B \lor D$ Given
2. $-(A \supset -B) \supset -C$ Given
3. $C \cdot A$ Given
4. C 3, simp
5. $A \supset -B$ 2, 4, mt
6. A 3, simp
7. $-B$ 5, 6, mp
8. D 1, 7, elim

4. a)
1. $A \lor -C$ — Given
2. $B \supset C$ — Given
3. $A \supset -B$ — Given
4. B — Given
5. $-A$ — 3, 4, mt
6. $-C$ — 1, 5, elim
7. $-B$ — 2, 6, mt
8. $-A \cdot -B$ — 5, 7, conj

c)
1. $-F \cdot E$ — Given
2. $C \supset F$ — Given
3. $(-C \cdot E) \supset C$ — Given
4. $-F$ — 1, simp
5. $-C$ — 2, 4, mt
6. E — 1, simp
7. $-C \cdot E$ — 5, 6, conj
8. C — 3, 7, mp
9. F — 2, 8, mp

e)
1. $A \supset (B \equiv C)$ — Given
2. $B \supset -C$ — Given
3. $A \cdot C$ — Given
4. C — 3, simp
5. $-B$ — 2, 4, mt

6. A — 3, simp
7. $B \equiv C$ — 1, 6, mp
8. $(B \equiv C) \cdot -B$ — 7, 5, conj

g)
1. $B \supset (-C \supset A)$ — Given
2. $-A \cdot B$ — Given
3. $C \supset (D \lor A)$ — Given
4. B — 2, simp
5. $-C \supset A$ — 1, 4, mp
6. $-A$ — 2, simp
7. C — 5, 6, mt
8. $D \lor A$ — 3, 7, mp
9. D — 8, 6, elim

i)
1. $(B \equiv C) \lor D$ — Given
2. $-D \cdot E$ — Given
3. $(B \equiv C) \supset F$ — Given
4. $(F \cdot E) \supset -B$ — Given
5. $-D$ — 2, simp
6. $B \equiv C$ — 1, 5, elim
7. F — 3, 6, mp
8. E — 2, simp
9. $F \cdot E$ — 7, 8, conj
10. $-B$ — 4, 9, mp

3.2

1. a)
1.
2.
3. imp
4. $-A \lor D$
5. $-A$, 4
6. 5, imp
7. imp
8. 6, 7, trans

c)
1.
2. imp
3. $-B$
4. 3, comm
5. $C \lor A$, dist
6. 5, simp
7. $-B \lor C$
8. $B \supset C$

e)
1.
2. A, dn
3. $B \supset C$, 2, exp
4. $-A$, 3
5. C, imp
6. $-A$, 5, comm
7. $-B$, 6, assn
8. $-A \lor C$, 7
9. B, 8, imp
10. $A \supset C$

g)
1. Given
2.
3. C, 1, dist
4. A, imp
5. D, 4, 2
6. $-A$, transp
7. imp

i) 1.
   2. 1, bic
   3. 2, simp
   4. $D \vee C$, imp
   5. $B \vee D$, assn
   6. $B \vee D$, 5, comm
   7. $-C$, imp
   8. $-B$, simp
   9. imp
   10. $-D \cdot -C$, 9
   11. $-D$, comm
   12. $-D$, $-B$, 11, dist
   13. 12
   14. B, 13, imp

k) 1.
   2.
   3. $-D$, 1, dist
   4. $-E$, comm
   5. $D \vee E$, 4
   6. $D \vee E$, imp
   7. $F \cdot G$, 6, 2
   8. imp
   9. $-(D \vee E) \vee G$
   10. 9, simp
   11. $D \vee E$, 10, imp
   12. transp

m) 1. Given
   2.
   3. 1, exp
   4. 2, simp
   5. $A \vee B$, 3, 4
   6. B, $-C$, dem
   7. $-(A \vee B)$, comm
   8. C, imp
   9. 2, simp
   10. 9, add
   11. 8, 10, mt

o) 1. Given
   2.
   3. $A \supset C$, exp
   4. $-D$, 2
   5. $-A \vee D$
   6. imp
   7. A, 3, 6, mt
   8. $-A$, imp
   9. A, dem
   10. 9, simp
   11. 2, simp
   12. $-E$, 10
   13. 4, simp
   14. 13, 12, conj

2. a)
   1. $A \supset (B \supset D)$ Given
   2. $-A \vee (B \supset D)$ 1, imp
   3. $-A \vee (-B \vee D)$ 2, imp
   4. $(-B \vee D) \vee -A$ 3, comm
   5. $-B \vee (D \vee -A)$ 4, assn
   6. $-B \vee (-A \vee D)$ 5, comm
   7. $B \supset (-A \vee D)$ 6, imp
   8. $B \supset (A \supset D)$ 7, imp

c)
   1. $A \cdot (B \cdot C)$ Given
   2. $(A \cdot B) \cdot C$ 1, assn
   3. $(B \cdot A) \cdot C$ 2, comm
   4. $B \cdot (A \cdot C)$ 3, assn

e)
   1. $-E \supset B$ Given
   2. $C \supset B$ Given
   3. $E \vee B$ 1, imp
   4. $-C \vee B$ 2, imp
   5. $(E \vee B) \cdot (-C \vee B)$ 3, 4, conj
   6. $(E \cdot -C) \vee B$ 5, dist
   7. $-(E \cdot -C) \supset B$ 6, imp
   8. $(-E \vee C) \supset B$ 7, dem

g) 1. $-C \cdot -(A \cdot B)$ Given

2. $(A \equiv B) \equiv (C \cdot D)$ Given

3. $[(A \supset B) \cdot (B \supset A)] \equiv (C \cdot D)$ 2, bic

4. $\{[(A \supset B) \cdot (B \supset A)] \supset (C \cdot D)\} \cdot \{(C \cdot D) \supset [(A \supset B) \cdot (B \supset A)]\}$ 3, bic

5. $[(A \supset B) \cdot (B \supset A)] \supset (C \cdot D)$ 4, simp

6. $-C$ 1, simp

7. $-C \vee -D$ 6, add

8. $-(C \cdot D)$ 7, dem

9. $-[(A \supset B) \cdot (B \supset A)]$ 5, 8, mt

i) 1. $-A \supset (C \supset D)$ Given

2. $-A \supset (E \equiv F)$ Given

3. $-A \supset [(E \supset F) \cdot (F \supset E)]$ 2, bic

4. $A \vee [(E \supset F) \cdot (F \supset E)]$ 3, imp

5. $[A \vee (E \supset F)] \cdot [A \vee (F \supset E)]$ 4, dist

6. $A \vee (E \supset F)$ 5, simp

7. $A \vee (C \supset D)$ 1, imp

8. $[A \vee (C \supset D)] \cdot [A \vee (E \supset F)]$ 6, 7, conj

9. $A \vee [(C \supset D) \cdot (E \supset F)]$ 8, dist

10. $-A \supset [(C \supset D) \cdot (E \supset F)]$ 9, imp

3. a) 1. $-(A \cdot B)$ Given

2. B Given

3. $-A \vee -B$ 1, dem

4. $-A$ 3, 2, elim

5. $-A \vee C$ 4, add

6. $A \supset C$ 5, imp

c) 1. $(F \supset B) \supset H$ Given

2. $H \supset (L \cdot W)$ Given

3. $(F \supset B) \supset (L \cdot W)$ 1, 2, trans

4. $-(F \supset B) \vee (L \cdot W)$ 3, imp

5. $[-(F \supset B) \vee L] \cdot [-(F \supset B) \vee W]$ 4, dist

6. $-(F \supset B) \vee L$ 5, simp

7. $-(-F \vee B) \vee L$ 6, imp

8. $(F \cdot -B) \vee L$ 7, dem

9. $(F \vee L) \cdot (-B \vee L)$ 8, dist

10. $F \vee L$ 9, simp

e) 1. $C \supset -(M \cdot B)$ Given

2. $-C \vee -(M \cdot B)$ 1, imp

3. $-C \vee (-M \cdot -B)$ 2, dem

4. $(-C \vee -M) \cdot (-C \vee -B)$ 3, dist

5. $-C \vee -M$ 4, simp

6. $-(C \cdot M)$ 5, dem

7. $-(C \cdot M) \vee -B$ 6, add

8. $(C \cdot M) \supset -B$ 7, imp

g)   1. $F \lor (R \cdot -U)$ Given
     2. $(F \cdot R) \supset C$ Given
     3. $(F \lor R) \cdot (F \lor -U)$ 1, dist
     4. $-(F \cdot R) \lor C$ 2, imp
     5. $(-F \lor -R) \lor C$ 4, dem
     6. $F \lor -U$ 3, simp
     7. $-U \lor F$ 6, comm
     8. $U \supset F$ 7, imp
     9. $-F \lor (-R \lor C)$ 5, assn
    10. $F \supset (-R \lor C)$ 9, imp
    11. $U \supset (-R \lor C)$ 8, 10, trans
    12. $U \supset (R \supset C)$ 11, imp
    13. $(U \cdot R) \supset C$ 12, exp

i)   1. $(E \equiv P) \lor F$ Given
     2. $-P$ Given
     3. $[(E \supset P) \cdot (P \supset E)] \lor F$ 1, bic
     4. $[(E \supset P) \lor F] \cdot [(P \supset E) \lor F]$ 3, dist
     5. $(E \supset P) \lor F$ 4, simp
     6. $(-E \lor P) \lor F$ 5, imp
     7. $(P \lor -E) \lor F$ 6, comm
     8. $P \lor (-E \lor F)$ 7, assn
     9. $-E \lor F$ 8, 2, elim
    10. $E \supset F$ 9, imp

3.3

1. a)   1. $-A \lor B$ Given
         2. $-B / -A$ Assumed
         3. $-A$ 1, 2, elim
         4. $-B \supset -A$ 2, 3, cp

    c)   1. A Given
         2. $-(A \cdot B) / A \cdot -B$ Assumed
         3. $-A \lor -B$ 2, dem
         4. $-B$ 3, 1, elim
         5. $A \cdot -B$ 1, 4, conj
         6. $-(A \cdot B) \supset (A \cdot -B)$ 2, 5, cp

    e)   1. $B \supset C$ Given
         2. $B \supset D$ Given
         3. $B / C \cdot D$ Assumed
         4. C 1, 3, mp
         5. D 2, 3, mp
         6. $C \cdot D$ 4, 5, conj
         7. $B \supset (C \cdot D)$ 3, 6, cp

g) 1. $A \lor (B \lor C)$ Given
    2. $-(A \lor B)/A \lor C$ Assumed
    3. $-A \cdot -B$ 2, dem
    4. $-A$ 3, simp
    5. $B \lor C$ 1, 4, elim
    6. $-B$ 3, simp
    7. C 5, 6, elim
    8. $C \lor A$ 7, add
    9. $A \lor C$ 8, comm
    10. $-(A \lor B) \supset (A \lor C)$ 2, 9, cp

2. a) 1. $H \supset (K \supset Q)$ Given
           2. $H \supset K/H \supset Q$ Assumed
           3. H/Q Assumed
           4. $K \supset Q$ 1, 3, mp
           5. K 2, 3, mp
           6. Q 4, 5, mp
           7. $H \supset Q$ 3, 6, cp
           8. $(H \supset K) \supset (H \supset Q)$ 2, 7, cp

c) 1. $F \supset G$ Given
    2. $F \cdot S/G \lor C$ Assumed
    3. F 2, simp
    4. G 1, 3, mp
    5. $G \lor C$ 4, add
    6. $(F \cdot S) \supset (G \lor C)$ 2, 5, cp

e) 1. $E \lor (E \cdot L)$ Given
    2. $-E/L$ Assumed
    3. $E \cdot L$ 1, 2, elim
    4. L 3, simp
    5. $-E \supset L$ 2, 4, cp

g) 1. $A \supset (B \supset C)$ Given
    2. $B/A \supset C$ Assumed
    3. A Assumed
    4. $B \supset C$ 1, 3, mp
    5. C 4, 2, mp
    6. $A \supset C$ 3, 5, cp
    7. $B \supset (A \supset C)$ 2, 6, cp

3.4

2. a) 1. $E \supset (C \cdot -D)$ Given
           2. $(A \cdot D) \cdot E$ Given
           3. $-C$ Assumed
           4. E 2, simp
           5. $C \cdot -D$ 1, 4, mp
           6. C 5, simp
           7. $C \cdot -C$ 6, 3, conj
           8. C 3, 7, ip

c) 1. $(A \lor -C) \supset (D \cdot F)$ Given
    2. $(-A \supset E) \cdot -F$ Given

3. $-E$ Assumed
4. $-A \supset E$ 2, simp
5. A 4, 3, mt
6. $A \lor -C$ 5, add
7. $D \cdot F$ 1, 6, mp
8. F 7, simp
9. $-F$ 2, simp
10. $F \cdot -F$ 8, 9, conj
11. E 3, 10, ip

e) 1. $-(C \supset A) \cdot (B \cdot -G)$ Given
    2. $(A \lor -C) \lor [(B \cdot E) \supset G]$ Given
    3. E Assumed
    4. $-(C \supset A)$ 1, simp
    5. $-(-C \lor A)$ 4, imp
    6. $-(A \lor -C)$ 5, comm
    7. $(B \cdot E) \supset G$ 2, 6, elim
    8. $B \cdot -G$ 1, simp
    9. B 8, simp
    10. $B \cdot E$ 9, 3, conj
    11. G 7, 10, mp
    12. $-G$ 8, simp
    13. $G \cdot -G$ 11, 12, conj
    14. $-E$ 3, 13, ip

3. a) 1. $M \lor H$ Given
    2. $H \supset M$ Given
    3. $-M$ Assumed
    4. $-H$ 2, 3, mt
    5. H 1, 3, elim
    6. $H \cdot -H$ 5, 4, conj
    7. M 3, 6, ip

   c) 1. $(M \lor R) \supset (A \cdot F)$ Given
    2. $-A$ Given
    3. M Assumed
    4. $M \lor R$ 3, add
    5. $A \cdot F$ 1, 4, mp
    6. A 5, simp

       7. $A \cdot -A$ 6, 2, conj
       8. $-M$ 3, 7, ip

   e) 1. $(S \supset M) \supset C$ Given
       2. $-(-M \lor C)$ Assumed
       3. $M \cdot -C$ 2, dem
       4. $-C$ 3, simp
       5. $-(S \supset M)$ 1, 4, mt
       6. $-(-S \lor M)$ 5, imp
       7. $S \cdot -M$ 6, dem
       8. $-M$ 7, simp
       9. M 3, simp
       10. $M \cdot -M$ 9, 8, conj
       11. $-M \lor C$ 2, 10, ip

4. a) 1. $(-A \cdot B) \lor (-A \cdot C)$ Given
    2. $C \supset (-E \supset -D)$ Given
    3. $-A \cdot (B \lor C)$ 1, dist
    4. $(B \lor C) \cdot -A$ 3, comm
    5. $B \lor C$ 4, simp
    6. $-B \supset C$ 5, imp
    7. $-B \supset (-E \supset -D)$ 6, 2, trans
    8. $(-B \cdot -E) \supset -D$ 7, exp
    9. $-(B \lor E) \supset -D$ 8, dem
    10. $D \supset (B \lor E)$ 9, transp

   c) invalid
       $M \lor -O$
       $H \supset (O \equiv N)$
       $\dfrac{N \lor M}{-N \supset O}$

   e) invalid
       $G \supset S$
       $H \lor (-G \cdot M)$
       $\dfrac{S \supset H}{H}$

g)
1. $(T \cdot C) \vee (T \cdot H)$ — Given
2. $C \supset -T$ — Given
3. $-H$ — Assumed
4. $-H \vee -T$ — 3, add
5. $-(H \cdot T)$ — 4, dem
6. $-(T \cdot H)$ — 5, comm
7. $T \cdot C$ — 1, 6, elim
8. T — 7, simp
9. $-C$ — 2, 8, mt
10. C — 7, simp
11. $C \cdot -C$ — 10, 9, conj
12. H — 3, 11, ip

i)
1. $(L \cdot S) \supset T$ — Given
2. $T \supset H$ — Given
3. $S \cdot -H$ — Given
4. $-H$ — 3, simp
5. $-T$ — 2, 4, mt
6. $-(L \cdot S)$ — 1, 5, mt
7. $-L \vee -S$ — 6, dem
8. S — 3, simp
9. $-L$ — 7, 8, elim

k) invalid

m)
1. $-I \supset (G \supset L)$ — Given
2. $-(L \vee I)$ — Given
3. $-L \cdot -I$ — 2, dem
4. $-I$ — 3, simp
5. $G \supset L$ — 1, 4, mp
6. $-L$ — 3, simp
7. $-G$ — 5, 6, mt

o)
1. $A \vee (R \cdot E)$ — Given
2. $A \supset L$ — Given
3. $L \supset E$ — Given
4. $-E$ — Assumed
5. $-L$ — 3, 4, mt
6. $-E \vee -R$ — 4, add
7. $-(E \cdot R)$ — 6, dem
8. $-(R \cdot E)$ — 7, comm
9. A — 1, 8, elim
10. $-A$ — 2, 5, mt
11. $A \cdot -A$ — 9, 10, conj
12. E — 4, 11, ip

q) invalid
$N \supset (C \cdot D)$
$(-D \vee S) \cdot M$
$(J \cdot M) \vee S$
$\overline{S \supset -N}$

s)
1. $D \supset R$ — Given
2. $D \cdot E / R \vee B$ — Assumed
3. D — 2, simp
4. R — 1, 3, mp
5. $R \vee B$ — 4, add
6. $(D \cdot E) \supset (R \vee B)$ — 2, 5, cp

u)
1. $B \equiv F$ — Given
2. $T \supset B$ — Given
3. $(-B \vee C) \cdot -F$ — Given
4. $-B \vee C$ — 3, simp
5. $B \supset C$ — 4, imp
6. $(B \supset F) \cdot (F \supset B)$ — 1, bic
7. $-F$ — 3, simp
8. $B \supset F$ — 6, simp
9. $-B$ — 8, 7, mt
10. $-T$ — 2, 9, mt

w) invalid
$H \equiv L$
$E \supset G$
D
$\dfrac{-E \vee -L}{G}$

y)
1. $(B \supset -E) \vee -F$ — Given
2. $(A \equiv B) \supset C$ — Given
3. $E \cdot (A \equiv B)$ — Given
4. $B \vee -C$ — Given
5. $-F \vee (B \supset -E)$ — 1, comm
6. $F \supset (B \supset -E)$ — 5, imp
7. $(F \cdot B) \supset -E$ — 6, exp
8. E — 3, simp
9. $-(F \cdot B)$ — 7, 8, mt
10. $-F \vee -B$ — 9, dem
11. $A \equiv B$ — 3, simp
12. C — 2, 11, mp
13. B — 4, 12, elim

Chapter 4

4.1

3. a) no; c) yes; e) yes; g) no.   5. a) sentence; c) sentence;
   e) schema.

4.2

2. a) $(x)Qx$; c) $(Ex)(Qx \lor Rx)$;
   e) $(Ex)(Rx \cdot -Qx)$; g) Hg;
   i) $(x)(Hx \lor Fx)$;
   k) $(x)[(Rx \cdot Ax) \supset -Ox]$;
   m) $(Ex)(Cx \cdot Lx)$; o) $(x)(Bx \supset Gx)$;
   q) $Bk \lor -Gk$;

   s) $(x)[(Dx \cdot Gx) \supset (Dx \cdot Gx)]$;
   u) $(Gg \cdot Hg) \supset (Bg \cdot -Fg)$;
   w) $(Ex)(Cx \cdot Ax)$;
   y) $(Ex)(Cx \cdot -Lx)$; a') $(x)Bx$;
   c') $(x)(Ux \supset Ux)$.

4.3

2. a) $Rm \cdot Rn$;
   c) $(Rm \equiv Bm) \lor (Rn \equiv Bn)$;
   e) $[(Cm \cdot Dm) \lor Bm] \cdot$
      $[(Cn \cdot Dn) \lor Bn]$;
   g) $[(Am \cdot Bm) \cdot Cm] \cdot [(An \cdot Bn) \cdot Cn]$.

3. a) V; c) I; e) V;
   g) I; i) I.

4. a) valid
   $$(x)(Hx \supset Ax)$$
   $$(x)(-Ax \lor -Bx)$$
   $$\frac{(x)Bx}{(x)-Ax}$$

   c) invalid
   $$(x)(Ux \supset -Ax)$$
   $$(x)(-Ax \lor Xx)$$
   $$\frac{(x)(Ux \equiv Cx)}{(Ex)Xx}$$

   e) valid
   $$(x)(Fx \supset Xx)$$
   $$(x)(Tx \lor Rx)$$
   $$(Ex)(Rx \supset Tx)$$
   $$\frac{(Ex)(Rx \lor Xx)}{(Ex)(-Fx \supset Tx)}$$

   g) valid
   $$(x)(Ux \supset -Tx)$$
   $$(x)(Ox \equiv Ux)$$
   $$(x)(Tx \supset -Ox)$$
   $$\frac{(x)Ox}{(x)(Tx \lor Ux)}$$

   i) invalid
   $$(x)[Lx \supset (Jx \equiv Ox)]$$
   $$(Ex)(-Ox \cdot -Lx)$$
   $$\frac{(Ex)[-Lx \supset -(Jx \cdot Lx)]}{(Ex)Ox}$$

4.4

2. a) 1. $(x)[(-Ax \equiv Cx) \cdot -Dx]$ Given
      2. $(-Ae \equiv Ce) \cdot -De$ 1, US
      3. $-De$ 2, simp
      4. $-De \vee -Ae$ 3, add
      5. $-(De \cdot Ae)$ 4, dem

  c) 1. $Dh \cdot (-Fh \equiv Gh)$ Given
      2. $(x)(Cx \supset -Dx)$ Given
      3. $(x) -Gx$ Given
      4. $Ch \supset -Dh$ 2, US
      5. $-Gh$ 3, US
      6. Dh 1, simp
      7. $-Ch$ 4, 6, mt
      8. $-Ch \vee -Fh$ 7, add
      9. $(Ex)(-Cx \vee -Fx)$ 8, EG

  e) 1. $(x)[(Ax \supset Bx) \supset (Cx \supset Dx)]$ Given
      2. $-(Ae \cdot -Be) \cdot Ce$ Given
      3. $De \equiv He$ Given
      4. $(Ae \supset Be) \supset (Ce \supset De)$ 1, US
      5. $(De \supset He) \cdot (He \supset De)$ 3, bic
      6. $-(Ae \cdot -Be)$ 2, simp
      7. $Ae \supset Be$ 6, imp
      8. $Ce \supset De$ 4, 7, mp
      9. $De \supset He$ 5, simp
      10. $Ce \supset He$ 8, 9, trans
      11. Ce 2, simp
      12. He 10, 11, mp
      13. $(Ex)Hx$ 12, EG

  g) 1. $(x)\{Dx \supset [Hx \supset (Cx \supset Bx)]\}$ Given
      2. $(x)(Gx \supset Dx)$ Given
      3. $(x)[(Gx \cdot Hx) \cdot -Bx]$ Given
      4. $Dm \supset [Hm \supset (Cm \supset Bm)]$ 1, US
      5. $Gm \supset Dm$ 2, US
      6. $(Gm \cdot Hm) \cdot -Bm$ 3, US
      7. $Gm \cdot Hm$ 6, simp
      8. Gm 7, simp
      9. Dm 5, 8, mp
      10. $Hm \supset (Cm \supset Bm)$ 4, 9, mp
      11. Hm 7, simp
      12. $Cm \supset Bm$ 10, 11, mp
      13. $-B$ 6, simp
      14. $-Cm$ 12, 13, mt
      15. $(Ex) -Cx$ 14, EG

3. a) 1. $(x)(-Rx \equiv Dx)$ Given
    2. $(x)(Rx \supset Ax)$ Given
    3. $(x) -Dx$ Given
    4. $-Rm \equiv Dm$ 1, US
    5. $Rm \supset Am$ 2, US
    6. $-Dm$ 3, US
    7. $(-Rm \supset Dm) \cdot (Dm \supset -Rm)$ 4, bic
    8. $-Rm \supset Dm$ 7, simp
    9. Rm 8, 6, mt
    10. Am 5, 9, mp
    11. $(Ex)Ax$ 10, EG

c) 1. $(x)(Hx \supset -Dx)$ Given   6. $-Op$ 3, simp
    2. $(x)[(Hx \cdot Lx) \lor Ox]$ Given   7. $Hp \cdot Lp$ 5, 6, elim
    3. $-Op \cdot Lp$ Given   8. Hp 7, simp
    4. $Hp \supset -Dp$ 1, US   9. $-Dp$ 4, 8, mp
    5. $(Hp \cdot Lp) \lor Op$ 2, US   10. $(Ex) -Dx$ 9, EG

e) 1. $(Df \equiv Lf) \equiv Tf$ Given
    2. $(x)Tx$ Given
    3. $Df \cdot -Lf$ Given
    4. Tf 2, US
    5. $[(Df \equiv Lf) \supset Tf] \cdot [Tf \supset (Df \equiv Lf)]$ 1, bic
    6. $Tf \supset (Df \equiv Lf)$ 5, simp
    7. $Df \equiv Lf$ 6, 4, mp
    8. $(Df \supset Lf) \cdot (Lf \supset Df)$ 7, bic
    9. $Df \supset Lf$ 8, simp
    10. Df 3, simp
    11. Lf 9, 10, mp
    12. $(Ex)Lx$ 11, EG

g) 1. $(x)(Dx \supset Ox)$ Given
    2. $(x)(Ox \supset Tx)$ Given   7. $-Oj$ 6, 5, mt
    3. $(x)(Tx \supset Ax)$ Given   8. $-Oj \lor -Kj$ 7, add
    4. $(x)(Kx \supset Hx)$ Given   9. $-Kj \lor -Oj$ 8, comm
    5. $-Tj$ Given   10. $Kj \supset -Oj$ 9, imp
    6. $Oj \supset Tj$ 1, US   11. $(Ex)(Kx \supset -Ox)$ 10, EG

i) 1. $(x)(Fx \equiv -Ux)$ Given
    2. $(x)(Ux \cdot -Tx)$ Given
    3. $(x)[Fx \lor (Tx \lor Rx)]$ Given
    4. $Fm \equiv -Um$ 1, US
    5. $Um \cdot -Tm$ 2, US
    6. $Fm \lor (Tm \lor Rm)$ 3, US
    7. $(Fm \supset -Um) \cdot (-Um \supset Fm)$ 4, bic
    8. $Fm \supset -Um$ 7, simp
    9. Um 5, simp
    11. $-Fm$ 8, 9, mt

12. $Tm \lor Rm$ 6, 11, elim
13. $-Tm$ 5, simp
14. Rm 12, 13, elim
15. $(Ex)Rx$ 14, EG

4.5

1. a) $(Ex) -Sx$;   c) $(x)(Sx \supset -Px)$;
   e) $(Ex) -(-Sx \cdot Px)$;
   g) $(Ex)(Sx \cdot -Px)$;
   i) $(Ex)(Px \cdot -Sx)$.

2. a)
   1. $-(Ex)[(Ax \lor Cx) \cdot -(Gx \cdot Hx)]$ Given
   2. $(x)(-Hx \cdot Fx)$ Given
   3. $(x)(Dx \supset Cx)$ Given
   4. $(x) -[(Ax \lor Cx) \cdot -(Gx \cdot Hx)]$ 1, EQ
   5. $-[(Am \lor Cm) \cdot -(Gm \cdot Hm)]$ 4, US
   6. $-Hm \cdot Fm$ 2, US
   7. $Dm \supset Cm$ 2, US
   8. $-(Am \lor Cm) \lor (Gm \cdot Hm)$ 5, dem
   9. $-Hm$ 6, simp
   10. $-Hm \lor -Gm$ 9, add
   11. $-(Hm \cdot Gm)$ 10, dem
   12. $-(Am \lor Cm)$ 8, 11, elim
   13. $-Am \cdot -Cm$ 12, dem
   14. $-Cm$ 13, simp
   15. $-Dm$ 7, 14, mt
   16. $(Ex) -Dx$ 15, EG

   c)
   1. $(x)\{-[-(Ax \supset Bx) \supset (Cx \supset Dx)] \supset (Hx \supset Fx)\}$ Given
   2. $-(Ex) -[(Hx \cdot -Fx) \cdot -Bx]$ Given
   3. $Ce \cdot -De$ Given
   4. $-[-(Ae \supset Be) \supset (Ce \supset De)] \supset (He \supset Fe)$ 1, US
   5. $(x)[(Hx \cdot -Fx) \cdot -Bx]$ 2, EQ
   6. $(He \cdot -Fe) \cdot -Be$ 5, US
   7. $He \cdot -Fe$ 6, simp
   8. $-(-He \lor Fe)$ 7, dem
   9. $-(He \supset Fe)$ 8, imp
   10. $-(Ae \supset Be) \supset (Ce \supset De)$ 4, 9, mt
   11. $-(-Ce \lor De)$ 3, dem
   12. $-(Ce \supset De)$ 11, imp
   13. $Ae \supset Be$ 10, 12, mt

e)   1. $(x)[-Fx \supset (-Ax \cdot -Bx)]$ Given
     2. $-(Ex) -[(Gx \cdot Fx) \supset Dx]$ Given
     3. $(x)Ax$ Given
     4. $(x)(Fx \equiv Gx)$ Given
     5. $(x)[(Gx \cdot Fx) \supset Dx]$ 2, EQ
     6. $-Fm \supset (-Am \cdot -Bm)$ 1, US
     7. Am 3, US
     8. $Fm \equiv Gm$ 4, US
     9. $(Gm \cdot Fm) \supset Dm$ 5, US
    10. $-Fm \supset -(Am \lor Bm)$ 6, dem
    11. $Am \lor Bm$ 7, add
    12. Fm 10, 11, mt
    13. $(Fm \supset Gm) \cdot (Gm \supset Fm)$ 8, bic
    14. $Fm \supset Gm$ 13, simp
    15. Gm 14, 12, mp
    16. $Gm \cdot Fm$ 15, 12, conj
    17. Dm 9, 16, mp
    18. $(Ex)Dx$ 17, EG

3. a)   1. $(x)(Xx \equiv Rx)$ Given
             2. $(x)(Ax \equiv -Xx)$ Given
             3. $(x)(Cx \equiv Rx)$ Given
             4. $-(Ex) -Cx$ Given
             5. $(x)Cx$ 4, EQ
             6. $Xm \equiv Rm$ 1, US
             7. $Am \equiv -Xm$ 2, US
             8. $Cm \equiv Rm$ 3, US
             9. Cm 5, US
            10. $(Cm \supset Rm) \cdot (Rm \supset Cm)$ 8, bic
            11. $Cm \supset Rm$ 10, simp
            12. Rm 11, 9, mp
            13. $(Xm \supset Rm) \cdot (Rm \supset Xm)$ 6, bic
            14. $Rm \supset Xm$ 13, simp
            15. Xm 14, 12, mp
            16. $(Am \supset -Xm) \cdot (-Xm \supset Am)$ 7, bic
            17. $Am \supset -Xm$ 16, simp
            18. $-Am$ 17, 15, mt
            19. $Rm \cdot -Am$ 12, 18, conj
            20. $(Ex)(Rx \cdot -Ax)$ 19, EG
        c)   1. $(x)(Ix \supset -Tx)$ Given
             2. $(x)(Bx \supset Hx)$ Given
             3. $(x)(Hx \supset Tx)$ Given
             4. $-(Ex) -Bx$ Given
             5. $(x)(-Ix \equiv Ox)$ Given
             6. $(x)Bx$ 4, EQ

7. $Im \supset -Tm$	1, US
8. $Bm \supset Hm$	2, US
9. $Hm \supset Tm$	3, US
10. Bm	6, US
11. $-Im \equiv Om$	5, US
12. Hm	8, 10, mp
13. Tm	9, 12, mp
14. $-Im$	7, 13, mt
15. $(-Im \supset Om) \cdot (Om \supset -Im)$	11, bic
16. $-Im \supset Om$	15, simp
17. Om	16, 14, mp
18. $(Ex)Ox$	17, EG

e)

1. $(x)(Hx \supset -Lx)$	Given	
2. $(x)(Vx \supset -Cx)$	Given	
3. $(x)(Hx \lor Vx)$	Given	
4. $-(Ex) -Lx$	Given	
5. $(x)Lx$	4, EQ	
6. $Hm \supset -Lm$	1, US	
7. $Vm \supset -Cm$	2, US	

8. $Hm \lor Vm$	3, US
9. Lm	5, US
10. $-Hm$	6, 9, mt
11. Vm	8, 10, elim
12. $-Cm$	7, 12, mp
13. $(Ex) -Cx$	12, EG

4.6

3. a)

1. $(x)[(-Cx \lor -Dx) \lor -Hx]$	Given
2. $(x)(Hx \cdot -Gx)$	Given
3. $(x)[-Dx \supset (Fx \cdot Gx)]$	Given
4. $(-Ca \lor -Da) \lor -Ha$	1, US
5. $Ha \cdot -Ga$	2, US
6. $-Da \supset (Fa \cdot Ga)$	3, US
7. Ha	5, simp
8. $-Ca \lor -Da$	4, 7, elim
9. $-Ga$	5, simp
10. $-Ga \lor -Fa$	9, add
11. $-(Ga \cdot Fa)$	10, dem
12. Da	6, 11, mt
13. $-Ca$	8, 12, elim
14. $(x) -Cx$	13, UG

c)

1. $-(Ex) -[(Dx \cdot Cx) \cdot (Fx \cdot Gx)]$	Given
2. $(x)(-Bx \supset -Cx)$	Given
3. $(x)(Hx \supset -Gx)$	Given
4. $(Ex)[(Bx \cdot -Hx) \supset Kx]$	Given
5. $(x)[(Dx \cdot Cx) \cdot (Fx \cdot Gx)]$	1, EQ
6. $(Ba \cdot -Ha) \supset Ka$	4, ES
7. $(Da \cdot Ca) \cdot (Fa \cdot Ga)$	5, US

	8. $-Ba \supset -Ca$	2, US
	9. $Ha \supset -Ga$	3, US
	10. $Da \cdot Ca$	7, simp
	11. Ca	10, simp
	12. Ba	8, 11, mt
	13. $Fa \cdot Ga$	7, simp
	14. Ga	13, simp
	15. $-Ha$	9, 14, mt
	16. $Ba \cdot -Ha$	12, 15, conj
	17. Ka	6, 16, mp
	18. $(Ex)Kx$	17, EG
e)	1. $(x)\{[Fx \supset (Hx \lor Kx)] \lor Bx\}$	Given
	2. $(x)(Bx \equiv Gx)$	Given
	3. $(x) -Gx$	Given
	4. $[Fa \supset (Ha \lor Ka)] \lor Ba$	1, US
	5. $Ba \equiv Ga$	2, US
	6. $-Ga$	3, US
	7. $(Ba \supset Ga) \cdot (Ga \supset Ba)$	5, bic
	8. $Ba \supset Ga$	7, simp
	9. $-Ba$	8, 6, mt
	10. $Fa \supset (Ha \lor Ka)$	4, 9, elim
	11. $-Fa \lor (Ha \lor Ka)$	10, mp
	12. $(-Fa \lor Ha) \lor Ka$	11, assn
	13. $(Fa \supset Ha) \lor Ka$	12, imp
	14. $-(Fa \supset Ha) \supset Ka$	13, imp
	15. $(x)[-(Fx \supset Hx) \supset Kx]$	14, UG
g)	1. $(x)[Hx \supset -(Fx \cdot -Cx)]$	Given
	2. $-(x)(Hx \supset Tx)$	Given
	3. $(x)[(Cx \supset Gx) \cdot Fx]$	Given
	4. $(Ex) -(Hx \supset Tx)$	2, EQ
	5. $-(Ha \supset Ta)$	4, ES
	6. $Ha \supset -(Fa \cdot -Ca)$	1, US
	7. $(Ca \supset Ga) \cdot Fa$	3, US
	8. $Ha \supset (Fa \supset Ca)$	6, imp
	9. $(Ha \cdot Fa) \supset Ca$	8, exp
	10. $-(-Ha \lor Ta)$	5, imp
	11. $Ha \cdot -Ta$	10, dem
	12. Ha	11, simp
	13. Fa	7, simp
	14. $Ha \cdot Fa$	12, 13, conj
	15. Ca	9, 14, mp
	16. $Ca \supset Ga$	7, simp
	17. Ga	16, 15, mp
	18. $(Ex)Gx$	17, EG

4. a) 1. $(x)(Bx \supset Lx)$ — Given
2. $(x)(Ax \equiv -Ux)$ — Given
3. $(x)(Lx \supset Ux)$ — Given
4. $(x)Ax$ — Given
5. $Bm \supset Lm$ — 1, US
6. $Am \equiv -Um$ — 2, US
7. $Lm \supset Um$ — 3, US
8. Am — 4, US
9. $(Am \supset -Um) \cdot (-Um \supset Am)$ — 6, bic
10. $Am \supset -Um$ — 9, simp
11. $-Um$ — 10, 8, mp
12. $-Lm$ — 7, 11, mt
13. $-Bm$ — 5, 12, mt
14. $Am \cdot -Bm$ — 8, 13, conj
15. $(Ex)(Ax \cdot -Bx)$ — 14, EG

c) 1. $(x)[(Bx \cdot Ix) \supset Hx]$ — Given
2. $Ie \cdot Te$ — Given
3. $(x)(Tx \supset Bx)$ — Given
4. $(Be \cdot Ie) \supset He$ — 1, US
5. $Te \supset Be$ — 3, US
6. Te — 2, simp
7. Be — 5, 6, mp
8. Ie — 2, simp
9. $Be \cdot Ie$ — 7, 8, conj
10. He — 4, 9, mp
11. $(Ex)Hx$ — 10, EG

e) 1. $(Ex)\{[Bx \supset (Cx \supset Dx)] \supset Ax\}$ — Given
2. $(x)(-Bx \vee Hx)$ — Given
3. $(x)[(Hx \equiv -Ax) \cdot -Dx]$ — Given
4. $[Ba \supset (Ca \supset Da)] \supset Aa$ — 1, ES
5. $-Ba \vee Ha$ — 2, US
6. $(Ha \equiv -Aa) \cdot -Da$ — 3, US
7. $-Aa$ — Assumed
8. $-[Ba \supset (Ca \supset Da)]$ — 4, 7, mt
9. $-[-Ba \vee (Ca \supset Da)]$ — 8, imp
10. $Ba \cdot -(Ca \supset Da)$ — 9, dem
11. $-(Ca \supset Da)$ — 10, simp
12. $-(-Ca \vee Da)$ — 11, imp
13. $Ca \cdot -Da$ — 12, dem
14. Ca — 13, simp
15. $-Aa \supset Ca$ — 7, 14, cp
16. $(Ex)(-Ax \supset Cx)$ — 15, EG

g) invalid
$(Ex)(Bx \cdot Dx)$
$(x)(Qx \supset -Wx)$
$(Ex)(Ax \equiv Dx)$
$(x)(Dx \supset Qx)$
$\overline{(Ex)Wx}$

i)
1. $(x)(Gx \lor Dx)$ — Given
2. $(Ex)[(-Kx \lor Ax) \lor -Dx]$ — Given
3. $(x)[-Gx \cdot (-Ax \lor Fx)]$ — Given
4. $(-Ka \lor Aa) \lor -Da$ — 2, ES
5. $Ga \lor Da$ — 1, US
6. $-Ga \cdot (-Aa \lor Fa)$ — 3, US
7. $-Ga$ — 6, simp
8. Da — 5, 7, elim
9. $-Ka \lor Aa$ — 4, 8, elim
10. $-Aa \lor Fa$ — 6, simp
11. $Ka \supset Aa$ — 9, imp
12. $Aa \supset Fa$ — 10, imp
13. $Ka \supset Fa$ — 11, 12, trans
14. $(Ka \supset Fa) \lor -Ha$ — 13, add
15. $-Ha \lor (Ka \supset Fa)$ — 14, comm
16. $Ha \supset (Ka \supset Fa)$ — 15, imp
17. $(Ex)[Hx \supset (Kx \supset Fx)]$ — 16, EG

k)
1. $(x)[Wx \supset (Bx \lor Hx)]$ — Given
2. $(x)(Bx \supset Ox)$ — Given
3. $(Ex)(Wx \cdot -Ox)$ — Given
4. $Wa \cdot -Oa$ — 3, ES
5. $Wa \supset (Ba \lor Ha)$ — 1, US
6. $Ba \supset Oa$ — 2, US
7. Wa — 4, simp
8. $Ba \lor Ha$ — 5, 7, mp
9. $-Oa$ — 4, simp
10. $-Ba$ — 6, 9, mt
11. Ha — 8, 10, elim
12. $Wa \cdot Ha$ — 7, 11, conj
13. $(Ex)(Wx \cdot Hx)$ — 12, EG

m) invalid

o)
1. $(x)(Qx \supset -Wx)$ — Given
2. $(x)(Bx \supset Wx)$ — Given
3. $(x)(Wx \equiv Fx)$ — Given
4. $Qa \supset -Wa$ — 1, US
5. $Ba \supset Wa$ — 2, US
6. $Wa \equiv Fa$ — 3, US
7. $(Wa \supset Fa) \cdot (Fa \supset Wa)$ — 6, bic
8. $Fa \supset Wa$ — 7, simp
9. $-Wa \supset -Fa$ — 8, transp
10. $Qa \supset -Fa$ — 4, 9, trans
11. $Wa \supset Fa$ — 7, simp
12. $Ba \supset Fa$ — 5, 11, trans
13. $(Qa \supset -Fa) \cdot (Ba \supset Fa)$ — 10, 12, conj
14. $(x)[(Qx \supset -Fx) \cdot (Bx \supset Fx)]$ — 13, UG

q)   invalid

$(x)[Bx \supset (Wx \equiv Fx)]$

$(x)(Dx \supset Lx)$

$(Ex)Qx$

$(x)(Wx \supset Lx)$

$(x)(Fx \lor -Bx)$

$\overline{(Ex)(Qx \supset -Bx)}$

s)

1.	$(x)[(Wx \lor Qx) \supset Fx]$	Given
2.	$(x)[(Fx \lor Ux) \supset Bx]$	Given
3.	$(Wa \lor Qa) \supset Fa$	1, US
4.	$(Fa \lor Ua) \supset Ba$	2, US
5.	Wa	Assumed
6.	$Wa \lor Qa$	5, add
7.	Fa	3, 6, mp
8.	$Fa \lor Ua$	7, add
9.	Ba	4, 8, mp
10.	$Wa \supset Ba$	5, 9, cp
11.	$(x)(Wx \supset Bx)$	10, UG

Chapter 5

5.1

3.   a)   quantitative;   c)   qualitative;
    e)   quantitative;   g)   qualitative;
    i)   qualitative.

5.2 a–b(i)

3. $\frac{1}{4}$.

4. $\frac{1}{10}$.

5.   a) $\frac{1}{6}$;   c) $\frac{1}{6}$;   e) $\frac{1}{3}$.

6. $\frac{3}{8}$; $\frac{5}{8}$.

7.   a) $\frac{1}{4}$;   c) $\frac{5}{8}$;   e) $\frac{3}{40}$;   g)   1;
    i) $\frac{7}{20}$.

5.2 b(ii)–c

2.   a)   S1·S3;   c)   S2.

3.   a)   S2·S5·S6·S8;   c)   S2·S5;
    e)   S3·S7;
    g)   S1·S2·S4·S5·S6·S8;   i)   S1.

4.   a)   64;   c)   16,384.

5.   a)   ii) and iii);   b)   i), ii), and iii);
    c)   none.

6.   a) $\frac{1}{2}$;   c) $\frac{5}{6}$;   e) $\frac{2}{3}$;   g) $\frac{1}{3}$.

7.   a) $\frac{1}{2}$;   c) $\frac{1}{4}$;   e) $\frac{5}{6}$;   g) $\frac{3}{4}$;
    i) $\frac{1}{6}$.

5.3

8. a) $\frac{3}{10}$; c) $\frac{3}{20}$; e) $\frac{1}{10}$; g) $\frac{9}{20}$.

9. a) $\frac{1}{4}$; c) $\frac{3}{10}$; e) $\frac{3}{40}$; g) $\frac{1}{20}$;
    i) $\frac{11}{20}$; k) $\frac{2}{11}$; m) $\frac{2}{9}$.

10. a) $\frac{1}{7}$; c) $\frac{1}{5}$; e) $\frac{3}{70}$; g) $\frac{1}{28}$;
    i) $\frac{19}{70}$; k) $\frac{9}{28}$; m) $\frac{3}{28}$;
    o) $\frac{13}{140}$; q) $\frac{15}{38}$; s) $\frac{1}{22}$;
    u) $\frac{10}{23}$; w) $\frac{1}{2}$; y) $\frac{10}{19}$.

5.4

3. $\frac{4}{5}$; $\frac{1}{5}$.

4. 1,000,000/1,000,001.

5. a) $\frac{5}{9}$; c) $\frac{3}{5}$; e) $\frac{5}{7}$; g) $\frac{2}{3}$;
    i) $\frac{8}{11}$; k) $\frac{9}{17}$; m) $\frac{5}{6}$; o) $\frac{1}{6}$;
    q) $\frac{3}{11}$; s) $\frac{1}{5}$.

Chapter 6

6.1

5. a) $+, B, 1$; c) $\geq$; e) $\frac{5}{8}$.

8. $\frac{12}{25}$.

10. 0.0016.

12. $\frac{5}{36}$.

14. 0.072.

15. a) C, A; c) B, A, B, P, C;
    e) $A, C, A \cdot B$.

17. 0.24.

19. 0.00072.

6.2

4. 0.89.

6. $\frac{3}{10}$.

8. 0.88.

9. a) 1; c) $1 - P(A)$; e) $B, P(A)$.

10. 0.6, 0, 1.

12. a) 0.991; c) 0.32; e) 0.045.

13. 0.06.

15. 0.2.

17. 0.7.

19. 0.09.

21. $\frac{3}{8}$.

6.3

3. 0.64.

5. 0.6.

7. 0.42.

9. 0.6.

11. 0.6.

20. 0.84.

23. a) 0.3; b) 0.57; c) 0.13.

25. a) 0.24; b) 0.43; c) 0.33.

26. a) 0.28; c) 0.16; e) 0.42; g) 0.24.

6.4

2. $\frac{2}{3}$.

4. $\frac{3}{5}$; $\frac{2}{5}$.

6. $\frac{10}{1013}$.

18. $\frac{3}{11}$.

20. $\frac{7}{22}$.

22. $\frac{2}{67}$; $\frac{65}{67}$.

Comprehensive review of Chapter 6

1. 0.76.

3. a) 0.32; b) 0.18; c) 0.5.

5. a) 0.42; b) 0.12; c) 0.78; d) 0.22.

6. a) 0.23; c) 0.29; e) 0.76; g) 0.56; i) 0.76.

7. a) 0.7; c) 0.12; e) 0.16; g) 0.14; i) 0.2; k) 0.26.

Chapter 7

7.1

2. 110; 115; 120; 125; 130.

3. 5.

5. 122.3; 122.5; 122.

8. a) $\frac{1}{10}$; c) $\frac{4}{15}$; e) $\frac{1}{6}$.

9. a) $\frac{5}{12}$; c) $\frac{1}{6}$; e) $\frac{2}{3}$.

15. 19; 29; 39; 49; 59.

16. 10.

17. a) 24, 23.5, none; c) 42.4, 43, 43.

19. a) $\frac{1}{25}$; c) $\frac{3}{50}$; e) $\frac{3}{25}$.

20. a) $\frac{9}{50}$; c) $\frac{3}{50}$; e) $\frac{3}{50}$.

21. a) $\frac{2}{9}$; c) $\frac{1}{3}$.

7.2

2. a) 6; c) 6; e) 5.8.

3. a) $\frac{3}{10}$; b) $\frac{1}{5}$; c) $\frac{3}{5}$.

4. a) 118; c) 123; e) 41.2.

5. $\frac{3}{10}$.

6. a) 14; c) 27.4; e) I.

7. a) 19, 6, 4; c) 10, 12, 17.

9. a) $\frac{3}{4}$; c) $\frac{15}{16}$; e) $\frac{35}{36}$; g) $\frac{99}{100}$.

10. a) 75; c) 93.8; e) 97.2;
g) 99.

11. a) 0.94; b) 0.75; c) 0.98.

12. at most 0.01.

14. a) 99; c) 84; e) 67; g) 52;
i)   at most 0.03.

7.3

5. 720.

6. 3,628,800.

8. a) 72; c) 3024.

9. a) $\frac{1}{72}$; c) $\frac{1}{504}$; e) $\frac{1}{3024}$;
g) $\frac{1}{90}$, 720.

10. 336.

12. 12.

13. a) 336; c) 6720.

14. a) $\frac{1}{56}$; c) $\frac{1}{336}$.

15. 1.

19. 3003.

21. 3432.

23. 15,504.

26. a) 10; c) 165; e) 1716.

27. $\frac{1}{84}$; $\frac{1}{42}$.

28. a) $\frac{1}{11}$; b) $\frac{1}{22}$; c) $\frac{1}{66}$.

7.4

2. a) $\frac{1}{2}$; c) $\frac{1}{4}$; e) $\frac{5}{16}$.

3. $\frac{5}{16}$.

5. 0.06.

7. 0.17.

10. a) $r^4 + 4r^3s + 6r^2s^2 + 4rs^3 + s^4$;
c) $r^7 + 7r^6s + 21r^5s^2 + 35r^4s^3 +$
$35r^3s^4 + 21r^2s^5 + 7rs^6 + s^7$.

11. a) 1   9   36   84   126   126   84
36   9   1.

12. a) $r^{30} + 30r^{29}s + 435r^{28}s^2$.
c) $r^{1000} + 1000r^{999}s + 499,500r^{998}s^2$.

15. a) 0.68; b) 0.14; c) 0.02.

17. a) 0.005; b) 0.84.

19. a) 0.02; b) 0.01.

Chapter 8

8.1

4. high probability.

7. high weight.

8. high probability.

8.2

5. a) $\frac{2}{15}$; c) $\frac{1}{15}$; e) $\frac{3}{31}$; g) $\frac{5}{29}$;
   i) $\frac{14}{29}$; k) $\frac{11}{31}$.

7. a) 15; c) 42; e) 28.

8. a) 28; b) 34; c) 61.

10. a) 52; b) 52; c) neither.

11. a) 22; c) 42.

8.3

5. believe.

7. insure.

9. A_3.

12. escape.

14. A_3.

8.4

2. do not copy.

4. A_1.

7. fight.

9. A_1 and A_3, A_4, A_2.

8.5

3. Washington Ave.

5. a) sell next year; c) insure;
   e) attend all lectures.

8.6

2. a) 5.2; b) 4.4;
    c) try to cure 10.

4. a) 42; b) 32; c) wait.

6. a) 86; b) 76; c) use *x*.

8. a) 380; b) 280;
    c) "shave" points.

10. a) 4.6; b) 3.6;
    c) attend all lectures.

8.7

2. a) 6.5; b) 5.5; c) ask Fred.

4. a) 5.5; b) 5; c) A.

6. a) 4; b) 3; c) use brand *x*.

9. a) 7.2; b) 5.6; c) ask Fred.

11. a) 5.2; b) 3.2; c) *A*.

13. a) 3.7; b) 3.3; c) use brand *x*.

Chapter 9

9.1

3. difference.

5. agreement.

7. agreement.

10. negative correlation.

11. a) perfect positive correlation;
    c) no correlation;
    e) no correlation.

9.2

4. a) warranted; b) unwarranted;
    c) warranted.

7. less probable.

9. *a* and *c*.

9.3

4. a) warranted; b) warranted;
    c) unwarranted.

5. a) warranted; c) unwarranted;
    e) warranted.

6. more by B_2.

Chapter 10

10.1

2. a) amphiboly;
    c) begging question;
    e) wrong reason;
    g) equivocation; i) accident;
    k) begging question;

    m) continuum;
    o) complex questions;
    q) division; s) composition;
    u) accent.

10.2

2. a) special pleading;
    c) straw man; e) abusing man;
    g) force; i) authority;
    k) special pleading;

    m) abusing man;
    o) faulty analogy; q) force;
    s) authority.

Chapter 11

11.1

2. a) lexical; c) stipulative;
    e) lexical.

11.2 (a–d)

3. a) contextual; c) synonymous;
    e) abbreviative; g) contextual;
    i) synonymous.

11.2 (e–g)

4. a) denotative; c) ostensive;
    e) denotative.

Author Index

Subject Index

Boldface page numbers indicate the place where the words are defined.